STUDIA THEOLOGICA LUNDENSIA

SKRIFTER UTGIVNA AV
TEOLOGISKA FAKULTETEN I LUND

25

NATURE AND THE SUPERNATURAL
IN THE THEOLOGY
OF HORACE BUSHNELL

by

WILLIAM ALEXANDER JOHNSON

CWK GLEERUP · LUND 1963

BERLINGSKA BOKTRYCKERIET

LUND 1963

TABLE OF CONTENTS

Preface   7

Introduction   9

Chapter I. *An Introduction to the Development of Horace
  Bushnell's Thought*   15

Chapter II. *A Language for the Theology of Experience*   46

Chapter III. *Nature and the Supernatural: The One System of God*   63

   1. Definitions   66
   2. The Supernatural as Distinct from the Natural   69
   3. The Nature of Good and Evil   72
   4. The Nature and Consequences of Sin   78
   5. The Supernatural Work of Redemption   84
   6. The Character of Jesus Christ, the "Supernatural Divine
      Ministration"   88
   7. The Argument for Miracles   96
   8. The World Governed Supernaturally in the Interest of
      Christianity   99

Chapter IV. *An Organic Theory of Christian Education*   108

   1. The Nature of Christian Nurture   111
   2. Scriptural Basis for Christian Nurture   117
   3. "Household Baptism"   119
   4. The "Organic Unity" of the Family   122
   5. Theory of Depravity   129

Chapter V. *A Trinity of Manifestation*   138

   1. The Doctrine of Christ   140
   2. The Nature of the Trinity (preliminary)   143
   3. The Mode of Revelation   147
   4. Divine Logos   156
   5. Plurality of Persons   159
   6. The Trinity and Orthodoxy   170
   7. The Trinity and Human Sensibility   174

Chapter VI. *The Atonement and the Possible God*   179

   1. "Moral" View of the Atonement   180
   2. The Atonement and the Moral Power of God   185
   3. Law, Right and Government   194
   4. Forgiveness and Justice   199
   5. Christ and the Law   202
   6. God's Rectoral Honor   207
   7. The Atonement and Justification by Faith   209
   8. The Vicarious Sacrifice (Revised)   212
   9. The Passible God   217

Chapter VII. *Conclusion: The Accomplishment of Horace Bushnell*   225

   1. American Liberal Theology in the 19 Century   225
   2. The Transition to the "New Theology" (The Social Gospel)   236

Bibliography   258

General Index   273

6

PREFACE

This work of theological analysis belongs specifically to the New England theological scene. However, it has been brought to completion within the context of the Theological Faculty of Lund University. The single reason for this unusual undertaking is that I was encouraged to continue my Swedish theological education, and to write a doctor's thesis dealing with an American theologian.

Horace Bushnell's influence upon the development and direction of American theology has been substantial. More than any other individual, he was the transition figure between the Calvinism of early New England and the Liberalism which developed in the latter part of the 19 Century in the United States. In recent years, however, there has been little critical work done on Bushnell. The need to resuscitate interest in Bushnell and his contribution to ongoing discussions within American theology, appeared to be a relevant and timely project.

Professor Gustaf Wingren has guided the research for this book. Docent Harry Aronson has been especially helpful in enabling me to identify and construct a thesis in the Swedish tradition. I acknowledge their assistance with warm appreciation.

This thesis would not have been completed without the encouragement of Mrs. Austin Cheney of Manchester, Connecticut, wife of Horace Bushnell's grandson. Along with her many gracious acts of kindness, she permitted me the rare opportunity to use Bushnell's own library, which is now located in her home. Furthermore, in her home I experienced the warmth and hospitality of the Bushnell family. It is proper that this book be dedicated to her.

The libraries of the Hartford Seminary Foundation, Yale Divinity School and Harvard University permitted extensive use of their Bushnell materials. Most significant, however, was the invitation of Dr. James F. English, Superintendent of the Congregational Churches of Connecticut, to use the documents pertaining to 19 Century Congregationalism housed in the Congregational House, Hartford,

Connecticut. These materials enabled me to look at Bushnell from the vantage point of the New England Church, and to evaluate better the impact he had upon the ecclesiastical milieu of his time.

Miss Carol Steiman of the Religion Department of Trinity College typed most of the manuscript two times.

Finally, my wife, Carol Johnson, helped with the manuscript from the earliest days of its inception to its completion. As with other projects, without her helpfulness this work would never have been brought to published form.

William A. Johnson

Hartford, Connecticut, June, 1963

The quoted material from Bushnell is taken from the following editions:

Christian Nurture, 1861. Revised and Enlarged Edition of the earlier published *Discourses on Christian Nurture*, 1847 and *Views of Christian Nurture and of Subjects Adjacent Thereto*, 1848.

God in Christ, 1849.

Christ in Theology, 1851.

Nature and the Supernatural, 1858.

Sermons for the New Life, 1858.

Christ and His Salvation, 1864.

Work and Play, 1864.

The Vicarious Sacrifice, 1866.

Moral Uses of Dark Things, 1868.

Sermons on Living Subjects, 1872.

Forgiveness and Law, 1874.

Building Eras in Religion, 1881.

The Spirit in Man, 1903.

INTRODUCTION

To understand and appreciate Horace Bushnell, and his contribution to the development of American theology, one must recognize that he was primarily a preacher, and his work as a theologian was dependent directly upon the problems a Congregational clergyman had to face in a 19 Century New England pastorate. Furthermore, his qualifications for the role of a theologian were limited to the intellectual and academic preparation one received as a preacher in the Congregational Church at that time. He never held an academic position, neither was he involved in the training of candidates for the ministry of the Church. He aspired for the Hollis Chair of Moral Philosophy at Harvard, but an invitation was not forthcoming.

A sympathetic critic has said of Bushnell that "the designation of a theologian cannot in any technical sense ... be applied to him."[1] He was recognized as an eminent minister during his lifetime, but he was always involved in controversy and often charged with embracing heretical ideas. After his death, his thought directly influenced a significant segment of the Christian community, and subsequent uniquely American theological emphases would claim Bushnell as their spiritual ancestor. The Social Gospel movement in America, although making obeisance to Bushnell, soon became more activistic than analytical, and Bushnell's *direct* contribution to the thought of such men as Lyman Abbot and Walter Rauschenbusch was forgotten.

In the early part of the 20 Century, Horace Bushnell was considered to be the father of the Liberal Theology in the United States which at that time was rapidly passing away, and the prestige of which had waned in the face of such modern developments as Theological Realism and Neo-Orthodoxy. In the Nineteen Thirties, the most important fact of American theology was the disintegration of

---

[1] S. S. Drew, "An Estimate of Horace Bushnell," *Contemporary Review*, (August, 1879) p. 823.

Liberalism.[2] Liberalism had provided a coherent pattern of theological assumptions, all based upon the one great idea of an immanent God, whose presence might be intuitively apprehended throughout the length and breadth of nature, and in all the institutions of civilized society. This optimism was now breaking down before the onslaught of the new theologies. Horace Bushnell appeared thereby to be a relic of the past, a theological antique who had no relevancy for the modern world. However, this estimation of the Hartford minister is an unfair one, because as one judges Bushnell by subsequent history, he, more than any other of his time, was *the* creative force in New England theology in the 19 Century. It is correct to say that Bushnell was the greatest figure in American theology in his century, as Jonathan Edwards was in the 18. From Bushnell's work, American theology derived courage and inspiration and a vision of the truth of historic Christianity. Bushnell's theology served as the "bridge" between the Orthodox Calvinism of the 17 and 18 Centuries, and the later liberalizing developments within New England. Like his contemporaries, Bushnell could not avoid Calvinism, and he was forced to deal with categories which were informed by Edwards and the "New England Theology." But Bushnell addressed himself to a larger audience, to the "New Light" revivalistic ministers, Unitarians, transcendentalists, and the Episcopalians. His position as a Hartford pastor was transcended by the influence he has had upon the world of theological thought. His story is the narrative of the strengths and weaknesses, struggles and victories of American Christianity.

Nonetheless, there are certain deficiencies in Bushnell's theological perspective. He lacked an understanding of historical knowledge, and had been characterized as someone who thought first and read afterward. After having written his work on the Trinity, he reviewed his contribution to the study of this doctrine and wrote: "On a careful study of the creed prepared by the Nicene council, as interpreted by the writings of Athanasius in defense of it, I feel obliged to confess that I had not sufficiently conceived its import, or the title it has to respect as a Christian document."[3] It was only after his book on the Trinity had been written that he discovered the meaning of the Nicene formula, and then reinterpreted it in his

---

[2] John Bennett, "After Liberalism – What?," *Christian Century*, Vol. L, no. 45, (Nov. 8, 1933), pp. 1403–1406.
[3] *Christ in Theology*, p. 177.

own broad "comprehensive" way. Bushnell had failed also to comprehend fully the meaning of the theological controversies in New England Christianity, those controversies to which he contributed so substantially. He failed, too, to see the relationship of his own thought and the solutions to problems he provided within the broad sweep of Christian history. This latter criticism might be anticipated because Bushnell was not a professional scholar, but it does not weaken the argument that Bushnell's insights and conclusions were provisional and provincial, and at times immature. Bushnell's large and permanent influence in the world of theology must be considered in the context of this serious limitation.

Another serious criticism might be directed to Bushnell, and that is, that as a theologian he was inclined to the method which he employed as a preacher, the method of intuition. For this reason, judged by the standards of system and consistency, Bushnell cannot be termed a great theologian. He was a prophet, or a poet, rather than a theologian. He received a vision of truth, "fresh light" was given him; but, he did not laboriously reason out his theological position. He experienced and discovered the truths of theology. He failed to treat his "discoveries" as hypotheses and to subject them to criticism and rational scrutiny. Instead, he proclaimed them as truths to an expectant public. As an illustration, there was one period in his life when he allowed himself to revise a theory he had propounded. The reason for this alteration in his approach was because, as he said, "the truth appears to be outgrowing my published expositions." The volume which followed was Bushnell's attempt to catch up with his intuition of truth. One commentator on Bushnell said that his first and greatest contribution to the world of thought was himself.[4] In a real way, this is the only way to comprehend Bushnell, the theologian. His theology is dependent upon the independence of his spirit and the fertility of his mind. He felt compelled to deal with every doctrine from its foundation, and for the most part, he followed this inward compulsion to its conclusion. But he thought first, and reasoned afterwards. His "Essay on Language" showed that the thinking employed in the pursuit of theology had to be original thinking, that is, the production of the thought by the student's own mind. Therefore, the true method of theological teach-

[4] Frank Hugh Foster, *A Genetic History of the New England Theology* (Chicago: University of Chicago Press, 1907), p. 404.

ing is that of suggestion, that of re-creating truth for one's own self by the intuitive processes of the mind:

Thus, as form battles form, and one form neutralizes another, all the insufficiencies of words are filled out, the contrarieties liquidated, and the mind settles into a full and just apprehension of the pure spiritual truth. Accordingly we never come so near to a truly well rounded view of any truth, as when it is offered paradoxically; that is, under contradictions; that is, under two or more dictions, which, taken as dictions, are contrary one to the other.[5]

With rare exception, Bushnell wrote on a theological subject only once. He asserted what he believed to be the truth of a particular doctrine of belief, and then let time vindicate or deny his position. He took every opportunity to preach on similar theological concepts, but these occasions did not provide a large audience for him. He rarely entered into dialogue with the theologians of New England, rather, he digested their reviews and criticism, and went on to another subject. There is evidence that he was troubled by misunderstanding and a refusal on the part of his contemporaries to seek for new light as he had done. But, for the most part, his entire theological productivity may be seen in the light of the major books he published, *Christian Nurture, God in Christ, Nature and the Supernatural,* and *The Vicarious Sacrifice.* These four volumes highlight his major theological concerns—the nature of religious education, religious language, the doctrine of the Trinity, a conception of the relationship of nature to the supernatural, and the doctrine of the Atonement. In all of these works, we discover Bushnell's original and characteristic emphasis on the *religious life* as the source and guiding principle in theology. Because he was a preacher, and had to deal daily with the religious life of his congregation, he was forced to devise theological categories which might be adapted to the experiential side of man.

Bushnell's thought moved continuously between two poles – the incomprehensibility of the transcendent God and the necessary accomodation of the revelation of God to our human experiences. Theological truth, Bushnell said, must contribute to life. Any theory or concept in theology which did not contribute to life could not thereby be characterized as truth. In a real sense, this is Bushnell's apologetic for the Christian faith. It is this theme, that theology must

[5] *God in Christ,* p. 55.

12

be experiential, that theological doctrine must be taken from the realm of speculative logic to the place where life can be transformed, which is characteristic of Bushnell. He presented a view of the universe which included the natural and the supernatural as its major constituents, to enable him to present the truth of theology in this way. In his major work in the area of "apologetics," *Nature and the Supernatural*, Bushnell distinguished nature as the realm of *force* and *law*, and the supernatural as the realm of *personality* and *freedom*. This distinction permitted man to belong primarily to the supernatural realm, without at the same time deprecating his place in the natural realm. The supernatural is that realm which manifests the operation of personality. Nature and the supernatural are co-factors in the one system of God. When viewed in this light, the natural and the supernatural are not two realms worlds apart, but both are functions of the divine. This was a revolutionary hypothesis, and Bushnell employed it vigorously throughout his teological program, with the result that every major idea was colored by it. As persons, Bushnell reminds us, we are powers not in the line of cause and effect, but we can set causes in nature at work in new combinations, which nature could never produce by her own internal action. All of nature could be used in the service of personality for this reason. Bushnell drew the logical conclusion and asserted that what is more significant for the Christian faith is that "the world is governed supernaturally in the interest of Christianity." This presupposition forms the basis for Bushnell's discussion of religious language, Christian education, and the doctrines of the Trinity and the Atonement. It is *Nature and the Supernatural* which provides the underlying motif for all of Bushnell's theological conclusions.

In this thesis, *Nature and the Supernatural in the Theology of Horace Bushnell,* I have attempted to demonstrate that Bushnell's conception of the natural and the supernatural realms, and the inter-relationship between them, is constitutive for his entire theological system. Each theological subject he dealt with ultimately went back to the basic presupposition that the natural and the supernatural are co-factors in the one system of God.

To deal with this topic adequately, I have structured this thesis in the following way, (believing that it best encompasses the thought of Horace Bushnell):

Chapter I: An Introduction to the Development of Horace Bushnell's Theological Thought, which is the attempt to look at Bushnell in terms of the theological climate of 19 Century New England.

Chapters II–VI: Bushnell's Conception of Nature and the Supernatural as Constitutive for his Theological System, which together comprise the major expository work of the book. Bushnell's thought is dealt with in terms of the specific theological problems which confronted him during his pastorate in Hartford and later.

Chapter II: A Language for the Theology of Experience, which is the starting point for Bushnell's theology and the indispensable tool which Bushnell used to articulate his system.

Chapter III: Nature and the Supernatural: The One System of God, which is a major section of the book, describing how Bushnell looked at the universe, as it related to man, nature, the supernatural, revelation and Jesus Christ.

Chapter IV: An Organic Theory of Christian Education, which is Bushnell's pastoral concern to find a place for children within the "community of the faithful," and which speaks of Christian nurture rather than cataclysmic conversion as the basis for the Christian life.

Chapter V: A Trinity of Manifestation, which is Bushnell's attempt to describe the Trinity, avoiding a metaphysical tritheism on the one hand, and making the Trinity relevant to experiential faith on the other.

Chapter VI: The Atonement and the Passible God, which is Bushnell's final theological concern, an attempt to make the doctrine of the Atonement a truly "ethical" theory.

Chapter VII: Conclusion: The Accomplishment of Horace Bushnell, which is made up of two parts, one a description of the effect Bushnell's conception of nature and the supernatural had upon New England Theology in the 19 Century, and second, a suggestion of Bushnell's impact upon subsequent theological developments in the United States, particularly the Social Gospel, and such theologians as George A. Gordon, Lyman Abbott, Washington Gladden, and Walter Rauschenbusch.

14

CHAPTER I

An Introduction to the Development
of Horace Bushnell's Thought

Horace Bushnell [1] was born in 1802 in Bantam, Connecticut, where his parents and grandparents had been farmers. His early life was spent in New Preston, Connecticut, where the Bushnells achieved a certain degree of social standing and a relative amount of prosperity. The Bushnell family was religious, but in an untheological way, insisting upon "industry, order, time, fidelity, reverence, neatness, truth, intelligence, prayer," [2] rather than strict conformity to orthodox beliefs. Horace Bushnell's father had been a Methodist, his mother an Episcopalian, but both were now faithful members of the Congregational church, which was the only place of worship in New Preston. It was not until the age of twenty that Horace Bushnell made a public confession of faith and joined the church in New Preston. Horace Bushnell entered Yale University in 1823,

---

[1] The standard biographies are: Mary Bushnell Cheney, *Life and Letters of Horace Bushnell* (New York: Harper Brothers, 1880); Theodore T. Munger, *Horace Bushnell, Preacher and Theologian* (Boston and New York: Houghton, Mifflin Co., 1899); Warren Seymour Archibald, *Horace Bushnell* (Hartford: Edwin Valentine Mitchell, 1930); Barbara M. Cross, *Horace Bushnell, Minister to a Changing America* (Chicago: The University of Chicago Press, 1958); also, "Horace Bushnell, A Great Man," an address delivered by Dean Charles R. Brown at the opening of the Horace Bushnell Memorial Hall, Hartford, Conn.; Bushnell Centenary, Minutes of the 193 Annual Meeting, General Association of Connecticut, Hartford, June 17, 18, 1902 (Oxford Press, 1902); Short biographies of Horace Bushnell may be found in: H. Clay Trumbull, "Goodness and Greatness among all: Horace Bushnell," *My Four Religious Teachers* (Philadelphia: The Sunday School Time Co., 1903), pp. 70–125; Williston Walker, *Great Men of the Christian Church* (Chicago: University of Chicago Press, 1908), pp. 357–370; Ernest Trice Thompson, "Horace Bushnell and the Beginning of American Liberalism," *Changing Emphases in American Preaching* (Philadelphia: The Westminster Press, 1943), pp. 4–49; Washington Gladden, "Horace Bushnell and Progressive Orthodoxy," in *Pioneers of Religious Liberty in America*, (Boston: American Unitarian Association, 1903), pp. 227–263; cf. also William Warren Sweet, *Makers of Cristianity*, (Henry Holt and Co.), 1937, pp. 288–299; Roland Bainton, *Yale and the Ministry* (New York: Harper and Bros., 1957), pp. 113–126.
[2] Cheney, *Life and Letters of Horace Bushnell*, p. 29.

aware immediately of his awkwardness as a boy from the country.[3]
His college career was marked by intellectual conflict and doubt and
a degree of deliberation which did not permit him to become an
outstanding student.[4] Bushnell feared that religion could not be
demonstrated by the understanding. His daughter describes Bushnell's college experience in the following way:

A year to two before entering college, while still under the strong habitual
influences of home, he had accepted, rather than wrought out, the faith
of his youth. Now for the first time, the great untried world of thought
opened before him, and his active mind launched out upon a sea of doubt.[5]

Bushnell's problem of adjustment at Yale was a reflection of
the societal changes in New England in the nineteenth century. An
urban society was emerging from a predominantly farm economy.
The new society possessed its own mores and behavior patterns.
The *nouveau riche* attempted to create for themselves standards
relevant to what they felt was a dignified status in society. In
general, the people from the farming areas were those who could
maintain the traditional religious faith of the past, while the newly
formed classes looked for more sophisticated ways of expressing their
religion.[6]

After graduation from Yale, Bushnell began teaching school in
Norwich, Connecticut. It was here that Bushnell recognized the
distinction between his former "homespun" manner and his growing
urbanity.[7] Neither happy nor successful as a teacher, Bushnell attempted to enter the New York journalistic world and became a
member of the editorial staff of the *Journal of Commerce*. He found
this kind of life also distasteful. Next, he believed that he should
prepare himself for a legal career, and in 1831, completed his law
examinations at Yale. In addition, he tutored at the university.
During all of this period, his religious doubts were obvious, and

[3] Cross, *Horace Bushnell, Minister to a Changing America*, p. 4.
[4] Cheney, p. 208. "I was brought up in a country family, ignorant of any but
country society, where cultivated language in conversation was unknown. I
entered college late, . . . when the vernacular type of language is cast . . . I had no
language, and if I chanced to have an idea, nothing came to give it expression."
[5] Cheney, pp. 36, 37
[6] Cf. Cross, p. 7.
[7] "There was a rigor in their piety, a want of gentle feeling . . . The mothers of
the homespun age had a severe limit on their culture and accomplishments . . . We
demand a delicacy and elegance of manners impossible to them." Bushnell, *Work
and Play*, pp. 396–400.

16

at one point he found that he could not lead college prayer, a duty which every tutor was required to fulfill. A revival swept through Yale, but Bushnell was unaffected. Nonetheless, he was able to write later—

I was graduated, and then, a year afterwards, when my bills were paid, and when the question was to be decided whether I should begin the preparation of theology, I was thrown upon a most painful struggle by the very evident, quite incontestable fact that my religious life was utterly gone down. And the pain it cost me was miserably enhanced by the disappointment I must bring on my noble Christian mother by withdrawing myself from the ministry. I had run to no dissipations; I had been a churchgoing, thoughtful man. My very difficulty was that I was too thoughtful, substituting thought for everything else, and expecting so intently to dig out a religion by my head that I was pushing it all the while practically away.[8]

His religious conversion came about, he later wrote, from an awareness that there was one certainty: the distinction between right and wrong.[9] He was convinced that he was worthy enough to choose God, and equated this confidence with the Christian doctrine of salvation. He entered Yale Divinity School soon after this experience of "conversion."

In the time immediately following his arrival at Yale Divinity School, Bushnell came under the influence of Nathaniel Taylor, the outstanding representative of the New England School of Theology, which since the days of Jonathan Edwards had sought to defend Calvinism against all foes. He found Taylor to be a vigorous and stimulating teacher. However, he could not accept everything in the "New Theology," but he did believe that Taylor had taught him to think critically for himself.[10] Taylor's theological system, which was called the "New Divinity," was based upon the epistemology and ethical absolutism of the Scottish common-sense philosophy. Christian theology was, for Taylor, an intellectually demonstrable system. The moral obligation which belonged to religious faith was universal and demanding. His theology was very effective for preaching.[11] In

---

[8] Cheney, p. 32.
[9] Cheney, p. 59. "If there is a God, . . . he is a right God. If I have lost him in the wrong, perhaps I shall find him in the right." He prayed to the "dim God, dimly felt" and was "borne up into God's help . . . After this all troublesome doubt of God's reality is gone."
[10] Cheney, p. 59.
[11] Cross, p. 17, describes Taylor's God in the following way: "The world was so dominated by His benevolence that His nature was crossed and thwarted by

Taylor's theology, man was depraved, but this fact did not need to discourage the sinner. His happiness came about in obedience to God's law, which freed him from bondage to his selfishness. The saving change could come about instantaneously and, as was claimed, could transform the sinner into a saint. As a result, the awesome and awful *Deus absconditus* of early New England theology had been transformed in a genial, rational, and reliable divine being. God was characterized by benevolence, and His function was to bring about good government and human happiness.[12]

Bushnell, however, was finally unsatisfied with Taylor's theological system and was convinced that it was simply a continuation of an antiquated theological tradition. A new starting point for theology had to be found. Theology had to speak to the modern world in terms which were consonant with the contemporary developments in thought. Taylor's God and his theological system seemed for Bushnell a regression to the Christian faith of his childhood. Taylor did not provide a theological idiom which could address itself to the major individual and social concerns of New England man.

Samuel T. Coleridge's *Aids to Reflection* offered Bushnell the starting-point for his new theology. He discovered that the *Aids* permitted man to doubt the very basis of his faith.[13] Sophisticated doubt (that is, "doubt in order that you may end in believing the truth") had been recommended by Coleridge. The interpretation of religion was based upon a Kantian theory of knowledge which distinguished between the Reason and the Understanding. The Understanding, which was dependent upon the senses, could not

---

sin. He had permitted evil in the world not wilfully but because the world with its evil was the best alternative available to His choice, and He offered for man's approval the best of all possible universes. Under God's benign administration, happiness was good and suffering was evil. Since all men sought their own happiness, self-interest was divinely sanctioned. Thus God's just equation of human nature and moral duty made man's obligation and pleasure alike the blithe pursuit of happiness. Sin was only the error that happiness and selfishness were identical. Thus defined as folly, sin called less for reprobation than enlightenment, and through the scourges of natural evil God pressed upon erring man the recognition that he had won not happiness but pain. Under this vigorous and salutary discipline, the faltering creature was led toward salvation."

[12] Cross, pp. 18–19.

[13] "Never be afraid to doubt," the *Aids* told him, "if you only have the disposition to believe, and doubt in order that you may end in believing the truth." Samuel T. Coleridge, *Aids to Reflection* (London: Bohn Library, 1913), p. 66; cf. Cross, pp. 22 f.

handle adequately the "spiritual realities" which existed beyond the natural world. The Understanding was able to construct theological systems, but it could not deal with the "spiritual nature" of human existence. Reason was able to transcend the phenomenal world and was able to conceive of the moral law and man's spiritual nature. Reason, furthermore, provided man with a conscience and with the possibility of religious insight. Reason was conceived to be individualistic, which meant that man did not have to rely upon universal consent for truth.

Morality was based upon an immediate apprehension of the Absolute, which had no reference to space and time or sense-experience. Man was free to perform the Good, which was revealed to him as the Moral Law. His obedience was based upon the acknowledgement of his duty to do the Good. The moral law was based upon reason, for man was able to perceive those ideas which were the necessary premises of the moral life. After reading the *Aids to Reflection*, Bushnell realized that he now had a theology with which he could work.[14]

Bushnell read Coleridge from the point of view of the American Romantic movement, which was gaining momentum in New England at that time. It would be his task, so he expressed it in later life, to change the course of American Protestantism by means of Coleridge's *Aids to Reflection* and the American Romantic movement. The Christian faith, said Bushnell, could never be based upon any system which demanded intellectual demonstration. Religion appeals ultimately, he insisted, to the heart and to feeling. Bushnell wrote:

When the preacher touches the Trinity and when logic shatters it all to pieces, I am all at the four winds. But I am glad I have a heart as well as a head. My heart wants the Father; my heart wants the Son; my heart wants the Holy Ghost—and one just as much as the other. My heart says the Bible has a Trinity for me, and I mean to hold by my heart.[15]

---

[14] Cross, p. 26, says: "Coleridge offered a new vocabulary when established modes of expressions seemed inadequate; "Reason," the "supernatural," "subjective," "elections of the will," usurped the place of "self-interest," "common sense," "moral government," "pleasures and pains." Centering on questions different from those of the New England tradition, and justifying belief through an esoteric epistemology, the *Aids* mediated escape from worn theological controversies. The release was the more intoxicating in that the ideas were largely pre-empted without the epistemological structure behind them."

[15] Cheney, p. 56.

In February of 1833, the North Church in Hartford called Bushnell to be its pastor. He left Yale and New Haven to become pastor of a unique church in the center of Connecticut Congregationalism, and brought his wife, Mary Apthorp, whom he had recently married, with him. In the North Church, Bushnell found all of the varieties of New England theology represented. The controversy between the Old and New Schools of theology was raging. The two leading deacons were opposed to each other on every point of theology.[16] The conservative members of the church were critical of the theology which Yale and New Haven represented. However, his congregation liked him in spite of the differences, and Bushnell could write, "I begin to feel that God has confided to me a noble work, and, with his aid, I shall aim to follow it faithfully."[17] Theodore Munger, a theological disciple of Bushnell and his earlist biographer, described Bushnell's early ministry in the following way:

Neither side heard what it expected. Old School and New School were ignored, or gently set aside to make room for a discussion that had nothing to do with their differences except to supercede or rather to absorb them in a more comprehensive view of the subject. Nothing was said of natural ability, or moral ability, or gracious ability, except that 'they raise a false issue which can never be settled.' To thus dismiss a controversy which had raged since Edwards, and was now embodied in the neighboring divinity schools, would have been regarded as a jest if his treatment of it had not been so serious. Instead of sinking himself and his hearers in 'the abysmal depths of theology,' he carried them into the world of human life and Christian experience, where all was so much a matter of fact that there was small room for question. Arminius and Edwards, Taylor and Tyler, would have listened without dissent—bating a phrase or two—and for the time would have forgotten their differences; or possibly, as often happens with contestants when a greater truth is forced upon them, they might have said, 'We always thought so.' For in truth, Bushnell thus early was 'passing into the vein of comprehensiveness' of which he afterwards spoke—a phrase that defines better than any other the method and spirit of the man.[18]

Hartford during this early period in Bushnell's ministry was economically dependent upon the trade that the Connecticut River brought to its docks. Bushnell, at first, readily identified himself

[16] *Ibid.*, p. 68; he felt had been "daintily inserted between an acid and an alkali, having it for his task both to keep them apart, and to save himself from being bitten by one or devoured by the other."
[17] *Ibid.*, p. 70.
[18] Munger, *Horace Bushnell, Preacher and Theologian*, p. 53.

with the commercial interests of the town.[19] But Bushnell also had to speak to the financial and social elite who were in his church. However, Hartford, which had anticipated great financial success, found that the railroad threatened the prosperity of the city, and it was now on the verge of economic ruin.[20] The uncertainty of the economic situation in Hartford continued throughout Bushnell's pastorate there. It was quite natural for Bushnell to try to relate religion and commerce in his sermons, and to preach on the duties of the Christian to bring about economic progress.

When an economic slump came, the more revivalistic-type minister suggested that this was only an example of divine judgement. Bushnell did not know what to make of revivals, which he found

[19] Samuel Goodrich, in *Recollections of a Lifetime* (New York: 1857), I, p. 436, described Hartford as a "small commercial town . . . dealing in lumber and smelling of molasses and old Jamaica, . . . strongly impressed with a plodding, mercantile, and mechanical character." Among the "few merchants and many shopkeepers" some "dainty patricians still held themselves aloof." Cf. Cross, p. 31; there was a recognition from the very beginning of Bushnell's ministry that there was a relationship between the Christian faith and the economy.

[20] Cross, pp. 32–34. Cross reports that in the early 1800's, Hartford capital was largely invested in commerce, the expectations of which often failed to materialize. The great wealth anticipated from the steam-boat trade was lost with the opening of the Boston and Springfield Railroad. By 1846, the *Courant* dolefully recorded that the city merged on economic ruin. Other financial strains on Hartford during Bushnell's time included the tendency of her business men to invest money outside of the city. Some of the most well-known families became financially embarrassed, although a fairly steady group of the controlling powers prospered. Money became localized in the insurance companies and many who found economic prosperity there established themselves as the city's aristocracy. Cf. also, pp. 37, 45, 46. "The ethos of the business community shaped his way of thinking. In spite of his rural past, he often used the imagery of finance and business. He described God's final profit calculation in His dealings with humanity; the 'conquest of grace' seemed like gaining a good credit position. God's free gift of salvation and the destitution of the elect without His mercy figured difficultly within an imagery drawn from rationalized capitalism. God's confidence in the humanity in which He had invested was rational rather than 'visionary'; it was that 'of a banker whose fund is in.' Bushnell encouraged a well-secured and enterprising Christian hope. 'As certainly . . . as you succeed you can be saved.' . . . Religion, he taught, should not intrude upon business. The law of self-interest prohibited charity in trade; commerce was properly conducted by strict accounting. During the hours of business, merchants were to act 'under the laws of trade,' reserving 'their charities–all their symphaties, allowances, mitigations, merciful accomodations–for a separate chapter of life.' Repeatedly, Bushnell called upon the metaphor of flight to convey the religious life to his congregation. The Sabbath served less as a critique of all experience than as an escape from the usual 'low torments' of the mind into a temporary freedom, where the soul might 'ascend to things congenial to its higher affinities.'"

always followed a business crisis. Revivals, in themselves, had some value, he conceded; but to equate them with the whole of the Christian religion and experience was to warrant disaster, he felt.[21] The most successful revivalist was Joel Hawes, pastor of the First Church, Hartford. He was determined to "restore orthodoxy" and to "convert" every member of his congregation to Jesus Christ. However, his revivalistic techniques did not always win adherents. At one point, a new church, the North Congregational Church, was formed, made up of the discontents from Hawes' church. When called upon to dedicate the new church, Hawes noted that there was present, "a taste . . . for a superficial and showy kind of preaching," which "regales the fancy and the taste, rather than searches the heart and conscience—that deals in pretty thoughts and fine sayings, rather than in the doctrine which is called salvation." [22] It was to this church that Bushnell had been called to be pastor. The initial period in a New England Congregational pastor's ministry was always a probationary one, and Bushnell had "to follow a tortuous line." He was sure that he would be dismissed by his church.

His first published sermon was entitled "The Crisis of the Church." In it, Bushnell attempted to demonstrate in what ways Protestantism and democracy were allied. He believed that the chief dangers to the country were "slavery, infidelity, Romanism, and the current of our political tendencies."

[21] Cheney, pp. 82–83; Bushnell wrote: "Nature is multiform and various on every side. She is never doing exactly the same thing at one time which she has done at another. She brings forth all her bounties by inconstant applications and cherishments endlessly varied. A single thought extended in this direction were enough, it would seem, to show us that, while God is unchangeable, he is infinitely various–unchangeable in his purposes, various in his means. And so it is instructive to advert to the various and periodical changes of temperament which affect men in other matters than religion. These fluctuations are epidemical, too, extending to whole communities, and infecting them with an ephemeral interest in various subjects, which afterwards they wonder at themselves, and can in no way recall. No observing public speaker ever failed to be convinced that man is a being, mentally, of moods and phases which it were as vain to attempt the control of as to push aside the stars. . . . These remarks bring us to conclude that there is in what we call revivals of religion something of a periodical nature, which belongs to the appointed plan of God in his moral operations; but as far as they are, what the name imports, revivals of *religion* (that is, of the principle of love and obedience), they are linked with dishonor; so far they are made necessary by the instability and bad faith of Christ's disciples. But here it must be noted that the dishonor does not belong to the revival, but to the decay of principle in the disciple, which needs reviving."

[22] Joel Hawes, *A Sermon Delivered at the Dedication of the North Congregational Church of Hartford* (Hartford: 1825), pp. 15–16.

Early in his career in Hartford, Bushnell described his people as "moral, honorable . . . beneficient and habitually reverent." However, the congregation was always wary of anything extravagant in theological and ecclesiastical matters. Salvation, dependent upon a change of heart, was difficult to accept; "total depravity" was an odious idea; sin and the conviction of sin were equally objectionable. The Scriptures seemed much too vulgar, and the sacrifice of Christ appeared unnecessary.[23]

Bushnell, for the most part, addressed himself to the religious and spiritual preferences of his congregation. Religion, he insisted, did not destroy the "zest for life," which he defined in terms of "a triumph over the unknown." Bushnell could, however, stand up to his congregation and accuse them of moral failure. He said of them: "Probably there was never any class of Christians in the world . . . so little penetrated by Christian love."[24]

Bushnell struggled to make religion meaningful to his divided congregation. There were constant grumblings among his members and accusations flew back and forth. A Professor of Theology in the seminary in East Windsor was extremely critical of what he called Bushnell's "heresies." His church was continuously split into factions, and other Hartford churches gladly took into its memberships any of Bushnell's malcontents.

The sure mark of a New England Congregationalist pastor's success during this period was the number of converts ("the fruits of a minister's labors") he could bring into the church. Revivals had an important place in New England religion, and were determinative of a minister's appointment to a specific church. Bushnell tried his

[23] Cf. *Sermons for the New Life,* pp. 108, 206–209; *Christ and His Salvation,* p. 74; *Sermons on Living Subjects,* pp. 53, 112.

[24] *Christ and His Salvation,* pp. 130–131; *Moral Uses of Dark Things,* pp. 314–315. Cf. Cross, p. 49: "As Bushnell's experience gradually turned his imagination to the figure of Christ, he found a judgment on the world. In the midst of Hartford propriety he pondered on the image of Christ with such lonely and narrow scrutiny that he wondered whether he himself, confronted with a man so alien, odd, and exiled, would not turn away. Eternally separate from the world, Christ was not a popular Savior. 'Christ did not wrest victories from fate by the energy of His will, but by a loving, passive submission.' Meek, disreputable, scorning propriety, the figure and message of Christ aligned at no point with the successful merchant. No one could discern the Gospel but the 'meek and humble.' Who, then were the world's Christians? Those whom the laws of population had doomed to extinction, the outcast, the animal–the Negroes were now 'the true Nazarenes and Galileans of the world.'"

hand at revivals, but was not successful.[25] During all of this time, Hawes continued to fill his church with the "regenerate." The Episcopal Church, at the same time, was constant in its denouncement of "revivalistic crudeness". Completely frustrated, Bushnell thought to return to teaching. However, in 1836 he published an article entitled, "The Spiritual Economy of Revivals of Religion," in which he attempted to destroy the commonly accepted formula that equated religion with revivals. Because of this article, his preaching was suspected of doctrinal errors by the more conservative elements of the congregation.[26] It was believed that Bushnell had "deflected from the true faith." Bushnell had recognized that there were dangers which might come from a successful revival. Invariably he found that a revival was followed by a "religious deadness." [27] As time went on, more and more people who had left Hawes' church affiliated with Bushnell's. Bishop Brownell of the Episcopal Church of Connecticut, enumerated to the clergy the "Errors of the Times," which he felt were: the extravagant quest for the "new birth," the neglect of the Sacraments, including baptism, the idea of Christian nurture, and the alternating enthusiasm and apathy of New England Congregationalism.[28]

[25] It is reported that in 1834, 41 new members "by profession," become part of his church; in 1835, only 4; in 1836, 12; cf. Cheney, p. 7.

[26] Cheney, p. 92: "Deacon Seth Terry, once before alluded to as the chief representative of the Old School in the North Church, wrote him in January, 1839, a letter of kind remonstrance on this subject. He said, 'I have for some time been exceedingly pressed in my mind respecting my duty to yourself and the church of which you are pastor, and I an unworthy member, regarding my views of your public ministrations... Between our views of many of the important doctrines and principles of the Scriptures, I have been more and more convinced of late, and especially since your recent exposition in your doctrinal discourses, there is a wide difference. Had this difference been on minor points, or on those of a controverted nature, I should have had less difficulty, and perhaps have remained silent; but, as I view it, you hold many things which affect and subvert long-established and well-established doctrines and principles, and those in which our churches are at rest and in union.' He fears that the letter may seem disrespectful to his pastor (a fault which his respect for the ministry would forbid), and adds, 'If, in my endeavor to be plain and explicit, I schould seem to be harsh, I assure you that such are my feelings towards you personally, arising from your gentlemanly and Christian deportment, that I should regret it.' "

[27] Unitarians and medical men were warning a health-conscious public of the unfortunate results of excessive religious ardor. Letter to Charles Finney, from George Gale, quoted in Arthur Cole, *Social Ideas of the Northern Evangelists* (New York: 1854), p. 80; North Church *Records* (State Historical Library, Hartford), Vol. I; L. Eaton, "Eli Todd," New England Quarterly, XXVI (1853), pp. 435–453.

[28] Thomas Brownell, *Errors of the Times* (Hartford: 1843).

Bushnell wrote the following about revivals and revivalism:

The merit is that it displaced an era of dead formality, and brought in the demand of truly supernatural experience. The defect is, that it has cast a type of religious individualism, intense beyond any former example. It makes nothing of the family, and the church, and the organic powers God had constituted as vehicles of grace. It takes every man as if he had existed *alone;* presumes that he is unreconciled to God until he has undergone some sudden and explosive experience in adult years, or after the age of reason; demands that experience, and only when it is reached, allows the subject to be an heir of life. Then, on the other side, or that of the Spirit of God, the very act or *ictus* by which the change is wrought is isolated or individualized, so as to stand in no connection with any other of God's means or causes—an epiphany, in which God leaps from the stars, or some place above, to do a work apart from all system, or connection with his other works. Religion is thus a kind of transcendental matter, which belongs on the outside of life, and has no part in the laws by which life is organized—a miraculous epidemic, a fire-ball shot from the moon, something holy, because it is from God, but so extraordinary, so out of place, that it cannot suffer any vital connection with the ties, and causes, and forms, and habits, which constitute the frame of our history. Hence the desultory, hard, violent, and often extravagant or erratic character it manifests. Hence, in part, the dreary years of decay and darkness, that interspace our months of excitement and victory.[29]

A major problem presented itself to Hartford in the 1830's.[30] The children of the Hartford elite began to demonstrate a lack of moral concern. As a result of the growth of large cities in New England in the 19 Century, there was a constant move from the rural areas to the larger cities and their "many temptations." [31] Within such a context, social mobility brought about severe religious problems. Often an attempt was made to save the young sinner by an appeal to his sentimental nature, and he was urged to return home to Mother and to God. Bushnell was extremely sensitive to the need to help the young person, now living in Hartford or one of

[29] Bushnell, *Christian Nurture,* pp. 187, 188.
[30] Cross, p. 57.
[31] James Alexander lists the lures of the cities as follows: ". . . the night cellar, the low concert, the ball, the equivocal show, . . . the billiard room, and the den of infamy . . ." In the *Christian Spectator* we have a reporter unhappily telling of many friends who had gone to New York and not become a Christian "or even a Sabbath-School teacher." Instead, they had "cast off the . . . fear of sin" which had been theirs in childhood. James Alexander, "The Merchants' Clerk Cheered and Counselled," William Sprague (ed.), *The Man of Business Considered in His Various Relations* (Philadelphia, n.d.), p. 35; "Large Cities," *Christian Spectator,* I² (1828), p. 21.

the other large cities, to find a vital, realistic religious faith. The Calvinistic origins of New England theology had always included the child in the household of faith. When the child was pledged to the church, he became a member of the visible church. Within the New England churches, however, this older Calvinistic view was challenged by the unique Congregational ideal, that a regenerate individual who presented himself for church membership had to show evidence of his conversion. The revival movement in America, of course, strengthened this latter viewpoint. It emphasized the transforming and regenerative change, that is, the conscious struggle of the individual with sin before a peace with God could be found. The child was viewed as a "child of wrath" until the divine Spirit could make him into a "child of God." All of religious education was directed towards the "cataclysmic upheaval" of the religious orientation of the child. Ernest Thompson characterized the movement in the following way:

The Churches generally felt that progress and development were impossible without the emotional excitement and the spasmodic success of a revival. For more than a hundred years, up to the eve of the Civil War, the evangelical Churches of America made revivals their chief dependence for bringing children as well as adults into the Christian life. The approved method of becoming a Christian was to be converted in a protracted meeting. Periods between revivals were considered periods of spiritual dearth, during which the Church could only wait for the next outpouring of the divine power.[32]

Bushnell's first book appeared in 1846 and was entitled *Christian Nurture*.[33] In it, Bushnell urged that the life of childhood should be part of the life of the Christian family, which in turn was part of the organic unity of the church. His thesis was that the child was to grow up a Christian, and never know himself as being otherwise. With proper Christian nurture, asserted Bushnell, no child would ever be lost:

In other words, the aim, effort, and expectation should be, not, as is commonly assumed, that the child is to grow up in sin, to be converted after

[32] Thompson, *Changing Emphases in American Preaching*, pp. 20, 21.
[33] Cheney comments on Bushnell's thesis, p. 178. "The philosophy which underlies 'Christian Nurture' is likely to be lost sight of in the greater attraction of its practical lessons. It is opposed to the *individualism* of the then prevalent theology, and recognizes and emphasizes the *organic* life of the family, the Church and society at large, wherein no soul lives or acts alone as a unit, but all as parts of a living organism, interdependent and mutually helpful."

he comes to a mature age; but that he is to open on the world as one that is spiritually renewed, not remembering the time when he went through a technical experience, but seeming rather to have loved what is good from his earliest years.[34]

There were immediate repercussions to the treatise in New England. A "Letter" appeared, sanctioned by the North Association of Hartford County, which accused Bushnell of "dangerous tendencies." [35] The book was suppressed by its original publisher, the Massachusetts Sunday School Society. Bennett Tyler, a professor of theology at East Windsor Seminary, rejected the thesis of the book in its entirety. The soul of the child was depraved, and it could not be won from its initial state without the intervention of divine grace, Tyler said.[36] Other critics came forward and rejected the book because it was "naturalistic," that is, that it implied a man could become a Christian by education rather than by a direct change of the heart as wrought by God's power. Bushnell seemed "to resolve the entire matter into organic laws, explaining away both depravity and grace," Dr. Charles Hodge of Princeton said.[37] The Sunday School Union decided to suppress the book. By 1848, Bushnell was the author of a book which had stirred theological interest like none had done for a century! His name became known everywhere.[38]

Although Bushnell's book had a positive effect upon the New England religious scene, nevertheless, he became more and more of a controversial figure. On the one hand, he did not satisfy the revivalists who looked for the immediate conversion experience as the basis for the religious life, and on the other hand, he did not satisfy the liberals who did not appreciate his concept of the organic relationship between the family and the church, and his insistence that the church was at the center of all genuine Christian experience.

Bushnell was next to concern himself in his ministry with the

[34] *Christian Nurture,* pp. 10 f.

[35] Cheney, p. 179.

[36] "Educated by angels, amid the glories of heaven," the child would remain a sinner. In Tyler's caustic attack upon Bushnell, New England Calvinism was attempting to maintain itself. Bennet Tyler, *Letters to Dr. Bushnell on Christian Nurture* (Hartford, 1848), pp. 6 ff; cf. Bushnell's letter to his daughter (1848), Cheney, pp. 188–189.

[37] Cf. Charles Hodge, "Bushnell on Christian Nurture," *The Biblical Repertory and Princeton Review,* XIX (October 1847), pp. 502–539.

[38] Cf. the reviews by G. W. Briggs, "Bushnell on Christian Nurture," *Christian Examiner and Religious Miscellany,* XLIII (1847), and Noah Porter, Jr., "Bushnell on Christian Nurture," *New Englander,* VI (1848), pp. 126–134.

social and economic problems of his community, which, he felt, reflected the problems of his country. He proposed to study the "foundation of civic obligation."[39] He became a political activist in the city of Hartford and soon associated himself with the Protestant Alliance, a group which proposed to bring about religious liberty and Protestant unity.[40] Bushnell wrote an open letter to the pope, in which he demanded religious liberty for all Roman Catholics. Later, he attended an international meeting of the Alliance, and much to his disappointment discovered that even there creedal loyalty was demanded of its members. He grew tired of the Alliance and demanded rather that America "be saved from Catholicism." His sermon, "The Crisis of the Church," reflected his insistence that religion and politics could not be divorced from one another: "Rise then O Men of Christ! And Thou O God of the land, arise! Fire in us the spirit of our fathers! . . . TILL OUR COUNTRY AND THY GLORY ARE SAFE!"[41] He was very much impressed with the idea of a "Holy Community," in which Americans could bring about the perfect society. At times, however, he despaired of any vital involvement of religion in the political sphere. In terms of the slavery question, Bushnell was adamant—slavery was a sin and had to be abolished. However, the abolition of slavery was to come about according to God's plan, *not* man's. Bushnell asked men to await the activity of God's will in history to eradicate slavery. Man, however, was not to interfere even if it were a matter of conscience to him.[42]

Bushnell was convinced that the ministry must guide the affairs of the state. An articulate ministry was necessary for a virtuous nation, he insisted. The clergy had the task of leading the people

[39] Cf. Cross, Chapter VI: "The Expedient of Eloquence." Cross describes his criticism of society: "Convinced that society and government were founded in God's decree, Bushnell criticized the social contract theory that lay behind the American Constitution and the more recent triumph of the Democrats in Connecticut. Denying the sovereign 'rights of the people,' Bushnell announced that an organic social order preceded and determined any written covenant. Men never existed in a Lockean 'state of nature,' with rights they could insure by compact, and they should therefore accept the status quo that Providence had established. Against militant Jacksonian individualism, Bushnell, like most of the northern ministry, sanctioned political conservatism."
[40] Cf. Bushnell, "The Evangelical Alliance," *New Englander*, V (1847), pp. 113, 121–123.
[41] Bushnell, "Christ of the Church," (Hartford, 1835), p. 36.
[42] Bushnell, "The Northern Iron," (Hartford, 1854), p. 10; "The Census and Slavery" (Hartford, 1860), p. 4; "A Discourse on the Slavery Question," (Hartford, 1839), p. 21.

into "the holy republic." In the last analysis, however, Bushnell's congregation was unwilling to have their minister act as a political monitor. His *Politics under the Law of God,* which was used as a campaign document against the Whigs in 1844, made Bushnell extremely unpopular. Thereafter he remained silent until the Civil War, when the conditions of the time insisted that he speak out again as a political mentor to a people whom he believed were ignorant of the will of God.

Invited in 1848 to give lectures at Harvard, Yale, and Andover, Bushnell dealt in these with the doctrines of the Trinity and the Atonement.[43] These lectures were incorporated into the book *God in Christ,* published in 1849, which included an introductory chapter on the nature and role of language. Bushnell was concerned with the problem of the relation of religious truth to language and symbol. Part of the reason for this concern was due to the unique phenomenon known as "The Golden Age of American Oratory," which forced the preacher to be eloquent in order to be understood.[44] Theology can be delivered, said Bushnell, from the morass into which it had floundered, only if there be a reassessment of the nature of language. All language is divisible into two components, a physical and an intellectual:

[43] Cf. Bushnell, *God in Christ,* p. 185. "You have called me to occupy, this evening, a singular, and, in the same view, difficult and responsible office; which office, however, I most readily undertake, because I seem to have a subject and a duty appointed me also. It cannot be improper, in the circumstances, to say that when your letter came inviting me to perform this exercise, I had just emerged from a state of protracted suspense, or mental conflict, in reference to what is called, theologically, the doctrine of Atonement; that is, of the life and death of Jesus Christ as the Saviour of the world. The practical moment of Christ's work had been sufficiently plain, but the difficulty had been to bring its elements into one theologic view. The subject had for many years been hung up before me, and I had been perusing it on all sides, trying it by manifold experiments, and refusing to decide by the will what could only be cleared by light, till now, at last, the question had seemed to open itself and display its reasons."

[44] Cross, pp. 91–92: "The lectures which later became *God in Christ* assigned theology a new role; properly interpreted, theology was poetry, suited to the finest minds; no longer the domain of unremitting logic, it became the very instrument of eloquence. To the lectures thus interpreting Christian dogma, Bushnell prefaced a treatise on language. Contemporaries had provided a compendious manual on oratorical knowhow; Bushnell investigated the relation of religious truth to the premises and nature of effective language. The love of coherence was inherent in the New England tradition; Bushnell's need to analyze and comprehend proved stronger than his rejection of New England's provincial rationalism." Cheney says that this chapter on "Language" is the key to Horace Bushnell; (p.203).

Words of thought or spirit are not only inexact in their significance, never measuring the truth or giving its precise equivalent, but they always affirm something which is false, or contrary to the truth intended. They impute *form* to that which is really out of form. They are related to the truth, only as form to spirit—earthen vessels in which the truth is borne, yet always offering their mere pottery as being the truth itself.[45]

Language is inexact and inadequate in its representation of spiritual truth. It also changes its meaning and often reflects varying points of view. Different symbols, therefore, have to be employed in order to express the richness of the Christian experience. For this reason, Bushnell said that Christian truth could never be brought under the mold of a dogmatic statement:

Considering the infirmities of language, all formulas of doctrine should be held in a certain spirit of accommodation. They cannot be pressed to the letter for the very sufficient reason that the letter is never true. They can be regarded only as proximate representations, and should therefore be accepted not as laws over belief, or opinion, but more as badges of consent and good understanding. The moment we begin to speak of them as guards and tests of purity, we confess that we have lost the sense of purity.[46]

God in Christ was Bushnell's attempt to express the doctrines of the Trinity and the Atonement in a new way, thereby avoiding the hackneyed phraseology usually associated with these doctrines. The speaker, Bushnell believed, could move the listener to accept religious truth simply by speaking about divine truth: "Christian truth itself emerged as the expression of God—God coming into expression through histories and rites, through an incarnation, and through language—in one syllable, by the WORD." [47]

I know no better method than to accept these great truths of trinity and atonement as realities or verities addressed to faith; or what is not far different, to feeling and imaginative reason—not any more as logical and metaphysical entities for the natural understanding . . . The essential matter seems to be that some trinity shall be held, such as will answer the practical uses of the life, and bring God into a lively, glowing, manifold power over the inner man—Father, Son, Holy Ghost, historically three, and also really one;—some scheme of atonement that upholds laws, as eternal

[45] *God in Christ,* p. 48.
[46] *Ibid.,* p. 81.
[47] Cheney, pp. 201, 202, describes the reception Bushnell received after his address at Yale. See also *God in Christ,* p. 74.

verity and sanctity; delivering still from bondage under it, and writing it as a law of liberty in the heart.[48]

Bushnell did not try to solve the metaphysical problem of the relation of the human to the divine nature in Christ. Christ was different from man:

... not in degree, but in kind ... He is in such a sense God, or God manifested, that the unknown term of his nature, that which we are most in doubt of, and about which we are least capable of any positive affirmation is the human.[49]

The Trinity became for him, therefore, a trinity of manifestation, a trinity that resulted of necessity from the revelation of God. Bushnell described his approach to this problem:

I do not undertake to fathom the interior being of God, and tell how it is composed. That is a matter too high for me, and I think for us all. I only insist that, assuming the strictest unity and even simplicity of God's nature, He could not be efficiently or sufficiently revealed to us, without evolving a trinity of persons, such as we meet in the Scriptures. These persons or personalities are the *dramatis personae* of revelation, and their reality is measured by what of the infinite they convey in these finite forms. As such, they bear, on the one hand, a relation to God, who is to be conveyed or imported into knowledge; on the other they are related to our human capacities and wants, being that presentation of God which is necessary to make Him a subject of thought, or bring Him within the discourse of reason; that also which is necessary to produce mutuality, or terms of conversableness between us and Him, and pour His love most effectually into our feeling.[50]

Christ for Bushnell was a manifestation in human form of the eternal life of the Father. By his incarnate love, Bushnell said, he re-united man's love to God. Jesus Christ came to reveal God to man. Man's task therefore was to experience His manifested godness, love, and suffering. God entered "into human feeling, by his incarnate charities and suffering, to re-engage the world's love and re-unite the world, as free, to the Eternal life." *God in Christ* presented a new approach to Christian theology. Christian doctrine was appropriated not by the understanding, but by "the imaginative reason". "The endeavor is, by means of expression, and under the laws of expression, to set forth God—His providence, and His government, and,

[48] *God in Christ*, p. 111.
[49] *Ibid.*, p. 123.
[50] *Ibid.*, p. 137.

what is more and higher than all, God's own feeling, His truth, love, justice, compassion." [51]

The book had a mixed reception, although most of the reviewers were extremely critical of it, primarily, of course, the orthodox theologians. [52] Bushnell was accused of being a German transcendentalist "befogging, bloating, and spoiling the clear Anglo-Saxon mind." He was charged with the heresies of Sabellianism, Docetism, Apollinarianism, Eutychianism, Pelagianism, and semi-Pelagianism. [53] Clergymen and seminary professors banded together to remove Bushnell from his pastorate. [54] A period of isolation followed. A neighboring ministerial Association, the Fairfield West, attempted to bring him to trial for heresy by presenting a "Remonstrance and Complaint to the Hartford Central Association." [55] Even those who

[51] *Ibid.*, p. 74.

[52] Cheney, pp. 214, 215. "At the time of the publication of 'God in Christ,' the atmosphere was sensitively tremulous with suspicions in respect to the orthodoxy of the author, a state of things of which he himself was not ignorant. On the issue of the book from the press in February, 1849, a few of the religious newspapers and magazines spoke of it tolerantly, one or two perhaps kindly, but the larger number with decided expressions of dissent and denunciation. The May number of the *New Englander* for that year contained a notice of 'God in Christ' from the pen of Dr. Leonard Bacon, kindly in tone, and marked by discrimination and fairness in the statement of its teachings. Two ministers residing in Hartford, afterwards abundantly friendly to Dr. Bushnell, published lengthy reviews, more or less dissenting from its statements of truth.

"But these criticisms, and others such as these, were the milk of human kindness itself, compared with the language employed by another class of writers. No sooner did the book see the light than it became apparent that the theological authorities were determined to strangle the infant in its very cradle. It was extensively believed, and publicly charged at the time, that the fierce and systematic onset which was made upon the author and his new work was the result of a concerted plan, originating in Hartford and its vicinity. As a part of this plan, the leading theological centres were to furnish each a champion to assist in crushing the man, who, though he had denied none of the cardinal doctrines of Christianity, had ventured to express his faith in them under formulas and philosophic explanations somewhat different from those which were assumed to be canonically settled for all time."

[53] Cf. Cross, p. 111; also, review of *God in Christ, in Biblical Repository,* V³ (1849), pp. 371 ff; review of the Reverend Robert Trumbull's *Theopany, ibid.,* p. 564; Enoch Pond, *Review of Dr. Bushnell's "God in Christ"* (Bangor, 1849), p. 113; Charles Hodge, *Essays and Reviews* (Bangor, 1849), p. 113.

[54] Cheney, p. 215, also p. 222, Bushnell's letter to this wife.

[55] *Ibid.*, cf. Cheney, p. 225; p. 234: "in January, 1850, the Association of "Fairfield West," a ministerial body in the western part of the State, presented a "Remonstrance and Complaint to the Hartford Central Association" upon their action in the case of Dr. Bushnell. 'Various considerations,' they said, 'have caused us to fear lest the doctrines of that book *(God in Christ)* may be already gaining a dangerous ascendency, especially over the minds of the young, and

were loyal to Bushnell determined to find out if he *was* orthodox. Two years later, Bushnell attempted to articulate his orthodoxy in a volume entitled *Christ in Theology*.[56]

By 1850, Bushnell was a middle-aged man. He was a lonely man, considered theologically dangerous by both the Calvinists and the Unitarians.[57] The matter of whether the charge of heresy could be established was still a live question. His "comprehensive" approach did not satisfy the disputants.

During the winter of 1851–52 there was still another revival of religion in Hartford, this one brought about by the evangelistic preaching of Charles Finney of Oberlin. Bushnell, however, was not permitted to participate in the revival services held in Hawes' Center Church.[58] Further attempts were made to try Bushnell, now before the General Assembly of the Congregational Church.[59] Secretive

---

preparing the way for a widespread error, captivating to the carnal mind, but destructive of the faith, and ruinous to the souls of men.'

"The Hartford Association delayed their reply until March, and then merely reiterated their former statements concerning the book, and declined to present Dr. Bushnell for trial."

[56] From Bushnell's Preface to *Christ in Theology*, pp. i-vi: "This volume contains the matter of an answer made to the ministerial association of which I am a member, for the doctrines of my book, 'God in Christ,'—a book in which it was rumored and extensively believed that I had published dangerous or even fundamental errors. This answer was made, and the inquiry itself formally terminated, more than a year ago . . . Indeed, my intention was not so much to defend as to complete my doctrine, but a fuller exposition of certain points, and by a reference to the opinions of others, and of the Church in this and other ages. My principal endeavor in it is to make my positions more intelligible; in accomplishing which, I rely to a great extent on tracing their import comparatively, which in my book I had scarcely done at all.

"As my former volume was called 'God in Christ,' I have called the present 'Christ in Theology,' with a design that will be sufficiently obvious. To complete the descending series begun, there is wanted another volume, showing the still lower, and, as it were, sedimentary subsidence of theology itself, precipitated in the confused mixtures of its elements."

[57] Cross, p. 115, reports that: ". . . his revelation had merely kindled the fury of the conservatives and the timidity of the Connecticut liberals. Neither Unitarians nor Congregationalists took up his cause. No Unitarian nor Harvard advances interrupted his provincial pastorate, and he was left to attend the meetings of the Congregational Associations, a suspect and controversial figure. He stood under constant threat of excommunication. Only the church he had thought of leaving stood firmly behind him."

[58] Cheney, pp. 253, 254.

[59] *Ibid.*, pp. 258; 259: "'It is hardly to be expected, in such a case, that I will come before you protesting my orthodoxy; but I wish you to be notified of the confidence I have that, when the smoke of these agitations is blown away, it will be discovered by any competent scholar and critic in Church history who

overtures were made to members of Bushnell's church who would speak out against his heretical tendencies. Finally, at the initiation of some of the leading men of Bushnell's church, the church withdrew from the Hartford North Consociation, and the attack on Bushnell appeared to be at an end.[60]

In 1853, Horace Bushnell had been pastor of the North Church in Hartford for twenty years. On the anniversary of this appointment in Hartford, he preached a Commemorative sermon, summarizing his entire ministry up to this point. In the sermon he called attention to his theological methodology, or his theological "comprehensiveness" as he called it:

Accordingly, the effect of my preaching never was to overthrow one school and set up the other; neither was it to find a position of neutrality midway between them; but, as far as theology is concerned, it was to comprehend, if possible, the truth contended for both; in which I had, of course, abundant practice in the subtleties of speculative language, but had the Scriptures always with me, bolting out their free, incautious oppositions, regardless of all subtleties. Having it for a law never to act on the policy of concealment or suppression for the sake of peace, in respect to any subject in which I was ripe enough for a declaration, I took my stand openly on all the vexed questions, preaching both sides; or rather showing, in effect, that if both were to condense all they hold into one faith, they would probably not have any too large a faith to be Christian. But as all the language applicable to the subjects in question was preoccupied by the former uses, and the much debated subtleties of our New England rationalism, I had many difficulties making myself intelligible. The two parties heard me, as it were, across the fence, and the main question appeared for a long time to be, not what I was teaching, but on which side I was. If I preached a sermon, for example, that turned more especially on the absolute dependence of sinners, or their inability apart from God, to renew and sanctify themselves, the Old-School hearers, taken by the

may undertake to settle the precise merit or relative import of my supposed defections that I was really in a closer agreement of doctrine and a closer sympathy of evangelic sentiment with the acknowledged fathers and teachers of the Church, than my brethren who are testifying so great concern on my account. The verdict will be, not that I raised any banner of revolt against orthodoxy, but that, on the contrary, I only sought to restore its equilibrium, and keep it fitly adjusted to the varying currents of thought and opinion involved in human progress, as it has been in all ages, and, if it is to be "the everlasting gospel," must be in all ages to come . . .'"

[60] Cheney, p. 261: "*Voted*, that we, the North Church in Hartford, not regarding a consociated connection with other churches as essential to good order, fellowship, and standing among them (which we earnestly desire to preserve and cherish), do hereby withdraw from all connection with the North Consociation of Hartford County."

sound of certain right words and phrases which I must use, of course, but having no care to follow the arguments and explanations by which alone their meaning was determined, put on a look of visible satisfaction, which seemed to say, 'We have him with us.' If I preached a sermon that called to action, asserting a complete power, under God, to cast off sin and be renewed in righteousness, my New-School hearers were sure that it was right; for the main thing cared for by them was, not so much any point of theory as that men should not be shut up in sin, to wait for some prevenient grace that God's sovereignty may never bestow ... To make myself intelligible at once to both parties was difficult, for the reasons already assigned; but I was able, in general, to retain your confidence. In this I had no difficulty except upon the Old-School side; for with them it was a point not merely to resist the new theology of the day, but, as by a kind of necessary implication, to see that nothing was varied from the manner and form in which they had been taught; and they were not easily satisfied, even if the variation took them backward towards a more genuine antiquity. Though even this jealousy of variation, I am certain, would never have made even one of them restive, had there been no instigators of suspicion without, actuated themselves by rumor and hearsay, to disturb the impressions otherwise received under the unobstructed teachings of my ministry. As it was, I had always my strong personal friends and confidants, even among the pillars of their side. Indeed, I had a certain peculiar sympathy with the style of piety in the Old-School brethren, especially in all the points where it was contrasted with the flashiness of a super-active, all-to-do manner, such as then distinguished the movement party of the times. I loved their deep-drawn sentiments, and the sense of God that reverberated in their Christian expressions. I was drawn to their prayers, and to them personally by their prayers; and it has always been my conviction that if they had been a little more Old-School, if they had been able to comprehend in their antiquity more than one century, they would have been as much drawn to me as I was to them. But a few became satisfied that I was not exactly in what they took for the Old (viz., the 'New Light' metaphysical) theology in which they had been trained, grew more uncomfortable as they were more set upon from without, and withdrew; not in any manner of protest or disaffection, but silently, as connected with a change of residence, or with only some temperate avowals of dissatisfaction. Others, who had breadth enough to allow some variations of form when the substance was so manifestly preserved, stood by me firmly to their death; and others still remain, doubly endeared to me by the persistence of their confidence.

The only difficulty I have ever encountered in my ministry, that cost me a real and deep trial of feeling, related to the matter of evangelist preachers, and what may be called the machinery system of revivals. Things had come to such a pitch in the churches, by the intensity of the revival system, that the permanent was sacrificed to the casual, the ordinary swallowed up and lost in the extraordinary, and Christian piety itself reduced to a kind of campaigning or stage-effect exercise. The spirit of the pastor was broken, and his powers crippled by a lack of expectation; for it was becoming a fixed impression that effect is to be looked for only under instrumentalities that are extraordinary. He was coming to be scarcely more than a church clock for beating time and marking the years, while the effective ministry of the word was to be dispensed by a class of professed revivalists. It was even difficult for the pastor, saying nothing of conversions, to keep alive in Christians themselves any hope or expectation of holy living, as an abiding state, in the intervals of public movement and excitement left to his care; because everything was brought to the test of the revival state as a standard, and it could not be conceived how any one might be in the Spirit, and maintain a constancy of growth, in the calmer and more private methods of duty, patience, and fidelity, on the level of ordinary life. Others felt the mischiefs accruing to the cause of religion as I did, and remained silent. I took my ground, cautiously, as I knew how, and spoke my convictions. The result was painful for a time; not because any storm was raised, but because of the very great difficulty I found in making my position understood and appreciated, and because many appeared to be perplexed or embarrassed in their prayers, as if able to be sure no longer of any practical way of advance or success . . .

My sole object was to raise a distinction between the reviving of religion when it wants reviving, and a religion which places everything in scenes or spiritual campaigns, and tests all Christian exercise by the standards of the extraordinary.

I wish it were possible, also, to speak of the way in which he has led me on out of the difficulties and reserved questions which encompassed my early ministry. I will only say that Christianity is opened to me now as a new heaven of truth, a supernatural heaven, wide as the firmament, possible only to faith, to that luminous, clear and glorious. This one thing I have found, that it is not in man to think out a gospel, or to make a state of light by phosphorescence at his own centre. He can have the great mystery of godliness only as it is mirrored in his heart by an inward revelation of Christ. Do the will and you shall know the doctrine—this is the truth I have proved by my twenty years of experience.[61]

At this time, too, he struggled with ill health, which increasingly prevented his full-time participation in the activities of the church. Even with this fact, however, there were further attempts at trying Bushnell for heresy. One member of the Connecticut General Association, which met in Waterbury in 1853, asserted that:

We have come to a crisis in the history of the churches of Connecticut. Obscure it as you will, the foundations are touched. The question is whether a man charged with treason against the truth of Christ and the throne of God can be tried.[62]

[61] Cheney, pp. 282–287.
[62] Cheney, pp. 306–307: "In Hartford Central Association there had been for years a dissatisfied minority; dissatisfied because they believed there was fundamental error in Dr. Bushnell's books; dissatisfied because he was not brought

The division of the Congregational Associations in Connecticut, which occurred during Bushnell's time, and largely because of him, troubled him a great deal. The Christian faith in the Hartford Community was seriously aggravated by these further attempts at "heresy-hunting."

In 1854 he campaigned for a city park.[63] At the same time, he sought for a reconciliation with Dr. Hawes, who was his constant adversary in the Hartford religious community, in order to bring about, as he said, "God's truth in our community."[64] In so doing,

to trial; dissatisfied because his vital ministry, powerful preaching, and new ideas were a continual stumbling-block in the way of the old established habits and standards of their ancient churches. Finding that their minority was powerless in Hartford Central Association, and desiring some organization through which they could control the action of those who sympathized with their views, they conceived the idea of separating from their old Association and of forming a new one, to be called the Hartford Fourth, and to consist exclusively of such pastors and churches as they knew to be anti-Bushnell."

[63] Cheney, p. 312: "This piece of ground was a little less than a half a mile long, and comprised between thirty and forty acres; and the fine college grounds adjacent, arranged to harmonize with the plan, would make up a virtual park range of fifty acres. On the whole, the amount of space obtained would do very well for a small city, and being central, it would be taken care of and kept in constant use.

"Determined thus in the matter of locality, I had none the less been appalled by the god-forsaken look of the premises . . . at the extreme north bend of the river, and directly off Asylum Street, in front of the new Park Church, all the garbage und truck of the city were dumped, as in a Gehenna without fire–shavings, underbed fillings, tin-waste, leather-cuttings, cabbage stumps, hats without tops, old saddles, stove-pipes rusted out, everything, in short, that had no right to be anywhere else . . .

"Much anger and severity have been, of course, encountered, and I have had my share of it. Shortly after the ground had been taken it happened that the huge old grist-mill at one end, and the soap-works at the other, were burnt down; whereupon it was even charged upon me, in apparent sincerity, by an anonymous letter, that I had set these fires to help on my project. Now the park is universally popular–I do not know that it has an enemy. Millions of dollars would not buy the property. And I hear of it as being said, every few days, by one or another of the old economic gentlemen that opposed it with most feeling, *"After all, the best investment our city has ever made is the park."* This one thing is now clear to us all, that everything in the outward look of our city has been improving since the park was made. Our endeavors have courage in them; for we see that we can have a really fine city. Indeed, the park has already added millions to the real estate values of our property . . ." Letter from Bushnell to Donald G. Mitchell, Cheney, pp. 313–319.

[64] Cheney, p. 327. ". . . I knew that you were wanting something which you could accept as a valid and substantial assent to the great points of doctrine supposed to have been controverted by me; something, too, which you could use in a public way. In this view I gave you in two sentences [1] an explicit assent to the Nicene doctrine of the Trinity, as reaffirmed by the Westminster Assembly;

he had to compromise with Hawes' orthodoxy. But he did so in order to bring about "the peace and the restored unity of the body of Christ." [65]

In 1855, recognizing a serious break in his health, he began to travel. He went to New York; Cuba; Savannah, Georgia; Charleston, South Carolina; yet all the time being in anguish because of "my dear home, my deserted pulpit, my dear flock and work." [66] He was continually preoccupied with the thought of death. [67] In 1856 he decided to journey to California, not, however, before announcing that he was completing a series of lectures on "Supernaturalism," which was later to become the book *Nature and the Supernatural*. While in California he was offered the presidency of the College of California, but he decided to "wait upon providence" before accepting. Although it was obvious to him that the moist climate of the East contributed to his illness, he nonetheless formally declined the position in 1861. He did, however, establish the location of the College and made appeals that "the leading men in California" might permit it to make "claims upon their consideration." [68]

Nature and the Supernatural, the most thorough and complete treatise he ever wrote, dealt with the problem of revelation. "Does God make direct revelations to men now? Did he of old, then why not now? Does not the personality of God imply it?" he questioned. The book was directed specifically to the enlightened American public which he felt had been overwhelmed by "science and trans-

(2) an assent equally explicit to the 'equivalent expression' doctrine of the work of Christ,–the same which is commonly held in New England in terms entirely convenient or consonant to what I hold as a part of the true doctrine. Meeting you in terms like these, I only took care to set the statements in such a connection or framework that if you should have a mind to publish them it might read, not like something dictated or prescribed, but like something spontaneously offered. And now you reply, taking no notice whatever of these advances for which alone my letter was written, that if I 'will give you something on which you can stand, some presently avowed platform which shall accord with the common faith,' you will endeavor to meet me! My dear brother, on what can you stand? What is your orthodox platform? If you cannot meet me in the Westminster Assembly doctrine of Trinity, or the current terms of the New England doctrine of equivalent expression, just where you must accept the vast majority of your brethren or not at all, then where can you meet me?" Letter from Bushnell to Hawes, Cheney, pp. 331–332.

[65] Cheney, p. 337; cf. Cheney's comment about his orthodoxy, p. 338; and Austin Phelps of Andover, p. 339.
[66] *Ibid.*, p. 351.
[67] *Ibid.*, p. 354; also pp. 357, 362.
[68] *Ibid.*, p. 386, p. 404; cf. the sermon on his return to North Church, p. 407.

38

cendentalism." "From the first moment ... of modern science," *Nature and the Supernatural* declared, "it has been clear that Christianity must ultimately come into the grand issue of life and death with it." [69] The Christian faith, Bushnell maintained, was challenged by enemies—science, Biblical criticism, Unitarianism and transcendentalism, as well as others. Science and its methodology for discovering the truth, challenged the idea of divine creation and revelation. Bushnell spoke directly to the scientistis, (as he had to the transcendentalists), and always in terms of the categories they employed. Bushnell's project was ultimately the reconciliation of reason and faith, of science and revelation, and of nature and the supernatural. The Christian who had always regarded the natural and the supernatural as two distinct realms, which were antithetical to one another, did not realize that "a suspension of the laws of nature" could no longer be accepted by modern "scientific" man. The supernatural was defined in such a way that it could not possibly be defended. In regard to this question, Bushnell wrote:

We define miracles to be suspensions of the laws of nature, and make it impossible, *gratis*, from that time forth, to offer an argument for them, which any bravely rational person, or mind well grounded in science can ever be expected to admit ... We surrender, in fact, the credibility of anything supernatural or miraculous by renouncing the credibility of any such thing occurring now. [70]

It was Bushnell's thesis that nature and the supernatural were not antithetical, but rather complementary—coeternal factors in the universal system of God. We do not need to look for miracles to find the supernatural, for we find it, as Bushnell said:

... in what is least transcendent and most familiar, even in ourselves. In ourselves we discover a tier of existences that are above nature, and in all their most ordinary actions are doing their will upon it. The very idea of our personality is that of a being not under law of cause and effect, a being supernatural ... It is not said, be it observed, as is sometimes done,

[69] *Nature and the Supernatural*, p. 19. Cf. Cross, p. 119; p. 120: "All three of the public's new interests undermined inherited faith; geology contradicted the Mosaic account of creation and suggested to some that organic life might have developed slowly from the lowest forms up to man; technological progress fostered human pride and challenged the Christian pattern of history; finally, transcendentalism by scoffing at miracles, enthusing over human progress, and denying man's need of intercession, seemed to sum up the time's heresies and offer the public a faith adapted to its credulity. Bushnell set himself the task of answering these infidelities by a reformulation of Christian divinity."
[70] *Nature and the Supernatural*, pp. v, vi.

that the supernatural implies a suspension of the laws of nature, a causing them, for the time, not to be—that perhaps is never done—it is only said that we, as powers, not in the line of cause and effect, can set the causes in nature at work, in new combinations otherwise never occurring, and produce by our action upon nature results which she, as nature, could never produce by her own internal acting.[71]

What Bushnell had done in *Nature and the Supernatural* was to direct Christian theology away from its defensive position, to a new positive expression of the nature of divinity, within the Christian faith. The battle between science and religion seemed to have been won by science. Religion could no longer assert the verifiability of miracles. The Mosaic account of creation and the new geology contradicted one another. The public wanted to believe but could not in the face of the discoveries of science. Transcendentalism, which had earlier rejected miracles, and which built a faith on human progress, easily won the convictions of the intellectual. Science and transcendentalism therefore threatened to destroy for all times in New England the historic Christian faith. Bushnell responded by reformulating the Christian conception of *revelation,* for it was this doctrine which had been most seriously challenged. Revelation was in clear opposition to the scientific approach of discovery and evaluatory truth. Either the Bible and its revelation or science and its discoveries—these had appeared to be the only alternatives.

In *Sermons for the New Life,* published the same year as *Nature and the Supernatural,* Bushnell asserted that faith was a commitment which could not be justified on the basis of natural evidences. Knowledge came from trust. He had decided that it was no longer possible to accumulate evidence for the Christian faith. Rather, faith was a commitment which transcended scientific arguments

---

[71] *Ibid.,* p. 43. Cf. Cross, pp. 131, 132, and her comments on *Nature and the Supernatural:* "With *Nature and the Supernatural* Bushnell entered a new field, . . . seeking to rationalize man's history and experience within a Christian framework. Attempting to re-establish the Christian view of man, he called upon the testimony of science and made man as creator and inventor of the protagonist of the human drama. Yet he challenged contemporary humanism, even as he took account of it. He no longer, he wrote, longed to be thought a 'liberal.' With his final resolution to remain a Hartford preacher, he had moved this much closer to Connecticut theology and orthodox Christianity. He had spoken of a fallen world and a corrupted humanity, of the foolishness of atomic individualism. He refused to see the history of the world as the steady ascension to nineteenth-century virtue, and he restricted human hope to a brief, remote break in history."

and evidence. "One being, a sinner," he said, "commits himself to another being, a Savior"—this is the basis for the Christian life. Knowledge, proof, and evidence might ensue, but they were no longer necessary for the Christian life.

He finally resolved that he would spend the rest of his ministry in Hartford (though he had hoped during his younger years to receive a call from Harvard to become Hollis Professor of Moral Philosophy). The reviews of his books were unfavorable; Bushnell felt "pelted all around." His health collapsed and he was unable to preach. However, by New Year's Day of 1859, he was well enough to tell a friend that "I think the day is at hand when something can be done for a better conception of the work of Christ." [72] He proposed to write a treatise on "the laws of God's Supernatural kingdom." Having resigned from his church in Hartford in 1859, he gave himself entirely to the writing of this book, in which he hoped to set forth the meaning of the Atonement.

Civil war broke out between the states during the period of Bushnell's "Water Cure" at Clifton Springs, New York. He felt a vindication of his prophetic role. He had to take on once again the prophet's obligation to interpret, sustain, and direct the nation, which had become a conscious moral entity. [73] Slavery is barbarism, he shouted, and "it is dreadfully mortifying to our American feel-

[72] Cheney, p. 420: "I will try to comfort myself in the hope that I am about right when you, on one hand, set me down as the demolisher of nature and the *New Englander* complains, on the other, that I defer too much to nature, and am too much under her power." And again: "It is really hard times with a poor fellow. The *New Englander* tries me all through by the New Haven theology, and Dr. James makes me a ninny for being in the New Haven theology..." "My day has not yet come, and will not till after I am gone. So, by a kind of foolish conceit, it may be, I contrive to think. I should fare better if I would get up a school or sect, or raise a party of *ites*, have a publication, etc. But the work I am called to do moves slowly, and yet it moves." Cheney, pp. 420, 422.
[73] Cheney, pp. 423–424: "The hand of God is upon me, and I must go, I have struggled long with this dark necessity, and you on your part have also detained me. Were I dislodged by you, I should probably go with greater pains and fewer regrets.... I ought, perhaps, to say it is not merely to gain a lengthened lease of life that I am induced to make this trying sacrifice. If I had nothing to live for, I certainly would not wish to live a day longer. But I am encouraged in the hope of being so far recovered in health that I may prosecute, in a careful way, objects and themes of study that appear to me to have no secondary importance. In this hope I consent to go into exile, though to sever these ties and tear myself away costs me a struggle which I will not trust myself to describe; a struggle which I try to compose, by indulging the further hope that I may yet return to Hartford, and here may close my days... The grace of our Lord Jesus Christ be with you all: in this, Farewell."

ing."[74] Christian duty pointed directly to the abolition of slavery. He set the war within the Hebraic-Christian tradition, and discovered within it "comdemnation and atonement." "We have, at last, come to the point where only blood ... can resanctify what we have so loosely held and so badly desecrated."[75] For Bushnell, the war meant that tragedy and bloodshed were eternally necessary, but they also pointed away from history to Christ's eternal sacrifice.

Vicarious Sacrifice repeated many of the basic ideas of *God in Christ*, but with significant distinctions.[76] His own "Christly experience" influenced his theological concepts:

> I never saw so distinctly as now what it is to be a disciple, or what the key-note is of all most Christly experience. I think, too, that I have made my *last* discovery in this mine. First, I was led along into initial experience of God, socially and by force of the blind religional instinct in my nature; second, I was advanced into the clear moral light of Christ and God, as related to the principle of rectitude; next, or third, I was set on by the inward personal discovery of Christ, and of God as represented in him; now, fourth, I lay hold of and appropriate the general culminating fact of God's vicarious character in goodness, and of mine to be accomplished in Christ as a follower. My next stage of discovery will be when I drop the body and go home, to be with Christ in the conscious, openly revealed friendship of a soul whose affinities are with him. God help me in this expectation, that it may be fulfilled.[77]

There is "nothing strange as regards the principle" of the vicarious sacrifice of Christ, "no superlative, unexampled, and therefore unintelligible grace," asserted Bushnell. He went on to say:

[74] Cheney, p. 442.

[75] Bushnell, *Building Eras in Religion*, p. 311. Cf. Cheney, pp. 447, 448 regarding Lincoln.

[76] Cf. Cheney, p. 435; Bushnell, writing in a letter where he attempts to formulate a definition of Christian love says: "I suspect that your difficulty is not so much that you are selfish, precisely, in the matter of your love to Christ's goodness and beauty, as that you love him only artistically. There are two modes of love, admiration and felt affinity, the practical or practically Christian and the artistic, neither of which is at all selfish. When you admire a landscape, or love a beautiful child, there is no self-seeking in it, no computation of self-advantage, and yet it is not Christian. It is a distinterested, artistic, or aesthetic love. You may be a selfish person, thus loving, but this is not your selfishness. In the same way, we may love Christ artistically, as being the perfect beauty and good, where there is nothing selfish in the love, but only full room left to be a selfish person. Now the practical love, the Christian love, is being joined to Christ so as to be in self-sacrifice with him, and be, in so far, an unselfish person."

[77] *Ibid.,* p. 445.

Nothing is wanting to resolve the vicarious sacrifice of Jesus but the commonly known, always familiar principle of love, accepted as the fundamental law of duty, even by mankind. Given the universality of love, the universality of vicarious sacrifice is given also. Here is the centre and deepest spot of good, or goodness, conceivable. At this point we look into heaven's eye itself, and read the meaning of all heavenly grace.[78]

Bushnell concentrated his attention upon the suffering love of Christ, and sought, in this way, to awaken the religious sensibilities of man. God was love; his sacrifice revealed this love to a fearful humanity. Man responded to this love through his emotions. This was a difficult response, for the Christ of faith was hard to apprehend. Christ's life was one characterized by "sorrow, suffering, sacrifice, death, a paradox of ignominy and grandeur."[79] The life of Christ exhibited a sacrificial love, which was to be expressed by every man in his own life.

Bushnell was making the claim that all love was vicarious love, whether it was expressed in heaven or on earth. Love which suffered, with and for the sake of others, is vicarious love. Such a love, when associated with the mission of Christ, involved no mysterious or incomprehensible transaction, no legal or governmental procedure by which Christ enabled God to become gracious to men. Bushnell wrote:

In what is called his vicarious sacrifice [Christ] simply engages, at the expense of great suffering and even of death itself, to bring us out of our sins themselves, and so out of their penalties; being himself so profoundly identified with us in our fallen state, and burdened in feeling with our evils.[80]

The saving power came from the life and death of Christ. It was, however, not omnipotent power that compelled the will of men, but the power of God that renovated character, reconciled men to God, and induced them to love sacrificially.

The second volume of the *Vicarious Sacrifice,* entitled *Forgiveness and Law,* was written ten years later, and indicated Bushnell's ability to accept new opinions and new "light":

It seems to be required of me by the unexpected arrival of fresh light, that I should make a large revision of my former treatise entitled *The*

[78] *Vicarious Sacrifice,* p. 48.
[79] *Vicarious Sacrifice,* pp. 117, 197, 215, 216, 218; cf. Cross, pp. 145–6.
[80] *Ibid.,* p. 41.

Vicarious Sacrifice . . . Having undertaken to find the truth on this great subject at whatever cost, I am not willing to be excused from further obligation because the truth appears to be outgrowing my published expositions . . . There is no reason, personal to myself, why I should be fastened to my own small measures when larger measures are given me. Besides, how shall man ever get rid of his old sins, when he cannot let go his little outgrown opinions? [81]

During the winter and spring of 1863, he prepared two volumes, one entitled *Work and Play,* the other a collection of sermons, *Christ and His Salvation.* The following years were marked by a number of articles and essays which Bushnell wrote on a great variety of topics. *Moral Uses of Dark Things* is probably the most important from this last period of his life. He preached often during this time in the churches of Hartford, as well as in a wider Connecticut area, and also in Massachusetts and New York.

In 1875 he began a book on the Holy Spirit, which was to be entitled, "Inspiration: Its Modes and Uses, whether as related to Character, Revelation, or Action," [82] but did not have enough strength to finish it. He died on February 17, 1876. [83]

[81] *Forgiveness and Law,* p. 11.
[82] Cheney, p. 547; Bushnell says about this book: "I begin this day, January 22, 1875, a tract or treatise on the Holy Spirit and his work, which I have long been desiring to prepare, but have been detained formerly by other engagements, and of late by advanced age and the growing incapacity of disease. It does not seem to me that I can ever fully execute so heavy a work; but I can begin it, and God will permit me to go on, or stop me short when he pleases, and to him I gladly submit the result. Only, considering how much of divine insight will be needed to speak worthily of a subject so interior and deep, and so far removed from the mere natural intelligence of men, I invoke most earnestly his constant presence with me, and the steady oversight of his counsel. Help me, O Eternal Spirit, whose ways I am engaged to interpret, to be in the sense at all times of thy pure teaching, and to speak of what thou givest me to presently know!"
[83] Cross, p. 154, describes his last years: "Bushnell passed the last two decades of his life in the freedom of many finalities. His career had taken fixed form; he had few driving professional fears or expectations. The pugnacity of orthodoxy had waned with time, and, despite orthodoxy, a substantial number of books testified to his originality and his fame. If he had known failure, hatred, and frustrated ambitions, he also felt that he had known God. A white beard and long white hair framed the bony, emaciated face; the eyes, remote and unappeased, dominated his sharp, prominent nose and straight, thin mouth. If his pictures do not present the face of complete success, neither do they suggest defeat, but rather an austere resignation, hardly won. 'His general bearing was that of one whom life had chastened to the utmost.'"
Cheney, pp. 564, 565; His funeral sermon was preached by his successor at the North Church (now Park Church), the Rev. Dr. Burton, in which he said:

"Those of us who were personally and closely acquainted with this man will very sadly miss him. His humor; the fine insistence of his voice; the sinew, pith, and splendor of his diction, which never failed him even in his most extemporaneous utterances; his rich, inspired prejudices and frank contempt for several things on earth; his very quotable, sententious sayings, some last one of which was always likely to be circulating in this community; his sharp outlook continually upon the moving, great world; his beautiful ability to revise his own opinions, so that, meeting him any day, you were not unlikely to be told by him of some more felicitous, and comprehensive and unanswerable statement of some old point of truth which he had just worked out; his prayers, so rich and fresh with thought, so direct, true, and sweet in feeling; the power of various kinds, by which in his day he made the pulpit of the North Church to be one of the thrones of the world; his perfectly undaunted outlook into eternity; his high-hearted fight with disease and death for the last ten years; the youthfulness which beat irrepressible under his old age; his wiry form, determined and energetic to the last; his face so softened by years, and the chastisement of disease; and the inworking of God in his ripening soul,–yes, all that went to make Horace Bushnell, as he appeared among men and played off his magnetism upon them, some of us will affectionately, and sorrowfully, and also joyfully remember, until we meet him again in God's great other world . . .

"What a mind his must be to enter heaven, and start out upon its broad-winged ranges, its meditations and discoveries, its transfigurations of thought and feeling, its eternal enkindlings of joy as the mysteries of redemption unfold! I look forward with immense expectation to a meeting again with this man in his resurrection life. I want to see Horace Bushnell in his glorified immortal body, and note the movements of that mighty genius and that manful and most Christian soul when thus clothed upon and unhindered.

"Meanwhile, and until then, farewell, O master in Israel, O man beloved! God give thee light on thy dark questions now! God give thee rest from thy tired body! God bring us to thee when the eternal morning breaks."

CHAPTER II

A Language for the Theology of Experience

Horace Bushnell became anxious about Christianity. "Is it now to be found," he asked "that Christianity is only another form of myth, and is it so to be resolved into the mere 'history of nature' as the other religions before it?" Will the Christian faith be reduced to mere natural occurrences, "under the unchangeable laws of an endless cycle?" He found that there was a "new infidelity" present in his world, "a general progress toward mere naturalism", which was "in one way or another, extinguishing the faith of religion in the world." [1] He wrote: "All pretenses of a supernatural revelation, inspiration, or experience, it rejects; finding a religion, beside which there is no other, within the terms of mere nature itself; a universal, philosophic, scientific religion." [2] He found that this "philosophic, scientific religion" allowed for genuine religious experience—it permitted sacred scripture, and testified to the profoundest admiration for Jesus Christ, but only "in common with Numa, Plato, Zoroaster, Confucius, Mohammed, and others." This new religion insisted upon universal brotherhood and love and worship, but all of this on a naturalistic level. There could be no miracles, no Incarnation, no Resurrection, no new creation, and nothing which in any way defied the natural laws of the universe. Supernaturalism in all of its forms and manifestations had to be rejected outright. "Redemption itself, considered as a plan to raise man up out of thraldom, under the corrupted action of nature, rolling back its currents and bursting its constraints,—is a fiction. There is no such thraldom, no such deliverance, and so far Christianity is a mistake; a mistake, that is, in everything that constitutes its grandeur as a plan of salvation for the world." [3]

For Bushnell, the Christian faith was the Gospel of Salvation to

[1] Horace Bushnell, *Nature and the Supernatural* (as together constituting The One System of God), p. 16; cf. Bushnell's fear in *Work and Play*, pp. 100–101; *Sermons for the New Life*, p. 427; *Building Eras in Religion*, p. 52.
[2] *Nature and the Supernatural*, p. 17.
[3] *Ibid.*, p. 18.

the world. As such, it was inevitable that it should come into conflict ("a grand issue of life and death") with science. But Bushnell
was insistent that it was not that the Christian faith conflicted with
science. Both the Christian faith and science have their "common
root and harmony" in God. He spoke of Christianity as "the natural
foster-mother of science," and science as "the certain handmaid of
Christianity."[4] The Christian faith and science constitute one complete system of knowledge.

Nonetheless, Bushnell recognized the difficulty that "we see things
only in a partial manner." Because of the two great modes of thought,
Christianity, always conceived of in a supernaturalistic way, as
related to God's transcendent plan, science, as belonging to the
human and naturalistic. It was inevitable, he wrote, that a final
collision would take place and "a struggle necessary to the final
liquidation of the account between them."[5] Bushnell found that in
the intellectual current of his day there was widespread the idea
that one believed in nature simply, and in Christianity only in so
far as it conformed to nature and was able to find "shelter under
its laws." The mind of the Christian world was becoming more and
more saturated with naturalism, Bushnell feared, which he discovered led to real unbelief in the Christian faith.[6] He wrote: "Never

[4] *Ibid.,* p. 19; cf. the sermon "In and By Things Temporal are given Things
Eternal", *Sermons on Living Subjects,* pp. 268–284. Bushnell wanted to demonstrate that there was a "fixed relation between the temporal and the eternal,
such that we shall best realize the eternal by rightly using the temporal", p. 270;
cf. also the sermon, "Our Advantage in being Finite", *Sermons on Living Subjects,*
pp. 329–351.
[5] *Nature and the Supernatural,* p. 19; cf.: "Thus, from the time of Galileo's and
Newton's discoveries, down to the present moment of discovery and research
in geological science, we have seen the Christian teachers stickling for the letter
of the Christian documents and alarmed for their safety, and fighting, inch by
inch and with solemn pertinacity, the plainest, most indisputable or even demonstrable facts. On the other side, the side of science, multitudes, especially
of the mere *dilettanti,* have been boasting, almost every month, some discovery
that was to make a fatal breach upon revealed religion." Bushnell also objected
to what he called "bondage under the method of science." He contrasts this with
"the method of faith" which is "a verification by the heart, and not by the notions
of the head." *Ibid.,* p. 20.
[6] Bushnell listed a number of ways in which naturalism had affected the mind
of the age: first, there was "the relics of the old school of denial and atheism,
headed most conspicuously by Mr. Hume and the French philosophers"; but
there was also those "naturalizing critics in the Christian scriptures," Strauss,
Hennel, Newman, Fronde, Fox, Parker, who had virtually annihilated the gospels;
then there was "the schools of pantheists, who identify God and nature", as
well as "the large and vaguely-defined body of physicalists", the best example

before, since the inauguration of Christianity in our world, has any so general and momentous issue been made with it as this which now engages and gathers to itself, in so many ways, the opposing forces of human thought and society. Before all these combinations the gospel must stand, if it stands; and against all these must triumph, if it triumphs. Either it must yield, or they must finally coalesce and become its supporters." [7]

Bushnell did not intend to destroy the sciences and the scientific method and in this way vindicate the supernaturalistic character of the Christian faith. Rather, he began by insisting that there was an element of truth in all of the discoveries of modern science. "David Hume's argument," he wrote, "contains a great and sublime truth; viz., that nothing ever did or will take place out of system, or apart from law—not even miracles themselves." What Bushnell proposed was rather to find a legitimate place for the supernatural within "the one system of God", and to demonstrate that the supernatural belonged as a necessary part to the divine system itself. In this way, Bushnell believed that the supernatural in Christianity would maintain, "first, the rigid unity of the system of God; secondly, the fact that everything takes place under fixed laws." [8] Bushnell purposed to do the following:

of which are the phrenologists; with them were "the very intelligent, influential body of Unitarian teachers of Christianity," who were characterized by a maintenance of the truth of the scriptural miracles but also by a denial of human depravity and the need for supernatural grace. Such a faith led to an ethical theism instead of the Gospel of Salvation. Christ became a teacher and an interpreter of nature: "God, they say, has arranged the very scheme of the world so as to punish sin and reward virtue; therefore, any such hope of forgiveness as expects to be delivered of the natural effects of sin by a supernatural and regenerative experience, is vain; because it implies the failure of God's justice and the overturning of a natural law. Whoever is delivered of sin, must be delivered by such a life as finally brings the great law of justice on his side. To be justified freely by grace is impossible." *Nature and the Supernatural*, p. 24; also there were the "myriad schools of Associationists", who assumed that human nature belonged to the general order of nature; the "magnetists or seers of electricity" who described religion as "the revelations of natural clairvoyance and scientific necromancy ... illuminated by magnetic revelations"; also those physicians who were "continually occupied with the phenomena of the body", and finally those individuals in modern politics who insisted that civil government was grounded in a social contract, which "has the advantage ... of accounting for the political state, atheistically, under mere nature".

[7] *Nature and the Supernatural*, p. 29.
[8] *Ibid.*, p. 31; cf. also pp. 33 ff.; it is interesting to note that Bushnell recognized the difficulties of "a punctually infallible and verbal inspiration." He maintained that these difficulties were "insuperable".

48

I shall make out a conception both of nature and of supernatural redemption by Jesus Christ, the incarnate Word of God, which exactly meets the magnificent outline-view of God's universal plan, given by the great apostle to the Gentiles,—'And He is before all things, and by Him (in Him, it should be,) all things consist.' Christianity, in other words, is not an afterthought of God, but a forethought. It even antedates the world of nature, and is 'before all things'—'before the foundation of the world.' Instead of coming into the world, as being no part of the system, or to interrupt and violate the system of things, they all *consist,* come together into system, in Christ, as the center of unity and the head of the universal plan.[9]

The world must include Christianity, which ". . . becomes a proper and complete frame of order; to that crystalizes, in all its appointments, events, and experiences; in that has the design or final cause revealed, by which all its distributions, laws, and historic changes are determined and systematized."[10]

But in order to carry out his plan, Bushnell first had to develop a theory of language adequate to express his belief that Christianity existed "before the foundation of the world", and that, "instead of coming into the world, as being no part of the system, or to interrupt and violate the system of things, they all *consist,* come together into system, in Christ, as the center of unity and the head of the universal plan."

Bushnell effected a transformation in New England theology by an exposé of the deficiency and incapacity of language to serve as a medium of religious truth. This was a simple, readily understandable, but very radical critique of theology. Bushnell not only criticized theological language because of its implicit rationalistic structure, but criticized the claim that theology could be a speculative science. He articulated his criticism in the famous "Dissertation on Language" which formed the introduction to *God in Christ,* as well as in the chapter "Language and Doctrine" in *Christ in Theology.* In the article, "Our Gospel a Gift to the Imagination", Bushnell wrote:

[9] *Ibid.,* p. 31.
[10] *Ibid.;* cf. *The Spirit in Man,* p. 62: "God governs systematically which is the same as to say that he governs comprehensively. Either all things transpire in a plan as relatives in a grand whole, or else there is no whole. By his providential sway and the secret sway of his spirit then, we find him turning the courses of mind and matter together as a comprehensive whole, part answering to part, mind to matter and matter to mind, thoughts to events and events to thoughts, all things to all in a chime of universal order and law."

Human language is a gift to the imagination so essentially metaphoric, warp and woof, that it has no exact blocks of meaning to build a science of. Who would ever think of building up a science of Homer, Shakespeare, Milton? And the Bible is not a whit less poetic, or a whit less metaphoric, or a particle less difficult to be propositionized in the terms of the understanding. Shall we then have nothing to answer, when the sweeping question is put, why philosophy and every other study should make advances, and theology be only spinning its old circles and revising and re-revising its old problems? It must be enough to answer that philosophy, metaphysical philosophy, having only metaphor to work in, is under exactly the same limitation; that it is always backing and filling, and turning and returning, in the same manner; that nobody can name a single question that has ever been settled by all the systems it has built and the newly contrived nomenclatures it has invented. Working always in metaphors and fooling itself, how commonly, by metaphor, it gets a valuable gymnastic in words, and prepares to a more full and many-sided conception of words. So far it is fruitful and good, and just so far also is the scientific labor of theology. After all it is simple insight in both, and not speculation, that has the true discernment. Words give up their deepest, truest meaning, only when they are read as images of the same.[11]

Bushnell rejected the idea that God taught men language simply by the direct pronunciation of words. Language, he believed, was a by-product of the development of the races throughout the centuries. God was involved in the creation of language only in the sense that he created in all human beings the power of self-representation or expression.[12] Language was best understood when it was conceived to be a human product and a vehicle of thought. Bushnell offered the following as a suggestion as to how languages originated:

[11] *Building Eras in Religion,* p. 272.
[12] *God in Christ,* p. 17, article "Preliminary Dissertation on the nature of Language as related to Thought and Spirit". Bushnell was dependent, for his theory of language, upon an article by Prof. Josiah W. Gibbs in *The Christian Spectator,* Vol. IX, (1837). Bushnell suggested that languages are created even in Connecticut: "I hope it will not offend the romantic or marvelling propensity of my readers, if I affirm that a new language has been created and has perished, in Connecticut, within the present century. A very distinguished citizen, whose name is familiar to the country at large, himself a scholar and a keen philosophic observer, had a pair of twin boys, who were drawn to each other with such a mysterious and truly congenital fondness as to be totally occupied with each other, and thus to make little or no progress in learning the language of the family. Meantime, they were constantly talking with each other in a language constructed between them, which no one but themselves could understand. In this language they conversed at their plays as freely as men at their business, and in a manner that indicated the most perfect intelligence between them."

There is no difficulty in perceiving how our two unlanguaged men will proceed, when thrown together in the manner supposed, as far as the naming of sensations or physical objects is concerned. For the object is always present as a mediator or interpreter between them, so that when a sound is uttered as a name for it, or in connection with it, they may always know to what the sound or name refers. Thus all sights, sounds, smells, tastes, and touches, or feelings, or what is the same, their objects, are easily named, and their names will come into currency without difficulty, when sounded as representatives of the objects. As to the sounds adopted, they will generally be determined arbitrarily, or, at least, by causes so occult or remote that we must regard them as arbitrary.[13]

Bushnell spoke of a noun-language, which was a grouping of names to designate things. The noun-language also included the names of actions, which are called verbs. This kind of language was a physical language.

There was, however, another sphere of language which was wholly distinct from the physical language, which Bushnell called the language of intelligence. This was the language which served the mind, and which lay outside of the sense world. This was the kind of language which served to express a thought or an emotion. But the question remained, how to exhibit these internal states (thoughts, emotions) to other individuals? The only possible way, Bushnell said, was through the mediation of things; that is, by means of objects and acts which are part of the sensible world. These may act as "signs" of thought and may aid in the interpretation of these internal states. He wrote:

It is only as there is a Logos in the outward world, answering to the logos or internal reason of the parties, that they can come into a mutual understanding in regard to any thought or spiritual state whatever. To use a more familiar expression, there is a vast analogy in things which prepares them, as forms, to be signs or figures of thoughts, and thus, bases or types of words. Our bodily mechanism, and the sensible world we live in, are, in fact, made up of words, to represent our thoughts and internal states;—they only want naming, and then, passing into sound, to be reproduced or have their images called up by sounds, they drop out, so to speak, their gross material quality, and become words of spirit, or what the poet calls "winged words;"—cursitating forms of life, that fly out in sound upon the air, as interpreters and messengers of thought between the minds of men.[14]

[13] God in Christ, pp. 19, 20.
[14] Cf. ibid., pp. 20, 21: "It has been easy for our language-makers to agree in the use of sounds standing for outward objects and acts because these outward

The language-maker therefore employed an image or figure in the sensible world which was an adequate representation for a thought or emotion. The image became, in this way, a common sign or conception of the internal state, and as a result an intellectual world was generated. But, Bushnell added:

A very large share of the signs by which they [children] interpret their thoughts one to the other, will consist of bodily gestures and actions—all as natural to the internal activity as a blush, or any flush of passion, to the inner state, represented and depicted by it in the face. For the body is a living logos, added to the soul, to be its form, and play it forth into social understanding. It will also be found that a very large share of the words which represent our emotions and thoughts, are, in fact, as their etymology declares, derived from the psychological expressions or demonstrations made through the body. Or when thoughts and emotions are represented by figures drawn from the physical creation above us and around us, the principle is the same: it is not done artificially, but by the simple force of nature. The soul that is struggling to utter itself, flies to whatever signs and instruments it can find in the visible world, calling them in to act as interpreters, naming them at the same time, to stand, ever after, as interpreters in sound, when they are themselves out of sight.[15]

Bushnell had discovered therefore that every language contained two distinct departments, the physical department—that which provided names for *things*—and the intellectual department—that which provided names for *thought and spirit*. The physical aspect of language used names simply as representations of things, the intellectual as representatives of thought. It is the latter which can only be learned by intelligent beings, that is, beings who can comprehend the inner sense or content of words, that is, beings in whom the Logos of the creation finds a correspondent logos, or reason, to receive the types it offers.

The origin of grammar, or the framing of words into sentences was not necessarily a later development, he said, for there was "a rudimental tendency to grammar, in the first efforts of speech."

objects and acts can be so fixed upon, or the mind so directed towards them, that a mutual understanding may be had in regard to the object which it is designed to name, before the name to be adopted is uttered. But if, now, one of them has a thought or emotion in his mind, or wishes to speak of a spiritual being or world, this, it will be seen, is not capable of being shown or pointed at, because it lies out of sense. The thought or emotion cannot be taken out and exhibited to the eye: how, then, can the two parties come to any such understanding as will enable them to name it?"

[15] *Ibid.*, p. 23.

The tendency to grammar was completed only under specific conditions of time and use.

In this view, which it is not rash to believe will sometime be fully established, the outer world is seen to be a vast menstruum of thought or intelligence. There is a logos in the forms of things, by which they are prepared to serve as types or images of what is inmost in our souls; and then there is a logos also of construction in the relations of space, the position, qualities, connections, and predicates of things, by which they are framed into grammar. In one word, the outer world, which envelops our being, is itself language, the power of all language. Day unto day uttereth speech, and night unto night showeth knowledge; there is no speech nor language where their voice is not heard,—their line is gone out through all the earth, and their words to the end of the world.[16]

The outer world, therefore, possessed an intelligence; "an organ throughout of Intelligence." It was, however, God's intelligence which was found in the outer world which made possible the correspondence between word and object. Bushnell maintained that man was always in the presence of Divine thoughts and meaning in this way. Every word was illumined by Divinity, and became subjects of love and reverence: "For, in what do we utter ourselves, what are the words and the grammar, in which we speak, but instruments of a Divine import and structure? Such a discovery, received in its true moment, were enough to make a thoughtful Christian stand in awe, even of his own words." [17]

[16] *Ibid.,* pp. 24–30.
[17] *Ibid.,* p. 32; cf. p. 37; Bushnell was impressed by the fact that Locke's theory of language was similar to his. Bushnell quoted from Locke: "It may also lead us a little towards the original of all our notions and knowledge, if we remark how great a dependence our words have on common sensible ideas; and how those which are made use of to stand for actions and notions, quite removed from sense, have their rise from thence, and from obvious sensible ideas are transferred to more abstruse significations, and made to stand for ideas that come not under the cognizance of our senses, e. g., to imagine, apprehend, comprehend, adhere, conceive, instill, disgust, disturbance, tranquillity, etc., are all words taken from the operations of sensible things, and applied to certain modes of thinking. Spirit, in its primary signification, is breath; angel, a messenger; and I doubt not, but, if we could trace them to their sources, we should find in all languages, the names which stand for things that fall not under our senses, to have had their rise from sensible ideas. By which we may give some guess what kind of notions they were, *and whence derived, which filled their minds who were the first beginners of languages;* and how nature, even in the naming of things, unawares suggested to men *the originals and principals of all their knowledge;* whilst to give names which might make known to others any operations they felt in themselves, or any other ideas that come not under the cognizance of the senses, they were fain to borrow words from ordinary known ideas of

Bushnell went on to distinguish two distinct "departments" within every language. There was first the *literal* department, in which sounds were provided as names for physical objects and appearances. There was, second, the department of *analogy,* or figure, as Bushnell called it, in which physical objects and appearances were named as images of thought or spirit. The words got their power, as words of thought, by means of the physical images received in and through them. Bushnell warned the theologian that he must be aware of this distinction between the literal and the analogical departments of language. One of the major reasons for the infinite multiplications of opinions in the church was that the theologians had not distinguished properly between the literal and the figurative meaning of a term. Bushnell wrote: "There are no words, in the physical department of language, that are exact representatives of particular physical things. For whether we take the theory of the Nominalists or the Realists, the words are, in fact, and practically, names only of genera, not of individuals or species. To be even still more exact, they represent only certain sensations of sight, touch, taste, smell, hearing—one or all. Hence the opportunity in language, for endless mistakes and false reasonings, in reference to matters purely physical." [18]

In the same way, there were no terms in the spiritual department of language which were exact representatives of thought. The words used were only the names of a genus of a physical image, and were to be applied only to signify a genus of a physical image. Only in this way would the word signify a specific thought or sentiment with qualities peculiar to itself.

sensation; by that means to make others the more easily to conceive those operations they experimented in themselves, which made no outward appearance."

[18] Bushnell in *Christ in Theology,* p. 15, stated very specifically what is the "single principle" about which all of his theological ideas revolve, that is, "that all religious truth, as well theological as practical, is and must be presented under conditions of form of analogy from the outward state."

"The truth-feeling power of the soul may have truth present immediately to it, or may directly intuit truth, without symbols or representations of language. But the moment it will think discursively, or represent to another any subject of thought, that subject must be clothed in forms that are only signs or analogies, and not equivalents of the truth. Even definitions and the most abstract modes of terminology will be true only in a sense more or less visibly formal and analogical. They will carry their sense, not by simple notation, as in arithmetic or algebra, but as offering it to the critical power of the eye and heart in symbols naturally expressive."

54

Bushnell reminded his reader how difficult it was for a word to emerge from so many ambiguities and complications and for an exact meaning to be given to a word. The same was always true, said Bushnell, for the great mass of words employed in moral and spiritual discussions—words such as love, gentleness, contentment, patience, wisdom, justice, order, pride, and charity, etc. Words, when applied to moral subjects, "are legitimately used as the signs of thoughts to be expressed."

They do not literally convey, or pass over a thought out of one mind into another, as we commonly speak of doing. They are only hints, or images, held up before the mind of another, to put *him* on generating or reproducing the same thought; which he can do only as he has the same personal contents, or the generative power out of which to bring the thought required. Hence, there will be different measures of understanding or misunderstanding, according to the capacity or incapacity, the ingeniousness or moral obliquity of the receiving party—even if the communicating party offers only truth, in the best and freshest forms of expression the language provides.[19]

Only one class of intellectual words was able to have a perfectly determinate significance, and they were those which were related to "necessary ideas", such as time, space, cause, truth, right, arithmetical numbers, and geometrical figures. Language in reference to these ideas was a perfectly exact "algebra of thought."

Words of thought or spirit could never give a precise equivalent of the truth, Bushnell said. They attempt to impute form to that which really had no form. "They are related to the truth, only as form to spirit—earthen vessels in which the truth is borne, yet always offering their mere pottery as being the truth itself."[20] How closely related to theology:

A very great share of our theological questions, or disputes, originates in the incapacity of the parties to separate truths from their forms, or to see how the same essential truth may clothe itself under forms that are repugnant. There wants to be a large digestion, so to speak, of form in the teacher of theology or mental philosophy, that he may always be aware how the mind and truth, obliged to clothe themselves under the laws of space and sensation, are taking, continually, new shapes or dresses —coming forth poetically, allegorically, dialectically, fluxing through definitions, symbols, changes of subject and object, yet remaining still the same; . . .[21]

[19] *God in Christ*, p. 46.
[20] *Ibid.*, p. 48.
[21] *Ibid.*, pp. 49–50; Bushnell suggested some examples, cf. pp. 50 ff.

Revelation is, therefore, truth given us in forms or images naturally expressive. But the forms or images are not the truths of revelation themselves.

Bushnell conceived of thinking as nothing more than the treatment of thoughts by means of their forms. He wrote: "And so necessary is this, that, if we make use of a word whose original form is lost or unknown, we shall be found, in every case, to give the word, instinctively, an outward representation ourselves; that is, we shall image it, or give a form to the thought, in order to bring it into mental contemplation, or under the discourse of the mind." [22]

The Christian conceptions of the Incarnation and the Trinity are mysteries or paradoxes, wrote Bushnell, and belong to the same laws or conditions which belong to all language. "All words are, in fact, only incarnations, or insensings of thought." He insisted that, "if we investigate the relations of their forms to the truths signified, we have the same mystery before us; if we set the different, but related forms in comparison, we have the same aspect of repugnance or inconsistency. And then we have only to use the repugnant forms as vehicles of pure thought, dismissing the contradictory matter of the forms, and both words and the Word are understood without distraction,—all by the same process." [23] The Gospel of John, was called by Bushnell, "the most contradictory book in the world," but just for this reason it "contains more and loftier truths than any other." When the truth was being expressed, one did not have to be afraid of inconsistencies and self-contradictions in his language:

[22] *Ibid.*, p. 52; *Christ in Theology*, pp. 40 ff.
[23] *God in Christ*, p. 56; cf. also the article "The Christian Trinity a Practical Truth," in *Building Eras in Religion*, pp. 106–149, "we must avoid all practices of logic on the persons. We must take them as we take the one, which if we will put our logic on the term, will immediately turn out to be only a finite being,—a man. They are to be set before the mind at the outset as a holy paradox, that only gives the truth in so great power of expression that it defies all attempts at logic or definition. Seizing thus upon the living symbols, we are to chant our response with the Church and say: 'God of God, Light of Light, very God of very God;' and, if we cannot reason out the paradox, to like it the better that it stops the clatter of our speculative mill-work and speaks to us as God's great mystery should, leaving us to adore in silence. Not that we are here to disown our reason. God is no absurdity as three persons more than as one. Fully satisfied of this, we are only to love the grand abyss of God's majesty thus set before us and rejoice to fall into it, there to bathe and submerge our finite love, rejoicing the more that God is greater than we knew, taller than our reach can measure, wider than our finite thought can comprehend." (p. 147). Also the article "Our Gospel a Gift to the Imagination," pp. 249–285.

56

It is nothing to him that a quirk of logic can bring him into absurdity. If at any time he offers definitions, it is not to get a footing for the play of his logic, but it is simply as multiplying forms or figures of that which he seeks to communicate—just as one will take his friend to different points of a landscape, and show him cross views, in order that he may get a perfect conception of the outline. Having nothing but words in which to give definitions, he understands the impossibility of definitions as determinate measures of thought, and gives them only as being *other forms* of the truth in question, by aid of which it may be more adequately conceived.[24]

Logic was, therefore, a "defective, and often a deceitful instrument." "No turn of logical deduction," Bushnell wrote, "can prove anything, by itself, not previously known by inspection or insight."[25] However, there was always that group of sophists, who, "having neither a large observation, nor a power of poetic insight, occupy themselves as workers in words and propositions, managing to persuade themselves and others that they are great investigators, and even discoverers of truth."[26] A symbol or a formula had only analogical value, and had to be received by *intuition* or *insight* or

---

[24] *God in Christ,* p. 57.

[25] Logic was not "logic as a science, but ... that deductive, proving, spinning method of practical investigation, commonly denoted by the term *logical." Ibid.,* pp. 57–58; *Christ in Theology,* p. 85, "the logical expounder can make it certain by almost no degree of caution that he is not imposing on himself by spinning a theory that is really of some word or latent form of grammar in his language and not of the consciousness itself." Bushnell thought it was easy to "spin" a coherent system of unified thought which was entirely based upon the partiality and prejudices of the mind; cf. *God in Christ,* p. 93; cf. also *Christ in Theology,* pp. 16–17.

[26] *God in Christ,* p. 59; "It seems to be supposed, or rather assumed, by the class of investigators commonly called logical, that after the subject matter of truth has been gotten into propositions, and cleared, perhaps, by definitions, the faculty of intuition, or insight, may be suspended, and we may go on safely, to reason upon the forms of the words themselves, or the "analogy the words bear to each other." And so, by the mere handling of words and propositions, they undertake to evolve, or, as they commonly speak, to *prove* important truths. They reason not by or through formulas, but upon them. After the formulas are got ready, they shut their eyes to all interior inspection of their terms, as in algebra, and commit themselves to the mere grammatic laws or predications of their words–expecting, under these, by inversion, evolution, equation, *reductio ad absurdum,* and the like, to work out important results. And this is popularly called *reasoning.* They do not seem to be aware that this grammatic, or constructive method, while it is natural as language itself, having its forms in what I have called the grammar of the soul and of the creation, is yet analogical only to truth and spirit–a warp that is furnished out of form and sense, for the connecting into speech of symbols or types that lie in form and sense; on which account, propositions are called *formulas,* or little forms."

"interior inspection." The faculty of *insight* could not be suspended, however, when one drew up a conclusion. This requirement is not relevant to the pure algebraic process, said Bushnell, because the terms stand for exact quantities. This fact was particularly true for theology. Subjects such as man, life, self-active being, God and religion, could not be described by means of a formula. Bushnell spoke of the human will in this context:

> ... the writer will be overpowered by the terms and predicates of language; which being mostly derived from the physical world, are charged, to the same extent, with a mechanical significance. And then we shall have a sophism, great or small, according to his capacity—a ponderous volume, it may be, of formulas, filled up, rolled about, inverted, crossed and twisted—a grand, stupendous, convoluted sophism—all a mere outward practice, however, on words and propositions, in which, as they contain a form of cause and effect in their own nature, it is easily made out that human liberty is the liberty of a scale-beam, turned by the heavier weights. Meantime, the question is only a question of consciousness, one in which the simple decision of consciousness is final;—to which, argument, whether good or bad, can really add nothing, from which nothing take.[27]

When one became *alive* in God, that is, when the individual was truly united to Him, all theological discussions passed out of "the realm of mechanism and the empire of dead atoms." Bushnell wrote: "We look at the whole body as a vital nature, and finding every function alive, every fibre active, we perceive that all the parts, even the minutest, exist and act as mutual conditions one of another. And so it is in spiritual life."[28] The Bible must be considered in the same way:

> There is no book in the world that contains so many repugnances, or antagonistic forms of assertion, as the Bible. Therefore, if any man please to play off his constructive logic upon it, he can easily show it up as the absurdest book in the world. But whosoever wants, on the other hand, really to behold and receive all truth, and would have the truth-world overhang him as an empyrean of stars, complex, multitudinous, striving antagonistically yet comprehended, height above height, and deep under deep, in a boundless score of harmony; what man soever, content with no small rote of logic and catechism, reaches with true hunger after this, and will offer himself to the many-sided forms of the scripture with a perfectly ingenuous and receptive spirit; he shall find his nature flooded

[27] *God in Christ*, pp. 62–63.
[28] *Ibid.*, p. 64; on this basis, Bushnell rejected the "design" argument for God's existence. *Ibid.*, pp. 64–65.

with senses, vastnesses, and powers of truth, such as it is even greatness to feel.[29]

Bushnell reminded his reader that one does not destroy the inconsistencies and contradictions of the Bible; rather, we allow them to stand, "offering our mind to their impressions, and allowing it to gravitate inwardly, towards that whole of truth, in which they coalesce."

And when we are in that whole, we shall have no dozen propositions of our own in which to give it forth; neither will it be a whole which we can set before the world, standing on one leg, in a perfectly definite shape, clear of all mystery; but it will be such a whole as requires a whole universe of rite, symbol, incarnation, historic breathings, and poetic first, to give it expression,—in a word, just what it now has.[30]

Poets are, therefore, the true metaphysicians. The science of the future will be discovered by the poets. Religion, however, Bushnell believed, had a natural and profound alliance with poetry. Furthermore, much of the Bible was made up of poetic expression. The teachings of Christ were "utterances of the truth," and never argumentation about it. They contained no definitions and no proofs. Truth shone by its own evidence in the life of Christ. It was this same truth which found us; we could never find it. Bushnell reminded us that Paul was no dialectician, nor did he attempt to create a theological system, nor was he a dogmatizer. Paul wrote under inspiration. He was a prophet and a seer: "Under so many illatives and deductive propositions, he is emitting fire, not formulas for the mere speculative understanding; rolling on, in the vehement power of a soul possessed with Christ, to declare the mystery that hath been hid for ages."[31]

Bushnell believed that it was impossible to get a complete and sufficient Christian dogmatic system. There could be no such thing as scientific theology. Language was not adequate to such a purpose. He wrote:

[29] *Ibid.,* pp. 69–70.
[30] *Ibid.* "And then, it will not be strange if we drop our feeble, bloodless sentences and dogmas, whether of belief or denial, and return, duly mortified, into the faith of those august and magnificent forms of scripture-incarnation; Father, Son, and Holy Ghost; atonement as blood, life sacrifice, propitiation, ransom, liberty, regeneration, wisdom, righteousness, sanctification, and redemption–the great mystery of godliness."
[31] *Ibid.,* p. 76.

Can there be produced, in human language, a complete and proper Christian theology; can the Christian truth be offered in the molds of any dogmatic statement? What is the Christian truth? Pre-eminently and principally, it is the expression of God—God coming into expression, through histories and rites, through an incarnation, and through language —in one Syllable, by the WORD. The endeavor is, by means of expression, and under the laws of expression, to set forth God—His providence, and His government, and, what is more and higher than all, God's own feeling. His truth, love, justice, compassion. Well, if it be something for a poet to express man, it is doubtless somewhat more for a book to be constructed that will express God, and open His eternity to man. And if it would be somewhat difficult to put the poet of humanity into a few short formulas, that will communicate all he expresses, with his manifold, wondrous art, will it probably be easier to transfer the grand poem of salvation, that which expresses God, even the feeling of God, into a few dull propositions; which, when they are produced, we may call the sum total of the Christian truth? [32]

Bushnell described New England theology as essentially rationalistic, in the sense that it had been believed that the Christian faith could be reduced to neat systems and formulas. However, the Christian faith for Bushnell could not be understood in terms of the "loss-and-gain style of religion, the stern, iron-limbed speculative logic" of New England theology.[33] "It has not been held as a practical, positive, and earnest Christian truth that there is a PERCEPTIVE POWER in spiritual life, an unction of the Holy One, which is itself a kind of inspiration—an immediate, experimental knowledge of God, by virtue of which, and partly in the degree of which, Christian theology is possible." [34]

The use of logic will, therefore, be deprecated in Bushnell's theological exposition. The scriptures cannot be considered as "a maga-

---

[32] *Ibid.*, p. 83; in reference to creeds, Bushnell said that "the best creed is that which stays by the concrete most faithfully, and carries its doctrine as far as possible, in a vehicle of fact and of real life." "This is the peculiar excellence and beauty of what is called the "Apostle's Creed." If, however, creeds of theory, or systematic dogma, must be retained, the next best arrangement would be to allow assent to a great number of such creeds at once; letting them qualify, assist, and mitigate each other. And a virtual allowance of this is, in fact, one of the best points in our Saybrook Platform, which accepts the acknowledgment, either of its own Articles, or of the "Doctrinal Articles of the Church of England" or of the "Westminster Confession," or of the "Confession agreed on at the Savoy"; and if it be indifferent which of the four is received, there can be no objection, certainly, if all are received."
[33] *Ibid.*, p. 96.
[34] *Ibid.*, p. 93.

zine of propositions and mere dialectic entities", but only as "inspirations and poetic forms of life." But this will allow Bushnell to write:

Our opinions will be less catechetical and definite, using the word as our definers do, but they will be as much broader as they are more divine; as much truer, as they are more vital and close to the plastic, undefinable mystery of spiritual life. We shall seem to understand less, and shall actually receive more. No false *pre-cision,* which the nature and conditions of spiritual truth forbid, will, by cutting up the body of truth into definite and dead morsels, throw us into states of excision and division, equally manifold. We shall receive the truth of God in a more entire organic and organific manner, as being itself an essentially vital power. It will not be our endeavor to pull the truth into analytic distinctions, as if theology were a kind of inorganic chemistry, and the last end of discovery, an atomic theory; but we shall delight in truth, more as a concrete vital nature, incarnated in all fact and symbol around us—a vast, mysterious, incomprehensible power, which best we know, when most we love.[35]

With his theory of language Bushnell replaced the rationalism and dogmatism of New England theology with, at least, the possibility of a theology of experience, in which intuition took the place of system. The long-sanctioned theological terms which had held Christian theology in New England in its iron grip for generations had been challenged, and it had been challenged in terms of its fundamental premise, that is, that theological language was competent to express the nature of theological ideas. Words were mere "airy symbols" which had arisen from physical objects and relations. Words were "inexact in their significance, never measuring the truth

---

[35] *Ibid.,* p. 94; Bushnell maintained that such a position did not result in a "confused" mysticism: "If any should be apprehensive that the views here offered may bring in an age of mysticism, and so of interminable confusion, they will greatly misconceive their import, and also the nature of mysticism itself. A mystic is one who finds a secret meaning, both in words and in things, back of their common or accepted meaning—some agency of Life, or Living Thought, hid under the forms of words and institutions, and historical events. Hence, all religious writers and teachers, who dwell on the representative character of words and things, or hold the truths of religion, not in mechanical measures and relations, but as forms of life, are so far mystics." Quoting from Neander, Bushnell made no disavowal of the fact that there was a mystical element in the views he held of Christian life and doctrine: "Man is designed, in his very nature, to be a partially mystic being; the world to be looked upon as a mystic world. Christ himself revealed a decidedly mystic element in his teachings. There is something of a mystic quality in almost every writing of the New Testament. In John, it is a character. In 'the dialect' Paul, there are very many passages quite as mystical as any in John." *Ibid.,* p. 95.

or giving its precise equivalent." Words imputed form to that "which is out of form." But then grammar aggravated language, and made more confusing what was already inexact. Logic was deceptive, because the user of logic was often uninformed regarding the meaning of a word or how it was used in a sentence.

What Bushnell had implied, was that theology, when conceived of as systematic or scientific theology, was impossible. There was more truth in the mystic's insight; although he recognized the difficulties of communication which existed when the mystic began to articulate his ideas. Theology must become "Divinity" or a higher kind of theology, a theology which allowed for inspiration in the discovery of truth and did not rely simply upon reflection.

The student then will be a student, not of theology but, in a proper sense, of divinity. The knowledge he gets will be divinity, filling his whole consciousness—a Living State and not a scheme of wise sentences. He will be a man who understands God as being indoctrinated or inducted into God, by studies that are themselves inbreathings of the divine love and power.[36]

[36] *Christ in Theology*, p. 67. Theodore T. Munger in his book *Horace Bushnell, Preacher and Theologian* (Boston: Houghton, Mifflin and Co., 1899), p. 108 wrote: "It was by this gate that he went out from the world about him into the world of spiritual reality and freedom where his work lay. It must not be supposed that he abjured theology as a science because he refused to be bound by definition, nor that he slighted reason because he set aside the forms of logic. He simply refused to put infinite things into finite forms as wholly containing them. He protested against treating thought and spirit as measurable by sense; he asserted that spiritual and moral realities lie behind language, and that words have their origin in these realities, though they do not define them, but only suggest their scope and significance. It is under such a conception of language that he explains his use of creeds."

CHAPTER III

Nature and the Supernatural: The One System of God

If all human language is found under conditions of form, but if truth itself, which is spiritual, is out of form or does not have any form, then it does *not* follow that Christian doctrine is to be despaired of. But Bushnell felt that the very insufficiency of words to convey the meaning of spiritual things forced us to take them "as signs offered to candor and the interpreting power of sympathy and spiritual insight." Although words in themselves are inadequate to express divine truths, they can be employed, as Bushnell wrote, if there is present "a sympathy with God." But this condition of sympathy requires "a large infusion of the Divine Spirit, which is itself a divine experience and an immediate knowledge." [1] How then may a theology be constructed? Bushnell wrote:

> What, though language can tell us nothing true concerning him, save as in forms that need to be interpreted by feeling and can open their light only to a spiritually discerning sympathy; what, though there be in them no real notation for truth, in which, by definitions, equations, inversions and such like operations, we may pile up a scheme of theology or divine knowledge from below, that shall stand and be true, like a treatise in mathematics, simply as being what it is; is it therefore nothing that we can know God as being with us and in us, filling our argumentations, opening to us the senses and powers of words, imparting himself to our secret experience as the light of all seeing, and molding us ever to that state of divine consciousness, which is, at once, the condition and principal substance of knowledge? I certainly think otherwise. Indeed, if it were possible to get religious truth into shapes and formulas having an absolute meaning, like the terms of algebra, as clear even to the wicked as to the pure, and requiring no conditions of character in the receivers, it would very nearly subvert, it seems to me, all that is most significant and sublime in the discipline of life. [2]

Is it possible then for theology ever to become a science or to attain to a fixed and properly authoritative statement? [3] If it is

[1] *Christ in Theology*, pp. 65, 66.
[2] *Ibid.*, p. 66.
[3] *Ibid.*, p. 86.

impossible for the literal meaning of theological terms to be stated; if the needs of Christendom are softened, to allow for the spirit of accomodation, that is to allow for the possible sufficiency of other creedal formulations, then it would appear that there could not be a Christian theology. Then every man could possess a spiritual freedom, "to see visions and dream dreams, and offer his licentious vagaries as the veritable inspirations of God." [4]

It is to the honor of Bushnell's catholic mind that he was able to doubt whether there could be such a thing as theology, and although he wavered in his answer to the question, "Is it probable that theology can ever become a science or attain to a fixed and properly authoritative statement?", he answered it in the affirmative. But he did so in terms of what he believed to be the "true organific principle of Christianity," that is, God himself—"the Divine Nature incarnate outwardly, and so inserted inwardly in human faith and consciousness." Every confession of faith, therefore, had to be an extension of the Incarnation proposed as a creed of fact:

And if we ask for the best and healthiest and least uncertain forms of truth, under which (in connection with the divine presence in the consciousness of the disciples, and by that consciousness interpreted) the organizing power the Christian grace may become most effective, indestructible, and harmonious; I would say that we ought to adhere as closely as possible, in all catechisms and confessions, to the simple historic matter of the gospel. This is the real substructure, the pillar and ground of all truth—it is the gospel as God shapes it. [5]

Nonetheless, every system which man creates, displays man's limitations. This is particularly true of theological systems, which attempt to grasp the reality of God, but by the use of human forms. But the system may be of some value "to collect his knowledges and frame them into some intelligible order."

This will comfort his intelligence. It will give him the method, also, by which to teach what he knows, and learn what he does not. If our generalizations are only General Thumbs, if our systems are only pocket systems of the infinite, they are yet necessary as accommodations to ourselves, and, possibly, are good for what they exclude, as well as for what they contain. They are to the disciple what the iris is to the eye, drawing its opaque and variously-colored curtains round the aperture of sight, that only just so much of the light may enter as will make the tiny picture within distinct and clear.

[4] *Ibid.*, p. 69.
[5] *Ibid.*, p. 78.

It is also conceivable, and is probably a serious and momentous truth, that the exercise of system or the endeavor after system, is commonly a greater benefit than the actually resulting systems prepared. Instigated, in this effort or exercise, by the natural instinct of system, the disciple is made stronger and more competent by his exercise; though he reaches no veritable system of God at all. He is drawn toward a closer coherency and compactness of thought; his religious convictions are comforted and fortified; he is better guarded, also, against fantastic experiences and wild illusions, that might otherwise confound the dignity of his life, and separate even his duties from the respect that is necessary to their value.[6]

Bushnell, therefore, not only refrained from a final condemnation of theology, but rather conceded its value and contributed to its advance. The reason for this was that Bushnell believed that one could distinguish between a closed or merely reasoned system and an open and free system, which allowed for the discovery which is always of God; "between an incrustation on the outside, to keep and imprison the life, and a cell or point of embryonic tissue begun at the center of life itself." This is the distinction between theology and divinity.

Divinity has its basis in fact and being—God as in the creation, God in history. It meets us in all outward objects; and again in the Scripture, in the form of political and religious annals, the biographies of distinguished saints, the teachings of prophets, the incarnate life and death of the Word made flesh. Here opens a vast realm of divine fact, radiant in every part with the light of God. But this all is body, not spirit; the face of divinity, but not the power. By divinity we mean what may be derived to us from this and made conscious within us, by an immediate experience of God, in connection with this. It is what of God a regenerate man may receive, in virtue of the new inner sense awakened in him. It is that influx and intergrowth of the divine nature that is consciously experienced, when every inlet of the soul is opened by love, and faith, and prayer, and holy living, and patient waiting upon God. It is interpretation made by experience,—a knowledge had of God, through the medium of consciousness, and resembling the knowledge we get of ourselves in the same manner; or, it is not a doctrine or system of doctrine, but a Living State, the Life of God in the soul of man.[7]

But there was another reason why Bushnell finally accepted theology, and that was because of the principle which lay at the very basis of his theory of language, that is, that this is "a *logos* world," that is: "There is a logos in the form of things, by which they are

[6] *Ibid.*, p. 80.
[7] *Ibid.*, pp. 82–83.

prepared to serve as types or images of what is inmost in our souls." [8]

It is this principle which led him to his massive study of the relattionship between nature and the supernatural. He wrote in the preface to *Nature and the Supernatural (as together Constituting the One System of God)* that this book contained:

... a wide hypothesis of the world, and the great problems of life and sin and supernatural redemption and Christ and a Christly Providence and a divinely certified history and of superhuman gifts entered into the world and finally of God as related to all, which liquidates these stupendous facts in issue between Christians and unbelievers and gives a rational account of them. [9]

I. *Definitions*

Bushnell defined nature as "that created realm of being or substance which has an acting, a going on or process from within itself, under and by its own laws." [10] The supernatural was that which is "either not in the chain of cause and effect, or which acts on the chain of cause and effect, in nature, from without the chain." [11] Bushnell wanted to demonstrate that God had erected "another and higher

---

[8] *God in Christ,* p. 30.

[9] *Nature and the Supernatural,* pp. iii, iv.

[10] *Nature and the Supernatural,* p. 36: "Or, if we say, with some, that the laws are but an other name for the immediate actuating power of God still it makes no difference, in any other respect, with our conception of the system. It is yet *as if* the laws, the powers, the actings, were inherent in the substances, and were by them determined. It is still to our scientific, separated from our religious contemplation, a chain of causes and effects, or a scheme or orderly succession determined from within the scheme itself." Cf. *The Spirit in Man,* pp. 74 ff.

[11] *Nature and the Supernatural,* p. 37: "Thus if any event transpires in the bosom, or upon the platform of what is called nature, which is not from nature itself, or is varied from the process, nature would execute by her own laws, that is supernatural, by whatever power it is wrought." "So if the processes, combinations, and results of our system of nature are interrupted, or varied by the action, whether of God, or angels, or men, so as to bring to pass what would not come to pass in it by its own internal action, under the laws of mere cause and effect, the variations are, in like manner, supernatural." Cf. pp. 36, 38. Cf. also p. 43, "... nature is that world of substance, whose laws are laws of cause and effect, and whose events transpire, in orderly succession, under those laws; the supernatural is that range of substance, if any such there be, that acts upon the chain of cause and effect in nature from without the chain, producing, thus, results that, by mere nature, could not come to pass." Cf. the extract from the sermons "The Great Time Keeper," pp. 301–310, and "The Preparations of Eternity," pp. 331–340, *The Spirit in Man.*

system, that of spiritual being and government, for which nature exists." There was, he believed, a constant action and reaction between these two realms, and together they formed the "one system of God." But Bushnell was very careful to insist that a God who is superior to nature, but, who, at the same time, acted *through her laws,* did not permit a genuine supernaturalism. Christianity, as a supernatural religion, insisted upon the affirmation that God is "acting from without on the lines of cause and effect in our fallen world and our disordered humanity, to produce what, by no mere laws of nature, will ever come to pass." Christianity is a supernatural religion because it "acts regeneratively and new-creatively to repair the damage which those laws . . . would otherwise perpetuate," and not because it "acts through the laws of nature, limited by, and doing the work of, the laws." [12] The Christian faith must be considered as a redemptive agency, which attempts to "reverse and restore the lapsed condition of sinners."

Bushnell believed that man was far from being a "proper item" of nature. He was under no law of cause and effect in the choices he made: "He stands out clear and sovereign as a being supernatural, and his definition is that he is an original power acting, not in the line of causality, but from himself":

He [man] is not independent of nature in the sense of being separated from it in his action, but he is in it, environed by it, acting through it, partially sovereign as regards his self-determination, and only not completely sovereign as regards executing all that he wills in it. In certain parts or departments of the soul itself, such as memory, appetite, passion, attention, imagination, association, disposition, the willpower in him is held in contact, so to speak, with conditions and qualities that are dominated partly by laws of cause and effect; for these faculties are partly governed by their own laws, and partly submitted to his governing will by their own laws; so that when he will exercise any control over them, or turn them about to serve his purpose, he can do it, in a qualified sense and degree, by operating through their laws. As far as they are concerned, he is pure nature, and he is only a power superior to cause and effect at the particular point of volition where his liberty culminates, and where the administration he is to maintain over his whole nature centers. [13]

[12] *Ibid.,* p. 42. In the sermon, "God's One Family," *The Spirit in Man,* p. 342, Bushnell wanted ". . . to show that the whole spiritual empire of God is homogeneous, that whatever distinctions of era and world and power may exist, they are all such as will emerge in a common unity and brotherhood."
[13] *Nature and the Supernatural,* p. 51. See the development of Bushnell's argument, pp. 42 ff, *Moral Uses of Dark Things,* p. 38.

Man's self-determination, his will, his power of volition, is the central attribute of his personality, and it is this which distinguished man from nature. Bushnell wrote about man: "In every friend we distinguish something more than a distillation of natural causes; a free, faithful soul, that, having a power to betray, stays fast in the integrity of love and sacrifice. We rejoice in heroic souls, and in every hero we discover a majestic spirit, how far transcending the merely instinctive and necessary actings af animal and vegetable life. He stands out in the flood of the world's causes, strong in his resolve, not knowing, in a just fight, how to yield, but protesting . . ." [14] It is only man who possesses the ability to rise above the level of "every-day forces," to become a great man, to become "a free cause in himself." This is man as a supernatural creature. However, man can only be a supernatural creature when he acts upon the realm of nature from outside of nature. Man is able to do this because he is a moral being, a being who can transcend his environment; that is, a being who can act as a free agent. [15]

[14] *Ibid.*, p. 56; cf. "Every Man's Life a Plan of God," *Sermons for the New Life*, pp. 9–28, particularly pp. 21, 22.
[15] *Nature and the Supernatural*, pp. 58; 59, 60. Cf. Bushnell's allusion to Washington: "Were our Washington conceived in that course of good and great action, by which he became the deliverer of his country, to be the mere distillation of natural causes, who of us would allow himself to be thrilled with any such sentiments of reverence and personal homage? It is no mere wheel, no link in a chain, that stirs our blood in this manner; but it is a man, the sense we have of a man, rising out of the level of things, great above all *things,* great as being himself." Bushnell became ecstatic at times: "So that, after all which has been done by the sensuous littleness, the shallow pride, and the idolatry of science, to make a total universe, or even a God, of nature, still it is nothing but the carpet on which we children have our play, and which we may only use according to its design, or may cut, and burn, and tear at will. The true system of God centers still in us, and not in it; in our management, our final glory and completeness of being as persons, not in the set figures of the carpet we so eagerly admire and call it science to ravel." He insisted, however, that there seemed to be a difference in degree of moral capacity in various individuals; "How different the power of two men, creatures though they be of the same order; a Newton, for example, a Watt, a Fulton; and some wild Patagonian or stunted Esquimaux. So, if there be angels, seraphim, thrones, dominions, all in ascending scales of endowment above one another, they will, of course, have powers supernatural, or capacities to act on the lines of causes in nature, that correspond with their natural quantity and degree. What wonder, then, is it, in the case of Jesus Christ, that he reveals a power over nature, appropriate to the scale of his being and the inherent supremacy of his divine person." Cf. *Moral Uses of Dark Things*, p. 56; *Building Eras in Religion*, pp. 94, 295, 305.

II. *The Supernatural as Distinct from the Natural*

"God is expressed but not measured by his works,"[16] Bushnell wrote. Nature was not to be considered as "the proper and complete system of God," but God must always be more than nature, separate and distinct from nature. God cannot be contained in cause and effect relationships, nor in natural law formulations. The supernatural can never be reduced to the natural.[17]

Bushnell believed that the history of Western civilization gave vivid support for his assertion that human nature craves the supernatural. He referred, in this context, to "the immense array of mythologic and formally unrational religions . . . that have been accepted by the populations of the world," and also to the Greeks and Romans who ultimately accepted Christianity.[18] He spoke of the poet Shelley who, after he became an atheist, could not be content until he populated his world with a whole host of mythological beings. But there was also the Mormon faith, Bushnell said, which basically was a religious attempt to find the sense of the miraculous and the mysterious in life. It could be considered a universal fact of history, he asserted, that "man is a creature of faith, and cannot rest in mere nature and natural causality," but seeks for some kind of religious truth in his life.[19]

Bushnell asserted, too, that the new science of geology pointed to the existence of the supernatural: "Now to show the existence of a God supernatural, a God so far separated from nature and superior to it as to act on the chain of natural cause and effect from without the chain, the new science of geology comes forward, lays open her

[16] *Nature and the Supernatural,* p. 64.

[17] Neither can the will of God be identified with causal relationships; cf. *Nature and the Supernatural,* pp. 60, 61, 66–67; cf. *Moral Uses of Dark Things,* pp. 107 ff; *Building Eras in Religion,* pp. 78 ff, 302.

[18] Bushnell remarked that Christianity ". . . if not supernatural enough, was corrupted by the addition of still new wonders pertaining to the virgin, the priesthood, the sacraments, and even the bones of the saints; indicated all, and some of them (such as that Mary is the Mother of God,) generated even, by dialectic processes." *Nature and the Supernatural,* p. 66.

[19] *Ibid.,* pp. 71–72; Bushnell found, furthermore, that there was a "world immaterial" within the bounds of cause and effect. "We speak here, it will be understood, of what is called inorganic chemistry, and vital chemistry, the chemistry of matter out of life or below it, and of that which is in it and by it. The lives that construct and organize the bodies they inhabit, are the highest forms of nature, and are set in nature as types of a yet higher order of existence; viz., spirit, or free intelligence."

stone registers, and points us to the very times and places where the creative hand of God was inserted into the world, to people it with creatures of life." [20] The earth had been in a molten state at some remote period in history. As it emerged from this state by a cooling process, there was no vestige of life on it. However, the "vast cinder," the earth, eventually became inhabited with creatures of life: "Finally man appears, last and most perfect of all the living forms; for, while so many successive orders and types of living creatures, vegetable and animal, show us their remains in the grand museum of the rocks, no vestige, or bone, or sign of man has ever yet been discovered there. Therefore here, again, the question returns, whence came the lordly occupant?" [21] Bushnell answered this question by reference to a power outside of nature, which initiated these "new forms of organized life." [22] The existence of life cannot be accounted for on the basis of dead matter. "We are brought, then, to the conclusion," Bushnell wrote, "which no ingenuity of man can escape, that the successive races of living forms discovered by geology are fresh creations, by a power out of nature and above it acting on nature; which, it will be remembered is our definition of supernaturalism itself." [23]

Bushnell went on to distinguish between *things* and *persons,* or *things* and *powers.* "All free intelligences . . . the created and the uncreated, are, as being free, essentially supernatural in their action; having all, in the matter of their will, a power transcending cause and effect in nature, by which they are able to act on the lines and vary the combinations of natural causalities." They are therefore *powers,* and not things, because they can act from themselves, uncaused. *Things,* on the other hand, can propagate effects only under certain fixed laws. [24] Bushnell summarized the distinction:

At the head of one class we conceive is God, as Lord of Hosts; who, in virtue of his all-originating power as Creator, is called the First Cause; having round him innumerable orders of intelligence which, though caused to exist by Him, are as truly first causes in their action as He,—starting

[20] *Ibid.,* p. 76; cf. *Moral Uses of Dark Things,* p. 230 and *Building Eras in Religion,* p. 314.
[21] *Ibid.,* p. 77.
[22] *Ibid.;* cf. the refutation of the developmental theory, which asserted that organic life developed out of matter by inorganic forces, pp. 78–81; cf. *The Moral Uses of Dark Things,* pp. 186 f.
[23] *Ibid.,* p. 82; cf. *Building Eras in Religion,* pp. 64, 66, 69.
[24] *Ibid.,* p. 84; cf. *Building Eras in Religions,* pp. 21 ff, 50, 60, 63.

all their trains of consequences in the same manner. In the other class, we have the immense catalogue of what are called the natural sciences,—the astronomical bodies, the immaterial forces, the fluids and solids of the world, the elements and atoms of chemistry, the dynamics of life and instinct,—in all of which, what are called causes are only propagations of effects under and by fixed laws. Hence they are second causes only; that is, causes whose causations are determined by others back of them; never, in any sense, originative, or first causes.[25]

Bushnell could then conclude that nature was not to be equated with the universe, because there was "another kind of existence in ourselves, which consciously does not fall within the terms of nature":

First, we recognize in the grand inventory our own human race. We call them persons, spirits, souls, minds, intelligences, free agents, and we see them moving out from nature and above it, consciously superior; streaming into it in currents of causality from themselves; subduing it, developing or detecting its secret laws, harnessing its forces, and using it as the pliant instrument of their will; first causes all, in a sense, and springs of action, side by side with the Creator, whose miniatures they are, whose footsteps they distinguish, and whose recognition they naturally aspire to. Next adjacent to those we have the intelligent powers of the astronomic worlds, and all the outlying populations of the sky; so numerous that we shall best conceive their number, not by counting the stars and increasing the census obtained by some factor or multiplier greater than the mind can definitely grasp, but by imagining the stellar spaces of infinity itself interfused and filled with their prodigious tides of life and motion. All these, like us, are creatures of admiration, science, will, and duty; able to search out the invisible in the visible, and find the footsteps of God in his works. Then again, also, we recognize a vast and gloriously populated realm of angels and departed spirits, who, when they are sent, minister, unseen, about us; mixed, we know not how, in the surroundings of our state, with unsaintly and demoniacal powers of mischief, not sent nor suffered even to come, save when they are attracted by the low affinities we offer as open gates to their coming. To which, also, we are to

[25] *Ibid.;* cf. pp. 85 ff. Bushnell elaborated (p. 86): "Powers, acting in liberty, are capable of a double action,–to do, or not to do, (God, for example, in creating, man in sinning;) things can act only in one way, viz., as their law determines.

"Powers are perfectible only by exercise, after they are made; things are perfect as made.

"Powers are perfected, or established in their law, only by a schooling of their consent; things are under a law mechanical at the first, having no consent.

"Powers can violate the present or nearest harmony, moving disorder in it; things are incapable of disorder, save as they are disordered by the malign action of powers.

"Powers, governed by the absolute force or fiat of omnipotence, would in that fact be uncreated and cease; things exist and act only in and by the impulsion of that fiat."

add those unknown, dimly-imagined orders or intelligences, of which we are notified in the terms of revelation,—seraphim, living creatures, thrones, authorities, dominions, principalities, and powers.[26]

III. *The Nature of Good and Evil*

What then of the possibility of evil? If God had created a realm of powers, or free agents, and that realm of powers, was not governed by the realm of things, why was there evil and misery in the world? In the answer to this question, Bushnell made the assumption that God's omnipotence was not power, "in the sense of influence, or moral impression, but [as] mere executive force." God, as omnipotent, "is in force to do all that force can do—this and nothing more." Bushnell wrote: "But force has no relation to the doing of many things. It can overturn mountains, roll back the sea, or open a way through it; but manifestly it has nothing to do in the direct impulsion of a soul; for a soul is a power, capable of character and responsibility, as being clear of all causation and acting by its own free self-impulsion. Therefore, to say that powers, or free agents, cannot be swayed absolutely by omnipotent force, is only to deny the applicability of such force, not to place it under limitation."[27] Such a conception of omnipotence, involved *no* limitation to the power of God. Rather it indicated that "the reason of God's empire excludes, at a certain point, the absolute dominion of force." God's force, however, "consents to the sovereignty of his eternal reason, and the counsel of wisdom in his purposes." But then: "Is it any impeachment of God that he did not care to reign over an empire of stones? If he has deliberately chosen a kind of empire not to be ruled by force, if he has deliberately set his children beyond that kind of control, that they may be governed by truth, reason, love, want, fear, and the like, acting through their consent; if we find them able to act even against the will of God, as stones and vegetables can not, what more is necessary to vindicate his goodness, than to suggest that he has given them, possibly, a capacity to break allegiance, in order that there may be a meaning and a glory in allegiance, when they choose it?"[28]

[26] *Ibid.*, pp. 87, 88. Cf. *The Spirit in Man*, pp. 224 ff.
[27] *Ibid.*, p. 95.
[28] *Ibid.*, pp. 95–96. Bushnell referred to Anselm's question, in terms of the seeming limitation of God's omnipotence because of the sacrifice of Christ: "To

Because there is the possibility of right, we must have the possibility of wrong, concluded Bushnell. The possibility of wrong is therefore inherent within the system of powers. It may be the very plan of God, suggested Bushnell, "to establish his powers in the right, by allowing them an experiment of the wrong, in which to school their liberty." The system of God will be, therefore, "one that systematizes the caprices and discords of innumerable wills, and works results of order, through endless complications of disorder." The highest expression of the system of God is that it brings together the powers which transcend nature, and includes even those disorders which are found within nature itself. God's system is a "comprehensive order" which takes up many antagonistic parts. Bushnell said: "The higher unity is not gone because discord has come in points below, and would not be, even if the discord were eternal. Still it remains, comprehends every thing, moving still on its ends, as little diverted or disturbed, as if the powers all came to wed themselves to it in loving obedience. There is a real universe now as before, because the universal *nisus* of the plan remains, and because the regulative order that comprehends so great irregularity retains its integrity unbroken, its equilibrium undisturbed." [29]

The great problem of existence is, therefore, the problem of how best to perfect one's freedom; i. e., "the schooling of our choice, or consent, as powers, so that we may be fully established in harmony with God's will and character":

They are to be trained, formed, furnished, perfected; and to this end are to be carried through just such scenes, experiences, changes, trials, variations, operations, as will best serve their spiritual perfection and their final fruition of each other and of God. If there are necessary perils in such a trial of their liberty, then they are to be set upon the course of

show for what necessity and cause God, who is omnipotent, should have assumed the littleness and weakness of human nature, for the sake of its renewal;" or, as he had just been saying how he did this to restore the world, when, for aught that appears, "he might have done it merely by his will."

[29] *Ibid.*, pp. 97–98; Bushnell drew an analogy between the system of God and the American republic: "Thus how meager an affair to thought were our American republic, if it were nothing but the run of causes in the climate and soil, and the mere physiology of the men; but, when it is considered as containing so many wills, acting all from themselves, incomputable in their action because they are uncaused in it; reducing so many mixtures of contrarieties and discords to a beautiful resultant order and social unity; striving still on, by the force of its organice *nisus*, toward a condition of historic greatness hitherto unknown to the world–considered thus, how truly sublime and wonderful a creation does it appear to be." Cf. *Building Eras in Religion*, pp. 256, 316.

such perils. Nor will it make any difference if the perils are such as breed the greatest speculative difficulties. God does not frame his empire to suit and satisfy our speculations, but for our practical profit; to bring us up into His own excellence, and establish us eternally in the participation of his character.[30]

This "training of consent" is a preparation for society; that is, a preparation "in truth, in purity, in justice, in patience, forgiveness, love, . . ." Powers, therefore, by their very nature, are *social*. Man must have training as powers among other powers:

And thus it is that we find ourselves embodied in matter, to act as powers upon, for, with, and, if we will, against each other, in all the endless complications of look, word, act, art, force, and persuasion; in the family and in the state, or two and two upon each other; in marriage, fraternity, neighborhood, friendship, trade, association, protection, hospitality, instruction, sympathy; or, if we will, in frauds, enmities, oppressions, cruelties, and mutual temptations,—great men moving the age they live in by their eloquence; or shaping the ages to come by their institutions; or corrupting the world's moral atmosphere by their bad thoughts, their fashions and vices; or tearing and desolating all things by irruptions of war, to win a throne of empire, or the honors of victors and heroes. By all these methods do we come into society, and begin to act, each one, upon the trains of cause and effect in nature; thus, upon each other, from our own point of liberty.[31]

Meanwhile, God reigns over society, and relates himself in a social way to every human being. He governs and trains every member of society in the use of his own liberty. Nature is, therefore, the universal medium by and through which this training takes place: "The powers act on each other, by acting on the lines of cause and effect in nature; starting thus new trains of events and consequences, by which they affect each other, in ways of injury or blessing." Bushnell continued: "All doings and misdoings are, in this view, a kind of discourse in the terms of nature, by which these supernatural agents, viz., men, answer to each other, or to God, in society. Their blasphemies and prayers and songs and threats, their looks and gestures, their dress and manners, their injuries and alms, their blows and barricades and bullets and bombs, these and such like are society, the grand conversation by which our social discipline is carried on. And it is all a supernatural transaction."[32]

[30] *Ibid.*, p. 99.
[31] *Ibid.*, pp. 99–101.
[32] *Ibid.*, p. 102.

74

Man is involved in what Bushnell called a "condition privative," which involves him in evil. The certainty of sin as related to man is involved in man's spiritual training as a power. A "condition privative" does not imply any positive ground, or cause, or necessity for sin, for if there were, then it would not be sin. Sin cannot be referred to a first principle. A "condition privative" is a "moral state that is only inchoate, or incomplete, lacking something not yet reached, which is necessary to the probable rejection of evil." Bushnell discussed the nature of the "condition privative" in the following way: [33]

1. "In the necessary defect of knowledge and consequent weakness of a free person, or power, considered as having just begun to be." A power is not necessarily, by its very nature, strong or perfect. Free agents are weak because they are free and ". . . left to act originatively, held fast by no superior determination, bound to no sure destiny; save as they are trained into character, in and through their experience." An existence merely begun, must, of necessity, be deficient in knowledge. And, yet, the man is guilty if he makes the wrong choice. But no one is obligated to choose the wrong. [34]

2. "It is another condition privative, as regards the moral perfection of powers, that they require an empirical training or course of government, to get them established in the absolute law of duty, and that this empirical training must probably have a certain adverse effect for a time, before it can mature its better results." Justice, truth, beauty, right, require the process of experience to be matured into characters. The process of experience requires two "economies," the first, law, the second, liberating grace and redemption. [35]

---

[33] *Ibid.,* pp. 109–123.

[34] *Ibid.,* pp. 110–114; Bushnell used the example of Adam: "As we look upon him, raising the question whether he has moral strength to stand, we observe, first of all, that being in a perfect form of harmony, uncorrupted, clean, in one word, a complete integer, he must of course be spontaneous to good, and can never fall from it until his spontaneity is interrupted by some reflective exercise of contrivance or deliberative judgment. But this will come to pass, without fail, in a very short time; because he is not only spontaneous to good, but is also a reflective and deliberative being." "What then is this wrong he is debating, what does it signify? He does not ask whether it will bring him evil or good for what these are, experimentally, he does not know. Enough that here is some great secret of knowledge to be opened; how can he abstain, how refuse to break through the mask of this unknown something, and know! He is tempted thus, we perceive, not by something positive, placed in his way, but by a mere condition privative, a perplexing defect of knowledge incident to the fact of his merely begun existence."

[35] *Ibid.,* p. 120, cf. Bushnell's description of law and liberty in relationship to

Bushnell believed that the law was a necessary idea, which commanded man from eternity to "do right," without making any specifications regarding the nature of the right. The reception of the law in this manner "supposes a mind and temper already configured to it, so as to be in it in mere love and the spontaneous homage that enthrones it . . ." The problem is, therefore, how to produce this configuration: "God, as a power and a force extraneous, undertakes for it, first of all, to enforce it empirically, by motives extraneous; those of reward and fear, profit and loss. He takes the law absolute down into the world of prudence, re-enacting it there and preparing to train us into it, by a drill-practice under sanctions." The result is, however, "habitual and wearisome selfishness"; for, as long as the mind is occupied by empirical sanctions, it can only be interested in itself. There is a certain benefit, however, in these sanctions: ". . . it gives adhesiveness to the law, which otherwise, as being merely ideal, we might lightly dismiss; that the friction it creates, like some mordant in the dying process sets in the law and fastens it practically, or as an experimental reality; that the woes of penalty wage a battle for it, in which the soul is continually worsted and so broken in; that it develops in short a whole body of moral judgments and convictions, that wind the soul about as cords of detention, till finally the law to be enforced becomes an experimental verity fully established. Just here the soul begins to feel a dreadful coil of thraldom around it." To escape from the law is impossible; but to keep the law is also impossible. Because of this situation, man's sin appears to be more severe than ever. The discipline under which he exists only aggravates his knowledge of sin. He is, thereby, prepared for the "second economy," that of liberating grace and redemption: "For now, in Christ," Bushnell said, "the law returns, a person, clothed all in personal beauty, and offers itself to the choice, even as a friend and deliverer; so that, being taken with love to Christ, and drawing near at his call in holy trust, the bondman is surprised to find that

the practical life; Bushnell also related law and liberty to law and gospel, cf. p. 122: "It [the law] is said to have its value in the development of knowledge; for by the law is 'the knowledge of sin'—'that sin by the commandment might become exceeding sinful.' It is bondage introducing and preparing liberty. 'The law gendereth to bondage,' but the gospel, "Jerusalem that above, is free."' 'If there had been a law that could have given life, verily righteousness should have been by the law'; but that was impossible. 'It is the schoolmaster to bring us to Christ,' and then, having embraced him, he becomes a new inspiration in our love, after which we no more need 'to be under a scholmaster.'"

he is loving the law as the perfect law of liberty". The whole operation of law and liberty presupposes, said Bushnell, a "condition privative" in the subject; that is, that the subject suffers a kind of repulsion by the law, and is won to it only by embracing the goodness of it in a personal deliverer.

3. "There appears to be yet another condition privative, as regards our security against sin, in the social relation of power and their trial in and through that relation; viz., that they are, at first, exposed to invasions of malign influence from each other, which can nowise be effectually prevented, save as they are finally fortified by the defenses of character." The great problem of existence consists in what Bushnell called "the fencing of powers," that is, to assort and separate the good from the bad and to render one inaccessible to the other.

Bushnell concluded on the basis of the above discussion that sin cannot be accounted for in terms of anything positive. The "conditions privative" allow for the possibility of understanding the nature of sin: "These conditions privative are in the nature of perils, and while they excuse nothing, for the law of duty is always plain, they are yet drawn so close to the soul and open their gulfs, on either hand, so deep, that our expectation of the fall is really as pressing as if it were determined by some law that annihilates liberty. Liberty we know is not annihilated. And yet we say, looking on the state of man made perilous, in this manner, by liberty, that we can not expect him to stand." [36]

What then of the existence of Satan, or the devil? God might create a realm of things and have it stand firm in its order. But if he created a realm of powers, what then "of their outbreak in evil." Bushnell had to insert some kind of diabolic personality to explain the incidence of evil in the world. Two principles have existed together from eternity, one of which is the cause of good, the other, the cause of evil. The good principle we call God and make it into a being, Bushnell believed, and the bad principle we call a "condition privative." One is a positive and real cause, the other is a bad possibility that influences God from eternity, waiting to become a fact, whenever the opportunity is given:

[36] *Ibid.*, pp. 127, 128; Bushnell made reference to "ministering angels" and "bad spirits," evil demons etc., in this argument, pp. 124 ff. See his discussion of the medium, p. 127. Bushnell was convinced of the scriptural truth of "good angels," the existence of which seemed to conflict with his conception of free beings who never sin; cf. also pp. 129 ff.

And then it follows that, the moment God creates a realm of powers, the bad possibility as certainly becomes a bad actuality, a Satan, or devil, *in esse;* not a bad omnipresence over against God, and His equal—that is a monstrous and horrible conception—but an outbreaking evil, or empire of evil in created spirits, according to their order. For Satan, or the devil, taken in the singular, is not the name of any particular person, neither is it a personation merely of temptation, or impersonal evil, as many insist; for there is really no such thing as impersonal evil in the sense of moral evil; but the name is a name that generalizes bad persons of spirits, with their bad thoughts and characters, many in one. That there is any single one of them who, by distinction or preeminence, is called Satan, or devil, is wholly improbable. The name is one taken up by the imagination to designate or embody, in a conception the mind can most easily wield, the all or total of bad minds and powers.[37]

Evil, once it exists, inevitably becomes organic, and builds a kingdom over against God. Satan is, threrefore, "a bad possibility, eternally existing prior to the world's creation." But Bushnell asserted that it is the plan of God to regenerate the bad powers loosened by his creation:

The cross of redemption is no afterthought, but is itself the grand all-dominating idea around which the eternal system of God crystallizes; Jesus Christ, the "appointed heir of all things"—"the Lamb slain from the foundation of the world." Here stands out the final end or cause of all things, here emerge the powers made strong and glorious. Weak, at first, unperfect, incomplete, they are now completed and glorified—complete in him, who is the head of all principality and power.[38]

IV. *The Nature and Consequences of Sin*

Sin exists, Bushnell concluded. Over against those individuals who tried to deny the existence of sin,[39] Bushnell maintained that there was such a thing as properly blamable action, the transgression of right, or of law, a positive disobedience of God—or "any

[37] *Ibid.,* pp. 134, 135; Bushnell quoted Davenport, "the ablest theologian of all the New England Fathers," who asked the question, "What is the devil?" in his *Cathechism:* "The multitude of apostate angels which, by pride, and blasphemy against God, and malice against man, became liars and murderers, by tempting him to that sin."

[38] *Ibid.,* pp. 136, 138, 139. "The stability of Satan and his empire consists, not in the force of some personal chieftainship, but in the fixed array of all bad minds, and even of anarchy itself, against what is good."

[39] *Ibid.,* pp. 142 ff. Bushnell named the following culprits: the phrenologists, Theodore Parker, Fourier, Strauss, Carlyle, and Emerson, and the whole host of naturalists of his time.

78

thing that rationally connects with remorse, or carries the sense of guilt as a genuine reality."

The first proof for the fact of sin must be made by an appeal to observation. We impute blame, by inevitable necessity, to acts of injury done to us by others. Bushnell was so confident about this fact that he could write: "... if there be any man living who undertakes to be consistent in the denial of sin, setting it down however firmly, as a point of will, never to blame any injury done to others or to himself, we will engage, in case he is able to spend four waking hours without any single thought or feeling of blame as against any human creature, to admit the truth of his doctrine." [40]

Another proof for the fact of sin is that man blames himself for a sin committed. Bushnell wrote: "And here we are bold to affirm that every person of a mature age, and in his right mind, remembers turns, or crises in his life, where he met the question of wrong face to face, and by a hard inward struggle broke through the sacred convictions of duty that rose up to fence him back." Man commits sin individually, and recognizes that there is no determinative for his sin. He cannot rid himself of the fact in his consciousness which tells him that he committed the sin. Bushnell believed that the sense of sin pervaded all of mankind, and that everyone was plagued by "the foul demon of guilt." He wrote: "Men are under a subtle and tacit, but damning sense of blame, and can not bear ... to have subjects introduced that remind them of it, and stir again the guilt of their conscience." [41]

Still another proof of the fact of sin is that mankind acts on the assumption that wrong is done, or is likely to be done in the world. Everything in government presupposes the existence of sin. Why is it necessary to organize the civil state, why fence about society with

[40] *Ibid.*, p. 151.
[41] *Ibid.*, p. 152. "He remembers how it shook his soul and even his body; how he shrunk in guilty anticipation from the new step of wrong; the sublime misgiving that seized him, the awkward and but half-possessed manner in which it was taken, and then afterward, perhaps even after years have passed away, how, in some quiet hour of the day or wakeful hour of night, as the recollection of that deed—not a public crime, but a wrong, or an act of vice—returned upon him, the blood rushed back for the moment on his fluttering heart, the pores of his skin opened, and a kind of agony of shame and self-condemnation, in one word, of remorse, seized his whole person. This is the consciousness, the guilty pang, of sin; every man knows what it is ... men are under a subtle and tacit, but damning sense of blame, and can not bear, on all occasions, or any where but in the public assemblies of religion, to have subjects introduced that remind them of it, and stir again the guilt of their conscience." Cf. p. 155.

laws, and enforce them by severe punishments if there is no sin in the world? The whole superstructure of the civil order rests upon the conviction that there is sin and that it leads to a social behavior.[42]

And even another proof involves the experience of *forgiveness*. No one doubts the reality of forgiveness. But it is always the forgiveness of a wrong, a "blamable and guilty wrong" which is forgiven: "If there is nothing to blame—there is nothing to forgive. One of two things, then, must be true: either that there has been some blamable wrong in the world, or else that the forgiveness we think of, speak of, inculcate, and commend, is a baseless phantom, out of all reality, as destitute of dignity and beauty as of solidity and truth." [43]

Bushnell insisted that sin is not "misdirection," because such a view avoided all recognition of the blame and responsibility of man. Man is the "grand misdirector." It is he who turns God's world into "a hell of misdirection." This is his sin.

Sin effects the whole realm of nature. Man, who had been defined by Bushnell as a force, a being supernatural, and therefore outside of nature, is able to act upon the chain of cause and effect relationships. Nature is, in a very real sense, subordinate to man, and man is able to change it as he wants.[44] Man's sin, therefore, can also change the course of nature, and even can produce "new conjunctions of causes":

[42] *Ibid.*, p. 157; see the interesting use of the concept of checks and balances, p. 158. "Besides we are afraid even of the law; trying, by every method possible, to invent checks and balances against usurpations and abuses of power; so to make power responsible, and to hedge about even our tribunals of justice by penal enactments against bribery, connivance, and arbitrary contempt of law; as if wanting still some defense against even our defenders, and the more terrible wrongs they are like to perpetrate, in the abuse of those powers which have been committed to their hands."

[43] *Ibid.*, p. 159; additional proofs for the fact of sin may be found in the sentiments of man; "The staple matter of emotion, all that so profoundly moves our feeling in these records of fact and fiction, is that here we look upon the conflict of good and bad powers, the glory and suffering of one, the hellish art and malice of the other, followed or not followed by the sublime vindications of providential justice. It is the war, actual or imagined, of beauty and deformity, good and evil, in their higher examples. In this view, we have a deeper sense of awe, a vaster movement of feeling, in the contemplation of a man, a mere human creature, in a character demonized by passion than we have in the rage of the sea, or the bursting firestorm of a volcano; because we regard him as a power–a bad will doing battle with God and the world." (pp. 160, 161).

[44] *Nature and the Supernatural*, pp. 162 ff. Bushnell was primarily critical of Parker at this point, and in particular in terms of Parker's criticism of the slave trade as an "abuse and misdirection of human nature." Cf. Theodore Parker,

Sin, therefore, is . . . such a force as may suffice, in a society and world of sin, to vary the combinations, and display a new resolution of the activities, of nature. The laws remain, but they are met and provoked by a new ingredient not included in nature; and so the whole field of nature, otherwise a realm of harmony, and peace, and beauty, takes a look of discord, and, with many traces of its original glory left, displays the tokens also of a prison and a hospital.

In all these cases, the results of pain, disorder, and death are properly said to be unnatural; being, in a sense, violations of nature. The scheme of nature included no such results. They are disorders and dislocations made by the misconjunction or abuse of causes in the scheme of nature. And the same will be true of all the events that follow, in the vast complications and chains of causes, to the end of the world. Whatever mischief, or unnatural result is thus brought to pass by sin, will be the first link of an endless chain of results not included in the scheme of nature, and so the beginning of an ever-widening circle of disturbance. And this is the true account of evil.[45]

Man has a great power over the causes of the world, not only in the present time, but for all of the years to come. The scheme of nature "is marred, corrupted, dislocated by innumerable disturbances and disorders." Nature's laws continue, but the conjunctions between her laws are unnatural. Immense transformations therefore take place in nature. And it is this which represents the fact of sin in the world.

But the consequences of sin can also be seen in the human *soul*, which results in "perceptions discolored, the judgments unable to hold their scales steadily because of the fierce gusts of passion, the thoughts huddling by in crowds of wild suggestion, the imagination haunted by ugly and disgustful shapes, the appetites contesting with reason, the senses victorious over faith, anger blowing the overheated fires of malice, low jealousies sulking in dark angles of the soul, and envies baser still, hiding under the skim of its greenmantled pools—all the powers that should be strung in harmony, loosened from each other, and brewing in hopeless and helpless con-

Discourses of Religion (Boston: American Unitarian Association, 1842), p. 13; cf. also Bushnell's evaluation of the history of man: "Is it then given us, for our privilege, to look over the sad inventory of the world's history, the corruptions of truth and religion, the bloody persecutions, the massacres of the good, the revolutions against oppressions and oppressors, and the combinations of power to crush them, if successful, caste, slavery and the slave trade, piracy and war tramping in blood over desolated cities and empires–can we look on these and have it as our soft impeachment to say, that they are only the misdirections of discordant causes in human nature?" (pp. 163, 164).
[45] *Ibid.*, pp. 167 ff.

fusion; the conscience meantime thundering wrathfully above and shooting down hot bolts of judgment, and the pallid fears hurrying wildly about with their brimstone torches—these are the motions of sins, the Tartarean landscape of the soul and its disorder, when self-government is gone and the constituent integrity is dissolved." [46]

The consequences of sin are also seen in the *body*,[47] which results in a condition of "general intemperance." Bushnell suggested that "many of the sufferings and infirmities even of persons called virtuous, are known by all intelligent physicians to be only the groaning of the body under loads habitually imposed, by the untempered and really diseased voracity of their appetites"; that is, sin becomes a power disturbing the body, "shattering the nerves, inflaming the tissues, distempering the secretions, and brewing a general ferment of disease." Everything that is suffers from a "state of unnature" because of sin. Bushnell maintained that:

Self-centered now, every man in his sin, and having no ligatures of race and family and family affection to bind them together, the selfishness of their fall would be unqualified, softened by no mitigations. Spiritual love they can not understand, because they never have felt the natural love of sex, family, and kindred, by which, under conditions of propagation, a kind of inevitable, first-stage virtue is instituted; such as mitigates the severities of sin, softens the sentiments to a social, tender play, and offers to the mind a type, every where present, of the beauty and true joy of a disinterested, spiritual benevolence. They compose, instead, a burly prison-gang of probationers, linked together by no ties of consanguinity, reflecting no traces of family likeness, bent to each other's and God's love by no dear memories. Society there is none. Law is impossible. Society and law suppose conditions of organic unity already prepared. Every man for himself, is the grand maxim of life; for all are atoms together, in the medley of the common selfishness; only the old atoms have an immense advantage over the young ones fresh arrived; for these new comers of probation, come of course to the prey, having no guardians or protectors, and no tender sentiments of care and kindred prepared to shelter them and smooth their way. Besides, the world into which they come must have been already fouled and disordered by the sin of the prior populations, and must therefore be a frame of being, wholly inappropriate to their new-created innocence.[48]

[46] *Ibid.,* p. 172.

[47] Bushnell is not a dualist in the usual sense of the term, for he was able to write: "Body and soul, as long as they subsist in their organized state, are a strict unity. The abuses of one are abuses also of the other, the disturbances and diseases of one disturb and disease the other. The fortunes of the body must, in this way, follow the fortunes of the soul, whose organ it is." *Ibid.,* p. 174.

[48] *Ibid.,* pp. 180, 181, 182. Intimations of *Christian Nurture* are found in Bush-

Sin, finally, produces a disturbance in the material and physical world. If sin can affect the soul, the body and even society, reducing all nature to an unnatural state, it can also produce disorder in the material and physical world. Sin, being a supernatural force, can continually play itself "into the chemistries and external combinations of matter, converting shapes, reducing or increasing quantities, transferring positions, framing and dismembering conjunction, turning poisons into medicines, and reducing fruits to poisons, till at length scarcely any thing is left in its properly natural state." [49] Nature can become "a realm of deformity and abortion; groaning with the discords of sin and keeping company with it in guilty pains of its apostasy." Bushnell added:

After all the fine sentimentalities, lavished by rote and without discriminating thought on the works and processes of nature, he will be surprised to find that the world is not as truly a realm of beauty, as of beauty flecked by injury. The growths are carbuncled and diseased, and the children have it for a play to fetch a perfect leaf. Fogs and storms blur the glory of the sky, and foul days, rightly so called, interspace the bright and fair. The earth itself displays vast deserts swept by the horrid simoom; muddy rivers, with their fenny shores, tenanted by hideous alligators;

nell's argument at this point: "How much more, where the odor of a heavenly piety fills the house and sanctifies the atmosphere of life itself. Instead of being set forth as an overgrown man, issued from the Creator's hand to make the tremendous choice, undirected by experience, he is gently inducted, as it were, by choices of parents before his own, into the habit and accepted practice of all holy obedience; growing up in the nurture of their grace, as truly as of their natural affection." Cf. the address "God's Thoughts fit Bread for Children," pp. 70–89, and the sermon "A Great Life begins Early," pp. 90–102, *The Spirit in Man.*
[49] *Nature and the Supernatural,* p. 186; Bushnell asserted that nature did not represent the mind of God, that is, that not all the creations of God are beautiful. Cf. p. 187: "Not only do the poets and poetasters in prose go the round of nature, sentimentalizing among her dews and flowers, and paying their worship at her shrine, as if the world were a gospel even of beauty; but our philosophers often teach it as a first principle, and our natural theologians assume it also in their arguments, that the forms of things must represent the perfect forms of the Divine thought, by which they were fashioned. It would seem that such a conceit might be dissipated by a single glance of revision; for God is the infinite beauty, and who can imagine, looking on this or that half-dry and prosy scene of nature, that it represents the infinite beauty? The fact of creation argues no such thing." Bushnell also referred to Swedenborg in his discussion of creation, p. 188: "Swedenborg and his followers have a way of representing, I believe, that God creates the world through man, by which they understand that what we call the creation, is a purely gerundive matter–God's perpetual act–and that he holds the work *to man,* at every stage, so as to represent him always at his present point, and act upon him fitly to his present taste."

swamps and morasses, spreading out in provinces of quagmire, and reeking in the steam of death. In the kingdom of life, disgusting and loathsome objects appear, too numerous to be recounted; such as worms and the myriads of base vermin, deformed animals, dwarfs, idiots, leprosies, and the rot of cities swept by the plague; history itself depicting the mushrooms sprouting in the bodies of the unburied dead, and the jackals howling in the chambers, at their dreadful repast. Even more significant still is the fact, because it is a fact that concerns the honor even of our personal organism, that no living man or woman is ever found to be a faultless model of beauty and proportion. When the sculptor will fashion a perfect form, he is obliged to glean for it, picking out the several parts of beauty from a hundred malproportioned, blemished bodies in actual life. And what is yet more striking, full three-fourths of the living races of men are so ugly, or so far divested of beauty in their mold, that no sculptor would ever think of drawing on them for a single feature! [50]

Sin is, therefore, "a very great, world-transforming, world-uncreating fact." A far-reaching, all-comprehensive state of "unnature" is the consequence of sin.

V. *The Supernatural Work of Redemption*

But Bushnell asked that we look for some remedial agency or dispensation that shall restore the lapse and bring out those results of order and happiness, that were proposed by God in his act of creation. Man cannot help himself; only God is able to restore what has been disrupted by sin. Only God, in a supernatural manner, could bring about the original unity of man. Man cannot redeem himself, Bushnell asserted; "O, if there be a kind of life most sad, and deepest in the scale of pity, it is the dry, cold impotence of one, who is honestly set to the work of his own self-redemption!" This means that man is absolutely unable to do what is right before God: "No created being, of any world, not even the new-formed man before his fall, nor the glorified saint, nor the spotless angel, had ever any possibility of holiness, except in the embrace of God." [51] God is the source of all religious virtue, and man is unable to do any good without the grace of God. Bushnell wrote: "By mere working on himself and manipulating, as it were, his body of sin and death, he can do just nothing in the way of self-perfection; and, if he could even do every thing, as regards self-transformation, there would be no religious

[50] *Ibid.,* pp. 191, 192.
[51] *Ibid.,* p. 237.

character in the result, any more than if his works were done before the moon. Religious character is God in the soul, and without that all pretenses of religious virtue are, in fact, atheistic." [52]

But the freedom of the will involves, "freedom as volitional function," which presupposed for Bushnell the capacity to regenerate and to constitute a character. The execution of an action needs, therefore, divine help and grace, and this is the power of the will, in terms of man's moral recovery: "It may so offer itself and the subordinate capacities to God, that God shall have the whole man open to his dominion, and be able to ingenerate in him a new, divine, state, or principle of action." [53] Society cannot be restored either without a supernatural action. Progress under sin, by laws of natural development, remains a fiction, so Bushnell insisted.

The supernatural agency which is required to provide a remedy for sin must be wholly compatible with nature. The supernatural act of restoration cannot break the laws of the natural realm, nor can it disturb its systematic action. Even miracles, which are brought about by supernatural powers, do not remove or suspend nature's laws. Nature is subjected, by her laws, to God's activity and to ours, "to be thus acted on, and varied in her operation, by the new combinations or conjunctions of causes, they are able to produce." God acts perpetually upon the lines of causes in nature, and "doing his will supernaturally in it, or upon it . . .", he is, nevertheless, in per-

[52] *Ibid.,* pp. 238, 239, 240: "We have no ability at all, of any kind, to regenerate our own state, or restore our own disorders. Salvation is by faith, or there is none."

[53] *Ibid.,* p. 240; cf. Bushnell's use of Plato (whom he calls "the wisest heathen") to support his position; "If, in this whole disputation, we have rightly conceived the case, virtue is acquired, neither by nature's force, nor by any institutes of discipline or teaching, but it comes to those that have it, by a certain divine appointment (or inspiration) over and above the mind's own force or exertion." The reference is from the *Meno,* 89; cf. also, his evaluation of Plato's religion, p. 246: "What a condition of hunger for knowledge! a great and mighty soul, prying at the gates of light, to force them open, catching the faintest gleams of truth or opinion, and committing his all tenderly to them as to a slender raft upon the sea, only venting, with a sigh, the mysterious hint of a Divine Logos, who will possibly come to him within and be a surer light, a safer guide. And this dim hint of a better revelation is ventured more boldly in his *Alcibiades,* when he says–'We must wait patiently until some one, either a god or some inspired man, teach us our moral and religious duties and, as Pallas in Homer did to Diomede, remove the darkness from our eyes.' How little incredible was it to him, the highest philosophic intellect the world has ever seen, that some incarnate messenger of God, or teacher supernaturally sent, may sometime come to enlighten the world! What in fact does he tell us, but that he is waiting for Jesus the Christ."

fect compatibility with the laws and order of nature. Such a claim, Bushnell discovered, is supported by the "new science" of geology. He asked:

For when the geologists show that new races of animal and vegetable life have taken a beginning, at successive points in the history of the creation, that whole realms of living creatures disappear again and again, to be succeeded by others fresh from the hand of God, what does it signify but that the atoms and elemental forces of nature are so related to God, that they do, by their own laws, submit themselves to his will flowing into new combinations, and composing thus new germs of life? [54]

The "new births of life" of which the geologists speak, act according to their inherent properties and laws, but they are "instigated by a divine force not in its natural laws." Therefore, when we admit the existence of a supernatural world, we are not being superstitious. Rather, to assert that God acts upon the world does not in any way derange the scientific order of the universe. Bushnell was careful to maintain the scientific credibility of his position: "To serve this intent, two things manifestly are wanted, and one as truly as the other; viz., nature and the supernatural, an invariable, scientific order, and a pliant submission of that order to the sovereignty and uses of wills, human and divine, without any infringement of its constancy. For if nature were to be violated and tossed about by capricious overturnings of her laws, there would be an end of all confidence and exact intelligence." [55] God is, therefore, in a constant state of activity, in the same way as He was when He created the world. He is active from eternity to eternity. In all events and changes He has a present concern. He turns the "wheels of nature" by his ever-present power and government. Nature is subjected to His constant agency, but in terms of its laws, which laws He never suspends, *but only employs.* The great realm of nature is flexible to his will for all of time. But, He is also a living God, "with us and about us, filling all things with His potent energy and fatherly counsel."

Furthermore, insisted Bushnell, the supernatural agency of God is itself subject to immutable and fixed laws. Man, as an intelligent creature, can have no comfort under a world ruled by no law nor system which does not conform to a principle of intelligence. Everything in God's plan must stand within the strict unity of

[54] *Ibid.,* pp. 254, 255.
[55] *Ibid.,* p. 257.

86

reason. God can never violate the "instinctive opinion of law," because our intelligence insists that God's plan be in accord with law and systematic unity. God will never deviate from rules of universal application, because He himself is Sovereign Intelligence, and the Perfect Reason. Bushnell wrote: "The unity of God always perishes, when the unity of order and law is lost. And we may as well believe in God, acting on or against another, as in the same God acting outside of all fixed laws and terms of immutable order." [56]

[56] *Ibid.*, p. 262; Bushnell was insistent that the term "law" be used properly. First, it implied that which is uniform; "as that, in exactly the same circumstances, it will always and forever do, bring to pass, direct, or command precisely the same thing.", pp. 262, 263. Natural law is therefore, "the law by which any kind of being or thing is made to act invariably, thus or thus, in virtue of terms inherent in itself; as when any body of matter gravitates by reason of its matter, and according to the quantity of its matter.", p. 263. Moral law "pertains never to a thing, or to any substance in the chain of cause and effect, but only to a free intelligence, or self-active power. Its rule is authority, not force. It commands, but does not actuate or determine. It speaks to assent or choice, inviting action, but operating nothing apart from choice. It imposes obligation, leaving the subject to obey or not, clear of any enforcement, save that of conviction beforehand, and penalty afterward.", p. 263. The supernatural work of God in Christ and the Spirit are not fully reducible to natural or moral law, although to a certain extent God's nature will be a law to his action, i. e., ". . . if God is infinite in his nature, then it is a fixed law of his nature that he shall indicate infinity in his action, and if he has geometric ideas, that his works shall, by a necessary consequence, have some fixed relation to the laws of geometry; such as we discover in their spheres, and orbits, and projectile curves, and in the subtle triangulations of light.", pp. 263–264, and: "It is the eternal, necessary law of right, or of love; a law that he acknowledges with a ready and full assent forever; that which determines the immutable order, and purity, and glory of his character." Another conception of law must be introduced, that is, the law of one's end, or the law which reason imposes in the way of attaining his end: "Moral law, we have said, shapes the character of God, and that determines his end. Since he is a morally perfect being in his character, moral perfection or holiness will be the last end of his being, that for which he creates and rules; for, if he were to value holiness only as the means of some other end, such as happiness, then he would even disrespect holiness, rating it only as a convenience; which is not the character of a holy being, but only an imposture in the name of such a character. Regarding holiness then as God's last end, his world-plan will be gathered round the end proposed, to fulfill it, and all his counsels will crystallize into order and system, subject to that end. For this nature will exist, in all her vast machinery of causes and laws; to this all the miracles and supernatural works of redemption will bring their contributions. Having this for his end, and the supernatural as means to his end, the divine reason will of course order all under fixed laws of reason, which laws will be so exact and universal as to make a perfect system.", pp. 264, 265. It is in this sense that Bushnell meant that all of God's supernatural acts, providences and works, supernatural though they may be, will be dispensed by immutable, universal and fixed laws. It is this way because God's rule never varies and his reason is perfect. His

87

The supernatural work of redemption must take place systematically and under fixed laws. The Incarnation took place under an immutable and universal law. The doctrine of the Spirit and the doctrine of prayer are nothing more than the unfolding to us of the laws of the spirit and the laws of prayer, as they pertain to the supernatural kingdom of God:

> The glory, the true sublimity of God's architectural wisdom is that, while his work stands fast in immutable order, it bends so gracefully to the humblest things, without damages or fracture, pliant to all free action, both His and ours; receiving the common play of our liberty, and becoming always a fluent medium of reciprocal action between us; to Him a hand showing his handy work, or even a tongue which day unto day uttereth speech, and night unto night showeth forth knowledge of Him; to us the ground of our works, the instrument of our choices, and yet, in the order, all, of a perfect counsel and of laws as immutable as his throne. In this rests the doctrine of faith, the doctrine that justifies prayer, enables the disciple to believe that God can notice him, and move among causes to help him; raising him thus into a state of ennobled consciousness, how superior to the low mechanical skepticism which thinks itself dignified in the discovery that God, incrusted in the stiffness of his scientific order, has no longer any power to bend himself to man.
>
> Thus we conceive, alas! too feebly, the true scale of dignity in God's two realms. In one the order is superficial and palpable. In the other it is deep as eternity, mysterious and vast as the counsel that comprehends eternity, in its development. Still it is counsel, it is order, it is truth and reason.[57]

VI. *The Character of Jesus Christ, the "Supernatural Divine Ministration"*

Bushnell believed that he had now demonstrated the need for a supernatural, divine ministration which would restore the disorders of sin. Furthermore, he believed he had demonstrated that such a ministration was compatible with the order of nature, and was there-

world-plan will be an exact and perfect system of order, centered in the eternal unity of reason as his last end.

[57] *Ibid.*, pp. 272–273; pp. 275–276; p. 269: "Could we look into the history, too, of the innumerable other worlds God has comprehended in his reign, what a lesson might we thence derive from events counterpart to his of the incarnation, varied only to meet the varied conditions of their want, character, and destiny. Though we may not be able, creatures of a day, to unfold the law of this grand miracle, and reduce it to a formula of science, how little reason have we, in our inability, to question the fact of such a law."

fore a rational possibility. Bushnell then asked the question whether the "supernatural divine ministration" had actually come into being?

The answer to his question Bushnell found in the person of Jesus Christ.[58] He called Him "the central figure and power of Christianity." He had established on earth a celestial institution called the kingdom of God, which was a "perpetual, supernatural dispensatory of healing and salvation for the race." Christianity was, therefore, no scheme of doctrine, or ethical practice, but was, rather, a miracle, a power outside of nature which descended into it; "a historically supernatural movement on the world, that is visibly entered into it, and organized to be an institution in the person of Jesus Christ." Jesus Christ is the central figure of Christianity—the entire fabric of Christianity stands or falls with Him!

Jesus Christ, nonetheless, could not be classified with mankind, although He was a man. We discover in the New Testament, Bushnell said, that the life and character of Jesus Christ represented the truth of divine excellence and beauty: "Having our attention arrested thus by the impression made on our respect, we are put on inquiry, and the more we study it the more wonderful, as a character, it appears. And before we have done, it becomes, in fact, the chief wonder of the story; lifting all the other wonders into order and intelligent proportion round it, and making one compact and glorious wonder of the whole picture—a picture shining in its own clear sunlight upon us, as the truest of all truths—Jesus, the Divine Word, coming out from God, to be incarnate with us, and be the vehicle of God and salvation to the race." [59]

Bushnell looked at the life of Jesus, and remarked that his character was remarkable, even though he did not rely chiefly upon miracles to convince people that He was sent from God. The childhood of Jesus was perfect, he said, unspotted. It could best be characterized as a "kind of celestial flower." Everyone loved Him. He grew up in favor with God and man, "a child as lovely and beautiful that heaven and earth appear to smile upon him together." The

[58] Ibid.; cf. entire chapter X, entitled "The Character of Jesus Forbids His Possible Classification with Men," republished with minor changes by The Chautauqua Press (New York: 1888), 87 pgs., pp. 276–332.
[59] Ibid., p. 278: "On the single question, therefore, of the more than human character of Jesus, we propose, in perfect confidence, to rest a principal argument for Christianity as a supernatural institution; for, if there be in Jesus a character which is not human, then has something broken into the world that is not of it, and the spell of unbelief is broken."

grace and beautifying power of God was upon Him, and he unfolded "like a sacred flower." [60]

The mature life of Jesus was characterized by innocence. He was a perfectly harmless being, who was actuated by no destructive passions. The figure of a Lamb was appropriate to him: "Appearing in the grandeur and majesty of a superhuman manhood, he is still able to unite the impression of innocence, with no apparent diminution of his sublimity. It is in fact, the distinctive glory of his character, that it seems to be the natural unfolding of a divine innocence, a pure celestial childhood, amplified by growth." When his enemies were called upon to show what evil he had done, they could not specify any, except that he had offended them and their prejudices. Even Pilate could find no wrong in him. He died, "a being holy, harmless, undefiled. And when he hangs, a bruised flower drooping on his cross, and the sun above is dark, and the earth beneath shudders with pain, what have we in this funeral grief of the worlds, but a fit honor paid to the sad majesty of his divine innocence." [61]

His religious life was characterized by the fact that he never acknowledged sin and never expressed the least sense of unworthiness. Bushnell was much impressed with this characteristic of Jesus' personality. He wrote that we have in the person of Jesus, "a style of piety, withal, wholly unsuited to his real character as a sinner, holding it as a figment of insufferable presumption to the end of life, and that in a way of such unfaltering grace and beauty, as to command the universal homage of the human race!" His character remained the same throughout his life. He had no need of improvement in his personal life. He was never extravagant nor eccentric, disturbed nor maladjusted. [62]

Jesus claimed an inherent affinity and oneness with God. He assured everyone that He was "the Way, the Truth and the Life." "No man cometh to the Father but by me", was the claim He made. No one appeared offended when Jesus spoke in this way. There was

---

[60] *Ibid.*, pp. 281 ff.; Bushnell referred to the Apocryphal writers and their account of the childhood of Jesus.

[61] *Ibid.*, pp. 283–284: "Decisive, great, and strong, Christ is yet all this, even the more sublimely, that he is invested, withal, in the lovely, but humanly feeble garb of innocence."

[62] *Ibid.*, pp. 286–288; cf. p. 287: "He is the most unworldly of beings, having no desire at all for what the earth can give, impossible to be caught with any longing for its benefits, impassible even to its charms, and yet there is no ascetic sourness or repugnance, no misanthropic distaste in his manner."

no one to claim that He was vain or filled with conceit. Bushnell felt that the response of the part of man was completely otherwise: "For eighteen hundred years, these prodigious assumptions have been published and preached to a world that is quick to lay hold of conceit, and bring down the lofty airs of pretenders, and yet, during all this time, whole nations of people, composing as well the learned and powerful as the ignorant and humble, have paid their homage to the name of Jesus, detecting never by any thought of his extravagance. In which we have absolute proof that he practically maintains his amazing assumptions!" [63] This fact led Bushnell to assert that Jesus Christ was more than a man.

There is also a passive side to the character of Jesus. Jesus united the passive virtues of his being and made them part of his character.[64] Christ connected the "non-resisting and gentle passivities with a character of the severest grandeur and majesty." The superhuman nature of Christ's character consisted in the fact that He was perfect in spirit in terms of the small trials of existence but also in the momentous ones. He was always patient, and maintained a condition of serenity. Bushnell wrote: "He is poor, and hungry, and weary, and despised, insulted by his enemies deserted by his friends, but never disheartened, never fretted or ruffled." [65] He did not seem to have passions or temper or even self-will. But he was not a Stoic, for he experienced every ill. He had a "sacred and sovereign good" which allayed his ills. The passion scenes at the end of his life revealed his nature, which was more than human. Bushnell insisted Christ was composed, mentally and emotionally, during the crucifixion, whereas every other man would be in a state of extense distress. Christ possessed the "serenity of a spectator" during the tragedy of his crucifixion. The death scene became, therefore, a scence of a transcendent love. Bushnell described Christ's death in the following way:

But this one thing is clear, that no one of mankind, whether man or woman, ever had the sensibility to suffer so intensely; even showing the body, for the mere struggle and pain of the mind, exuding and dripping with blood. Evidently there is something mysterious here; which mystery is vehicle to our feling, and rigthfully may be, of something divine. What,

[63] *Nature and the Supernatural*, p. 291.
[64] Bushnell insisted that Christ and Socrates had entirely different characters. Socrates did not possess the character of submissiveness until the time of his death. *Ibid.*, p. 292.
[65] *Ibid.*, p. 294.

we begin to ask, should be the power of a superhuman sensibility? and how far should the human vehicle shake under such a power? How too should an innocent and pure spirit be exercised, when about to suffer, in his own person, the greatest wrong ever committed? [66]

But in dying Christ took upon himself the sins of others:

How then, if perchance Jesus should be divine, an embodiment of God's love in the world—how should he feel, and by what signs of feeling manifest his sensibility, when a fallen race are just about to do the damning sin that crowns their guilty history; to crucify the only perfect being that ever came into the world; to crucify even him the messenger and representative to them of the love of God, the deliverer who has taken their case and cause upon him! Whosoever duly ponders these questions, will find that he is led away, more and more, from any supposition of the mere mortality of Jesus. [67]

Christ demonstrated that he possessed a superhuman character by the display of His human traits during his lifetime. He also demonstrated his superhuman character in the works and teachings of his role as the Messiah. Christ proposed to organize the kingdom of heaven on earth. He attempted to bring about a new moral creation of the race, and a restoration of a spiritual kingdom of God. "The rustic tradesman of Galilee propounds even thus for his errand"; a universal kingdom, cemented in God. This plan was projected into future ages. Bushnell was extremely confident regarding the role Jesus would play in the future of civilization:

Is this great idea then, which no man ever before conceived, the raising of the whole human race to God, a plan sustained with such evenness of courage, and a confidence of the world's future so far transcending any human example—is this a human development? Regard the benevolence of it, the universality of it, the religious grandeur of it, as a work readjusting the relations of God and his government with men—the cost, the length of time it will cover, and the far off date of its completion—is it in this scale that a Nazarene carpenter, a poor uneducated villager, lays out his plans and graduates the confidence of his undertakings? [68]

This, however, was not a human project, but a project which only God could bring to fulfillment.

Bushnell believed that Christ's life and ministry was also related to social class. Jesus Christ took his place among the poor and lowly in society and anticipated that the kingdom would come in terms

[66] *Ibid.,* p. 296.
[67] *Ibid.,* p. 297.
[68] *Ibid.,* p. 301.

of the downtrodden and the rejected classes of the world. His manners, tastes and intellectual attainments outgrew his lowly origins, and if He were merely human, He would have suffered a painful distaste for the kind of society in which He had to live. Individuals from the highest circles of society came to Him to receive his instruction. Nonetheless, He remained with the poor and the outcast, and made them the primary concerns of His ministry. "The ingenuous babes of poverty" were ready to receive His message, Bushnell wrote. He loved the poor, and loved to be identified with them, although He never descended to the level of their crude behavior.[69]

Bushnell then attempted to relate Christ's life among the poor to the treatment of the poor by the great men of his day. He said that Christ's concern for the poor was to be contrasted with the contempt the great statesmen and philanthropists have had for the lowly classes of society throughout history. The poor were always the "conveniences and drudges of society," and any influence for the betterment of society was always in terms of the upper classes. Christ became for Bushnell, therefore, "the poor man's philoso pher":

Seeing the higher circles open to him, and tempted to imagine that, if he could once get footing for his doctrine among the influential and the great, he should thus secure his triumph more easily, he had yet no such thought. He laid his foundations, as it were, below all influence, and, as men would judge, threw himself away. And precisely here did he display a wisdom and a character totally in advance of his age. Eighteen centuries have passed away, and we now seem just beginning to understand the transcendent depth of this feature in his mission and his character. We appear to be just waking up to it as a discovery, that the blessing and upraising of the masses are the fundamental interest of society—a discovery, however, which is only a proof that the life of Jesus has at length, begun to penetrate society and public history. It is precisely this which is working so many and great changes in our times, giving liberty and right to the enslaved many, seeking their education, and encouraging their efforts by new and better hopes, producing an aversion to war, which has been the fatal source of their misery and depression, and opening, as we hope, a new era of comfort, light, and virtue in the world. It is a if some higher and better thought had visited our race—which higher thought is in the life of Jesus.[70]

[69] Ibid., pp. 302–303: "His patients are all below his level and unable to repay him, even by a breath of congenial sympathy; and nothing supports him but the consciousness of good which attends his labors."
[70] Ibid., pp. 303, 304–306; Christ was able to identify himself with the poor, said Bushnell, without at the same time, eliciting any feelings of partisanship in them.

As a teacher, Bushnell found Christ to be an original and independent thinker. But as he said, "the originality of Christ is uneducated." He had received no formal education, but He, nonetheless, did not reflect the age or country in which He lived. Whatever He taught was from Himself. He had borrowed from no one. "He is the high-priest of the divine nature, speaking as one that has come out from God, and has nothing to borrow from the world."[71] He never taught by human methods. He never revealed the infirmities of human teachers. He baffled His followers. He seemed to be exempted from the infirmities of human nature. He did not represent a school or party, and was never an extremist or revolutionary. He was neither a radical nor a conservative.[72] He held to no superstitions. He taught with a simplicity which could accomodate itself to all kinds of minds. At times, Bushnell became ecstatic about the person of Christ: "Call him then, who will, a man, a human teacher; what human teacher ever came down thus upon the soul of the race, as a beam of light from the skies—pure light, shining directly into the visual orb of the mind, a light for all that live, a full transparent day, in which truth bathes the spirit as an element. Others talk and speculate about truth, and those who can may follow; but Jesus is the truth, and lives it, and, if he is a mere human teacher, he is the first who was ever able to find a form for truth, at all adequate to the world's uses."[73]

In addition to all of this, the morality of Jesus had a practical superiority to that of all human teachers. His moral teachings were propounded in precepts that carried their own evidence. They were,

[71] *Ibid.,* p. 307. Bushnell was familiar with Biblical scholarship which asserted that Christ borrowed from "the Persians and the eastern forms of religion, or that he had been intimate with the Essenes and borrowed from them, . . .", but rejected this view as unsound.

[72] *Ibid.,* p. 313; Bushnell distinguished between liberality and charity. "Charity holds fast the minutest atoms of truth, as being precious and divine, offended by even so much as a thought of laxity. Liberality loosens the terms of truth; permitting easily and with careless magnanimity variations from it; consenting, as it were, in its own sovereignty, to overlook or allow them; and subsiding thus, ere long, into a licentious indifference to all truth, and a general defect of responsibility in regard to it. Charity extends allowance to men; liberality, to falsities themselves. Charity takes the truth to be sacred and immovable; liberality allows it to be marred and maimed at pleasure. How different the manner of Jesus in this respect from that unreverent, feeble laxity, that lets the errors be as good as the truths, and takes it for a sign of intellectual eminence, that one can be floated comfortably in the abysses of liberalism."

[73] *Ibid.,* p. 314.

said Bushnell, great spiritual laws which had ben ordained by God: "He simply comes forth telling us, from God, what to do." The morality of Christ, was, therefore, "about as firmly seated in the convictions of men, as the law of gravity in their bodies." Bushnell summarized:

He comes into the world full of all moral beauty, as God of physical; and as God was not obliged to set himself to a course of aesthetic study, when he created the forms and landscapes of the world, so Christ comes to his rules, by no critical practice in words. He opens his lips, and the creative glory of his mind pours itself forth in living precepts—Do to others as ye would that others should do to you—Blessed are the peace-makers—Smitten upon one cheek, turn the other—Resist not evil—For-give your enemies—Do good to them that hate you—Lend not, hoping to receive—Receive the truth as little children. Omitting all the deep spiri-tual doctrines he taught, and taking all the human teachers on their own ground, the ground of preceptive morality, they are seen at once, to be meager and cold; little artistic inventions, gleams of high conceptions caught by study, having about the same relation to the christian morality, that a statue has to the flexibility, the self-active force, and flushing warmth of man, as he goes forth in the image of his Creator, to be the reflection of His beauty and the living instrument of his will. Indeed, it is the very distinction of Jesus that he teaches, not a verbal, but an ori-ginal, vital, and divine morality.[74]

Christ simply told men how to live. He never dressed up a moral picture and then asked man to observe its beauty. He was never anxious for the success of his teaching. He was never jealous of contradiction. Neither was He ruffled or disturbed by the dullness and incapacity of His friends. Jesus was "a lonely uninstructed youth" who came forth from the moral darkness of Galilee, and who was "even more distinct from his age, and from every thing around him, than a Plato would be rising up alone in some wild tribe in Oregon." He assumed a position at the head of the world, and maintained it for eighteen centuries, by the pure self-evidence of His life and doctrine.[75]

[74] *Ibid.*, pp. 316, 317.
[75] *Ibid.*, p. 318; cf. also p. 321: "The most conspicuous matter therefore, in the history of Jesus, is, that what holds true, in all our experience of men, is inverted in him. He grows sacred, peculiar, wonderful, divine, as acquaintance reveals him. At first he is only a man, as the senses report him to be; knowledge, ob-servation, familiarity, raise him into the God-man. He grows pure and perfect, more than mortal in wisdom, a being enveloped in sacred mystery, a friend to be loved in awe–dies into awe, and a sorrow that contains the element of worship!" cf. also pp. 331–332: "This one perfect character has come into our world, and

Bushnell concluded his study of the character of Jesus with the assertion that He was a real historic person, Jesus of Nazareth, who bore the real character ascribed to him in history. And in all of life, furthermore, He was sinless.[76]

VII. *The Argument for Miracles*

Bushnell discovered that a problem remained for the Christian who took the life of Christ seriously. What about miracles? Are the miracles facts to be believed by the Christian, or are they intellectual burdens which the modern Christian had better discard? Bushnell believed that if miracles somehow could be verified, then it might be established that the Christian faith was a supernatural revelation of God.[77] Bushnell however stood overagainst those thinkers who maintained that miracles dishonor God because they add to or amend the revelation of God in nature, thereby breaking up the order of His work.[78]

Bushnell defined a miracle in the following way: "An act, which operates on the chain of cause and effect in nature, from without the chain, producing in the sphere of senses, some event which

lived in it; filling all the molds of action, all the terms of duty and love, with his own divine manners, works, and charities. All the conditions of our life are raised thus, by the meaning he has shown to be in them, and the grace he has put upon them. The world itself is changed, and is no more the same that it was; it has never been the same, since Jesus left it. The air is charged with heavenly odors, and a kind of celestial consciousness, a sense of other worlds, is wafted on us in its breath. Let the dark ages come, let society roll backward and churches perish in whole regions of the earth, let infidelity deny and, what is worse, let spurious piety dishonor the truth; still there is a something here that was not, and a something that has immortality in it. Still our confidence remains unshaken, that Christ and his all-quickening life are in the world, as fixed elements, and will be to the end of time; for Christianity is not so much the advent of a better doctrine, as of a perfect character; and how can a perfect character, once entered into life and history, be separated and finally expelled? It were easier to untwist all the beams of light in the sky, separating and expunging one of the colors, than to get the character of Jesus, which is the real gospel, out of the world. Look ye hither, meantime, all ye blinded and fallen of mankind, a better nature is among you, a pure heart, out of some pure world, is come into prison and walks with you."

[76] *Ibid.*, pp. 324 ff.
[77] *Ibid.*, p. 333.
[78] Bushnell mentioned Spinoza, Parker, Hume, and Strauss in this discussion, *ibid.*, pp. 334, 335; also Hennel, p. 339, Parker again, pp. 340, 357, Strauss, pp. 340–345; see pp. 355 ff. for Bushnell's criticism of "form criticism".

96

moves our wonder, and evinces the presence of a more than human power." A miracle was not therefore "any wonderful event developed under the laws of nature, or of natural causation"; nor, "an event transpired singly, or apart from system"; nor, a "contradiction of our experience," nor a "suspension, or violation, of the laws of nature." [79]

Bushnell attempted to prove that miracles exist by means of the following argument: [80]

1. Man acts supernaturally in all of his free accountable actions, that is, he acts upon the chain of cause and effect in nature. These acts are similar to God's acts up on the causes in nature:

If the sun darkens, or the earth shudders with Christ in his death, that sympathy of nature is just as appropriate for him, as it is for us that our skin should blush, or our eye distill its tears, when our guilt is upon us, or our repentances dissolve us. It is not cause and effect that blushes, or that weeps, but it is that cause and effect are touched by sentiments which connect with our freedom. Nature blushes and weeps, because she was originally submitted, so far, to our freedom, or made to be touched by our actions; but she could not even to eternity raise a blush, or a tear of contrition, if we did not command her. [81]

2. Sin approaches the status of a miracle because it is an act of a free being but in terms of the way in which he was not made to act. It is an act which is therefore not under the laws of cause and effect as established by God. What happens when sin enters the world?, Bushnell asked. There is:

[79] In this context, we must remember the distinction between the *natural* realm, the realm of cause and effect relationships, and the *supernatural* realm, the realm which acts upon the chain of cause and effect from outside the chain, which is not caused in its action, but acts from itself without any previous causality. Also *ibid.*, pp. 336–339, cf. this statement in reference to the last negative definition of a miracle: "Nature stands fast, with all her terms of cause and effect, as before, a constant quantity, interposed by God to be a medium between supernatural beings, in their relative actions. They are to have their exercise in it, and upon it, and so, by their activity, they are to make a moral acquaintance with each other; men with men, all created spirits with all, God with creatures, creatures with God; acquaintances also with the uses of laws by the wrongs they suffer, and with their own bad mind by seeing what wrongs they do–so by their whole experience to be trained, corrected, assimilated in love, and finished in holy virtue. There is no more a suspension of the laws of nature, when God acts, than when we do; for nature is, by her very laws, subjected to his and our uses, to be swayed, and modified, and made a sign-language, so to speak, of mutual acquaintance between us."
[80] *Ibid.*, pp. 345–359.
[81] *Ibid.*, p. 346.

A general disruption of every thing that belongs to the original para-
disiac order of the creation. The soul itself begins, at the first moment,
to feel the terrible action of it, and becomes a crazed and disordered
power. The crystal form of the spirit is broken, and it is become an opaque
element, a living malformation. The conscience is battered and trampled
in its throne. The successions of the thoughts are become disorderly and
wild; the tempers are out of tune; the passions kindle into guilty fires,
and burn with a consuming heat, the imagination is a hell of painful, ugly
phantoms; the body a diseased thing, scarred by deformity. Society is out
of joint, and even the physical world itself, as we have shown, is marred
in every part by abortions, deformities visible, and discords audible, so as
no more to represent the perfect beauty of its author.[82]

3. Nature, therefore, does in fact no longer exist. Sin has "un-
made" the world. Nature is disrupted; causes are co-joined falsely,
causality becomes a malign activity: "The whole machine is in disorder, though no one part is wanting. It is no longer a watch, or
time-keeper, but a jumble of useless and absurd motions. So nature,
under sin, is no longer nature, but a condition of unnature."[83]

4. Nature can never be restored until there is some "action sovereign as a miracle." The laws of nature are running as laws of sin and
death. The laws have no power of self-rectification.

As certainly therefore as sinners are to be restored, as certainly, that is,
as that all God's ends in the world and human existence are not to fail,
there will be, must be miracles, or puttings forth, at least, of a divinely
supernatural power. Every thing in the whole creation is groaning and
travailing in expectation of so great a redemption. The very plan was
originally, as we have shown, to bring out the grand results of spiritual
order and character intended, by means of a double administration; that
is by the creation and the new-creation, the creation disordered by sin,
the new-creation raised up and glorified by grace and its miracles.[84]

5. Nature is not the whole empire of God; nature is, rather only
a "field for the training of his children." Spiritual creatures, that is,
creatures supernatural, compose the real body and substance of his
empire. The existence of any form of life is a proof that God has
wrought a miracle upon nature.

6. The character of Jesus is a miracle. Here is a being who has
broken into the world, but who is not of it; one who has come out
from God as the Eternal Word of the Father incarnate. The laws of
nature are subordinated to His power. "The very laws of nature
themselves, having him present to them, as a new agent and a higher

[82] *Ibid.*, pp. 346, 347.   [83] *Ibid.*, p. 348.   [84] *Ibid.*, p. 349.

98

first term, would require the development of new consequences and incidents in the nature of wonders." Furthermore, "he declares that he has come out from God, to be a restorer of sin, a regenerator of all things, a new moral creator of the world; thus to do a work that is, at once, the hope of all order, and the greatest of all miracles." Christ is executing the true system of God which is above nature, "which is itself the basis of all stability and contains the real import of all things":

Dwelling from eternity in this higher system himself, and having it centered in his person, wheeling and subordinating thus all physical instruments as doubtless he may, to serve those better ends in which all order lies, it will not be in us, when he comes forth from the Father, on the Father's errand, to forbid that he shall work in the prerogatives of the Father. Visibly not one of us, but a visitant who has come out from a realm of spiritual majesty, back of the sensuous orb on which our moth-eyes dwell as in congenial dimness and obscurity of light, what shall we think when we see diseases fly before him, and blindness letting fall the scales of obscured vision, and death retreating from its prey, but that the seeming disruption of our retributive state under sin, is made to let in mercy and order from above. For, if man has buried himself in sense, and married all sense to sin, which sin is itself the soul of all disorder, can it be to us a frightful thing that he lays his hand upon the perverted causalities, and says, 'thou art made whole'? If the bad empire, the bitter unnature, of our sin, is somewhere touched by his healing power, must we apprehend some fatal shock of disorder? If, by his miraculous force, some crevice is made in the senses, to let in the light of heaven's peace and order, must we tremble lest the scientific laws are shaken, and the scientific causes violated? Better is it to say—'this beginning of miracles did Jesus make in Galilee, and manifested forth his glory, and we believe in him.' Glory breaks in through his incarnate person, to chase away the darkness. In him, peace and order descend to rebuild the realm below, they have maintained above. Sin, the damned miracle and misery of the groaning creation, yields to the stronger miracle of Jesus and his works, and the great good minds of this and the upper worlds behold integrity and rest returning, and the peace of universal empire secure. Out of the disorder that was, rises order; out of chaos, beauty.[85]

VIII. *The World Governed Supernaturally in the Interest of Christianity*

Bushnell insisted that Christianity superseded all of the philosophies of every age, and opened deeper truths regarding the problem of

[85] *Ibid.*, pp. 354, 355; for a discussion of the objections to miracles, see pp. 359–366.

human existence to man than had ever been discovered before. The Christian faith proclaimed in the simplest way possible that God had two ministrations for man, letter and spirit, law and grace. The first was a formal concept and is the basis for all perfection. Yet it is an abstraction, which, when enforced by power, can not make anything perfect. It is a schoolmaster, but a schoolmaster of loss and defeat and death. It is a ministration of *condemnation*. It holds us in bondage, and looses "retributive causes that set the whole creation groaning and travailing in pain together." Bushnell maintained that this "was understood as well at the beginning as afterward. For, if there had been a law given that could have given life, then verily righteousness should have been by the law. But that was inherently impossible, and the impossibility is recognized from the first. The legal state was instituted, not as a finality, but as a first stage in the process of training; to develop the sense of guilt and spiritual want, to beget a knowledge of sin, its exceeding sinfulness, and the insupportable bondage it creates.[86] But then there appeared a new ministration in the person of the incarnate Redeemer, which complemented and superseded the other:

Now he hath obtained a more excellent ministry, by how much also he is the mediator of a better covenant, which was established upon better promises. For, if that first covenant had been faultless, then should no place have been sought for the second. Now it is no more a question of works; there never could have been a rational expectation of human perfection on that basis; but it is a question of simple faith. The righteousness of God without, or apart from the law, is now manifested, even the righteousness of God which is by faith of Jesus Christ, unto all and upon all them that believe. What we call our virtue now is no more a will-work, or a something done according to law, but it is a continuous and living ingeneration of God, who has thus become a divine impulse or quickening in us, and so the life of our life. Therefore now we are free. Embracing the person of Christ, and yielding the homage of our hearts to him, we do, in fact, resume the law, in our deliverance from its bondage.[87]

When we embrace Christ, Bushnell said, we are free to the law, and we enter a liberty that fulfills all law which is the law of Christ. The bondage to sin is gone; liberty has come; man is free from the law of sin and death. This is the ministration of righteousness. It is striking, said Bushnell, that this doctrine appears only in the New Testament and nowhere else. It is the only true and real philosophy—"it bears

[86] *Ibid.*, p. 373.
[87] *Ibid.*, p. 374.

the eternal water-mark of divinity, and that ends all inquiry." Christianity is the highest, most perfect expression of the divine revelation in history! [88]

Bushnell's *Nature and the Supernatural* was his attempt to provide a "comprehensive" approach to Christian theology. But it was much more than that; it was the "wide hypothesis" of the world he had promised his readers in the preface to the volume. Bushnell wrote *Nature and the Supernatural* during a period of intense criticism of his ministry (which left him in a "poor bankrupt state"), and during a time when the intelligent among the populace were turning away from the Christian faith. The sense of an imperiled Christianity runs throughout its pages. *Nature and the Supernatural* is Bushnell's principal theological work, and held for him the "principal meaning of his life." [89] He did not rely upon the theological traditions of the past to find material for his book, rather he looked for new revelation.[90] He insisted throughout the book that God would continue to speak directly to men, and that this inspiration should be the source of theological truth.

Nature and the Supernatural betrayed Bushnell's fear of the great enemies of the Christian faith. The Christian world was moving to the "vanishing point of faith." Bushnell saw as his task to defend Christianity against all challengers. *Nature and the Supernatural* was to provide the defense. It was science and transcendentalism [91] which had beguiled the American public, and Bushnell saw as his role the vindication of the Christian faith in the midst of a hostile environment; the Christian faith must come ultimately into "a grand issue of life and death" with its opposition.

The reason why Christianity faced such great odds in the contemporary world, Bushnell believed, was because it had always restric-

[88] *Ibid.*, p. 377. Bushnell maintained that "the capital points or ideas of Christianity, frame into the supernatural, on one hand, in such beautiful order and facility, and without any strain of contrivance or logical adaptation; and into human experience, on the other, in a way so consonant to the dignity of reason, and the wants and disabilities of sin, that the signature of God is plainly legible in the documents."
[89] Mary Bushnell Cheney, *Life and Letters of Horace Bushnell*, pp. 361–362.
[90] *Ibid.*, p. 277.
[91] Science in this reference described the new science of geology, which contradicted the Mosaic account of creation and suggested that organic life developed slowly from the lower forms up to man; transcendentalism rejected miracles, believed passionately in human progress, and denied the fact of sin, and the need of a divine mediator.

ted the supernatural realm from the natural, and by so doing it gave the supernatural an arbitrary and unreal character. It had always been considered that which exceeded the mere terms of nature "was supernatural." New England theology was particularly responsible for this development in Christian thought. As a result, the Christian faith in New England grew rigid and strenuously dualistic. Bushnell saw this mistake and wrote *Nature and the Supernatural* in an attempt to rectify it. He did so, as we have seen above, by demonstrating that man himself belonged primarily to the supernatural realm. Bushnell began with man, and demonstrated that he was not similar to other organisms. He did this, as we have seen, by making the distinction between powers and things. As a power, man was free: "The very idea of personality is that of a being not under the law of cause and effect." When this principle was comprehended, all of the problems which New England theology raised regarding the segregation of the natural from the supernatural disappeared. Man was not determined by things as the rest of nature, but man was able to control his own destiny, to "set causes in nature at work in new combinations otherwise never occurring, and produce, by our action upon nature, results which she, as nature, could never produce by her own internal acting." [92]

Once Bushnell had perceived the priority and supernatural character of personality, he then molded his whole theory of nature to conform to the interests and aims of personality. In *Nature and the Supernatural*, Bushnell could easily draw the next conclusion that it is Christianity which best fulfills the intentions and demands of nature: "The world is governed supernaturally in the interest of Christianity." The passage which we quoted earlier is of decisive importance:

The world was made to include Christianity; under that becomes a proper and complete frame of order; to that chrystalizes, in all its appointments, events, and experiences, in that has the design or final cause revealed, by which all its distributions, laws, and historic changes are determined and systematized. [93]

This means, therefore, that the doctrines of the Christian faith inhere within the conception of nature and the supernatural that Bushnell proposed. Man, who was free, but who had his obligations

[92] *Nature and the Supernatural,* p. 43.
[93] *Ibid.,* p. 31.

decreed by the law of right, had chosen evil instead of good. Because of this fact, man was a damned being. Man's own sinful election stood at the center of all of history. The disorders and deformities of creation, which were disclosed by geology, were caused by human sin. These destructive tendencies in nature provided "anticipative consequences" of man's spiritual deformity. The "dark things" of nature, too—pain, disease, danger, plague, insanity, mutabilities—are the "disciplinary dispensations" provided for man to enable him to determine his moral responsibility. It is man who is in the center of the natural world and history. Miracles became, in Bushnell's treatment, manifestations of the spiritual order, for a miracle was only, as we have seen, a "supernatural act . . . which operates on the chain of cause and effect from without the chain." [94]

But Bushnell was ambitious for man. Man's dilemma was not created by an inherent evil in his will, rather by a "condition privative" of his virtue. Man knew the law, but he had to discover the meaning of right and wrong through experience. Experience served to fortify the will and to enable man to achieve, with the aid of grace, a state of righteousness. But the irreparable choice of evil by the will, initiated a shock that disturbed all of nature, and turned nature into "unnature": "A whole creation groaning and travailling in pain." [95] No restoration of man's fallen condition was possible. The situation brought about when man as "power" chose experience over the obligation of the law could not be changed from within nature, which was fallen with man. Salvation was not possible, as Bushnell reminded his contemporaries, by allegiance to a legal morality. Obedience based upon fear remained outside of the realm of redemption. Neither was salvation possible through self-reliance, for the individual was molded by a sinful society. Society served one positive function, however, and that was to introduce civilization in the midst of "the brutality of nature."

Salvation could come only by means of the divine entering the natural. [96] All hope of restoration depended upon God:

Christianity is . . . no mere scheme of doctrine, or of ethical practice, but is instead a kind of miracle, a power out of nature and above, descending into it; a historically supernatural movement on the world that is visibly entered into it, and organized to be an institution in the person of Jesus

[94] *Ibid.,* p. 336.
[95] *Ibid.,* p. 171.
[96] *Ibid.,* p. 250.

Christ. He therefore is the central figure and powers, and with him the entire fabric either stands or falls.[97]

The intruder into history, Jesus Christ, whose character forbade "his possible classification with men," was the Savior of man and nature. Bushnell wrote:

But . . . let us note more distinctly the significance of this glorious advent, and have our congratulations in it. This one perfect character has come into our world, and lived in it; filling all the molds of action, all the terms of duty and love, with his own divine manners, works, and charities. All the conditions of our life are raised thus, by the meaning he has shown to be in them, and the grace he has put upon them. The world itself is changed, and is no more the same that it was; it has never been the same, since Jesus left it. The air is charged with heavenly odors, and a kind of celestial consciousness, a sense of other worlds, is wafted on us in its breath. Let the dark ages come, let society roll backward and churches perish in whole regions of the earth, let infidelity deny, and, what is worse, let spurious piety dishonor the truth; still there is a something here that was not, and a something that has immortality in it. Still our confidence remains unshaken, that Christ and his all-quickening life are in the world, as fixed elements, and will be to the end of time; for Christianity is not so much the advent of a better doctrine, as of a perfect character; and how can a perfect character, once entered into life and history, be separated and finally expelled? It were easier to untwist all the beams of light in the sky, separating and expunging one of the colors, than to get the character of Jesus, which is the real gospel, out of the world. Look ye hither, meantime, all ye blinded and fallen of mankind, a better nature is among you, a pure heart, out of some pure world, is come into your prison and walks it with you. Do you require of us to show who he is, and definitely to expound his person? We may not be able. Enough to know that he is not of us—some strange being out of nature and above it, whose name is Wonderful. Enough that sin has never touched his hallowed nature, and that he is a friend. In him dawns a hope—purity has not come into our world, except to purify. Behold the Lamb of God, that taketh away the sins of the world! Light breaks in, peace settles on the air lo! the prison walls are giving way—rise, let us go.[98]

With Christ as the new premise (which can be received only by faith), Bushnell had provided the framework within which a Christian theology could be written. *Nature and the Supernatural* provided the outline for a systematic theology, a theology which might include the traditional doctrines of the church. He summarized his outlook in the following way: [99]

[97] *Ibid.*, p. 276.
[98] *Ibid.*, pp. 331–332.
[99] *Ibid.*, pp. 377–400.

1. The revelation of God in Christ is called a *Gospel;* that is, Christ came into the world from outside of nature, and brought with Him a new premise. This is the "Good News" of the Gospel, the report of the supernatural mission of Christ, the supernatural fact that "God was in Christ reconciling the world unto himself."

2. Christ's work is called *Salvation.* Christ declared that He had the power to save people from their sins. Salvation is, therefore, a "rescue from nature by a power above nature." It is this rescue which Christ accomplished.

3. Salvation is effected by *Faith.* Christianity is distinguished from every other philosophical and ethical system because it claims that all virtue rests upon faith. Grace is imported into nature from outside of nature. Christ came from above the world into the world. Salvation does not lie within the premises of natural fact and reason. For this reason, it cannot be logically deduced. It addresses itself to faith, not to reason. "It is only received, when faith comes, laden with sin and fettered by its iron bondage, to rest herself, in holy trust, on the transcendent fact of such an appearing, and to find by experiment that it is, in sacred reality and power, what it assumes to be." Salvation is by faith because it is a supernatural salvation.

4. *Justification by Faith* is another distinctive feature of Christianity. This means that "the transgressor, believing, has a righteousness generated in him, which is not built up under the law, by his own practice; and that something has been done to compensate the law, violated by his past offenses, and save it in honor, when his sin is forgiven."

5. Christianity sets up a *Kingdom of God* on earth. "It is called 'the kingdom of God' or 'of heaven,' because the organic force by which so many wills and finally all mankind are to be gathered into unity, is not in nature, but comes down out of heaven, in the person of Christ the king." Here we have a supernatural kingdom—a real, living community, organized by a real king, and propagated by the powers of truth and love. The kingdom grew out of the Incarnation. When Jesus appeared on earth, the kingdom of heaven was at hand.[100]

---

[100] *Ibid.*, pp. 384, 385. "This accordingly is the great thought of Christianity–the kingdom of God; the implanting of a divine rule in lost men, and the gathering in, at last, of all people and kindreds of the earth, into a vast, universal order of peace and truth under Christ the anointed king."

6. The *Holy Spirit* is a "supernatural indwelling force, by which Christ is perpetuated in the world." There is a necessity for the Holy Spirit in the miraculous advent of Christ.

Christ and the Spirit are complementary forces, and, both together, constitute a complete whole; such a kind of whole as no man, or myth, or accident ever invented. There was an inherent necessity that whatever supernatural movement, for the regeneration of man, might be undertaken, should include, both a moral, and an efficient agency; one before the understanding, and the other back of it, in the secret springs of the disordered nature; a divine object clothed in beauty, and love, and justice, to be a mold into which the soul may be formed, the type of a divine life in which it may consentingly be crystallized; an efficient grace, working within the soul, preparing it to will and to do and rolling back the currents of retributive causes in it, opening it to the power of its glorious exemplar and drawing it ever into that and a life proceeding from it.[101]

7. The doctrine of *Spiritual Regeneration* corresponds to "our human state and to the fact of a supernatural economy." This doctrine presupposes that the individual possesses no good in his character and cannot generate any good by himself. A radical change is necessary within ones' life in order to erase the radical defect within one's life. "Separated from God," wrote Bushnell, man "is a monster, and not a proper man." This is the effect of sin—it alienates the subject from the life of God. Salvation therefore presupposes a rebirth of the individual. The great change in character is the beginning of all true virtue, because it is the revelation of God in the soul. "To say that it is a change of the soul's love, is only another version of the same truth; for the love is changed by the entering in of God and his love, into the soul's faith. For love is of God, and every one that loveth is born of God, and knoweth God. Old things are passed away, and all things are become new; because God is revealed within, changing, of course, the principle of all action, and the meaning of all experience."[102]

8. The doctrine of *Providence* coincides with the fact of supernatural activity in the redemption of mankind. Christianity assumes that the world is governed in the interest of the Christian faith.

9. The doctrine of the *Trinity* coincides with the historical incarnate appearance of Christ. It is a conception generated by supernatural appearances—first, the Almighty Creator and Father, then Christ, the Word of God, and finally the Holy Spirit.

[101] *Ibid.*, pp. 386, 387.
[102] *Ibid.*, p. 390.

First, we have the Father, setting God before us as the author and ground of all natural things and causes. Then we have the Son and the Spirit, which represent what God may do, acting on the lines of causes in nature; one as coming into nature from without, to be incarnate in it, the other as working internally in the power of the Son, to dispense to the soul what he addressed outwardly to human thought, and configure the soul to him, as an exemplar embraced by its faith. Then, putting our trust in the Son, as coming down from God, offering himself before God, going up to Him, interceding before Him, reigning with Him, by Him accepted, honored, glorified; invoking also God and Christ to send down the Spirit, and let him be the power of a new indwelling life, breathing health into our diseases, and rolling back the penal currents of justice to free us of our sin, we are able to act ourselves before the new salvation, so as to receive the full force of it.[103]

The gospel, therefore, as a supernatural gospel, "stands in the compact order of a complete intellectual unity, because it was given by a comprehending mind equal to the reach of the plan." It remains now for Bushnell to elucidate the theological ideas which lie within his "wide hypothesis of the world." The analysis which follows will attempt to demonstrate how each of the theological problems Bushnell dealt with were handled from within the complete intellectual unity he called "Nature and the Supernatural." It must be recognized, however, that as we do this, we are looking at the theology of Horace Bushnell from the vantage point of Nature and the Supernatural. Bushnell's *Christian Nurture* and *God in Christ* were written prior to the publication of *Nature and the Supernatural*, but in each of these books, we shall find a correspondence with and a confirmation of the thesis proposed in this most "comprehensive" of his works. It is our thesis that Bushnell attempted to coordinate his theological ideas about the relationship of Nature to the Supernatural.

[103] *Ibid.*, p. 393.

CHAPTER IV

An Organic Theory of
Christian Education

"The child is to grow up a Christian, and never know himself as being otherwise." This is Bushnell's thesis in his first published theological work, *Discourses on Christian Nurture,* which appeared in 1847.[1] This book emerged directly from the problems which Bushnell experienced as he attempted to "win souls" for the Church of Christ during his early ministry in Hartford. During his first years as pastor of the North Church, he tried his hand at leading revivals and urged his congregation to accept Jesus Christ as its savior. However, no revival of religion followed at the North Church. It was reported that, in 1834, only forty-one came into the church on profession of faith; in 1835, only four; and, in 1836, twelve.[2] Bushnell wanted to establish a "higher and more solid confidence in revivals." He did not want to get rid of revivals altogether. Revivals could play a constructive role in the "spiritual economy of the church."[3] The existing revivalist system he considered to be extremely debilitating to the church. This was the result of a whole host of mistaken notions regarding revivals. It had always been assumed that the church must be in a constant state of revival. Furthermore,

[1] Cf. A. J. William Myers, *Horace Bushnell and Christian Education,* Chap. II, "The Genesis of the Book, *Views of Christian Nurture,*" pp. 7–33, in which the author traces the response of the Massachusetts Sabbath School Society (the original publishers), the Hartford Central Association, and the Rev. Bennet Tyler, to Bushnell's first book.

A number of early articles indicated the trend of Bushnell's thinking: "Spiritual Economy of Revivals of Religion", *The Quarterly Christian Spectator,* X, (February 1838), pp. 131–148 (republished in *Views of Christian Nurture and of Subjects Adjacent thereto* (1848) and *Building Eras* (1881); "Review of the Errors of the Times", *The New Englander Magazine,* (January 1844); in which Bushnell criticized Bishop Thomas C. Brownell's *Errors of the Times:* (A charge delivered to the clergy of the diocese of Connecticut, at the annual convention, holden in Christ Church, in the city of Hartford, June 13, 1843), Hartford, Case, Tiffany and Co., 1843; "The Kingdom of Heaven as a Grain of Mustard Seed", *The New Englander Magazine,* (October 1844); the sermon "Unconscious Influence," (1845) included in *Sermons for the New Life.*
[2] Mary Bushnell Cheney, *Life and Letters of Horace Bushnell,* p. 7.
[3] "Spiritual Economy of Revivals of Religion," *The Quarterly Christian Spectator,* X, (Feb., 1838), pp. 131–148.

it was believed that the church was not accomplishing anything unless there was an "artificial firework." And then Bushnell believed there was a basic misconception regarding the nature of the Christian life at the bottom of the entire revivalist's attempts. Because of these distorted ideas, and others, Bushnell concluded that revivals were primarily a liability to the churches. Because of Bushnell's inability to get a successful revival started, he considered himself a failure in the ministry. "The most disheartening impediment to the Christian minister," he said, "is the thought that religion depends only on revivals." [4]

Revivalists, Bushnell asserted, presupposed that the experience of conversion was relevant solely in the adult years. The adult, before he was to become a Christian, had to begin not with a sense of personal sin, but with a recognition of his lost condition through the original sin of Adam. The adult was a part of a race of people who lay under the righteous condemnation of God, totally depraved, and already doomed to everlasting punishment.[5] It was difficult to find a place for the child with such a conception of religion. The child was religiously anonymous, until such a time when, intellectually and emotionally, he had developed into an adult, a naturally depraved adult, and ready for conversion.[6]

Practically, what happened in New England was not too startling. The child was not won to Christ and the Church. Rather, he was drawn away into the big cities and their "many temptations." [7] Social mobility plus the rise of the large cities in New England created

[4] Cf. Bushnell's Commemorative Sermon, pp. 19–20.
[5] Cf. Theodore T. Munger's commentary on the system of total depravity, *Horace Bushnell, Preacher and Theologian*, p. 73.
[6] Bushnell, in the remarkable essay, "The Kingdom of Heaven as a Grain of Mustard Seed," offered the following alternative: "We hold that children are, in a sense, included in the faith of their parents, partakers with them in their covenant, and brought into a peculiar relation to God, in virtue of it. On this ground, they receive a common seal of faith with them, in their baptism; and God on his part, contemplates, in the rite, the fact that they are to grow up as Christians, or spiritually renewed persons. As to the precise time or manner in which they are to receive the germ of holy principle, nothing is affirmed. Only it is understood, that God includes their infant age in the womb of parental culture, and pledges himself to them and their parents, in such a way, as to offer the presumption, that they may grow up in love with all goodness, and remember no definite time when they became subjects of Christian principle. Christian education is then to conform to this view, and nothing is to be called Christian education which does not." *The New Englander Magazine*, (October 1844), pp. 600–619.
[7] Cf. Barbara Cross, *Horace Bushnell, Minister to a Changing America*, pp. 58 ff.

a need for religious security. A religious literature flourished, which urged a return to the piety of early childhood.[8] Religion became a religion of alternates—*either* you were saved or you were damned, *either* good or evil, innocent or corrupt.[9]

The original Puritans had proposed that the infant offspring of believers were eligible for baptism which was "the seal of the righteousness of faith." Though the child was later to "own the covenant" (which had been divinely established), and become a full member of the church, it was presupposed that he was already in the "household faith." He was to "grow up in the Lord." Of course, this "covenental" conception of Christian nurture disappeared with the revivalists. It was Bushnell's role to remind the Christian that the children of the Christian family participated already in the faith.

Into the theological situation of New England in the middle of the 19 Century, Bushnell offered his *Views of Christian Nurture, and of Subjects Adjacent Thereto.* In it he wrote: "There is then some kind of nurture which is of the Lord, deriving a quality and a power from Him, and communicating the same. Being instituted by Him, it will of necessity have a method and a character peculiar to itself, or rather to Him. It will be the Lord's way of education, having aims appropriate to Him, and, if realized in its full intent, terminating in results impossible to be reached by any merely human method." [10]

[8] *Ibid.,* pp. 59–60: "The *Friendship Offering* decided that angels must weep to see the soul "all pure and brilliant" descend to the earth–"that huge shadow of woe and crime–through which no winged thing . . . can penetrate unstained . . . Moved at the spectacle of infants so pure and doomed, the *Rose of Sharon* tenderly requested speedy deaths for the young." "The mother, . . . provided the key to salvation. . . . References to the failures of family government, to family tragedies, and to the wanton eagerness of young people to leave home suggest that their doubts were founded in familial instabilities. Some felt failure of tradition made women seek out authoritative counsel, the latest information, the reassurance of mutual confession in "maternal societies". Advisory novels and periodicals multiplied and sold . . . Perplexed and hopeful, women were emotionally sustained by the assurance that their training could triumph over the temptations of the world."

[9] Munger, *op. cit.,* p. 75: "The chief feature of this phase of religious experience was its unnaturalness. Great truths were involved in the system, and great results sprang out of them, but they were so defined and used that they almost lost the features of a gospel and wore the cast of a doom. It dealt with human nature only as depraved, and hence took little account of its varying characteristics or special needs, but loaded it with burdens that did not belong to it, and then required it to throw them off by processes that were drawn out of metaphysical subtilities buttressed by random quotations from Scripture."

[10] Horace Bushnell, *Christian Nurture,* p. 9.

I. *The Nature of Christian Nurture*

"The child is to grow up a Christian, and never know himself as being otherwise." Bushnell described the nature of Christian education in the following way: "... the aim, effort, and expectation should be, not, as is commonly assumed, that the child is to grow up in sin, to be converted after he comes to a mature age; but that he is to open on the world as one that is spiritually renewed, not remembering the time when he went through a technical experience, but seeming rather to have loved what is good from his earliest years." [11]

The entire purpose of Christian education, Bushnell wrote, presupposed that children were to grow up in Christ. It is a "baleful implication" to say that a child is to "reject God and all holy principles, till he has come to a mature age." Furthermore, it is absurd to believe that the Scriptures tell the child that he is not to love and obey God truly until after he has spent many years in "hatred and wrong", "old enough to resist all good, but too young to receive any good whatever."

Bushnell questioned the assumption that a child is a sinner, and cannot be a Christian until God has given him a new heart. He asked: "Who then has told you that a child can not have the new heart of which you speak? Whence do you learn that if you live the life of Christ, before him and with him, the law of the Spirit of Life may not be such as to include and quicken him also? And why should it be thought incredible that there should be some really good principle awakened in the mind of a child?" [12]

The Christian, Bushnell defined as "one who has simply *begun* to love what is good for its own sake." Why was it impossible, Bushnell asked, to believe that a child had the ability to love? Even presupposing a system of depravity, there was nothing, Bushnell said, "to forbid the possibility that a child should be led, in his first moral act, to cleave unto that what is good and right, any more than in the first or his twentieth year." The spirit of God so fills the world, Bushnell said, that He "... holds a presence of power and government in all objects, so all human souls, the infantile as well as the adult, have a nurture of the Spirit appropriate to their age and wants." Was it possible to conceive that the Holy Spirit had no

[11] *Ibid.*, p. 10.
[12] *Ibid.*, p. 16.

"agency in the miniature souls of children?" [13] It was a monstrous opinion, Bushnell believed, to believe that little children were growing up completely helpless and unconscious regarding the perils of their world.

It is to be asserted, Bushnell maintained, that Christian education must be different from that which is not Christian. Its sacred character is to be characterized by "the nurture of the Lord," and just for this reason it was to be different from all non-Christian education. "Un-Christian education," as Bushnell termed it, attempted to bring up the child in such a way that he was to be converted in the future. On the other hand, Christian parents, who were in "the nurture of the Lord," would naturally seek to rear their children in such a way that they will be partakers with them in the grace of life. Bushnell offered the following illustration:

> A young man, correctly but not religiously brought up, light and gay in his manners, and thoughtless hitherto in regard to any thing of a serious nature, happens accidentally one Sunday, while his friends are gone to ride, to take down a book on the evidences of Christianity. His eye, floating over one of the pages, becomes fixed, and he is surprised to find his feelings flowing out strangely into its holy truths. He is conscious of no struggle of hostility, but a new joy dawns in his being. Henceforth, to the end of a long and useful life, he is a Christian man. The love into which he was surprised continues to flow, and he is remarkable, in the churches, all his life long, as one of the most beautiful, healthful, and dignified examples of Christian piety. [14]

Such an illustration as this might suggest, as Bushnell said, that "Christian piety should begin in other and milder forms of exercise, than those which commonly distinguish the conversion of adults; that Christ himself, by that renewing Spirit who can sanctify from the womb, should be practically infused into the childish mind." [15] "Christian nurture" is the ideal form of Christian education. Bushnell described Christian nurture in the following way: "Something is wanted that is better than teaching, something that transcends mere effort and will-work—the loveliness of a good life, the repose of faith, the confidence of righteous expectation, the sacred and cheerful liberty of the Spirit—all glowing about the young soul, as a warm

[13] *Ibid.*, p. 17.
[14] *Ibid.*, pp. 18, 19.
[15] *Ibid.*, p. 19.

and genial nurture, and forming in it, by methods that are silent and imperceptible, a spirit of duty and religious obedience to God." [16]

Bushnell believed that all Christian parents desired their children to grow up in Christian piety. Probably, the better Christians they were, the more likely the child would display this piety at an early age. But, is it impossible, he asked, for Christian parents to desire that their children become Christians?:

... if it be generally seen that the children of such are more likely to become Christians early, what forbids the hope that, if they were riper still in their piety, living a more single and Christ-like life, and more cultivated in their views of family nurture, they might see their children grow up always in piety towards God? Or, if they may not always see it as clearly as they desire, might they not still be able to implant some holy principle, which shall be the seed of a Christian character in their children, though not developed fully and visibly till a later period in life? [17]

But if one assumed that human nature was corrupt, the question remained when the Christian faith might be introduced to the child? Is it better to introduce the Christian faith "when evil is young and pliant to good, or when it is confirmed by years of sinful habit?" Bushnell asked. Bushnell could see no alternative but the one which permitted the Christian faith to be embraced by the child and shared by Christian parents. He wrote: "Nay, the operative truth necessary to a new life may possibly be communicated through and from the parent, being revealed in his looks, manners, and ways of life, before they are of an age to understand the teaching of words; for the Christian scheme, the gospel, is really wrapped up in the life of every Christian parent, and beams out from him as a living epistle, before it escapes from the lips, or is taught in words. And the Spirit of truth may as well make this living truth effectual, as the preaching of the gospel itself." [18]

Goodness, Bushnell believed, could be communicated at any age— at infancy or at childhood, or whenever the individual was most pliant to good. It was not necessary to harden first "the plastic nature of childhood" into stone before a Christian character could be brought about.

Bushnell then asked whether his conception of Christian nurture suggested the doctrine of the radical goodness of human nature,

[16] *Ibid.,* p. 20.
[17] *Ibid.,* pp. 20–21.
[18] *Ibid.,* p. 22.

which affirmed that the task of Christian education was, "to educate or educe the good that is in us?" Bushnell rejected this theory of Christian education, and said that the "natural pravity of man is plainly asserted in the Scriptures, and if it were not, the familiar laws of physiology would require us to believe what amounts to the same thing." But even if neither the Holy Scriptures nor physiology taught man this doctrine, Bushnell insisted that spiritual education would necessarily involve "an experiment of evil." The growth of Christian virtue always involved a struggle with evil. He wrote: ". . . only as it passed round the corner of fall and redemption, ascending thus unto God through a double experience, in which it learns the bitterness of evil and the worth of good, fighting its way out of one, and achieving the other as a victory." *Sin*, however, was not derivative from the parents, but nonetheless the child did receive from his parents "some prejudice to the perfect harmony of this mold, a noxiousquality in the mold derived by descent; that is, some kind of pravity or obliquity which inclines him [the child] to evil." [19] Bushnell felt cetrain that this distinction did not permit the alternate conception of Christian education to be asserted, that which was based upon "the radical goodness of human nature." Such a conception of human nature, he believed, would make Christian education irrelevant and superfluous.

It was not to be denied, however, he said, that "if a child ever does anything in a right spirit, ever loves any thing because it is good and right, it involves the dawn of a new life." However, cannot the child submit himself to parental authority lovingly and simply because it was the right thing to do?, Bushnell asked. Bushnell suggested that the Scriptural injunction: "Children obey your parents in the Lord, for this is right" was an *absurd* passage. The love of a child for what is good and right must be "a fixed love" towards what is right. "He must love it for the sake of its principle," and it must not be "the mere excitement of a natural sensibility to pleasure in the contemplation of what is good." [20]

[19] *Ibid.*, p. 23.

[20] *Ibid.*, pp. 24–25.: "Nor is there any age, which offers itself to God's truth and love, and to that Quickening Spirit whence all good proceeds, with so much of ductile feeling and susceptibilities so tender. The child is under parental authority too for the very purpose, it would seem, of having the otherwise abstract principle of all duty impersonated in his parents, and thus brought home to his practical embrace; so that, learning to obey his parents in the Lord, because it is right, he may thus receive, before he can receive it intellectually, the principle of all piety and holy obedience."

There have been instances of children who had been so trained in a Christian home that they could not remember when they began to be religious. Bushnell reminded his readers that there were individuals in the church who could not remember a time when there was a "gracious change" in their character. There was, he said, "the sweeter comfort" in one who learned to love God early in life. The Moravian Brethren, for example, revealed "as ripe and graceful an exhibition of piety, as any body of Christians living on the earth," and they were able to make their churches "schools of holy nurture to childhood." [21]

Bushnell analyzed the relationship of parent to child from within the Christian community, and discovered that there was "something like a law of organic connection, as regards character, subsisting between them." The faith of the parent must, of necessity, be propagated to the child. Bushnell described the *organic* relationship between parent and child in the following way:

... for the child, after birth, is still within the matrix of the parental life, and will be, more or less, for many years. And the parental life will be flowing into him all that time, just as naturally, and by a law as truly organic, as when the sap of the trunk flows into a limb. We must not govern our thoughts, in such a matter, by our eyes; and because the physical separation has taken place, conclude that no organic relation remains. Even the physical being of the child is dependent still for many months, in the matter of nutrition, on organic processes not in itself. Meantime, the mental being and character have scarcely begun to have a proper individual life. Will, in connection with conscience, is the basis of personality, or individuality, and these exist as yet only in their rudimental type, as when the form of a seed is beginning to be unfolded at the root of a flower. [22]

A fuller elaboration followed:

At first, the child is held as a mere passive lump in the arms, and he opens into conscious life, under the soul of the parent streaming into his eyes and ears, through the manners and tones of the nursery. The kind and degree of passivity are gradually changed as life advances. A little farther on it is observed that a smile wakens a smile; any kind of sentiment or passion, playing in the face of the parent, wakens a responsive sentiment or passion. Irritation irritates, a frown withers, love expands a look con-

---

[21] *Ibid.,* p. 26.
[22] *Ibid.,* pp. 27–28; Bushnell described the relationship also in this way: "Perhaps I should rather say, such a connection as induces the conviction that the character of one is actually included in that of the other, as a seed is formed in the capsule; and being there matured, by a nutriment derived from the stem, is gradually separated from it."

genial to itself, and why not holy love? Next the ear is opened to the understanding of words, but what words the child shall hear, he can not choose, and has as little capacity to select the sentiments that are poured into his soul. Farther on, the parents begin to govern him by appeals to will, expressed in commands, and whatever their requirement may be, he can as little withstand it, as the violet can cool the scorching sun, or the tattered leaf can tame the hurricane. Next they appoint his school, choose his books, regulate his company, decide what form of religion, and what religious opinions he shall be taught, by taking him to a church of their own selection. In all this, they infringe upon no right of the child, they only fulfill an office which belongs to them. Their will and character are designed to be the matrix of the child's will and character. Meantime, he approaches more and more closely, and by a gradual process, to the proper rank and responsibility of an individual creature, during all which process of separation, he is having their exercises and ways translated into him. Then, at last, he comes forth to act his part in such color of evil, and why not of good, as he has derived from them.[23]

Christian education, began with nurture, or cultivation: "And the intention is that the Christian life and spirit of the parents, which are in and by the Spirit of God, shall flow into the mind of the child." Virtue is an individual category, but it is erroneous, insisted Bushnell, to conceive of virtue in terms of one act or a series of acts. Virtue is, rather, a state of being. The laws of an *organic* relation affect every part of our being. Bushnell's theory of the "organic" nature of life may be summarized as follows:

All society is organic—the church, the state, the school, the family; and there is a spirit in each of these organisms, peculiar to itself, and more or less hostile, more or less favorable to religious character, and to some extent, at least, sovereign over the individual man. A very great share of the power in what is called a revival of religion, is organic power; nor is it any the less divine on that account. The child is only more within the power of organic laws than we all are. We possess only a mixed individuality all our life long. A pure, separate, individual man, living *wholly* within, and from himself, is a mere fiction. No such person ever existed, or ever can. I need not say that this view of an organic connection of character subsisting between parent and child, lays a basis for notions of Christian education, far different from those which now prevail, under the cover of a merely fictitious and mischievous individualism.[24]

[23] *Ibid.*, pp. 28, 29.
[24] *Ibid.*, pp. 31–32; Bushnell referred to the Pauline passage, "I have begotten you through the gospel," in terms of the parent, who, "having a living gospel enveloped in his life, brings it into organic connection with the soul of childhood."

II. *Scriptural Basis for Christian Nurture*

Bushnell next inquired whether there was scriptural support for the concept of Christian nurture as he had described it. God has taught us, he said, "that children should grow up in piety, as earnestly as the parents can desire it." We know, furthermore, "on first principles," that God will bestow spiritual grace upon the child in such a measure as to bring about the moral renovation of the child. He will act in this manner for all children, unless there is a "collateral reason" why He cannot do so. But, such a conception of the nature of God necessarily presupposes that the parent will abide "to a life of Christian diligence." He wrote: "Let it be enough to know, on first principles in the character of God, that he will so dispense his spiritual agency to you and to your children, as to produce, considering the freedom of you both, the best measure and the ripest state of holy virtue." [25]

It is clear, too, from the Holy Scriptures, that God had pledged the Holy Spirit to man, and had commanded man "to be filled up with the Spirit." He appointed man to be a light to the world, and prepared man for this role with the assistance of the Holy Spirit. But, God's promises are always "to you and to your children," Bushnell assured his reader. Therefore, he asked, "what better assurance can you reasonably ask, to fortify your confidence in whatever spiritual grace may be necessary to your utmost success?" [26] Bushnell questioned whether a scheme of Christian education which was based upon the idea that it was necessary "to produce a first crop of sin, and then a crop of holiness" is in accord with the character of God as described in the Bible. "God appoints," wrote Bushnell, "nothing of which sin and only sin, is to be the proper and legitimate result." Rather, "holy virtue is the aim of every plan God adopts, every means he prescribes, and we have no right to look only for sin, in that which he has appointed as a means of virtue. We can not do it understandingly without great impiety." [27]

The Old Testament passage, "Train up a child in the way he should go, and when he is old he will not depart from it" is offered as evidence that the conception of Christian nurture which he is proposing has Biblical support. The New Testament, Bushnell said,

[25] *Ibid.*, p. 34.
[26] *Ibid.*, p. 35.
[27] *Ibid.*

is equally clear in terms of the definition of Christian nurture: "Bring them up in the nurture and admonition of the Lord." This passage suggested for Bushnell that there was "a Divine nature, that is to encompass the child and mold him unto God; so that he shall be brought up, as it were, in Him."[28] The Bible would indicate, therefore, said Bushnell, that the theory of religion prevalent in his day, which assumed that men were to grow up in evil, was a spurious understanding. Rather, Bushnell believed that there would be a time when "all shall know God, even from the least to the greatest." He insisted that this idea had been widespread in Christian churches in New England in the past. But if there were to be such a time as this again, he said, then children had to be brought up in the nurture of Christ.

There was a strange paradox rampant, too, Bushnell found. On the one hand, it was asserted that human society was advancing and that Christian virtue was becoming more prevalent; but on the other hand, the churches maintained a theory of religion which said that "men are to be dragged into the church by conquest." This appeared to be at least incongruous, said Bushnell. Nonetheless, Bushnell was optimistic about the future of American society:

Whereas there is a sober and rational possibility, that human society should be universally pervaded by Christian virtue. The Christian scheme has a scope of intention, and instruments and powers adequate to this: it descends upon the world to claim all souls for its dominion—all men of all climes, all ages from childhood to the grave. It is, indeed, a plan which supposes the existence of sin, and sin will be in the world, and in all hearts in it, as long as the world or human society continues; but the scheme has a breadth of conception, and has powers and provisions embodied in it, which, apart from all promises and predictions, certify us of a day when it will reign in all human hearts, and all that live shall live in Christ.[29]

Bushnell found many Scriptural passages which referred to the "organic law" of life, and which, he believed, maintained that "character in children often regarded as . . . derivative from their parents." By way of illustration, Bushnell used the following passages: "By the offence of one, judgment came upon all." In reference to Paul: "The unfeigned faith, which dwelt first in thy grandmother Lois, and thy mother Eunice, and, I am persuaded, that in thee also." God is repre-

[28] *Ibid.*, p. 36.
[29] *Ibid.*, p. 37.

sented as "keeping covenant and mercy with them that love him and keep his commandments, to a thousand generations." Passages as this one from Ezekiel, "the son shall bear the iniquity of the father," or, "the soul that sinneth, it shall die," are oftentimes used to disprove "the fact of an organic connection." However, Bushnell said, these passages refer rather to the historical fact that "the wickedness of parents propagates itself in the character and condition of their children." The Scriptures refer again and again to the organic relationship between the child and his parents: "For the promise is to you and to your children"; "for the good of them and their children after them."

III. *"Household Baptism"*

Bushnell repeated his assertion that the religion of his generation was out of step:

> Something has undoubtedly been gained to modern theology, as a human science, by fixing the attention strongly upon the individual man, as a moral agent, immediately related to God, and responsible only for his own actions; at the same time there was a truth, an important truth, underlying the old doctrine of federal headship and original or imputed sin, though strangely misconceived, which we seem, in our one sided speculations, to have quite lost sight of. And how can we ever attain to any right conception of organic duties, until we discover the reality of organic powers and relations? And how can we hope to set ourselves in harmony with the Scriptures, in regard to family nurture or household baptism, or any other kindred subject, while our theories exclude, or overlook precisely that which is the base of their teachings, and appointments? [30]

[30] *Ibid.*, pp. 39, 40. Cf. also pp. 49, 50, where Bushnell described the following scene: "I once took up a book from a Sabbath-school library, one problem of which was to teach a child that he wants a new heart. A lovely boy (for it was a narrative) was called every day to resolve that he would do no wrong that day, a task which he undertook most cheerfully, at first, and even with a show of delight. But, before the sun went down, he was sure to fall into some ill-temper or be overtaken by some infirmity. Whereupon, the conclusion was immediately sprung upon him that he "wanted a new heart." We are even amazed that any teacher of ordinary intelligence should not once have imagined how she herself, or how the holiest Christian living, would fare under such kind of regimen; how she would discover every day, and probably some hours before sunset, that she too wanted a new heart? And the practical cruelty of the experiment is yet more to be deplored, than its want of consideration. Had the problem been how to discourage most effectually every ingenuous struggle of childhood, no readier or surer method could have been developed.
Simply to tell a child, as he just begins to make acquaintance with words, that

Bushnell inisted upon "household baptism" or infant baptism. He felt that the rite of infant baptism presupposed an authentic organic connection of character between the parent and the child. It is "a seal of faith in the parent, applied over to the child, on the ground of a presumption that his faith is wrapped up in the parents' faith; so that he is accounted a believer from the beginning." The parent had in his character a power which, presumptively, was able to produce the similar power in his children. However, it was possible "by reason of some bad fault in itself, or possibly some outward hindrance in the Church, or some providence of death, [that] it may fail to do so." The rite of infant baptism saw the child in the parent, and counted him *presumptively* a believer and a Christian. However, the rite of infant baptism presumed that the child may not grow up to be a believer, and permitted him the freedom to do otherwise. God, however, wrote Bushnell, presumed that the child would grow up to be a believer and appointed the rite of infant baptism. Bushnell

he "must have a new heart before he can be good", is to inflict a double discouragement. First, he can not guess what this technical phraseology means, and thus he takes up the impression that he can do or think nothing right, till he is able to comprehend what is above his age–why then should he make the endeavor? Secondly, he is told that he must have a new heart *before* he can be good, not that he may hope to exercise a renewed spirit, *in* the endeavor to be good–why then attempt what must be worthless, till something *previous* befalls him? Discouraged thus on every side, his tender soul turns hither and thither, in hopeless despair, and finally he consents to be what he must–a sinner against God, and that only. Well is it, under such a process, wearing down his childish soul into soreness and despair of good, sealing up his nature in silence and cessation as regards all right endeavors, and compelling him to turn his feelings into other channels, where he shall find his good in evil–well is it, I say, if he has not contracted a dislike to the very subject of religion, as inveterate as the subject is impossible."

Cf. also pp. 59, 60, concerning revivals, a subject which Bushnell was not ready to leave: "I desire to speak with all caution of what are very unfortunately called revivals of religion; for, apart from the name, which is modern, and from certain crudities and excesses that go with it–which name, crudities, and excesses are wholly adventitious as regards the substantial merits of such scenes–apart from these, I say, there is abundant reason to believe that God's spiritual economy includes varieties of exercise, answering, in all important respects, to these visitations of mercy, so much coveted in our churches. They are needed. . . . But the difficulty is with us that we idolize such scenes, and make them the whole of our religion. We assume that nothing good is doing, or can be done at any other time. And what is even worse, we often look upon these scenes, and desire them, rather as scenes of victory, than of piety. They are the harvest-times of conversion, and conversion is too nearly everything with us. In particular we see no way to gather in disciples, save by means of certain marked experiences, developed in such scenes, in adult years."

took issue with the Baptists who asserted that nothing but sin could be expected of the child. He insisted that God had written His own name upon the child, and expected him to grow up in all duty and piety.[31]

When Paul baptized the household of Stephanas, one might assume, said Bushnell, that there were children in the household, "for a household generally contains children."[32] Another reference to infant baptism in the New Testament Bushnell believed to be: "Except a man be born of water *and of the Spirit,* he cannot enter the kingdom of heaven." But he thought that Jesus had given the rite a "higher sense" i. e.: "He had come to set up a spiritual kingdom, the kingdom of heaven." The proselyte who came to be baptized was baptized with his entire family. All were regenerated and naturalized together. It is understood, therefore, that children were to be included in the church with their parents. Paul tells us, said Bushnell, that "in the church of God, the believing party sanctifies the unbelieving."[33]

Bushnell found many references to infant baptism in the early church.[34] He quoted Justin Martyr: "There are some of us, eighty years old, who were made disciples to Christ in their childhood." This passage, taken in connection with the baptismal formula, "Go disciple all nations, baptizing," clearly referred to "the rite that introduced the subject into the Christian school as a disciple," Bushnell reported. Irenaeus also made reference to the rite of infant baptism when he said: "Christ came to save all persons through himself; all, I say, who through him are regenerated unto God: in-

---

[31] *Ibid.,* pp. 40–41.

[32] Cf. the careful argument of Bushnell, *ibid.,* p. 42. He was consciously attempting to challenge the Baptists' rejection of infant baptism. "Admitting the correctness of the translation, which some have questioned, the argument seems rather plausible as a turn of logic, than just and convincing; for, if we consider the more decisive position held in that age by the heads of families, and how, in common speech, they were supposed to carry the religion of the family with them, we shall be convinced that nothing was more natural than the very language used here. It was taken for granted, as a matter of common understanding, that, in a change of religion, the children went with the parents; if they became Jews, that their children would be Jews; if Christian believers, that their children would be Christians. Hence all the terms used, in reference to their religion, took the most inclusive form." Cf. also p. 47.

[33] *Ibid.,* pp. 43–44; Bushnell referred to the Jewish practice of baptizing "in token of cleansing"; he said that Jesus instituted the rite, not by any accident or historical basis.

[34] *Ibid.,* p. 45.

fants and little ones, and children and youth, and the aged." "Regenerated unto God" alludes to baptism, Bushnell thought, and specifically to parents and children. This fact verified for him the practice of infant baptism in the churches of Irenaeus' time: "You perceive, too, in this exposition, that the view of Christian nurture I am endeavoring to vindicate, is not new, but is older, by far, than the one now prevalent—as old as the Christian church. It is radically one with the ancient doctrine of baptism and regeneration, advanced by Christ, and accepted by the first fathers." [35]

The regeneration which takes place in the rite of infant baptism is only "presumptive" and *not* actual. Everything depended upon the organic law of character between the parent and the child, the church and the child, that is, upon duty and holy living and gracious example. Bushnell expressed his confidence in the rite of infant baptism: "The child is too young to choose the rite for himself, but the parent, having him as it were in his own life, is allowed the confidence that his own faith and character will be reproduced in the child, and grow up in his growth, and that thus the propriety of the rite as a seal faith will not be violated." [36]

IV. *The "Organic Unity" of the Family*

Bushnell recognized that there were objections to his view of Christian nurture, and he dealt with them in turn. To the "theoretical objection" that such a view left no room for the sovereignty of God, Bushnell maintained that it cannot be shown, "where the whole conduct of the parents has been such as it should be to produce the best effects, and where the sovereignty of God has appointed the ruin of the children." The sovereignty of God is always related to means, asserted Bushnell, and we are not authorized to think of it as separated from means. Another objection, this one from observation, that so many pious parents had been so unfortunate with their children, Bushnell answered by saying that many persons, who are noted for their piety, are yet disagreeable persons, and this is so because of some marked defect in their religious character: "They display just that spirit, and act in just that manner, which is likely to make religion odious—the more odious, the more urgently they

[35] *Ibid.*, p. 46.
[36] *Ibid.*

commend it. Sometimes they appear well to the world one remove distant from them, they shine well in their written biography, but one living in their family will know what others do not, and if their children turn out badly, will never be at a loss for reason." [37] Rather, Christian parents should teach a feeling rather than a doctrine about the Christian faith; that is, "to bathe the child in their own feeling of love to God, and dependence on him, and contrition for wrong before him, bearing up their child's heart in their own, not fearing to encourage every good motion they can call into exercise; to make what is good, happy, and attractive, what is wrong, odious and hateful; then as the understanding advances, to give it food suited to its capacity, opening upon it, gradually the more difficult views of Christian doctrine and experience." Bushnell criticized the church on this point, for it can be the divisions, the fanaticisms, the wordliness, and the orthodoxies of the church which counteract the religious training of the children by the parents. He wrote: "But when the school of Christ makes itself an element of sin and death, the child's baptism becomes as great a fiction as the church itself, and the arrangements of divine mercy fail of their intended power." [38]

Bushnell's conception of Christian nurture was dependent upon "a constant and careful discipline" on the part of the parents. The greatest virtue of a family was the "truly good and sanctified life." He warned parents that "a reign of brute force is much more easily maintained, than a reign whose power is righteousness and love." However:

There are, too, I must warn you, many who talk much of the rod as the orthodox symbol of parental duty, but who might really as well be heathens as Christians; who only storm about their house with heathenish ferocity, who lecture, and threaten, and castigate, and bruise, and call this family government. They even dare to speak of this as the nurture of the Lord. So much easier is it to be violent than to be holy, that they substitute force for goodness and grace, and are wholly conscious of the imposture. It is frightful to think how they batter and bruise the delicate, tender souls of their children, extinguishing in them what they ought to cultivate, crushing that sensibility which is the hope of their being, and all in the sacred name of Christ Jesus. By no such summary process can you dispatch your duties to your children. You are not to be a savage to them, but a father and a Christian. Your real aim and study must be to infuse into them a new life, and, to this end, the Life of God must perpetually reign

[37] *Ibid.*, pp. 48, 49. The chief mistake, however, is to insist upon "a new heart before he can be good"; cf. pp. 50, 51.
[38] *Ibid.*, pp. 51–52.

in you. Gathered round you as a family, they are all to be so many motives, strong as the love you bear them, to make you Christ-like in your spirit. It must be seen and felt with them that religion is a first thing with you.[39]

Bushnell contrasted Christian education, the "nurture of the Lord," with "a half-wordly, carnal piety, proposing money as the good thing of life; stimulating ambition for place and show; provoking ill-nature by petulance and falsehood; praying, to save the rule of family worship; having now and then a religious fit, and, when it is on, weeping and exhorting the family to undo all that the life has taught them to do; and then, when the passions have burnt out their fire, dropping down again to sleep in the embers, only hoping still that the family will sometime be converted!"[40] But Bushnell was also concerned with those parents who were not Christian:

Do not imagine that you have done corrupting them when they are born. Their character is yet to be born, and, in you, is to have its parentage. Your spirit is to pass into them, by a law of transition that is natural, and well nigh irresistible. And then you are to meet them in a future life, and see how much of blessing or of sorrow they will impute to you—to share their unknown future, and look upon yourselves as father and mother to their destiny. Such thoughts, I know, are difficult for you to meet; difficult because they open real scenes, which you are, one day, to look upon. Loving these your children, as most assuredly you do, can you think that you are fulfilling the office that your love requires? Go home to your Christless house, look upon them all as they gather round you, and ask it of your love faithfully to say, whether it is well between you? And if no other argument can draw you to God, let these dear living arguments come into your soul, and prevail there.[41]

Under the title "The Ostrich Nurture," Bushnell discussed the prevailing methods of religious education and especially the claim that children should be permitted to grow up in a spontaneous way, and to "generate their own principles." The child should be enabled to discover for himself how he is to live. "Having thus no artificial conscience formed to hamper his natural freedom, no religious scruples and superstitions inculcated to be a detention, or limitation, upon his impulses, he will grow up as a genuine character, stunted by no cant or affection; a large-minded, liberal, original, and beautiful soul."[42]

[39] *Ibid.*, pp. 56, 57.
[40] *Ibid.*, p. 58.
[41] *Ibid.*, p. 64.
[42] *Ibid.*, p. 67.

He criticized the over-use of "free moral agency," which did not permit distinctions between manhood and childhood. He protested against "notions of conversion that are mechanical" and against drilling into children "all the constraints separated from all the hopes and liberties of religion." God has instituted the reproductive order of existence, he said, including the parental and filial relationship, in order to mitigate the perils of free agency. Bushnell wrote: "One generation is to be ripe in knowledge and character, and the next is to be put in charge of the former, in the tenderest, most flexible, most dependent state possible, to be by them inducted into the choices where their safety lies." [43]

He protested again against bringing up children in expectation of revival seasons. But "a mere ethical nurture" is not to be identified with the Christian faith either. Children who are inducted in a mere ethical nurture, have no faith and are in no way dependent upon God. But the church must be alert to temper this kind of approach to faith by its constant insistence that Christ is the Savior of children, too. The Christian faith,

... has no conception that there can be a Saviour and salvation for all ages and stages of life; Christ is the Saviour of adults only! No! Christ is a Saviour bounded by no such narrow and meager theories—a Saviour for infants, and children, and youth, as truly as for the adult age; gathering them all into his fold together, there to be kept and nourished together, by gifts appropriate to their years; even as he himself has shown us go convincingly, by passing through all ages and stages of life himself, and giving us, in that manner, to see that he partakes the want and joins himself to the fallen state of each. Having been a child himself who can imagine, even for one moment, that he has no place in his fold for the fit reception of childhood? Dreadful insult, both to him an to childhood, and the greater insult, that the gospel even of heaven's love is narrowed to this by a supposed necessity of evangelism! What a position is given thus to children, growing up to look on an adult church, instructed into the opinion that what they look upon—Christ, ordinances, covenant vows—is only for adult people! [44]

"The organic unity of the family" was one of the most important concepts in Bushnell's theory of Christian nurture. He described this concept in the following way: "And so it is with all family transactions and feelings. They implicate ordinarily the whole circle of the house, young and old, male and female, fathers and mothers, sons and daughters. Acting thus together, they take a common

[43] *Ibid.*, p. 72.
[44] *Ibid.*, pp. 83–84.

character, accept the same delusions, practice the same sins, and ought, I believe, to be sanctified by a common grace."[45] How uncommon was this notion of organic unity, Bushnell suggested, in a society in which all modern notions and speculations had become individualistic. Bushnell found that in matters of religion we have the bonds of church authority, and erected the individual mind into a tribunal of judgment within itself. We have asserted free will as the ground for all proper responsibility, and framed our theories of religion to make it possible to treat persons as distinct units. The state, the church, and the family can no longer be considered as parts of an organic whole. They are rather "mere collections of units." There is no sense of the inter-relatedness of people. Rather, individuals are treated in such a way as to belong to the heap, or as seeds piled together. Bushnell's concern in *Christian Nurture* was to restore one of these organic forms, that is, the family.

The "organic unity of the family" was defined by Bushnell in terms of, "a power ... exterted by parents over children, not only when they teach, encourage, persuade, and govern, but without any purposed control whatever. The bond is so intimate that they do it unconsciously and undesignedly—they must do it. Their character, feelings, spirit, and principles, must propagate themselves, whether they will or not." In the early period of childhood (prior to the age of reason and deliberate choice), the control of parents must be regarded as an absolute force, and not as influence. Such an act of control must be considered an "organic" cause:

So too when the child performs acts of will, under parental direction, that involve results of character, without knowing or considering that they do, these must be classified in the same manner.

That is to say:

... we conceive the manners, personal views, prejudices, practical motives, and spirit of the house, as an atmosphere which passes into all and pervades all, as naturally as the air they breathe.[46]

There is nothing in this view, Bushnell wrote, which could conflict with the concept of the individuality of persons and their separate

---

[45] *Ibid.*, p. 90.
[46] *Ibid.*, pp. 93, 94: "The odor of the house will always be in his garments, and the internal difficulties with which he has to struggle, will spring of the family seeds planted in his nature."

responsibility. "The past we behold, living in the present, and all together we regard as one, inhabited by the common life. How much more true is this (though in a different way) in families, where the common life is so nearly absolute over the members; where they are all inclosed within the four walls of their dwellings, partakers in a common blood, in common interests, wants, feelings and principles." [47] The organic unity of families can be recognized by the fact that one generation is the natural offspring of another. "We shall find that there is a law of connection, after birth, under which power over character is exerted, without any design to do it." Immediately after birth, the child does not have the capacity to will or decide anything, and for this reason, he is not a complete individual. He is open to *impressions* from everything he sees. The character of the child is forming, under a principle, not of choice, but of nurture. "The spirit of the house is breathed into his nature, day by day. The anger and gentleness, the fretfulness and patience—the appetites, passions, and manners—all the variant moods of feeling exhibited round him, pass into him as impressions, and become seeds of character in him; not because the parents will, but because it must be so, whether they will or not. They propagate their own evil in the child, not by design, but under a law of moral infection." "The Spirit of the house" is infused into the members of the house by *nurture, not by teaching:* it is the air the children breathe. [48]

In all of the organic bodies known to man, Bushnell wrote, states, churches, sects, armies, there is a common spirit, by which they are pervaded and distinguished from each other. The term *Spirit,* as used by Bushnell, referred "to a power interfused, a comprehensive will actuating the members, regarding also the common body itself, as a larger and more inclusive individual." But it is the family spirit which is most evident, and it is the organic spirit of the home which shapes the character of its members.

The "organic working" of a family led Bushnell to the same conclusions:

The child begins, at length, to develop his character, in and through his voluntary power. But he is still under the authority of the parent, and has only a partial control of himself, in the development of which, he is

[47] *Ibid.,* p. 96.
[48] *Ibid.,* pp. 100–101.
[49] *Ibid.,* p. 107; cf. the examples Bushnell gave of the perverse effect this might have upon the child; p. 110: "Parents as late-risers."

gradually approaching a complete personality. Now, there is a perpetual working in the family, by which the wills, both of the parents and the children, are held in exercise, and which, without any design to affect character on one side, or conscious consent on the other, is yet fashioning results of a moral quality, as it were by the joint industry of the house.[49]

Bushnell found support for his conception of the "organic unity of the family" in the Bible. He said: "I observe that Christ is called a second Adam and a last Adam: language, to say the least, that suits the idea of a proposed union with the race, under its organic laws— as if, entering into the Christian family, his design were to fill it with a family spirit, which shall controvert and master the old evil spirit."[50] The seal of the covenant was a seal of *faith,* which applied to the whole house. The continuity of faith was somehow to be, or someway to be maintained, in a line that was parallel with the continuity of sin in the family. But the result was not to depend upon mere natural generation, but upon the organic causes which were involved in family nurture. Christ, the new "seed," was said to be of "the seed of Abraham," and "heir of the promise" made to him:

Thus the church has a constitutive element from the family in it still, as it had in the days of Abraham. The church life—that is, the Holy Spirit—collects families into a common organism, and then, by sanctifying the laws of organic unity in families, extends its quickening power to the generation following, so as to include the future, and make it one with the past. And so the church, in all ages, becomes a body under Christ the head, as the race is a body under Adam the head—a living body, quickened by him who hath life in himself, fitly joined together and compacted by that which every joint supplieth.[51]

The doctrine of organic unity, furthermore, "gives the only true solution of the Christian Church and of baptism as related to membership." If one did not maintain this doctrine, Bushnell warned, baptism became perverted, and was only a spectacle:

By a motion of his hand the priest breaks in, to interrupt and displace all the laws of character in life—communicating an abrupt, ictic grace, as much wider of all dignity and reason, than any which the new light theology has asserted, as the regenerative power is more subject to a human dispensation. A superstitious homage collects about his person. The child looks on him as one who opens heaven by a ceremony! The ungodly parent hurries to him, to get the regenerative grace for his dying child. The

[50] *Ibid.,* p. 112.
[51] *Ibid.,* p. 114.

bereaved parent mourns inconsolably, and even curses himself, that the neglected to obtain the grace for his child, now departed. The priest, in the eye, displaces the memory of duty and godliness in the heart.[52]

Baptism, on the basis of its organic unity with the parents, imparts and pledges a grace to sanctify that unity. The child is "potentially regenerate," and may be regarded as existing in connection with powers and causes that *contain* the fact, before time and separate from time:

> For when the fact appears historically, under the law of time, it is not more truly real, in a certain sense, than it was before. And then the grace conferred, being conferred by no casual act, but resting in the established laws of character, in the church and the house, is not lost by unfaithfulness, but remains and lingers still, though abused and weakened, to encourage new struggles.[53]

V. *Theory of Depravity*

Indicative of the theological climate of Bushnell's time were the reviews and comments of *Discourses on Christian Nurture*. Bennet Tyler of the East Windsor Seminary wrote a letter to Bushnell, which was soon published in pamphlet form, and which expressed his complete disapproval of it:

> That the child should grow up a Christian, it is necessary that he should become a Christian. And how is he to become a Christian? Is he made a Christian by education? You admit that there is no "radical goodness of human nature," and that "the work of Christian education" is not "to educe the good that is in us." No one is a Christian by nature; for all "are by nature children of wrath." Those to whom the privilege is given to become the sons of God, are "born, not of blood, nor of the will of the flesh, nor of the will of man, but of God." *Not of blood*—They are not Christians by natural descent. Grace is not hereditary. *Nor of the will of the flesh*—They are not converted by any efforts of their own, made in an unrenewed state. *Nor of the will of man*—They are not converted by moral suasion, or by any efforts of man. They are not made Christians by education. *But of God*—It is God's prerogative to change the heart. "We are his workmanship, created in Christ Jesus unto good works."[54]

---

[52] *Ibid.*, pp. 115, 116.
[53] *Ibid.*, pp. 117, 119; Bushnell admonished the parents: "Understand that it is the family spirit, the organic life of the house, the silent power of a domestic godliness, working, as it does, unconsciously and with sovereign effect–this it is which forms your children to God."
[54] *A Letter to Dr. Bushnell on Christian Nurture* (East Windsor Hill, June 7,

The reviewer of the *Discourses* in *The Christian Observatory*, regretted that Bushnell "does not properly recognize the truths of depravity and regeneration," and that Bushnell had been influenced by German thought:

The mass of them [the Germans] is ruined by vain philosophy, and corrupted by dead rationalism and ghostly transcendentalism, and all those hard and hateful names which designate the numerous shapes of Christian Infidelity which have swarmed from the fumes of their beer and tobacco, like the locusts from the smoke of the bottomless pit . . . It is really mortifying to see the pastor of a flock of Connecticut saints, leading them out of their fat valley into such lean and unwholesome pasture.[55]

Charles Hodge, Professor of Theology in Princeton Theological Seminary, supported Bushnell's thesis to a certain degree:

There is an intimate and divinely established connexion between the faith of parents and the salvation of their children; such a connexion as authorizes them to plead God's promises, and to expect with confidence, that through his blessing on their faithful efforts, their children will grow up the children of God. This is the truth and the great truth, which Dr. Bushnell asserts. This doctrine it is his principal object to establish. It is this that gives his book its chief value. This and its consequences render his discourses so appropriate to the present state of the church; for there is perhaps no one doctrine to which it is more important in our day to call the attention of the people of God.[56]

1847), p. 3. It was this *Letter* which made the publication committee of the Sabbath School Society cease printing the pamphlet Bushnell wrote defending the truth of his *Discourses on Christian Nurture*. The pamphlet was entitled, "An Argument for "Discourses on Christian Nurture" Addressed to the Publishing Committee of the Massachusetts Sabbath School Society" (Hartford, 1847). Cf. also Myers' comment, *op. cit.,* p. 50: "To this doctrine that a child may grow up a Christian, Tyler replied with what he believed to be one of his crushing syllogisms: 'And how is he to become a Christian?' And then he lays down one of his bedrock "Facts": "It is a fundamental principle of the Christian scheme," he alleges, "that every child born into the world, is by nature totally depraved, and must be born again in order to become a child of God, and an heir of heaven." Thus he meets argument and common sense by increased dogmatism. He was right to this extent, that either position had to be given up and there is now little dispute as to which it is." See also pp. 59–77.

[55] "Review of Horace Bushnell's *Discourses on Christian Nurture*," *The Christian Observatory*, I, (July 1847), pp. 323–330; cf. also *New England Religious Herald*, V, (August 7, 1847), pp. 383–393; (June, 1848), pp. 273–283.

"The New Theological Controversy," *The New Englander Magazine*, V, (1847), pp. 613–614; Noah Porter, Jr., "Bushnell on Christian Nurture," *The New Englander Magazine*, VI, (1848), pp. 126–134.

[56] Charles Hodge, "Bushnell on Christian Nurture," *The Biblical Repertory and Princeston Review*, XIX (October, 1847), pp. 502–539.

On the other hand, Hodge asserted, Bushnell was deficient on two points. Bushnell's concept of God's action upon nature was seriously defective. It recognized God as a power within nature, but not as a power above nature. There was nothing supernatural in the process of God's activity. There was no transcendent cause which was beyond and above nature. Second, Bushnell's conception of man's natural state was incorrect. It assumed, said Hodge, that man was not by nature the child of wrath, and that he was not involved in spiritual death. Bushnell had not taken the doctrine of natural depravity seriously, with the result that he had developed "a naturalistic doctrine of conversion."

The prominent theologian of the German Reformed Church, John W. Nevin, was asked by Bushnell to comment on the *Discourses*. Nevin wrote four articles analyzing Bushnell's theory of Christian education. He was appreciative of Bushnell's criticism of the "fanatical individualism" of the contemporary revivals. But he was also extremely critical of Bushnell's thesis because "it bases its theory of educational piety on the constitution of nature" rather than upon God's gift of grace. The major fault with Bushnell's argument was that it is too rationalistic, wrote Nevin. This appeared "in the first place, in the view which the tract takes of original sin or natural depravity. Dr. Bushnell assents fully to the doctrine of our general natural depravity; but it is certainly made to assume, under his hands, a form that robs it at least to a great extent of its proper force. If I have properly apprehended his meaning, he makes it to be a sort of necessary accident merely to our moral probation." [57]

There were other commentators who applauded Bushnell's concept of Christian nurture, and these represented a cross-section of the different denominations. [58] The theological question which Bush-

---

[57] John W. Nevin, "Educational Religion," *The Weekly Messenger of the German Reformed Church*, XII (July 7, 1847), p. 2.

[58] G. W. Briggs, "Bushnell on Christian Nurture," *The Christian Examiner and Religious Miscellany*, XLIII, (1847), pp. 435–451, in which the author notes a "growing harmony" in church doctrine, and applauds Bushnell for his views; "One generation, trained in the spirit of the view which Dr. Bushnell presents, might banish slavery and war, and many kindred sins. We rejoice, too, that parental influence is urged by him so strongly, as a divinely appointed agency for this great work. No combination of holy influences can compensate for its loss. We mourn, as we consider this, when we see how the children of numberless homes seem to be bereaved of their heaven-ordained teachers by the tendencies or the neglect to the time..." (p. 448).

Rev. William Heath, "The Baptist and Pedobaptist Theories of Church Mem-

nell's detractors had raised was that of natural depravity. Bushnell
appeared to want to avoid this problem, and to deal more with a positive theory of Christian nurture. However, as was pointed out to
him very quickly by Bennet Tyler, Charles Hodge, and John W.
Nevin, he had not taken seriously the doctrine of original sin. The
Discourses on Christian Nurture did not teach specifically that the
child was naturally depraved and that his corrupt heart had to be
changed into a new heart. No one is a Christian by nature, proclaimed Tyler; rather every child born into the world must be born
again in order to become a child of God. Furthermore, Bushnell's
thesis suggested that grace was hereditary and that the child was
already regenerate at the time of his baptism. It would appear then,
at least to the theologians mentioned above, that Bushnell's doctrine
of Christian nurture was too naturalistic, and the reason for this was
that he had lost sight of the doctrine that human nature was totally
depraved.

How did Bushnell's theory of Christian nurture differ from the
prevailing theories, particularly in reference to the doctrines of original sin and natural depravity? In one place, Bushnell asserted that
his view of Christian nurture "may be easily set in connection with

bership," *The Christian Review*, XII (December 1847), pp. 529–551; "Still we are
bound to express the highest respect and regard for Dr. Bushnell, as a man and
as a Christian. His system has carried him far; for the deeply logical structure of
his mind, and frankness of his character has led him to avoid all shirking of
legitimate consequences; but let it be here remarked that *this is the mildest
and most moderate theory of infant baptism* ever exhibited; the least offensive
to others, the most simple and consistent with itself. If it will not stand, nothing
will. Dr. Tyler's Letter in reply to it is but an argument for Baptist principles
from beginning to end." (p. 550.)

"Bushnell's Christian Nurture," *The Church Review and Ecclesiastical Register*,
I (1848–1849), pp. 228–245; "We may say of them (the Discourses), that they
are a series of efforts to place the work of promoting and extending religion on
a high philosophical ground, to unite and harmonize the various phenomena
connected therewith, and to correct the tendencies to fanaticism, which so
abundantly prevail in connection with the popular view on the subject. There
is a manliness, a comprehensiveness, a richness and fertility of thought in the
book, which commands respect and renders the whole attractive." (pp. 228–229).

The Methodist Quaterly Review, (January 1849); "Without pledging ourselves
to all Dr. Bushnell's views, we yet sympathize far more with him than with
the friends in New England he has so terrified. The doctrines of his book, or
similar ones, must be proclaimed from our house-tops. No part of the world
needs them as do the American churches, with whom baptized children seem
to be regarded as little heathens–just as if they has not been baptized at all....
We repeat it, from our hearts–on this subject *we need a great awakening*."
(p. 156.)

any of the existing theories of original sin," although some "more awkwardly than others." [59] However, he did not want to become involved in an argument on the theory of depravity and regeneration which had been "forever exploded" before the public. Nonetheless, Bushnell did deal with the question, and he did develop a theory of original sin.

In order to comprehend how Bushnell thought about these matters, we must refer back to his *Nature and the Supernatural*. In the discussion of the fall and original sin, Bushnell did not look for Scriptural support for these doctrines. Rather, he attempted to deal with them on a basis which might be acceptable to those theologians who questioned the authenticity of the Scriptures.

The question of the fall is closely related to what Bushnell termed the "condition privative." His entire discussion of Adam, as we have already seen in *Nature and the Supernatural,* was informed by this concept of "a moral state that is only inchoate, or incomplete, lacking something not yet reached, which is necessary to the probable rejection of evil." Adam's privative condition expressed itself in terms of three deficiencies. He was deficient in the knowledge of what to do experientially with the necessary ideas of the true and the good which he possessed as the law of his being. He was also deficient in moral power to make a law of duty from the idea of the good. Finally, he was deficient in the ability to deal with bad spirits and malign powers. These deficiencies are limitations in the human nature of Adam, and made certain his fall as well as that of mankind. Bushnell wrote: "These conditions privative are in the nature of perils, and while they excuse nothing, for the law of duty is always plain, they are yet drawn so close to the soul and open their gulfs, on either hand, so deep, that our expectation of the fall is really as pressing as if it were determined by some law that annihilates liberty. Liberty we know is not annihilated. And yet we say, looking on the state of man made perilous, in this manner, by liberty, that we can not expect him to stand." [60]

The certainty of the fall was asserted. But Bushnell insisted that sin and guilt were operative in the human sphere, because the fall resulted *not* from any positive cause, but only from that deficiency

[59] *An Argument for "Discourses on Christian Nurture,"* p. 23. H. Shelton Smith's *Changing Conceptions of Original Sin,* has informed the argument which follows.
[60] *Nature and the Supernatural,* p. 128.

inherent within the "condition privative." For this reason, no one is obligated to choose evil.

To understand fully Bushnell's conception of the fall, we must relate it to his idea of the consequences of the fall. It is at this point that Bushnell's conception of the structure of reality plays a major role. "The one system of God," which was made up of nature and the supernatural, is an organic whole. We have seen that the natural and the supernatural realms complement and interact with one another, even though they cannot be equated with each other. One is the realm of things, the stage or field, for the universe. The other, the realm of persons, spirits, including God the supreme spirit. The supernatural realm can assert its influence upon the natural realm in either creative or destructive ways. The human personality best exemplifies the power of the supernatural. Man is in nature and is conditioned by nature. But at the point of self-determination, man is supreme over nature. Man can then act in a supernatural way, that is, to act upon the natural chain of cause and effect, from outside of nature. He does so, Bushnell reminds us, only in conjunction with nature's laws, which he can apply in new combinations.

The effects of the fall, therefore, create a "wrong conjunction of causes" in nature. Sin cannot negate the laws of nature, but it can cause nature to act in an unnatural way, as it was not made to act. This condition subsequently affects every aspect of existence. But it affects the human first and causes him to act as if he were an unnatural being. His will, soul, passions, conscience and imagination are involved. Man's body is also affected. Bushnell wrote:

Nor is any thing better understood than that whatever vice of the mind—wounded pride, unregulated ambition, hatred, covetousness, fear, inordinate care—throws the mind out of rest, throws the body out of rest also. Thus it is that sin, in all its forms, becomes a power of bodily disturbance, shattering the nerves, inflaming the tissues, distempering the secretions, and brewing a general ferment of disease.[61]

The effects of sin involve more than the individual self, because the self is part of "an organic whole," the race. Therefore, the effects of Adam's sin will have a disturbing influence upon the natures of his offspring. But Bushnell did not believe that this included the doctrine of imputed sin. "The sin of no person can be transmitted, as a sin . . . ," but nonetheless there is an organic depravation of humanity

[61] *Ibid.*, p. 175.

because of the fall. As man is part of the organic whole, the human race, the effects of sin are propagated through all of humanity by the laws of heredity.[62] The effects of sin eventually become organic, and, as a result, a kingdom of evil is created overagainst God.

Bushnell's theory of depravity, then, involved the concept of hereditary depravity. It is this idea which informed his view of Christian nurture. He wrote:

> Could we enter into the mental habits of those children, who are spoken of in my text, and trace out all the threads of their inward character and disposition, we should doubtless find some color of idolatry in the fiber of their very being. They are not such as they would be, if their parents, of this and remote generations, had been worshipers of the true God. Their talents, dispositions, propensities are different. The idol god is in their faces and their bones, and his stamp is on their spirit. Not in such a sense that the sin of idolatry is in them—that is inconceivable; for no proper sin can pass by transmission—but that they have a vicious, or prejudicial infection from it, a damage accruing from their historical connection and that of their progenitors with it.[63]

The period of infancy, that period before the beginning of language, is the most important period for the child. It is during this "age of impression" that the child is most responsive to his parents. Sinful parents, therefore, propagate their own evil under the law of moral infection. This same evil may subsequently be propagated throughout the human race under the law of heredity.

We have seen how sin introduces a disorder even throughout the physical world. All of nature's disharmonies, and evidences of suffering have been caused by the impact of sin upon the physical universe. Bushnell introduced this concept of cosmic disharmony in order to highlight the destructive powers of the human will. The human will has the power, Bushnell said, to alter the conjunctions of causes found in the world as well as to disturb physical substances themselves. Sin, as it affects man, enables him, individually and corporately, to act supernaturally upon the universe and to bring about nature's disorders.[64] The consequences of sin, therefore, penetrate

---

[62] *Ibid.*, pp. 177–178.

[63] *Christian Nurture*, p. 99.

[64] H. Shelton Smith, *op. cit.*, p. 158, anticipates the criticism which might be made of Bushnell's doctrine. He distinguishes two kinds of consequences of the fall of man in Bushnell: "(1) those that follow upon the sin of man and (2) those that anticipate the sin of man." Bushnell was aware, however, of the objections that might be made: "As certainly as sin is to be encountered in his

the whole of reality. Sin is "that central fact, about which the whole creation of God and the ordering of his providential and moral government, revolves." [65]

Bushnell rejected finally the doctrine of total depravity as it was articulated by the theologians of his day, particularly Nathaniel Taylor and Bennett Tyler. Even though these men represented different theological schools of thought, they agreed that man came into the world in a state of total depravity. Man could be saved only when saving grace was interposed. Bushnell thought otherwise. There was a susceptibility to good in every man, he insisted. Man has within his soul that which may be appealed to by the right and the good. The child's first moral act, therefore, does not have to be evil, but it can be a good act. Furthermore, the child who is born into a Christian family ought to grow up to be a Christian. He has within himself that necessary moral ability to do so, although Bushnell recognized that every life involved a struggle with evil. But the good could overcome the evil, and had a practical advantage over it from the very outset of life. [66] Nevertheless, one had to be careful at this point to avoid misunderstanding. To say that a child is susceptible to the good does not mean that the child is morally good for this reason. There is no real goodness in the soul until it becomes united to the right. [67]

God's] plan," contended Bushnell, "its marks and consequences will appear anticipatively, and all the grand arrangements and cycles of time will be somehow preluding its approach, and the dire encounter to be maintained with it." Cf. *Nature and the Supernatural*, p. 201.

[65] *Nature and the Supernatural*, p. 214.

[66] Smith, *op. cit.*, pp. 160, 161, deals with the Unitarian criticism of Bushnell and indicates in what ways Bushnell was not a Unitarian in his doctrine of human nature; "His conflict with the Unitarian conception is evident in his thought at two points. In the first place, as against the Unitarians, he maintained that Adam's fall necessarily had a disordering effect upon the physical and mental characteristics of his offspring. . . . Since Bushnell disagreed with the Unitarian doctrine of original nature, he also disagreed with the Unitarian view of regeneration. For him, Christian regeneration was no mere process of eliciting the good within man."

Bushnell urged that Christianity "is not any doctrine of development, or self-culture; no scheme of ethical practice, or social re-organization; but it is a salvation; a power moving on fallen humanity from above its level, to regenerate and so to save." *Sermons for the New Life*, p. 109.

[67] *An Argument for "Discourses on Christian Nurture*, p. 26: "There is not and really can be no proper goodness in a soul till it practically embraces, as its final end and law, and thus becomes united to *the right*, or what is the same to *God and the principles of God*. Previously to this the power we have to feel the right and be attracted by the good are only the more conclusive proofs of

What Bushnell had accomplished with his theory of Christian nurture was three-fold:

1. He re-introduced the possibility of the child, who was reared by Christian parents, to be regenerate *in childhood*. This idea he maintained in the face of the revivalists and the advocates of the doctrine of human depravity.

2. He described evil in such a way that its effects were widespread, so widespread in fact, that the total structure of reality (and the fixed laws of nature) was distorted. When evil attained power in a race, it became a fixed law of nature or a "propagated quality" and was transmitted throughout the race from generation to generation.

3. He re-instated the Christian family as the central medium through which grace could be transmitted. Although Bushnell insisted that grace was always transmitted supernaturally, it is probably true that grace was also natural, at least to the extent that it was mediated through the laws of nature. In this way, according to the laws of nature, he believed that Christianity would eventually out-populate the un-Christian stock.[68]

depravity, inasmuch as we are found to reject what we practically approve, and to mortify the noblest wants of our being."
[68] *Christian Nurture*, pp. 195–207.

CHAPTER V

A Trinity of Manifestation

It is necessary to know something of Bushnell's private experience in order to comprehend the reasons why he wrote *God in Christ*. Bushnell's wife wrote about him in the following way (referring specifically to that period in his life immediately after the publication of *Christian Nurture*):

> The year 1848 was the central point in the life of Horace Bushnell. It was a year of great experiences, great thoughts, great labors. At its beginning he had reached one of those headlands where new discoveries open to the sight. He had approached it through mental struggles, trials, and practical endeavor, keeping his steadfast way amid all the side-attractions of his ceaseless mental activity. Five years before, God had spoken personally to him in the death of his beloved little boy, drawing his thoughts and affections to the spiritual and unseen, until, by slow advances, the heavenly vision burst upon him. He might well have said, what Edward Irving said of a like sorrow:—"Glorious exchange! He took my son to his own more fatherly bosom, and revealed in my bosom the sure expectation and faith of his own eternal Son." [1]

Bushnell read the life of the mystic, Madame Guyon and Uphaus' *Interior Life,* the works of Fenelon, and was attracted to the mystical developments which were taking place in New England theology. He rejected most of this emphasis, not, however, without retaining something of its value for theology. "I believed from reading, especially the New Testament, and from other testimony, that there is a higher, fuller life that can be lived, and set myself to attain it. I swung, for a time, towards quietism, but soon passed out into a broader, more positive state." [2] Thereafter, an incident occurred which remarkedly shaped his mind. It was reported that on an early morning in February, Bushnell's wife awoke to see that her husband had risen earlier. She asked him: "What have you seen?" He replied, "The Gospel." The Gospel had come, after great periods of thought

[1] Mary Bushnell Cheney, *Life and Letters of Horace Bushnell,* p. 191.
[2] *Ibid.,* p. 192.

and study, not as a logical conclusion to his study, but rather as a revelation and an inspiration. This experience he regarded as a crisis in his spiritual life, and he looked back upon it many years later as the period when he "passed the boundary":

I seemed to pass a boundary. I had never been very legal in my Christian life, but now I passed from those partial seeings, glimpses and doubts, into a clearer knowledge of God and into his inspirations, which I have never wholly lost. The change was into faith,—a sense of the freeness of God and the ease of approach to him.[3]

As a result, the Christian faith became for Bushnell "the faith of a transaction." "It is not," he said, "the committing of one's thought in assent to any proposition, but the trusting of one's being to *a being*, there to be rested, kept, guided, moulded, governed, and possessed forever." [4] The Christian faith became a divine experience, a personal discovery of Christ and of God as represented in Him. Christian knowledge became experimental knowledge. Bushnell was a new man but now with a "heavenly investiture."

He began immediately to give public expression to his private experience. A sermon appeared, entitled, "Christ the Form of the Soul," which was preached in the North Church, Hartford, based upon Gal. 4: 19, "Until Christ be formed in you." The sermon gave vivid expression to Bushnell's new experience:

If now we embrace him, we embrace the Divine Word. He becomes united to us and habited within us. Our love gives him a welcome in our soul and entertains him there. This we may call repentance, faith, conversion, regeneration, or by whatever name. The sublime reality is that the divine has made a junction with our nature, and Christ has begun to be formed within us—only begun. Henceforth the great object and aim of the Christian life is to have what is begun completed.[5]

He was invited by a number of schools, including Harvard Divinity School, Andover, and Yale College, to give the addresses at their graduating exercises. He immediately accepted these invitations, and looked at them as the opportunity to express further his newly-won faith in Christ. He began, thereafter, to look at Christian doctrine in terms of what he called "formulated Christian experience." The attempt to articulate in theological categories his religious experience

---

[3] *Ibid.*
[4] *Ibid.*, p. 192.
[5] *The Spirit in Man,* "Christ the Form of the Soul", p. 41.

formed the basis for the addresses which followed. He was aware of the fact that he was speaking *ad clerum,* and had to be responsible for "the thoroughness of the argument." But he reminded his audiences that to investigate God's own nature was the greatest presumption on his part, and the greatest levity on theirs. One cannot, he insisted, make the theology about God's interior nature comprehensible.[6]

I. *The Doctrine of Christ*

To deal with the doctrine of Christ in "A Discourse on the Divinity of Christ," which was delivered at the commencement exercises of Yale College, was to tread upon dangerous ground. We must always be aware, Bushnell said, that "God exceeds our measure, and must, until either He becomes less than infinite or we more than finite."[7] Nonetheless, Bushnell hoped that he might be able to apprehend Him in such a way that He would be clear of distraction in his understanding.

Bushnell considered Christ to be a "manifestation of the Life of God," but Christ was with the Father before the manifestation. For this reason, Bushnell could assert that Christ was God. Bushnell made this important distinction regarding the divinity of Christ: "By the *divinity* of Christ, I do not understand simply that Christ differs from other men, in the sense that he is better, more inspired, and so a more complete vehicle of God to the world than others have been. He differs from us, not in degree, but in kind; as the half divine parentage under which he enters the world most certainly indicates. He is in such a sense God, or God manifested, that the unknown term of his nature, that which we are most in doubt of, and about which we are least capable of any positive affirmation, is the human."[8]

[6] *God in Christ* (Three Discourses, delivered in New Haven, Cambridge, and Andover, with a preliminary dissertation on language), p. 122.
[7] *Ibid.,* cf. the sermon "God's Thoughts fit Bread for Children," *The Spirit in Man,* pp. 70–89; the sermon "The Finite demands the Infinite," *The Spirit in Man,* pp. 199–213; the sermons "The Gospel of the Face," pp. 73–95 and "The Immediate Knowledge of God," pp. 114–128, *Sermons on Living Subjects.*
[8] *God in Christ,* p. 122, Horace Bushnell chose 1 John 1:2 as his text for this discussion; cf. also *The Spirit in Man,* pp. 13 ff; cf. also the sermons "The Gentleness of God," pp. 28–50, "The Insight of Love," pp. 51–70, "The Fasting and Temptation of Christ," pp. 93–115, "Christ's Agony, or Moral Suffering," pp.

Bushnell catalogued a number of the proofs for the divinity of Christ: [*]

1. The pre-existence of Christ. "I came out from God"; "I came forth from the Father, and am come into the world"; "I came down from heaven"; "Ye are from beneath, I am from above"; "The glory which I had with thee before the world was." Bushnell believed that one could not read these passages from the New Testament and assert Christ's simple humanity. On the basis of them Christ was more than human.

2. The miraculous birth of Christ. Something more than humanity had come into man's history. The account in the New Testament of the miraculous birth of Christ had, for Bushnell, "the profoundest air of verity." Bushnell wrote: "If God were ever to be incarnate in the world, in what other manner, so natural, beautiful, and real, could He enter into the life of the race?"

3. The Incarnation. "The Word was made flesh"; "That which we have seen with our eyes, which we have looked upon, which our hands have handled of the word of Life"; "He that was in the form of God, and was made in fashion as a man"; these passages showed clearly, he said, that the Incarnation was not applicable to any mere man. The man referred to must be different from all other men. One could doubt his humanity more easily than his divinity.

4. The nature of the Godhead. Such passages as: "In whom dwelt all the fullness of the Godhead bodily"; "The church which is his body, the fullness of Him that is all in all"; "The express image of His person"; "The image of the invisible God"; "Complete in Him which is the Head of all principality and power"; transcend all human characterizations and are not consistent with the simple humanity of Jesus.

5. The relationship between the Father and the Son. Christ referred to this relationship in the following way: "I and the Father that sent me." "Ye neither know me nor my Father." "That which I have seen with my Father." "The Father is in me and I in him." "He that hath seen me hath seen the Father." Can we imagine, on the basis of these references, Bushnell asked, any other member of

225–247, "The Physical Suffering, or Cross of Christ," pp. 248–270, and "Heaven Opened," pp. 434–456, *Christ and His Salvation;* cf. also "Our Relations to Christ in the Future Life," *Sermons on Living Subjects,* pp. 442–468.
[*] *God in Christ,* pp. 123 ff; cf. the sermon "The Gospel of the Face," *Sermons on Living Subjects,* pp. 73–95.

our race referring to himself in the same way? It is Christ who "has the audacity . . . to promise that he and the Father—they two—will come to men together, and be spiritually manifest in them."

6. The comparison with God. Christ referred to himself in terms of the comparison between himself and God: "My Father is greater than I." Bushnell commented: "How preposterous for any mere human being of our race to be gravely telling the world that God is greater than he is!" [10]

7. The relationship of Christ to the world. Christ assumed a relation to the world which would be most offensive if he was merely a human being. He said, "I am the way, the truth, and the life." "I am the living bread that came down from heaven." "No man cometh unto the Father but by me." To assert this relationship to the world and not to be divine would also be preposterous, said Bushnell.

8. The sinless nature of Christ. Christ asserted a sinless nature when he said, ". . . which of you convinceth me of sin?" This is to Bushnell "stubborn evidence" of Christ's superhuman character. The only true reality of Christ in terms of his moral conduct is the divine within him. Christ, Bushnell said, "does not any longer act the man; practically speaking, the man sleeps in him."

9. The expectation of mankind. Jesus is divine, and not human: this is what mankind denies. Bushnell wrote:

[10] *God in Christ*, p. 125; Bushnell continued in reference to the Son of Man, "So, also, it is often argued from those numerous expressions of Christ, in which he calls himself the 'Son of man', that he there concedes his humanity. Undoubtedly he does, (for he does not appear to use the language in the lighter significance of the old prophets), but what kind of being is this who is *conceding* his humanity? Could there be displayed, by any human creature, a bolder stretch of presumption than to declare that God is superior to him, or to call himself 'the Son of man' by condescension?"; cf. *Christ and His Salvation*, pp. 357 ff: "It is very obvious, at the outset, that Christ can not be a true manifestation of God, when he comes in half the character of God, to act upon, or qualify, or pacify, the other half. He must be God manifest in the flesh, and not one side of God. If only God's affectional nature is represented in him, then he is but a half manifestation. And if we assign him, in that character, a special value, then we say, by implication, what amounts to the worst irreverence, that God is a being to be most desired when he is only halfpresented, and when his other half is either kept back, or somehow smoothed to a condition of silence. I take issue with all such conceptions of Christ. He is God manifested truly, God as he is, God in all his attributes combined, else he is nothing or at least no fair exhibition. If the purposes of God, the justice of God, the indignations of God, are not in him; if any thing is shut away, or let down, or covered over, then he is not in God's proportions, and does not incarnate his character."

It is God that we want, to know Him, to be near Him, to have His feeling unbosomed to us. As to the real human, we have enough of that. And, as to the unreal, superhuman human, that is, the human acted wholly by the divine, so as to have no action of its own, save in pretence, what is it to us but a mockery? What can we learn from it? True, we may draw from it the ideal of a beautiful and sinless life, and, in that, there may be a certain power. Still, it is an ideal, presented or conceived only to be despaired of. For this beautiful life, being sinless, is really not human, after all; and we'cannot have it, unless our nature is overborne and acted wholly by God in the same manner which, alas! is no longer possible, for we are deep in sin already. No! let us have the divine, the deific itself— the very feeling of God, God's own beauty, truth and love. Then we shall have both the pure ideal of a life, and a power flowing out from God to ingenerate that life in us. God; God is what we want, not a man; God, revealed through man, that we may see His Heart, and hide our guilty nature in the bosom of His love; God so identified with our race, as to signify the possible union and eternal identification of our nature with His.[11]

10. The formula of baptism. This baptismal formula gives the final evidence of the divine character of Christ. One is baptized "into the name of the Father, Son, and Holy Ghost." Each term in the formula is meant to denote the real divinity of the subject.[12]

II. *The Nature of the Trinity (preliminary)*

Bushnell dealt next with the doctrine of the Trinity. He provided what he called a "proximate conception" or preliminary definition: "It seems to be agreed by the orthodox, that there are three persons,

---

[11] *God in Christ,* p. 127.
[12] *Ibid.,* p. 129; Bushnell spoke of the "easy and free representations of the scripture and of the apostolic fathers . . . hardened into dogma" which caused the believer to question the real divinity of Christ. It is interesting to see how Bushnell dealt with the history of speculation about the Trinity: "In fact, it never was seriously questioned until after the easy and free representations of the scripture and of the apostolic fathers had been hardened into dogma, or converted by the Nicene theologues and those of the subsequent ages, into a doctrine of the mere human understanding; an assertion of three metaphysical persons in the divine nature. I do not say that such a mistake must not have been committed. And then, when a trinity of this kind was once inaugurated, it was equally necessary that speculation should rise up, sometime or other, to clear away the rubbish that speculation had accumulated. A metaphysical trinity must be assaulted by a methaphysical unity. And then, coming after both, and taking up the suspicion, that, possibly, dogma is not the whole wisdom of man; seeing, in fact, that it is wholly incompetent to represent the living truths of Christianity, we may be induced to let go a trinity that mocks our reason, and a unity that

Father, Son, and Holy Ghost, in the divine nature. These three persons, too, are generally regarded as belonging, not to the *machina Dei,* by which God is revealed, but to the very *esse,* the substantial being of God, or the interior contents of His being. They are declared to be equal; all to be infinite; all to be the same in substance; all to be one." [13] Bushnell recognized that the major problem associated with the Trinity arose when the term *person* was used to describe a member of the Trinity. Bushnell distinguished among those Christian teachers who held three real living persons in the interior nature of God; that is, three consciousnesses, wills, hearts, and understandings. These teachers found Biblical passages to support the idea of a "covenanting, co-operating, and co-presiding Trinity." But there were also other distinguished and living teachers who united the Father, the Son and the Holy Ghost in a "social way." By that phrase he meant that the members of the Trinity presided over the world as a kind of "celestial tritheocracy." The persons of the Trinity united as one God only in the sense that the three acted together with a perfect consent, or coincidence. This latter point of view, Bushnell believed, denied that the three persons of the Trinity were the same in substance, but maintained, rather, three separate and indivisible substances.

Bushnell decided that no one could assert the existence of three persons in the Trinity and mean that there were three consciousnesses, three wills, and three understandings. It would be impossible, he said, to speak about God as being one person in this way. The idea of a person, implied "an essential, incommunicable monad, bounded by consciousness, and vitalized by self-active will." [14] For this reason, it was impossible to speak of three units as one unit, "three sets of attributes inhering to a common substance," [15] or as

freezes our hearts, and return to the simple Father, Son, and Holy Ghost of the scriptures and the Apostolic Fathers; there to rest in the living and life-giving forms of the spirit. To this, it is my design, if possible, to bring you; for, in maintaining the essential divinity of Christ, there is no difficulty whatever, till we begin to speculate or dogmatize about the humanity, or find ourselves in contact with the more commonly accepted doctrine of trinity."

[13] *God in Christ,* p. 130.

[14] *Ibid.,* pp. 131–132; Bushnell gave some indication of this confusion existing in his time; "Thus, if the class I speak of were to hear a discourse insisting on the proper personal unity of God, it would awaken suspicion in their minds; while a discourse insisting on the existence of three persons, would be only a certain proof of orthodoxy; showing that they profess three persons, meaning what they profess, and one person, really not meaning it."

[15] *Ibid.,* pp. 132–133; Bushnell's criticism of this position was as follows: "Thus

"metaphysical and real persons." [16] The basic difficulty in this position is that when the word *person* is used, it means only a "threefold distinction." Bushnell clarified his rejection of this point of view:

Thus, they say that there is a certain divine person in the man Christ Jesus, but that when they use the term *person,* they mean not a person, but a certain indefinite and indefinable distinction. The later Unitarians, meantime, are found asserting that God is present in Christ, in a mysterious and peculiar communication of His being, so that he is the living embodiment and express image of God. If, now, the question be raised, wherein does the indefinable *distinction* of one, differ from the mysterious

it will sometimes be represented, that the three persons are three sets of attributes inhering in a common substance; in which method, the three intelligences come to their unity in a virtually inorganic ground; for if the substance supposed, be itself of a vital quality, a life, then we have only more difficulties on hand, and not fewer; viz., to conceive a Living Person having in Himself, first, the attributes of a person, and secondly, three more persons who are attributes, in the second degree,–that is, attributes of attributes. It can hardly be supposed that any such monster is intended, in the way of bringing the three persons into unity; therefore, taking the "substance" as inorganic, we have three vital personal Gods, and back of them, or under them as their ground of unity, an Inorganic Deity. I make no objection here to the supposition, that the persons are mere attributes of a substance not themselves; I ask not how attributes can be real enough to make persons, and not real enough to make substances; I urge it not as an objection, that our very idea of person, as the word is here used, is that of a living substance manifested through attributes–itself the most real and substantial thing to thought in the universe of God–I only call attention to the fact that this theory of divine unity, making it essentially inorganic, indicates such a holding of the three persons as virtually leaves no unity at all, which is more distinct than a profession of mental confusion on the subject."; also p. 134, "They [the worshippers] are practically at work, in their thoughts, to choose between the three; sometimes actually and decidedly preferring one to another; doubting how to adjust their mind in worship; uncertain, often, which of the three to obey; turning away, possibly, from one in a feeling of dread that might well be called aversion; devoting themselves to another, as the Romanist to his patron saint. This, in fact, is polytheism, and not the clear, simple love of God."

[16] *God in Christ,* p. 133; Bushnell described this theory: ". . . the three are sometimes compared, in their union, to the soul, the life principle and the body united in one person called a man–an illustration, which, if it has any point or appositeness, at all, shows how God may be one and not three; for the life and the body are not persons. Or, if the soul be itself the life, and the body is external development, which is possible, then, in a yet stricter sense, there is but one person in them all." Cf. also *Christ in Theology* (Being the Answer of the Author before the Hartford Central Association of Ministers, October 1849, for the doctrines of the book entitled *God in Christ*), pp. 140 ff. Bushnell criticized the position of "three metaphysical persons" by saying, *God in Christ,* pp. 134–135: ". . . though they are all declared to be infinite and equal, they really are not so. The proper deity of Christ is not held in this view. He is begotten, sent, supported, directed, by the Father, in such a sense as really annihilates his deity."

and peculiar *communication* of the other, or how does it appear that there is any difference, there is no living man, I am quite sure, who can invent an answer.[17]

The question remained, however: "How shall we resolve the divinity or deity of Christ . . . so as to make it consist with the proper unity of God?" There are two factors that must be dealt with, Bushnell said: first, the fact of the essential unity and supremacy of God, and second, the fact of a person who walked the earth, in human form, Jesus Christ, who was "a subject, suffering being." The highest and truest reality of this person Jesus Christ is that He is God, so Bushnell insisted.

The methodological principle Bushnell asserted regarding his investigation of the Trinity was: "The Trinity we seek will be a trinity that results of necessity from the *revelation* of God to man." Bushnell did *not* want to attempt to fathom the interior being of God, which he felt he could not do, and which he doubted was possible for anyone to do. He began by assuming the strictest unity and simplicity of God's nature. God could not be revealed to us, Bushnell said, without "evolving a trinity of persons." These persons or personalities are the *dramatis personae* of revelation. Their uniqueness is measured by the aspect of the infinite God which they convey to man. These persons are related to the Godhead, but are also related to our human capacities and needs. They are "that presentation of God which is necessary to make Him a subject of thought." [18] They are, therefore, necessary to produce mutuality between man and God, and to convey best His love to our feeling and experience. For this reason, Bushnell said, that God unrevealed was God existing simply as spirit and in Himself. God, before any "revealment," is the Absolute Being, the Infinite, the I Am that I am. He gives no sign that He is, other than that He is! God has no external form and has no activity. He may not be known by any color, sound, sign, or measure. He does not act or react as we do, neither does he deliberate, inquire, nor remember, believe, nor think, nor have emotions. This fact about God may be "a very unsatisfactory, unpleasant, unsignificant, and practically untrue representation of God," Bushnell remarked. But it must be this way. Without a Trinity, and an Incarnation, and a Revelation, God cannot be known.

[17] *God in Christ*, p. 135.
[18] *Ibid.*, p. 137.

III. *The Mode of Revelation*

When God decides to reveal Himself, He cannot be revealed as the One, the Infinite or the Absolute, but can only be revealed through human media. There are no infinite media through which he could make himself known. Therefore, it was necessary for the One to appear in the manifold; the Absolute to appear in the conditional; the Spirit in form; the Motionless in motion; the Infinite in the finite. Bushnell clarified this essential point:

> He must distribute Himself, He must let forth His nature in sounds, colors, forms, works, definite objects and signs. It must be to us as if Brama were waking up; as if Jehovah, the Infinite I am, the Absolute, were dividing off Himself into innumerable activities that shall dramatize His immensity, and bring Him within the molds of language and discursive thought. And in whatever thing He appears, or is revealed, there will be something that misrepresents, as well as something that represents Him. The revealing process, that which makes Him appear, will envelop itself in clouds of formal contradiction—that is, of diction which is contrary, in some way, to the truth, and which, taken simply as diction, is continually setting forms against each other.[19]

Thus the God who is revealed will move, make utterances, think, have emotions, and so forth. Only in this way is it possible for man to receive knowledge of Him. But this reception of knowledge will be limited by the degree of the finite's ability to receive knowledge of the Infinite. God can never be known until He is brought into our finite "molds of action." God is by definition a *Being* outside of man; a Being in whom the possibilities of every other being has its origin. Bushnell wrote:

> Taken in this view, as the absolute, all-comprehensive, being, we can know Him only *as* being; that is, by a revelation, or rather by revelations, giving out one after another, and in one way or another, but always in finite forms, something that belongs to the knowledge of God.[20]

In order for God to "generate" in us a knowledge of Himself, He must produce Himself in finite forms. Man's knowledge of God, therefore, is always a knowledge which involves the finite forms by which we know anything.[21] Bushnell illustrated this point by refer-

[19] *Ibid.*, p. 140.
[20] *Ibid.*, p. 141.
[21] *Ibid.*, p. 142; cf., "So, when we pray for the Holy Spirit, it is for the descent of the Holy Spirit–not that there is any descent or motion in the case; we only

ence to the Jewish state. The whole universe is a part of a theocracy, he said, but in Israel, a special theocracy is created. This was done in order to demonstrate the contrasts which exist between Israel and the universal theocracy.[22] In this way, God is revealed. God is the God of Egypt, Babylon and Philistia, as well as of Israel, but, for the benefit of all the nations, He selected Israel to be His people. They received a special discipline from Him, and by virtue of this discipline a special future. God is therefore considered by the Jews to be superior to the gods of the other nations. All victories in battle are attributed to Him. The final deliverance of the people is something He had brought about. But, this is only a preview of what will happen: "And so He will be known, at length, as the Great God and King above all gods." It is only by means of "relations, contrasts, actions, and reactions" that we come to a knowledge of God. Bushnell compared his method to philosophy: "Our method may be compared to that of resultant motions in philosophy. No one finite thing represents the Absolute Being; but between two or more finite forces acting obliquely on our mind, it is driven out, in a resultant motion, towards the Infinite. Meantime, a part of the two finite forces, being oblique or false, is destroyed by the mutual counteraction of forces."[23] When God is revealed, and if He is "efficiently revealed," Bushnell said, He will still possess an element of obscurity and mystery. He will not be a philosophic unity, which can be perfectly comprehended and measured. God never appears as simply as man might. If this were so, God would be only a larger man and not an Absolute Being. If it were possible for man to understand God perfectly, then it would not be the real God he understood. Rather, He would be all the more unknown. The Infinite can never be revealed away. Bushnell assured his readers: "But if we could see the last boundaries of God, and hold Him clear of a question

work our thought under the great law of action and reaction, which belongs to the finite quality of our nature."
[22] *Ibid.*, p. 143; Bushnell carried this idea of contrasts to the scripture writers; "The scripture writers, too, are continually working this figure of contrast, even setting God, if we compare their representations, in a kind of antagonism with Himself. Here, for example, is the great and broad sea–full of His goodness. Here it is a raging monster, whose proud and turbulent waves it is the glory of His majesty to hold in check. In one case, the sea represents Him. In the other, He is seen triumphing over His representative. Just so in the heavens, which, at one time, are His very garment; while at another, it is half His grandeur, that He sits upon the great circle above them, to mold and sway their motions."
[23] *Ibid.*, p. 144.

within the molds of logic and cognition, then He is not God any longer, we have lost the conception of God."

The reason that man can know God is because there is in God "a capacity of self-expression." God possesses a generative power of form and a creative imagination. By the implementation of these factors, He can produce Himself outwardly, and represent Himself in finite modes of being. Bushnell designated this God as the Logos, the Word, the Form of God. The Form of God is God "mirrored before His own understanding." As He is thus mirrored, He is mirrored in fragments before us. God "bodies" Himself in this manner: He "represents, expresses, or outwardly produces Himself."

Bushnell made it quite clear that God had appeared already in the human race, even though in fragmented form:

> The human person, taken as a mere structure, adapted to the high uses of intelligence and moral action, is itself a noble illustration of His wisdom, and a token also of the exalted and good purposes cherished in our existence. But there was yet more of God to be exhibited in the Human Form of our race. As the spirit of man is made in the image of God, and his bodily form is prepared to be the fit vehicle and outward representative of his spirit, if follows that his bodily form has also some inherent, *a priori* relation to God's own nature; such probably as makes it the truest, most expressive finite type of Him. Continuing, therefore, in a pure upright character, our whole race would have been a visible revelation of the truth and beauty of God.[24]

However, the whole race of mankind, which was to be an expression of God, became instead an expression of evil: "Truth has no longer any living unblemished manifestation in the world . . . Sin, prejudice, passion,—stains of every color—so deface and mar the race, that the face of God, the real glory of the Divine, is visible no longer." God, however, will reclaim what was lost, and will live in the "biographic history" of the world.[25]

But, before this general manifestation of God in history, there had been no revelation of the trinity in the appearances God made of Himself. But there is then the culmination or completion of revelation of God:

> Just here, accordingly, as the revelation culminates or completes the fullness of its form, many are staggered and confused by difficulties which

[24] *Ibid.*, pp. 146, 147.
[25] *Ibid.*, p. 147; Bushnell used the passage "And the word was made flesh, and dwelt among us; and we beheld his glory as the only begotten of Father, full of grace and truth," to support his argument.

they say are contrary to reason—impossible therefore to faith. I think otherwise. In these three persons or impersonations I see only a revelation of the Absolute Being, under just such relatives as by their mutual play, in and before our imaginative sense, will produce in us the truest knowledge of God—render Him most conversable, bring Him closest to feeling, give Him the freest, least obstructed access, as a quickening power, to our hearts.[26]

Bushnell was always conscious that he had to deal specifically with the doctrine of the Incarnation, and the problems presented by this doctrine, to verify his position on the Trinity. This was necessary because of the difficulties created by the relationship of the divine to the human in the person of Jesus Christ, and because of those difficulties which were implied by the relationship of His divine person to the other divine persons in the course of the process of revelation.

The first problem that Bushnell dealt with was the assertion that it is "an insult to reason" to assert an Incarnation of the divine nature, i. e., to say that the Infinite God is represented as dwelling in a finite human person, which is subject to its limitations and its evils. Bushnell attempted to respond to this difficulty by referring to several other religions which have believed or anticipated an Incarnation of their deity. If there have been these instances of belief in an Incarnation in the history of mankind, then it "would not seem to be wholly cross to natural reason to believe in such an event." Bushnell believed that there was a "true instinct" or "conscious want" on the part of the human race to receive a visitation of the Deity.[27]

The second difficulty Bushnell dealt with was the problem of the relationship of the human person who was "originally and specially related to the expression of God," and the revelation of God in history as Divine love. If we believe, said Bushnell, that the "human person will express more of God than the whole created universe," then is it any more absurd to believe that "the Word was made flesh?" The revelation of God in history becomes "much lovelier and holier as it exhibits more of His moral excellence and grandeur —His condescension, patience, gentleness, forgiveness, in one word, His love."

[26] *Ibid.,* p. 148.
[27] *Ibid.,* p. 149; Bushnell believed that the instances of belief in the Incarnation found in the history of man's religion is an evidence of "cultivated" forms of false religion.

Bushnell conceived of the revelation of Christ in the following way:

I am speaking, also, to such as believe the scriptures; and, therefore, it should be something to notice that they often represent the Saviour in ways that indicate the same view of his person: He is Emanuel, God with us—the Word made flesh—God manifest in the flesh—the express image of his person—the Life that was manifested—the glass in which we look to behold the glory of the Lord—the fullness of God revealed bodily—the power of God—the light of the knowledge of the glory of God in the face of Jesus Christ—the image of the invisible God. In all these, and in a very great number of similar instances, language is used in reference to Christ, which indicates an opinion that his advent is the appearing of God; his deepest reality, that he expresses the fulness of the Life of God.[28]

Christ is therefore more than a good man, or even a perfect man. The "hinge of the gospel" is Jesus Christ, who is the image of God, shining unto men. But, one might also object by asserting that the human person is limited, but God is not. Bushnell maintained that is was our knowledge of God which was limited. For us, it is incredible that God should take on human form to express himself. It is simply a matter of human limitation that we have difficulty conceiving of the Infinite becoming finite for us.

How do we respond when it is said that Christ is a living and intelligent person, who must, therefore, be seen in terms of the limitations belonging to a person? But, Bushnell reminded us, man does not have the right to measure the contents of Christ's person by his body: "A finite outward person, too, may as well be an organ or type of the Infinite as a finite thing or object; and God may act a human personality, without being measured by it, as well as to shine through a finite thing or a world, without being measured by that."[29]

How, then, do we deal with the assertion that Christ grows in wisdom and knowledge during his life? Such an assertion presupposed some kind of intellectual development, which implied in itself a limitation upon the person of Christ. Bushnell answered this difficulty in the following way: 1) "the language may well enough be taken as language of external description merely, or as only setting forth appearance as appearance"; or, 2) "the body of Christ evidently grew up from infancy; and that all his actings grew out . . .

---

[28] *Ibid.*, p. 150.
[29] *Ibid.*, p. 152.

with it; and if the divine was manifested in the ways of a child, it creates no difficulty which does not exist when it is manifested in the ways of a man or a world." [30] Bushnell believed that the question was whether it were possible for the divine to be revealed in the human. If it were possible, then there was no problem to assert that humanity grew and developed.

Nonetheless, there are other difficulties involved in the doctrine of the Incarnation. The Unitarians [31] insisted that Christ acts in such a manner that He demonstrates quite plainly that his internal nature is under a limitation. Therefore they maintain that He is only human. The Trinitarian believer, in order to counterattack the Unitarian argument, asserted that Jesus had a human soul, and it was only in the soul that any limitation was apparent. But the same Trinitarian Christian went on to say that Christ also had a divine soul which escaped all limitations. Bushnell rejected both of these positions. To assert that there was "a certain human soul called Jesus, born as such of Mary, obeyed and suffered," was to destroy the Scriptural witness of Christ. The New Testament maintained rather boldly, said Bushnell, "that he who was in the form of God, humbled himself and became obedient unto death, even the death of the cross." For Bushnell, the New Testament was extremely lucid when it reported that "He was in the Form of God." This meant that real divinity came into the finite and was subject to human conditions. It is the whole Christ, the Son, the Divine one, who is represented as being humbled, made weak, as divested of His glory, who existed under the limitations or conditions that do not belong to Deity. Bushnell could not find any support for the common Trinitarian theory of two distinct or distinctly active subsistences in the person of Christ. The theory, furthermore, denied the meaning of the Incarnation; i. e., "the union signified, and historically begun between God and man." Bushnell was adamant when he wrote:

The reality of Christ is what he expresses of God, not what he is in his physical conditions, or under his human limitations. He is here to express the Absolute Being, especially His feeling, His love to man, His placableness, conversableness, and His real union to the race; in a word, to communicate His own Life to the race, and graft Himself historically to it. Therefore, when we see him thus under the conditions of increase, obedience, worship, suffering, we have nothing to do but to ask what

[30] *Ibid.*
[31] *Ibid.*, p. 153; this reference indicated Bushnell's constant battle with the Unitarians; cf. also *Christ in Theology*, p. 128.

is here expressed, and, as long as we do that, we shall have no difficulty. But if we insist on being more curious, viz., on understanding the composition of the person of Jesus, and the relations of the infinite to the finite in his person, we can create as much of difficulty as we please.[32]

The person of Jesus was given to us, Bushnell said, to communicate God and His love to us. It cannot be a matter which one can investigate psychologically or physiologically, because the question of Christ's person does not lie within the categories of ordinary, natural humanity. Rather, Bushnell suggested, that one should receive what has been expressed by God in Christ than try to ascertain the make-up of the Christ. We are not to fool ourselves into believing that we can fathom the nature of Christ's person:

See, they say, Christ obeys and suffers, how can the subject be the supreme; the suffering man, the impassible God! Probably they toss off their discovery with an air of superior sagacity, as if by some peculiar depth of argument they had reached a conclusion so profound. They cannot imagine that even the babes of true knowledge, the simple children of Christian faith, who open their hearts to the reconciling grace of God in Christ Jesus, are really wiser and deeper than they. As if it were some

[32] *Ibid.,* pp. 154–157; Bushnell was vehement in his denial of the theory of two subsistencies. ". . . this theory of two distinct subsistencies, still maintaining their several kinds of action in Christ,–one growing, learning, obeying, suffering; the other infinite and impassible–only creates difficulties a hundred fold greater than any that it solves. It virtually denies any real unity between the human and the divine, and substitutes collocation or copartnership for unity. If the divine part were residing in Saturn, he would be as truly united with the human race as now. Instead of a person whose nature is the real unity of the divine and the human, we have two distinct persons, between whom our thoughts are continually alternating; referring this to one, that to the other, and imagining, all the while, not a union of the two, in which our possible union with God is signified and sealed forever, but a practical, historical assertion rather of his incommunicableness, thrust upon our notice, in a form more oppressive and chilling than it has to abstract thought. Meantime the whole work of Christ, as a subject, suffering Redeemer, is thrown upon the human side of his nature, and the divine side standing thus aloof, incommunicably distant, has nothing in fact to do with the transaction, other than to be a spectator of it. And then, while we are moved to ask of what so great consequence to us, or to the government of God, can be the obedience and suffering of this particular man Jesus, more than of any other, it is also represented, as part of the same general scheme, that he is, after all, scarcely more than a mere nominal man–that he is so removed from the fortunes and the proper trial of a man, by the proximity of the divine, as not even to unfold a human character! And thus, while the redemption even of the world is hung upon his human passibilities, he is shown, as a man, to have probably less of human significance than any other; to be a man whose character is not in himself, but in the custody that keeps him from being himself!"

special wisdom to judge that the Lord Jesus came into the world, not simply to express God, and offer Him to the embrace of our love, but to submit a new riddle to the speculative chemistry and constructive logic of the race! Indeed, you may figure this whole tribe of sophisters as a man standing before that most beautiful and wondrous work of art, the "Beatified Spirit" of Guido, and there commencing a quarrel with the artist, that he should be so absurd as to think of making a beatified spirit out of mere linseed, ochres, and oxides! Would it not be more dignified to let the pigments go and take the expression of the canvas? Just so are the human personality, the obedient, subject, suffering state of Jesus, all to be taken as colors of the Divine, and we are not to fool ourselves in practicing our logic on the colors, but to seize, at once, upon the divine import and significance thereof; ascending thus to the heart of God, there to rest, in the vision of His beatific glory.[33]

Nonetheless, Bushnell did not want us to believe something which was contradictory or absurd. But, we can believe, he said, "things that, taken in their form, are contrary one to the other—contrary in diction." The highest and most divine truths are often expressed in this way, he said. Oftentimes, this is the only way that divine truth can be communicated. Bushnell gave the example of the Gospel of John, which he said was the most contradictory book in the world, "one in which logic can make just what havoc it will—and this, because it is a book which embodies more of the highest and holiest forms of truth than any other."[34] This book discloses the divine mission of Christ, which is, as Bushnell said, "to express God ... to let all the repugnant terms pour their contents into our thought and feeling, suffering whatever of repugnance there is in the vehicles to fall off and be forgotten—just as in the viewing of a picture, the colors that are used to make shades, and thus to develop the forms, are disregarded and rejected when you consider the matter of complexion; or just as the flatness of the canvas is not insisted on, as contrary to the roundness of the forms; or just

---

[33] *Ibid.*, pp. 158–160, cf., "It is as if Abraham, after he had entertained as a guest the Jehovah angel, or angel of the Lord, instead of receiving his message, had fallen to inquiring into the digestive process of the angel; or, since he came in human form and spoke with a human voice, whether he had a human soul or not; and, if so, how the two natures were put together! Let alone thy folly and thy shallow curiosity, O Abraham! we should say, hear the Lord speak to thee; what he commands thee, do, what he promises, believe! Suspend thy raw guesses at His nature, and take His message!; again, making reference to Moses, "Instead of putting off their shoes before the burning bush, they would put out the fire rather– ..."

[34] *Ibid.*, p. 160.

as you disregard everything else, when you come to the moral expression, and offer your simple feeling to that, as the living truth of all." [35] We are to consider Christ's obedience in the same way, Bushnell said. We are not so much to consider the nature of the obedience itself, but rather what it expresses and signifies. In a similar way, when we speak of the "worship paid by Christ," Bushnell asked whether we can think of anything more clear than the Christ, who expressed what was perfect in God through the human.

The nature of the divine-human union in Christ remained a mystery for Bushnell. He insisted that one could not fathom the inner nature of God. However, he said that when one spoke about the sufferings and death of Christ, one should look at and see what the sufferings and death expressed: "The only question is, whether God, by a mysterious union with the human, can so far employ the element of His own Grace and Tenderness—whether, indeed, God can be allowed, in any way, to exhibit those Passive Virtues which are really the most active and sublimest of all virtues; because they are most irresistable, and require the truest greatness of spirit." [36] The agony of the garden and the passion of the cross prohibited, for Bushnell, the assumption of the Unitarians that God could not be connected with suffering. It also ruled out the usual Trinitarian assertion that there were two distinct natures in Christ, and it was only the human nature which suffered. We cannot intrude into the interior of God's mysteries, Bushnell insisted.[37] We are only to see the eternal Life approach our race. We can see, "Divine Love manifested and sealed; the Law sanctified by obedience unto death; pardon certified by the 'Father Forgive'; peace established and testified by the resurrection from the dead." Christ is that Holy Being in which "my God is brought to me," affirmed Bushnell. What is essential is that "I receive him in the simplicity of faith, as my one Lord and Savior." The Incarnation is not an isolated event in the history of mankind. It is a part of the grand and systematic work, which God had been directing in the history of the human race, ever since the world began.

[35] *Ibid.,* pp. 160–161.
[36] *Ibid.,* p. 162.
[37] *Ibid.;* cf. p. 163.

155

IV. Divine Logos

Bushnell next dealt with those difficulties involved in the relationship of Christ to the Father and the Holy Spirit.[38] He found that nowhere in the Scriptures was God mentioned as the Father until the coming of Christ.

There is, in fact, no real and proper development of the Father, which is older than Christianity, and here the designation is developed in connection with the Son and Holy Spirit as a threefold denomination of God. And this threefold denomination, again, (as I think must be evident), is itself incidental to, and produced by the central fact, or mystery of the incarnation, as an impersonation of God developed in time.[39]

He continued:

Thus, the Divine Word, or Logos, who is from eternity the Form or in the Form of God, after having first bodied Him forth in the creation and the government of the world, now makes another outgoing from the Absolute into the human, to reside in the human as being of it; thus to communicate God to the world, and thus to ingenerate in the world Goodness and Life as from Him. To make His approach to man as close, to identify Himself as perfectly as possible with man, he appears, or makes His advent through a human birth—Son of man, and Son, also, of God. Regarding him now in this light as set out before the Absolute Being, (who he representatively is,) existing under the conditions of the finite and the relative, we see at once that, for our sakes, if not for his own, he must have set over against him, in the finite, his appropriate relative term, or impersonation.[40]

---

[38] *Ibid.*, p. 167; cf. Bushnell's projected work on the Holy Spirit, *Inspiration by the Holy Spirit,* found in *The Spirit of Man,* pp. 3–55.

[39] This fact, wrote Bushnell, destroyed the Unitarian and Sabellian theory of the nature of God in relation to His revelation. Cf. *God in Christ,* pp. 167–168; cf. also *Christ in Theology,* p. 128, where Bushnell denied the Sabellian position.

[40] *God in Christ,* p. 168; cf. *Christ in Theology,* pp. 131 f., for a further discussion and clarification of *logos:* "I certainly supposed that every Christian scholar was so far acquainted with the historic doctrine of the Logos, as to know that so much is conceded, on all hands, and that when I spoke in this way, I was only referring to the fact thus conceded, that there is, at the least, a something in the divine nature called the Word, which is the fountain (whatever may be said of personality) of all the forms of things, and, in that sense, the medium of the creation of the worlds; something which is to the outward, in expression, what the inward life of God is to his being–a Form of God, a Mirror of Creative Imagination, in which he beholds and through which he may body forth images of this thought, or an 'express image of his person.'" Cf. also the sermon "Present Relations of Christ with his Followers," *Christ and His Salvation,* pp. 331–350, and even the sermon, "The Spirit in Man," *Sermons for the New Life,* pp. 29–49.

When Christ appeared in the human state, said Bushnell, and brought the divine into the human, there resulted, at one and the same time, a double "impersonation" of the Father and the Son. Both were "correspondent or relative terms." As Christ appeared in the finite, he called another representation of the Absolute into the finite, one that was conceived to reside in the heavens, as he himself was seen to walk upon the earth.

Therefore, he calls out into thought, as residing in heaven, and possessing celestial exaltation, the Father, who is, in fact, the Absolute Being brought into a lively, conversible, definite (therefore finite) form of personal conception, and sets himself on terms of relationship with him at the other pole; so that, while he signifies, or reveals the light and love of God, in and through the human or subject life, he is able to exalt and deify what he reveals, by referring his mission to one that is greater and higher in state than himself, viz., the Father in heaven.[41]

Bushnell discovered that Christ never said: "I came forth from the One, the Absolute; from Him that dwells above time, silent, never moving, without parts, or emotions." Christ gave us instead the conception of an active, choosing, feeling Spirit, which prompted Him to say: "I came forth from the Father." Nonetheless, there is an intimation of a *connection* between the Father and the Son because Christ can say: "My Father is greater than I." Furthermore, Christ expressed the essentially divine nature of His person when He referred to Himself and the Father as one and when He said: "He that hath seen me, hath seen the Father." But Christ added an element of mystery when He reported: "No man knoweth the Son but the Father, neither knoweth any man the Father, save the Son, and he to whosoever the Son will reveal him." The process of revelation is disclosing, but there remains an element of mystery to it all.

Meantime, it is by setting ourselves before this personal history of the Father in heaven, and the Son on earth, both as representatives standing out before the Absolute Being, watching the relative history they unfold in finite forms, their acting and interacting, and discovering what is expressed thereby,—cleared of all the repugnant and contradictory matter that is attributable to the vehicle, in distinction from the truth—it is thus that we are to ascend, as by a resultant of the two forces, into a lively realization, and a free, spiritual embrace of God, as our Friend, Redeemer, Peace, and Portion.[42]

[41] *God in Christ,* p. 169.
[42] *Ibid.,* pp. 170, 171.

There is, said Bushnell, the Logos in the creation, and also the Logos in the Incarnation. By means of these, God's character and personality are expressed. "He has," Bushnell wrote, "brought down the mercies of His Heart to meet us on our human level." The expression of God in revelation is moral.

But Bushnell believed that we did not have a complete apprehension of God at this point. In order to receive such a conception of God, a third personality, or the Holy Spirit, must appear. Another kind of expression, another distinct kind of impersonation of the Godhead is necessary to complete our understanding of God. We want to conceive of God, Bushnell said, "as in *act* within us, working in us, under the conditions of time and progression, spiritual results of quickening, deliverance, and purification from evil." Bushnell insisted upon this conception of the third person of the Trinity. Bushnell was impressed with the idea of "God's indwelling" within the human spirit. God must be given to man by another *finite* and *relative impersonation,* he said. This manifestation of God must occur in time and space. Thus, the Spirit of God is "clothed" with personality and activity.[43] The word "Spirit," Bushnell said, had been used before, but it had always referred to the "agency" of God. However, it had not been used before in the sense of divine personality or impersonation. The Holy Spirit is to be conceived of in the following way:

Now, the Divine Power, in souls, is to be developed under the form of a personal Sanctifier, related, in a personal way, to the Father and the Son, as they to each other. He is conceived, sometimes, as sent by the Father; sometimes, as proceeding from the Father and the Son; sometimes as shed forth from the Son in his exaltation; always as a Divine Agency, procured by the Son, and representing, in the form of an operation within us, that grace which he reveals as feeling and intention towards us.[44]

Bushnell clarified his definition:

Now, the Absolute Being, of whom we could predicate no motion or proceeding, becomes a Vital Presence, residing ever with us, to work in

[43] *Ibid.,* p. 172; "The word signifies air in motion, and as air is invisible, it becomes the symbol or type of unseen power exerted–quite transcendently, however, as regards our comprehension; for there is really no motion whatever." Bushnell referred to the activity of the Spirit "coming in a rushing, mighty wind; tipping the heads of an assembly with lambent flames; evidencing his power in souls, by opening the lips of men, and playing those utterances which are, themselves, expressions of the mind within; endowing men with gifts above their human capacity."
[44] *Ibid.,* p. 172.

us all that we need, and strengthen us to that which none but a divine power can support. What we should not dare to hope, and could not otherwise conceive—the Eternal Life, declared and manifested by Christ, liveth in us.[45]

V. *Plurality of Persons*

Bushnell is prepared now to describe the Trinity. There are three persons, or impersonations, all of whom exist under finite conditions, and which are expressed in human terms. They are relative persons, but taken representatively, they are infinites, because they stand for the Infinite. Each of them imparts something of God to us. By means of these relative concepts, therefore, we are elevated to proximity with God, who remains above our finite conceptions of Him. Bushnell summarized his position regarding the operations of the Trinity:

> The Father plans, presides, and purposes for us; the Son expresses his intended mercy, proves it, brings it down even to the level of a fellow feeling; the Spirit works within us the beauty he reveals, and the glory beheld in his Life. The Father sends the Son, the Son delivers the grace of the Father; the Father dispenses, and the Son procures the Spirit; the Spirit proceeds from the Father and Son, to fulfill the purpose of one, and the expressed feeling of the other; each and all together dramatize and bring forth into life about us that Infinite One, who, to our mere thought, were no better than Brama sleeping on eternity and the stars. Now, the sky, so to speak, is beginning to be full of Divine Activities, heaven is married to earth, and earth to heaven, and the Absolute Jehovah, whose nature we before could nowise comprehend, but dimly know, and yet more dimly feel, has, by these outgoings, waked up in us, all living images of His love and power and presence, and set the whole world in a glow.[46]

Bushnell found that the Holy Scriptures spoke of "a three-fold-ness," within the nature of God, which, he said, was a "vitalizing element offered to our souls." It was the instrument needed for man to ascend to the true greatness of God. We must not object to the term person used in reference to "threefoldness," he said, because the three persons of the Trinity appear under the grammatical forms appropriate to person. But we can never assign an interior, metaphysical nature to the three divine persons. The persons of the

[45] *Ibid.*, pp. 172, 173.
[46] *Ibid.*, pp. 173, 174.

Trinity have reality as they express "the wording forth of God." This is, therefore, what Bushnell called an Instrumental Trinity. The persons of the Trinity are, therefore, Instrumental Persons. Bushnell was most interested in showing that by means of these living persons, or impersonations, the Infinite One was brought down to the level of humanity. But, Bushnell insisted that there was to be no loss of God's greatness or reduction of His majesty in the process.[47]

Bushnell allowed a few years to elapse (1848—1851)[48] before answering the critics of his book *God in Christ*. He did so in his book, *Christ in Theology*, which was his answer to the charge brought before him. The book was directed to the Hartford Central Association of Ministers. He began by saying: "The time appears to have come when the heat of controversy and the pressure of assault are exhausted, and I publish now simply as regarding the truth." But it was not orthodox truth that Bushnell was concerned with. Rather, he insisted that he was not orthodox, according to any precise type of orthodoxy that he knew. However, Bushnell recognized that he was much closer to "real orthodoxy" than he had before believed, and that New England theology was much farther away from it

---

[47] *Ibid.*, p. 175; cf. *Christ in Theology*, pp. 130 ff, for a discussion of the charge of heresy regarding "an instrumental trinity." Cf. *The Spirit in Man*, pp. 78 ff; p. 201.

[48] *God in Christ*, p. 175. Reviews of *God in Christ* were found in *Biblical Repository*, (1849), *The New Englander Magazine*, (May 1848); three articles signed "Omicron" (gathered later into a pamphlet, entitled, "What Does Dr. Bushnell Mean?"), *New York Evangelist* (1848); *Biblical Repertory and Princeton Review*, (1848, also 1853); *Christian Observatory*, III (June 1849), Enoch Pond, "Review of Dr. Bushnell's *God in Christ*," (1849); also Charles Hodge, *Essays and Reviews*, (Bangor, 1849). Cf. Theodore Munger, *Horace Bushnell, Preacher and Theologian*, (Boston: Houghton, Mifflin and Co., 1899), Chapter IX, "Days of Accusation," especially pp. 142-148. The anguish which the proposed heresy trial effected in Bushnell is revealed very lucidly in his letters to the Rev. C. A. Bartol, a Boston Unitarian. Bushnell resolved not to be drawn into any controversy, "unless," as he said, "there is produced against me some argument of so great force that I feel myself required out of simple duty to the truth, either to surrender or to make important modifications in the views I have advanced," Munger, p. 145. The Rev. Mr. Amos S. Chesebrough, in a series of letters to the *Religious Herald*, which were signed C. C. (*Criticus Criticorum*), raised the question whether Bushnell was being understood correctly. These letters were published later in a pamphlet entitled *Contributions of C. C., Now Declared in full as Criticus Criticorum*, (by request), (Hartford: Brown and Parsons, 1849);

Cf. also, *Appeal of the Association of Fairfield West to the Associated Ministers connected with The General Association of Connecticut*, published by Baker, Goodwin and Co., (New York: 1852); and Edwin Pond Parker, *The Hartford Central Association and the Bushnell Controversy*, (Hartford, 1896).

than its theologians supposed. Bushnell had a real distaste for the word "orthodoxy," and considered it to be "characteristically un-christian." [49]

Bushnell reiterated his belief that no proper solution to the problem of the Trinity was possible. He, however, did attempt to account for "the external fact of trinity," and showed that God, the

[49] *Christ in Theology,* pp. IV–VI; he continued: "I have no victory to gain, and I see not that I have any to fear. As little have my brethren, who have been disturbed by my heresies. Whatever is now to be gained must be gained by truth and lost by error, and with that we may all be content." Bushnell referred to the theological battles of his day; "To see brought up, in distinct array before us, the multitudes of leaders and schools and theologic wars of only the century past,–the Supralapsarians, and Sublapsarians; the Arminianizers, and the true Calvinists; the Pelagians, and Augustinians; the Tasters, and the Exercisers; Exercisers by Divine Efficiency and by human Self-Efficiency; the love-to-being-in-general virtue, the willing-to-be-damned virtue, and the love-to-one's-greatest happiness virtue; no ability, all ability, and moral and natural ability distinguished; disciples by the new-creating act of Omnipotence, and by change of the governing purpose; atonement by punish-ment, and by expression; limited, and general; by imputation, and without imputation; trinitarians of a threefold distinction, of three psychologic persons, or of three sets of attributes; under a unity of oneness, or of necessary agree-ment, or of society and deliberative council;–nothing I think would more certainly disenchant us of our confidence in systematic orthodoxy, and the possibility, in human language, of an exact theologic science, than an exposition so practical and serious and withal so indisputably mournful,–so mournfully indisputable."

Also, *Christ in Theology,* p. 12: "Real orthodoxy," referred, for Bushnell, to the orthodoxy of the Reformation which is "connected with the previous times reaching back to the Nicene era." Cf. also pp. 71, 83.

Cf. also p. 13; Bushnell said in addition, "It [orthodoxy] presents an issue, not of truth, but of opinion, representing, as the word signifies on its face, that opinion may be a fit standard of Christian straitness or correctness; which, I do not hesitate to say, is a plain affront to that first and fundamental principle of the Christian doctrine, which disallows the test of mere natural judgment or opinion, and refers all truth to its final adjudication before the higher court of faith and spiritual discernment." See also p. 22: "And here, in the fate of this particular doctrine or dogma, you have, in small, a good illustration of all the wars of theology. We can not allow the Christian truth to hold those forms which are necessary to its expression; we must be more scientific; we must convert the forms into abstractions, overlay the abstractions with logical in-ferences, build the inferences into schemes and systems, and these we call doctrine or theology. Nothing was ever able to stand that was built in this way; but there is one remarkable advantage accruing to comfort us, that in so many dialectic buildings and destructions, our mind is sharpened, by what we suffer, to a closer, keener inspection of the forms of truth, and gradually convinces itself, by its own miscarriages, that real truth is to be found only by insight, and never by the extempore clatter of logical judgments. We seem, in this manner to be gravitating slowly toward the true position. Perhaps we shall sometime reach a point where God can teach us." Cf. also pp. 74 ff; and what Bushnell said about the creeds, p. 78.

Absolute One, revealed Himself to man in terms of the finite. This was necessary because the nature of language required it, he said. The process of revelation necessarily involved antagonistic symbols and pluralities of person. But the Trinitiy of the New Testament demands it, said Bushnell. The external fact of trinity did not permit one to pass over into the divine nature itself and attempt to show how the instrumental three of revelation were related to its interior distribution. This one could not do. The object of the instrumental three of revelation was "to give us the One," that is, to show us the One engaged in forms of action which were necessary for our redemption from sin. But the instrumental nature of revelation could not inform us about the transcendent properties and distributions of the divine substance. The subject of the Trinity was an impossible one, said Bushnell. This was why there were so many controversies regarding it. To attempt to determine a conception of the Trinity as pertaining immanently to the interior nature of God must remain a futile effort. The Trinity of revelation was given man, to use, and not to theorize about: "Any attempt to solve or conceive God's interior mystery, by reasonings cast in the molds and categories of our human consciousness, is presumptuous, possibly even absurd; an attempt, also, to clear that mystery, which it may have been one of the very objects of Scripture to present, as being itself the medium and highest power of expression for the infinite." [50]

Bushnell, in *Christ in Theology*, asserted that his position regarding the Trinity had a number of practical advantages for theology:

First, it assumed the strict unity of the Godhead. It also maintained that God was revealed under conditions of form and number, that is, that the Absolute was revealed by relatives. In the case of Incarnation, revelation took the form of relative persons. The unity of God had to be a fixed and immovable truth. Man received the "Divine Three in terms of love and workship, using them freely as media of thought concerning God and the way af his redeeming mercy."

Second, this was the mode of revelation by which the Trinity could be received by man. It enabled man to see the practical uses of the doctrine of the Trinity, and provoked him to the highest activity of thought concerning God. [51] God remained a mystery to

[50] *Christ in Theology*, p. 120.
[51] See *Building Eras in Religion*, chapter "The Christian Trinity, A Practical Truth," pp. 106–149.

man. But the human mind sought for God and His transcendence. Bushnell wrote: "It is one of the highest merits of the Christian expression of God under a threefold personality, that it would not allow the mind of the world to rest any longer in a conception so easy to thought and, in fact, so nearly finite; but compelled a new toil of exploration, and thus conducted to a new sense of the possibilities included in God and the mystery of finite being." [52]

Third, it showed exactly the location of the mystery of the Divine Three—Christ, the Son, was "God manifest under human conditions," and it was at this point of Incarnation that the Trinity appeared to man. The highest reality and truth of the Three is that they make themselves manifest, but are also the One. Whatever we receive, therefore, in the Trinity is not a knowledge of the One. It is, rather, a residuum of form and number that belongs to the medium and vehicle of truth, and not to the truth itself. Our interpretation of the Trinity must be a "dynamic" one:

> It certainly is more true for us, to take the Three as they are offered, and let them throw us into a maze by their cross relations; and in that maze, if we are in it in faith, longing only to be filled with God, we shall receive the largest possible communication of Him, as a being who can not be placed in the categories of our finite understanding. We shall have Him thus dynamically, or in virtual impression, when we can not make out a proper intellectual conception of Him. Here, then, when we come to the question, what is vehicle and what is truth, we neither affirm nor deny; but we say, here is the place for mystery, and she meets us only where the place for meeting is. We are not offended; we receive her gladly; perceiving in her shaded face and lineaments that, as she is the mother of Modesty, she is the sister also of Truth. [53]

Bushnell recognized, however, a certain "looseness" in his original argument in *God in Christ,* and proposed an elaboration of some major points: [54]

1. The personality of God.

One cannot state anything positive about God, Bushnell said. We can only approximate a conception of Him. But this must be done in a positive, rather than a negative way. We must take up certain

[52] *Christ in Theology,* pp. 123–124; Bushnell insisted that the Trinity remain "an open question forever." Cf. also p. 126.

[53] *Ibid.,* pp. 127, 128; Bushnell felt that such a *modus operandi* saved him from the heresies which had plagued the Christian Church for centuries, that is, as soon as an effort was made to comprehend "the interior mystery of God's nature," miscalculations were possible.

[54] *Ibid.,* pp. 134–177.

elements found in our own consciousness, and impute them to God. But in order to save His infinity, we must deny them again—"not conceiving exactly how much we mean by the denial, or what that Positive Infinite is whose infinity requires the denial." Bushnell gave an example: we discover, he said, that *will* is characteristic of our personality. We therefore ascribe this to God. However, we recognize that the will involves the determination of something which is undertermined, which is, as Bushnell said, "volition issued in time." God does not put forth new purposes in time. His choices and purposes are eternal, and are not part of time. Therefore, in the very act of attributing the will to God, and recognizing that it is an element in our own personality, we must take back the will in order to preserve His infinity. We must add negatives to save His infinity. This is so even when we ascribe to God "moral ideas and excellences." [55]

Is it possible for man to conceive of God?, Bushnell asked. The major problem we face is that God is "Absolute Being existing in himself and affirmed before himself, the infinite I AM." What possible conception can we give to Him? If we project elements of our own consciousness and make them applicable to God, the result is that we have a God subject to human categories, that is, a God of the genus Man. We may have a recognizable God as a result, but He will not be a God who meets the conditions of divine existence. [56] If, on the other hand, we apply negative characteristics to God, then we are left with an impersonal God, "the sleeping Brahma of the East." The idea of a living, acting God is lost. The real value of the Trinity conceived as a supernatural revelation is that it prevents, "our diminishing the One and conceiving Him to be only a man with magnifiers annexed, as in the feeble, undivine notion of a philosophic unity, it presents a Three. To shut away, at the same time, the second error—that which, to escape the first, turns itself toward the doctrine of the Brahmins and conceives Him to be only a vast impersonal abysm, or platitude; or, with the modern pantheists, to be the unconscious principle of an eternal Cosmos—it presents three Persons." [57] The Christian doctrine of the Trinity, by

[55] *Ibid.,* p. 135; the same result is evident if we attribute thought, deliberation, reasoning, invention, memory, emotion, and other characteristics to God.
[56] *Ibid.,* p. 136. Bushnell called such a God "The God of Priestly, a merely humanish, comprehensible unity ..." Cf. also p. 137.
[57] *Ibid.,* p. 137; cf. further, pp. 139, 140; "... when a human soul meets the

its insistence upon number and personality, maintains the conception of a *transcendent* God (who transcends the categories of our human understanding) and a *personal* God (who relates himself in a personal way to man).[58]

2. The unity of God.

Bushnell insisted upon the "strict simplicity" and the "one substance" and the "real unity" of God: "I conceived him as a properly individual being, included under one simply consciousness. And my argument was that, being one, or being thus assumed to be one, plurality of number and person will be involved in the process of his revelation and the work by which he redeems the world."[59] Bushnell rejected categorically the conception of three consciousnesses, wills, and understandings in the Godhead. It is impossible, he said, to insist upon a threeness of person, and at the same time retain any real belief in the divine unity. Bushnell, furthermore, rejected the idea of three distinct sets of attributes inhering in a common substance. He described the problem: "... for the sets of attributes are conceived, each and all, to be persons and not mere fascicles, and the common substance must be also as really a person, else it is only a platform of clay; and then, when the four persons begin to act—to send, go, think, suffer, descend, ascend, and the like, which is the matter to be explained—how will one set of attributes send another, or the person-general send any one of its three extra sets of attributes, without putting them on a distinct action that is not of, or possible, to the common substance?"[60] This solution

revelation of God, who, as the Infinite One, is certainly not within his plane of human thought and conception, and finds Him represented by three persons, which, as forms of thought and conception, are within his plane, would it not be more adequate and wiser to accept these persons rather as surfaces of the Infinite Person, boundaries and types of thought inclosing the vast unknown of solid being, otherwise only a dark, impersonal, unrepresentable abysm? And then, if he continues to say, chanting it ever as the doxology of praise and worship, 'Father, Son, and Holy Ghost,' professing it as his faith that God is three persons and one substance,–is it better for him to say it holding them as planes of description, or to settle it by wise deductions of logic that the planes are the very interior matter and chemistry of the substance?"

[58] *Ibid.*, p. 137; Bushnell referred to Luther, p. 139; " 'Reason (as related to God) is like a line which touches the whole sphere, but only at one point, and does not grasp the whole.' And then he answered not less wisely than wittily for the trinity revealed to faith, by saying, 'When logic objects to this doctrine, that it does not square with its rules, we must say, '*Mulier taceat in ecclesia*'."

[59] *Ibid.*, p. 142.

[60] *Ibid.*, pp. 143–144.

is ridiculous, he asserted. But he also rejected the Deistic and So-
cinian conception of the philosophical unity of God's nature.

As Bushnell affirmed the unity and strict simplicity of God, he
did not, however, exclude every possibility of number in the Godhead. Number, he said, has its *ground* in the divine nature. All
distinctions of law, order, form, genus and family have their root
in God. Bushnell ascribed all distribution of number to God:

> What thougthful soul, cleared of dullness toward what is familiar, and
> turned in its pure longings every way to search after God, has not some-
> time paused in a deep maze of bewilderment over the fact of bisexual
> existence universally observed in the living world, imagining what ground
> there may be, or not be, in God for such a distribution of organic life?
> It can not be said that there was *no* ground for it, save in the act of will
> by which it was appointed; for, in order to be willed, it must first be
> thought, and it could only be thought from eternity, the thoughts of God
> being, in some sense, necessary and coeval with his being.[61]

There is in the divine nature a property called the "Word." This
is an important feature of Bushnell's argument:

> The creation itself was manifestly possible, only on the ground of an
> originative power of Form, from which the created objects and frames
> of order deriving their mold, may issue as a true Cosmos; representing,
> as in a mirror, the thoughts of their Author. And this Word, this For-
> mative Power, is the "Wisdom" that is said to have "been with him in the
> beginning of his way before the works of old," "brought forth" or begotten
> from within "when there was no depth." This Word or Wisdom is next
> declared to have come forth from "the bosom of the Father" and declared
> Him to men; living, in a personal way, among men, as the incarnate Son
> of the Father.[62]

The Father, Son, and Holy Ghost, as persons which are conceptions
essentially finite, are, however, cast in molds derived from our own
personal consciousness. As such, they must be localized above or
below, descending and ascending, moving in space, sending and
being sent, suffering, deliberating, remembering, acting as logical
subjects upon and toward each other. They are all relative in form
to each other, however. As relative they are finite. Then, Bushnell
can assert that there certainly are not three finite persons in the
divine nature, corresponding to the manifestly finite terms or conceptions, Father, Son, and Holy Ghost. The nature of God must

[61] *Ibid.*, pp. 144–145.
[62] *Ibid.*, pp. 145–146.

remain inscrutable. God unrevealed is different from God revealed in the same way that truth is different from symbol. The Trinity proposes a nature transcending our plane of intelligence from a threefold presence in it.

3. Manner of the plurality.

God is represented in the Christian Scriptures by a "plurality" or "threeness." But because God is infinite, and every term or expression we use about Him is finite, what can we except, asked Bushnell, but an array of contrasts beyond the power of comprehension? Bushnell found that the representations of Scripture, and the ways of nature and Providence correspond by revealing God by symbols that are "various and formally repugnant." [63]

Bushnell found that the relation of the three persons could be interpreted in the following way on the basis of the Holy Scriptures: [64]

1. The class of *inequality;* the Father sending the Son and the Spirit; conceived relatively as holding the position of supernatural eminence and authority; declared, in that view, by the Son, to be greater than he,— representations, under countenance of which, the old theologians were accustomed to call the Father *fons trinitatis.*

2. The class of *equality,* demanding for the Son his right to be honored as the Father; quickening whom he will, from life in himself, even as the Father; one with the Father; equal without robbery.

3. The class of *concurrent action;* the Son doing whatsoever he sees the Father do; the grace of the Lord Jesus Christ, and the love of God, and the communion of the Holy Ghost, flowing in a common stream of good.

4. The class which makes the persons *subject and object,* acting terminatively upon or toward each other; the Son conceived by the Holy Ghost; the Father owning the Son at his baptism; the Spirit descending visibly upon him; the Spirit given to him without measure; Jesus breathing and sending the Holy Ghost; the Father hearing the Son; the Son glorifying the Father, ascending to the Father.

5. The class representing *each* to be God; worshipped and accepted in the prerogatives of God.

6. The class representing *all* to be God, as in the baptismal formula.

7. The class which represents the persons, *each to be other and different from each;* the Father loving the Son as other than Himself, giving the Spirit unto him without measure; the Son declaring that he does not his own will, teaches not his own doctrine; or, in a single utterance, repre-

[63] *Ibid.,* p. 152; Bushnell used as an example the passage "the God and Father of all, who is above all, and through all, and in you all"; cf. pp. 152 ff.
[64] *Ibid.,* pp. 155–156.

senting each and all the persons to be other in their mutual relationship; "I will pray the Father and *he* shall give you *another* comforter."

8. The class wherein *each* is represented, by cross affirmations, *to be each of the others.*[65]

The Three, therefore, summarized Bushnell, are "each to be each, as each to be greater or less, or each to be god, or all to be god, or all to be equal, or all concurrent, or all to be mutually subject and object toward each other, or each to be other and different." The Scriptures never acknowledge any restraints of system. They do not keep us within the bounds of a nice logical consistency. On the basis of a true Incarnation, antinomies must of necessity result:

...for the incarnate person, who is God localized in space and a body only *so far as* may serve a special purpose and work, and not absolutely— therefore God in a sense and not God in a sense—will be continually adjusting his position by contrarieties of word and act that correspond with the violent conditions he is under. Unable to conceive the interior mystery of the incarnation itself, we of course can not open the secret interior force and adjust the secret relation of the persons and the contrarious representations under which they appear; but it is something to know that they are offered more to our imagination than to our dialectic faculty; something also to know that the finite-infinite, subject-supreme, earthly-divine, God-man, implied in the simple idea of incarnation itself, must in word and act appear to be inferior, equal, concurrent, subject, God, not God, identical with and other than God the Supreme, or God as inward power and Spirit.[66]

Contradictions may remain in terms of our conception of the Trinity, but we must receive it practically in its true instrumental force: "A dialogue in the plane of our human understanding, through which

[65] Bushnell delineated a little more closely the meaning of the last point, pp. 156–157, "Christ is acknowledged, again and again, as being the Spirit–as when 'the law of the Spirit of life in Christ Jesus' is spoken of, in the eighth of the Romans; also in the frequent interchange of the terms "Christ" and "Spirit", which appears in the verses following, an interchange wholly inadmissible, save on the ground that the terms are, in some proper sense, convertible; also in the words, "the supply of the Spirit of Jesus Christ", "the Spirit of his Son"."

Bushnell alluded to the difficulties of the positions of the Unitarian and New England Trinitarian, pp. 160 ff. Bushnell asked what the Unitarian can do with the association of Christ and the Father under the pronoun "We"; how can the Trinitarian admit that Christ is the Father manifested; the Father, the Spirit, etc.?

[66] *Ibid.*, pp. 158, 159; cf. p. 160, Bushnell rejected "theological dogmatism" which he saw asserted in the following: "When Christ says, 'I will come to you,' which was interpreted to mean 'I will send a third person, who, your theologians will be able to show you, is constructively myself, because he acts for me'!"

the Infinite, incomprehensible One images to our thought his love and quickening grace, and so bestows upon our faith what passeth our understanding,—then the reconciliation is already accomplished, and the hostile terms coalesce in a manner so easy and natural, that we are scarcely conscious of their repugnance." [67] Bushnell favored the conception of the Trinity which identified the Son with the Father and with the Holy Spirit. In this way the second person of the Trinity was within the range of our experience. Therefore, we must identify Him fully with the Father and the Holy Spirit. By so doing, Bushnell said,

> ... we pass the spirit of the garden and the cross into the sky, and the power of the sky down into the tomb of Jesus so that he can not be holden of death, and both again through our own defiled nature, as a presence of all-sufficient power and crucified Love; and so, finding the Christ of God above, and the God of Christ below, and the Spirit of the Father and the Son every where, then the one link of a revolving chain which is drawing us up also into the sacred circle of the divine nature. [68]

The three members of the Trinity, thereby, all participate in real divinity, but they do so by mutual interchange of position.

4. The truth of what is expressed.

The instrumental expression of God in terms of the threeness of revelation never intends to communicate an ontological structure of God's nature. It does, on the other hand, intend to bring the one God into our knowledge and experience and, at the same time, give us the most distinct and adequate impression possible of His government, character, and feeling. In this way, we may be quickened and made partakers of the divine nature ourselves. [69]

[67] *Ibid.*, p. 161.
[68] *Ibid.*, p. 163–164: "What power is there to our feeling in the Spirit, the Sanctifier, for example, when conceived to be the same as the Christ of Gethsemane or the cross, now present within! How different is he to our thought from a mere inhabitation of divine efficiency or power!" But it is such a conception which was heretical in the churches. Bushnell's answer was: "But it is such a kind of heresy that the man who has it in him, receiving thereby of the fullness of God, grace for grace; beholding the throne in the cross and the cross also in the throne, and finding in his own bosom all the glories of divine majesty and the patient love of Calvary, blending in holy confluence and breathing gales of love to lift him to the skies–this is a kind of heresy for which he will be quite willing to suffer. No fire will burn it out of him."
[69] *Ibid.*, pp. 165, 166, 167; Bushnell asserted that "... if the revelation of the New Testament is false, because the three divine persons answer to no real threeness of person in God's interior nature, then the oneness of God's revelation in the

5. The eternity of the persons.

Bushnell found no difficulty in speaking of the persons, Father, Son, and Holy Ghost, as eternal. He wrote: "If the persons be regarded simply as incidental to the process of revelation, yet since God is an eternally self-revealing being in his very nature, we may well enough assume on that ground, if no other, that he is always to be known, even from eternity to eternity, as Father, Son, and Holy Ghost; that is, by a trinity of eternal generation, or a trinity eternally being generated, in virtue of his self-revealing activity." [70] What Bushnell was interested in was the "practical" conception of God. Bushnell meant by that term the conviction that "God will eternally and always be God." We can trust God, he said, to be now and always Father, Son, and Holy Ghost. It is not necessary for us to know the secret of his interior structure. What is necessary is for us to have the power to receive the Trinity and the modesty to bear it. Bushnell was obviously more concerned with the effect of the Trinity upon our person, than he was with the attempt to understand the interior structure of the Godhead.

VI. *The Trinity and Orthodoxy*

Bushnell insisted that his conception of the Trinity was orthodox and could be verified on the basis of history, in terms of 1) The Nicene Council, 2) The Reformation, 3) The Orthodox position.

1) Athanasius was Bushnell's interpreter of the Nicene Creed. Bushnell found that Athanasius insisted upon the unity and strict simplicity of God. God was "one substance," "the same in substance," "proper to the substance of the Father." He protested against all conceptions of partition or division and rejected any conception of the coincidences of wills. Furthermore, he denied that the Son or Word was called the image or likeness of the Father. And finally, he affirmed the strict monarchy of God against all conceptions of a threefold, co-presiding agency in government. The Nicene Council, concluded Bushnell, described the Trinity in terms of the Word as the invisible, incomprehensible nature of God, as Form is to Sub-

Old Testament and in nature is false, because it gives no intimation of his threeness."
[70] *Ibid.*, p. 168; cf. *God in Christ*, p. 113.

stance. The Son is to the Father as expression is to substance, and so is proper to the substance of the Father and *not* another Being.[71]

The clause, "begotten, not made," meant for Bushnell that "the Divine Word is necessarily and eternally *of* and *from* the Father"; the Son is "ever and from eternity being begotten"; ". . . the Divine Word is necessarily of the Father and proper to His Substance; that considered as in act, or self-conscious life,—creating, governing, revealing,—He as naturally generates the Word, or Son, . . ." Bushnell wrote:

> The persons had their personality in these conceptions of eternal generation and eternal procession, and apart from these they were nothing; these *were* the persons, and it was a fact as clearly perceived by them, as it ought to be by us, that three persons, or three co-existing agents, taken as a first truth, afterward to be conceived as one being, can by no possibility of thought be reduced to any thing better than a concilium of Gods,—a verbal and fictitious unity, affirmed as a cover to real and practical tritheism.[72]

Bushnell insisted that his conception of the Trinity did not differ in any major way from the Nicene formula. He did, however, take issue with the formulators of the Nicene Creed because they attempted "in their transcendental method" to go beyond the Holy Scriptures and describe the internal modes of the life and being of God. In addition, Bushnell could not affirm a Trinity of eternal generation, but began instead with "a Trinity generated in time." This led him to the conviction that the condition and ground out of which the Trinity was generated in time was eternal. For this reason, the Trinity itself was eternal. The affirmation of the eternal Sonship of Christ as a "personal conception of the Word," could not be found in the Scriptures. Instead, the eternity of the Word as proper to the One Substance was relevant in Bushnell's formulation.[73]

[71] *Christ in Theology*, pp. 180, 181; Bushnell quoted from Athanasius, "The Son is the Image and Radiance of the Father, and Expression, and Truth. For if, where Light exists, there be withal its Image, viz. Radiance; and a Subsistence existing, there be of it the entire Expression; and a Father existing, there be his truth, viz. the Son."

[72] *Ibid.*, p. 183; the important point in this entire discussion is "that the eternal generation is not a matter collateral to the conception of the trinity, but fundamental to it."

[73] *Ibid.*, pp. 185, 186; Bushnell went on to say in reference to Athanasius: "Though he does frequently speak of the eternal Sonship, as related to the opinions of Arius, and argues for it upon the language of scripture. Whether

2) Bushnell employed Calvin's definition of the Trinity from the *Institutes*. He quoted:

"This distinction [of the three] is so far from opposing the most *absolute simplicity and unity* of the divine being, that it affords a proof that the Son is one God with the Father, because he has the same Spirit with him; and that the Spirit is not a different substance from the Father and the Son, because he is the Spirit of the Father and of the Son. *For the whole nature is in each hypostasis,* and each has something peculiar to himself. * * * These distinctive appellations, ... denote their reciprocal *relations* to each other and not the substance itself, which is but one." [74]

Bushnell found in Calvin's conception of the Trinity the features of the "strict simplicity" of the Godhead, and the affirmation that the "whole nature is in each of the persons." The persons referred to in the Trinity denote reciprocal relations, that is, there is given the intimation that the "whole nature" becomes, in turn, each of the persons by means of "some peculiar property." This can occur, he said, only if something is *in act.* If the substance or nature is whole and the same in each, then there can be nothing but act to make a peculiar property. This conception, Bushnell said, was a Trinity of generation. He interpreted Calvin in such a way that Calvin could find no Trinity in the substance of God or the Godhead, but only a Trinity in act or economy. [75]

Bushnell found, too, that the disciples of Calvin agreed substantially with him. Bushnell cited John Howe. [76] The Westminister Confession supported his position, too, Bushnell believed. [77]

he means to affirm that Sonship as actual, or only potential in the Word, is, perhaps an open question."

[74] *Ibid.,* p. 187, the reference is from *Institutio,* Book I, Chap. XIII, Sec. 19. He referred also to Sec. 25, 6, 28; cf. also *Ibid.,* pp. 209, 210.

[75] *Ibid.,* p. 188; Bushnell in many places asserted the conception of a "threeness that lies in act;" cf. pp. 189 ff.

[76] *Ibid.,* pp. 189, 190. Bushnell quoted Howe: "And whereas the greatest quarrel is about personality, there can be nothing more plain than that one and the same man may sustain three persons; the person of a father, the person of a son, the person of a magistrate, and the like. Many persons may be sustained by one and the same man; the notion of person, in the strict and common sense, being only taken from the circumstances of their state and condition who are spoken of, and not as denoting this or that essence. And so to be a man and this or that person is not all one. The same man may endure and may *sustentare,* may put on and may bear several persons; and so it is no repugnancy to reason at all that the same God may do so too. And therefore this pretence of the irrationality or contradictiousness of this doctrine doth itself want a pretence." Bushnell insisted that Howe rejected a Trinity of the divine essence.

[77] *Christ in Theology,* p. 191. In reference to the Westminster Confession, Bushnell wrote: "The Westminster Assembly expressly defines the personality of the

3) Bushnell next compared his conception of the Trinity with two comtemporary champions of Orthodoxy, one from Germany and one from the United States. He chose Professor Twesten of Berlin because he possessed, so he said, very great theological ability. Bushnell found that Twesten began with "the absolute oneness of being in God," and maintained that there was a "subjective necessity" for the Christian fact of Father, Son, and Holy Ghost. The Christian Trinity was, therefore, the theological result of revelation. Bushnell concurred:

The trinity we found at the first point of agreements, was a trinity resting in expression, or occurring under the laws of expression; which I insisted could as little be subjected to mere logic as a poem or a painting, and the attempting of which, logically or ontologically, would even be absurd. Or, attempting to fence off logic by logic, I argued that, having assumed the absolute oneness of the divine essence, and found a trinity resulting under the conditions of revelation or expression within our plane of consciousness, we manifestly can not reason out or logically prove what has come to us only by the self-revelation of God; neither can we argue from the three of revelation to a transcendental three back of it; for, by the supposition, the transcendental substance back of it is the One. Therefore we are to accept the three as persons whose proper comprehensible verity is that they most adequately reveal the One, and there to rest;—only it is right for us to argue (this is the "single sentence" of addition just referred to) that, since God is an eternally active self-revealing being, he is likely to be eternally acted or revealed in this manner.[78]

persons, in that they are other than the One, as consisting in the active distinctions of generation and procession, and in nothing else. They do not refer to their own personal consciousness and say that the divine Three are distinct logical subjects, in the sense that they are themselves–this they well understand in a way to involve the whole subject in confusion." Bushnell also quoted from Baxter's *Practical Works*, to support his position, p. 193: "Perhaps we can do nothing better, but I believe there is yet more in the mystery of the trinity, because this is so intelligible . . . What a person in the trinity is, all the divines and school wits as good as confess they know not. It is the trinity as *related to us*, and *operative* in us, and *therein* notified that we must necessarily believe– . . . even as it is not our understanding of the essence of the sun, but our reception of its communicated *motion, light and heat,* that our nature liveth by."
[78] *Ibid.*, pp. 197 f; Bushnell used the *Bibliotheca Sacra* as his source for Twesten's works. Cf. also p. 196; Bushnell asked, "Is it that God is not as really and completely one as if no such relation of contrast between nature and grace had been discovered to us?" The answer of Dr. Twesten was "that God is in 'both relations the same being;' only 'we are obliged to form a *different conception* of this same Being.' The trinity then, is a different conception of God, suited to the plan of redemption and to our Christian experience under that plan." Cf. also pp. 197, 198; Bushnell said that when Twesten began to speculate about the interior nature of God, he left him behind, cf. also p. 201; Bushnell compared Twesten's speculation to someone wading through a desert of sand.

The second reference is to an article by Professor Moses Stuart on the "Sonship of Christ," published in the *Biblical Repertory and Princeton Review,* the orthodoxy of which Bushnell never questioned. Bushnell found an amazing similarity between the position maintained in this article and his own conception of the Trinity. The article complained of the "little attention...paid to the proper limits of knowledge." The writer said, and Bushnell agreed, that when religion had not yet "passed on from the heart to the head," the Trinity would be received in a purely simple and practical way, and therefore no difficulty was created. Bushnell asserted that we should go back to the simple statements of the Word of God and leave the inexplicable unexplained.[79]

VII. *The Trinity and Human Sensibility*

Bushnell had chosen to defend the Trinity against the direct challenges to it and its location within the corpus of Christian doctrine. To Bushnell it seemed perfectly natural to accept the Christian doctrine of the Trinity, provided it enabled the believer to grasp more of the truth about God. The Trinity permitted the "mysteries of law and grace, letter and spirit to enter practically into belief." The Christian faith, which could not be probed by the understanding but only by the imagination or the "imaginative reason," had to retain an element of mystery and paradox. Bushnell refused to attempt to penetrate the interior nature of the Godhead, and by so doing, he allowed the Christian faith to keep an element of transcendent mystery. The conception of the Trinity which Bushnell arrived at was a Trinity which resulted of necessity from the *revelation* of God to man. Father, Son and Holy Ghost were, for Bushnell, *dramatis personae* of revelation. The Trinity, therefore, is a neces-

[79] *Ibid.,* p. 206; Bushnell quoted from Moses Stuart's article "The Sonship of Christ," *The Biblical Repertory and Princeton Review* VI, 1835, p. 28, "With regard to theology, the uniformity with which the great cardinal doctrines of our faith have been embraced, is not less remarkable than the diversity which has prevailed in the mode of conceiving and explaining them. The fact that there is one God, and that the Father, Son, and Holy Ghost are this God; that there is such a distinction between the Father, Son, and Holy Spirit as to lay a sufficient ground for the reciprocal use of the personal pronouns, has been the faith of the Christian Church, from first to last. And yet there is probably no one doctrine contained in the scripture, which has been so variously defined and explained as this." Cf. also p. 208.

174

sary Christian truth, because it is the only way in which one can come to know God. Only by means of "a trinity, an incarnation, and other like devices of revelation" can one know God. God has a "capacity of self-expression—a generative power of form," by which He can represent Himself in the finite world. This is the Logos, the Word, the form of God, through which God will "live himself into the acquaintance and biographic history" of the world.

But the chief problem for Bushnell regarding the Trinity was the nature of the person of Christ. The orthodox doctrine of two distinct or distinctively active natures in Christ presented a theological perplexity which Bushnell sought to resolve. He attempted to do so by merging the personality of Christ into the Father. Then by refusing to penetrate the interior nature of God, he avoided all of those problems dealing with the metaphysical structure of the Godhead. Indeed, he could insist, that under a metaphysical tri-personality, the proper deity of Christ could not be held. The Trinity he sought for was based upon the belief that God put Himself under limitations in creation, so that He may act as a human personality without being measured by it as in other created forms. We meet God, therefore, through the *Logos*.

Bushnell went on, as we have seen, to reject "two distinct substances" in Christ, and contended instead that "the reality of Christ is what he expresses of God." His conception of Christ may be summarized as follows:

Perhaps it may be imagined that I intend, in holding this view of the incarnation, or the person of Christ, to deny that he had a human soul, or anything human but a human body. I only deny that his human soul, or nature, is to be spoken of, or looked upon, as having a *distinct* subsistence, so as to live, think, learn, worship, suffer, by itself. Disclaiming all thought of denying, or affirming anything as regards the interior composition or construction of his person, I insist that he stands before us in simply unity, one person, the divine-human, representing the qualities of his double parentage as the Son of God, and the son of Mary. I do not say that he is composed of three elements, a divine person, a human soul, and a human body; nor of these that they are distinctly three, or absolutely one. I look upon him only in the external way; for he comes to be viewed externally in what may be expressed through him, and not in any other way. As to any metaphysical or speculative difficulties involved in the union of the divine and the human, I dismiss them all, by observing that Christ is not here for the sake of something accomplished in his metaphysical or psychological interior, but for that which appears and is outwardly signified in his life. And it is certainly competent for God to work out the expression of His own feeling, and His union to the race in what way most approves itself to Him. Regarding Christ in this exterior, and, as it were, esthetic way, he is that Holy Thing in which my God is brought to me,—brought even down to a fellow relation with me. I shall not call him two. I shall not decompose him and label off his doings, one to the credit of his divinity, and another to the credit of his humanity. I shall receive him, in the simplicity of faith, as my one Lord and Saviour, nor any the less so that he is my brother.[80]

No theological theory was adequate to express fully the person of Christ. Christ ultimately expressed God in human form. This fact was capable of moving the human sensibility. Man's only task was to experience God's revealed goodness, love and mercy, through Christ. This was the reason why Christ came to the human race in the form He did. The Absolute God was always hidden from man's understanding. Christ came, as God revealed, to express divinity in a form man could understand. He revealed God's love in the Incarnation. He demonstrated the priority and sanctity of the law, by His perfect obedience to it. He showed the suffering heart of God in the midst of the evil of the world by the crucifixion. God in Christ entered into human experience, to attempt to win humanity back to eternal life with Him.

When Bushnell was accused of presenting a view of Christ that made Him "too exclusively divine," he answered by criticizing the theory which represented God as the Father by virtue of His creation and government of the world. God is not the Father "as one God," but as He is related to the central fact of the Incarnation. The self-expressing power of God is revealed in the Son, who in turn reveals the Father. When asked whether he meant to assert a "modal trinity, or three modal persons," he said that he must answer obscurely. The three persons of the Trinity are given *not* for the sake of an internal investigation of their internal contents, but rather for their external expression. They have a reality in me; they are the "wording forth" of God in my experience, Bushnell said. But the power of self-representation in God, or, as Bushnell also called it, "the distinction of the Word," is eternal. This is the permanent ground for the "three-fold impersonation" called the Trinity. God is therefore always revealing Himself to created minds as Father, Son, and Holy Ghost. Furthermore, this is the only form in which we shall get our impressions of God and have communion with Him.

[80] *God in Christ*, pp. 163–164.

Bushnell refused to be called a Sabellian, although there are obvious similarities between his view of the Trinity and the Sabellian. With the Sabellians, Bushnell asserted "a trinity of manifestations," but he did not choose to make any statement about whether God existed eternally as a "triad of persons." God may or may not exist as a Trinity of persons. He has, however, the self-expressive power to make Himself known in three forms. Bushnell would never enter the mystery of the interior nature of God. Bushnell's entire career was a protest against a form of theologizing which permitted man to know all there was to know about God's internal being. The best theologian is the poet, he was heard to say, and probably the best Christian was the individual who refused to fathom the depths of the Godhead.

Bushnell saw no reason to maintain an eternal triad in the divine being. But he did see reasons for asserting a Logos, an eternal self-expressing power within the Godhead which appeared as Father, Son and Holy Ghost. As he did this, he was giving his assent to the view of the universe which he had proposed earlier in *Nature and the Supernatural*. The universe was to be considered as the manifestation of a God who was constantly revealing Himself in nature. The Trinity, therefore, was an essential truth, a truth which gave full expression to the God of manifestation and revelation. A truth which embraced the universe was a divine truth, another evidence of God's revelation of Himself in the world. Bushnell said:

In the department of nature, we discover, as we think, a realm of complete systematic causation. All events proceed in right lines of invariable sequence under fixed laws. But as laws are only another name for God's will, or the action of forces representing his will, the system of nature becomes a symbol in its whole development of the regulative mind of God. What we call the natural consequences are determinations of that mind in the same manner. In this view it will be seen that, if the universal economy included nothing but nature, the single term or conception *God* would answer all our necessary uses. So far there would be no discoverable economic need of Trinity.

But the universal economy is larger and contains, of necessity, another and partially contending factor, supernaturalism, even as the balance of the firmament is settled between two natural factors or forces always contending with each other.[81]

God has instituted two realms of forces, a kingdom of nature and a kingdom of grace. Nature is "the presiding will of God," but so also

[81] *Building Eras in Religion*, pp. 126–127.

is the supernatural. The perfection of God's universe will consist in an orderly comprehension of both of these realms, under the principle of law. The Trinity may be termed "an economic Trinity" for this reason. That is, it is an instrument of a "supernatural grace or a redemptive economy." The Trinity saves the dimension of infinity which belongs to God, while at the same time permitting God to act according to His personality, that of sacrificial love. The universe expresses the nature of God. The natural and the supernatural are inter-dependent fields of God's activity. To attempt to speculate on the mystery of Trinity is to fail to comprehend the measure of God's revelation, that is, to provide an answer to the practical questions of religion. The Trinity gives man "the most vivid and intensest sense of his social and mutual relationship as a person." [82] Bushnell's allegiance to the world-view represented earlier is best expressed by this passage from *God in Christ:*

This Transcendent Being struggling out, so to speak, into the measures of human knowledge, revealing Himself through the petty modes and molds of our finite nature! He fills the whole universe with actions and reactions, such as will bring us into lively acquaintance with Him. He comes into the human itself, and melts into the history of man through agonies, sorrows, and tears. He kindles heaven and earth into a glow, by the relative activities of Father, Son, and Holy Ghost. And for what? Simply to communicate Himself, to express His nature and His feeling. [83]

[82] *Ibid.,* p. 122.
[83] *God in Christ,* pp. 180–181.

CHAPTER VI

The Atonement and the Passible God

The final major task Bushnell set for himself was to present a treatise on "the laws of God's supernatural kingdom," which would include a conception of the work of Christ. He wrote to his wife in 1861,

Things are now getting into some shape in this great field, where, you know, I have been toiling after *shape* for these two years. I mean to realize my original, heaven-given thought of a book on the Vicarious Sacrifice for Christian experience, and propose to make it possible by a volume, to precede, on the doctrine of the Sacrifice,—to precede, however, not in time, but in order, and to be published, both, as separate, and also as volumes I. and II. Call the one, say, "Vicarious Sacrifice in Christ;" and the other, "Vicarious Sacrifice in Believers," or by any such-like title.[1]

Bushnell referred to the stages in his life which led him to the point where he could write this book: first, the conversion in his youth; second, his experience while a tutor at Yale; third, the revelation of the meaning of the Gospel which caused him to write *God in Christ,* and, fourth, the conceptions of sacrifice which he had recently developed.

The doctrine of the Atonement was one of the most essential in the structure of New England theology. The theological "improvements" which New England contributed were largely centered about the "moral government theory of the Atonement." This was a theory of the Atonement which said that the atoning work of Christ maintained the general justice of God, whose moral law had been desecrated by man. Christ's Atonement made it possible for God to forgive man his sin, while at the same time, He was able to sustain His government. Christ had died to make divine forgiveness consistent with the moral law. But the sacrifice of Christ was irrelevant to the individual sinner. The Atonement was a legal transaction which fit into the total structure of God's moral government.

[1] Mary Bushnell Cheney, *Life and Letters of Horace Bushnell,* p. 445.

The chief purpose of the Atonement was to "maintain the rectoral honor of God."

Bushnell rejected the "moral government" theory while a student at Yale. It was not until the publication of *The Vicarious Sacrifice Grounded in Principles of Universal Obligation* that Bushnell could articulate his own contribution to the "improvements" to New England theology.

I. "Moral" View of the Atonement

Bushnell reminded us that no theory of the Atonement had won universal acceptance within the church. He discovered, however, that there was a recurring interest in what he called "the moral view" of the Atonement. He directed an attack against the penal theory of the Atonement:

> If Christ has simply died to even up a score of penalty, if the total import of his cross is that God's wrath is satisfied, and the books made square, there is certainly no beauty in that to charm a new feeling into life; on the contrary there is much to revolt the soul, at least in God's attitude, and even to raise a chill of revulsion. . . . No, the power which is so continually sought after in the unfolding and preaching of the cross— that which, to every really Christian preacher, is the principal thing—is not in, or of, any consideration of a penal sacrifice, but is wholly extraneous; a Christ outside of the doctrine, dwelling altogether in the sublime facts of his person, his miracles and his passion.[2]

Many of the unique theological features of Bushnell's thought may be seen at this juncture. There is "no beauty," he said, "to charm a new feeling into life" in the penal theory of the Atonement. Christ must truly remain outside of doctrine, "dwelling . . . in the sublime facts of his person, his miracles, and his passion."

The vicarious sacrifice of Christ meant, for Bushnell, that Christ "engages, at the expense of great sufferings and even of death itself, to bring us out of our sins themselves and so out of their penalties; being himself profoundly identified with us in our fallen state, and burdened in feeling with our evils." However, Bushnell asserted that the law at the center of existence was the law of love. Love itself is a principle vicarious in nature. Love identifies itself with others

[2] Horace Bushnell, *The Vicarious Sacrifice, Grounded in Principles of Universal Obligation*, p. 30; cf. the Address "A Discourse on the Atonement," (delivered before the Divinity School at Harvard University, July 9, 1848), in *God in Christ*.

in order to take on the burden of suffering and evil. Love clings itself to the evil and lost man, becomes afflicted for him, and is burdened by his incapacities and pains, and gladly bears suffering for his sake. He wrote: "Approving nothing wrong in him, but faithfully reproving and condemning him in all sin, it is yet made sin—plunged, so to speak, into all the fortunes of sin, by its friendly sympathy." [3]

The *usus loquendi* of all the vicarious and sacrificial language of the New Testament is found in Matthew 8: 7, Bushnell said: "That it might be fulfilled, which was spoken by Esias the prophet, saying —'Himself took our infirmities and bore our sicknesses.' " Christ, Bushnell believed, took our sicknesses upon Himself in the sense that he took them upon his feeling, and had his heart burdened by the sense of them. He bore the disgusts of the loathsomeness of their sin and felt their pains all over again.[4] The cross and vicarious sacrifice of Christ signify to man that God is a God of love, a suffering Saviour. One of Bushnell's most famous passages follows: "There is a Gethsemane hid in all love, and when the fit occasion comes, no matter how great and high the subject may be, its heavy groaning will be heard—even as it was in Christ. He was in agony, exceeding sorrowful even unto death. By that sign it was that God's love broke into the world, and Christianity was born!" [5]

[3] *Vicarious Sacrifice*, pp. 41–42; cf. the sermon, "The Finite demands the Infinite," *The Spirit in Man*, pp. 199–213, cf. p. 210, "God is our Redeemer also, and in order to this he must be a God who has power over nature, power to roll back its penal causes, tear us out of its bondage and cure the wounds of our sin by a healing of nature itself. If the resources of God, his power, love, beauty, feeling, will, were less than they are, we could not be redeemed from sin. If, then we cling to our sin, if we take it even as a disturbance to be called away from it, should we like it better if we could not get away? Do we want a God such as cannot help us out of our sin or heal the scars it has made? The worst man living would start in horror from himself if he knew that he must eternally be what he is."; also, "Loving God is but Letting God Love Us," *Sermons on Living Subjects*, pp. 31–54; cf. also Bushnell's use of the doctrine of the Atonement in reference to the Civil War, *Building Eras in Religion*, p. 311; cf. also "A Discourse on the Atonement," *God in Christ*, p. 189, "Christ enters into human feeling, by his incarnate charities and sufferings, to re-engage the world's love and reunite the world, as free, to the Eternal life."

[4] *Vicarious Sacrifice*, p. 44; cf. "A Discourse on the Atonement," *God in Christ*, p. 187, where Bushnell used 1 John 1: 2; cf. also pp. 188 ff.

[5] *Vicarious Sacrifice*, pp. 47 ff; cf.: "Nothing is wanting to resolve the vicarious sacrifice of Jesus, but the commonly known, always familiar principle of love, accepted as the fundamental law of duty, even by mankind. Given the universality of love, the universality of vicarious sacrifice is given also. Here is the center and deepest spot of good, or goodness, conceivable. At this point we look

Bushnell reported that the history of the doctrine of the Atonement has shown that, at times, the vicarious sacrifice of Christ had been considered a superlative kind of goodness. It was asserted that his sacrifice was "optional," that he might not have undertaken the sacrifice. The fact that He died, therefore, brought about the superlative merit, which could be used as substitution for our just punishment. Bushnell reminded his readers again that every attempt to schematize the work of Christ, and to put him in terms of our understanding, must result in a painful confusion of ideas. The conception of Christ's superlative merit falls into this category. What is a goodness over and above all standards of good?, he questioned. Goodness must be the same everywhere, and it is measured by the same universal and eternal standards. Then Bushnell made this remarkable statement: "God himself is not any better than he ought to be, and the very essence and glory of his perfection is, that he is just as good as he ought to be." [6]

In any conception of the vicarious sacrifice, Bushnell said, we must bring our ideas back under the standards of eternal virtue. We must discover that Christ was doing and suffering just what he ought, or felt that he ought, neither more nor less. [7] Every conception of a Saviour we have must be found under our laws of goodness. We cannot conceive of any other kind of Saviour. Bushnell could conclude, therefore, that Christ was under obligation to do and suffer what he did. But he was under obligation to Himself and to no one else. But He was God, as as such, He was fulfilling the obligations of God. Bushnell wrote:

All that he endures in feeling under them, he endures freely, and this it is that constitutes both his greatness and joy. There is an eternal cross

into heaven's eye itself, and read the meaning of all heavenly grace." Cf. also the sermon, "God preparing the State of Glory," *The Spirit in Man*, pp. 214–228, "Hence it is the great point of wisdom and goodness and condescension in his plans to be always doing what will express or glorify himself, that the earth may be full of his glory, 'that the glory of the Lord may be revealed and that all flesh may see it'; sending Christ to be the brightness of his glory in the world, shining into our hearts to give the light of the knowledge of the glory of God in the face of Jesus Christ, and in all this having ultimate reference also to a general communication of himself to the created minds of his universal kingdom.", p. 217; even the extract from the sermon, "The Eternity of Love," *The Spirit in Man*, pp. 240–245; cf. "A Discourse on the Atonement," *God in Christ*, pp. 191 ff.

[6] *Vicarious Sacrifice*, p. 58.
[7] *Ibid.*; cf. *The Spirit in Man*, pp. 245 ff, 256.

in his virtue itself, and the cross that he endures in Christ only reveals what is in those common standards of good, which are also eternally his.[8]

Love, then, is the principle of vicarious sacrifice. As such, it is related to Christ, but also to God, that is, the God who had revealed Himself before Christ's coming. Sacrifice is relevant to the nature of God even before the Christian era began, Bushnell believed. There is, therefore, no antagonism between the Old and New Testaments. God is God everywhere, always acting the same, "instigated by the same impulses, clothed in the same sympathies, maintaining the same patience, under the same burdens of love; acting, of course, in the Old Testament history, for the same ends of goodness that are sought in the New." [9]

Bushnell asserted that there could be no internal progress in God. God is never inferior to what He is now, and will never be superior. Nonetheless, Bushnell recognized the contrast in the ways of God as represented in the Old and New Testaments. However, this does not mean, he said, that the God of the Old Testament is a lower being or a different God from the God of the New Testament. There is no progress or development within God Himself, but there is, however, progress in His government of the world. God's plan is a plan of spiritual restoration, which unfolds according to a progressive revelation. Bushnell wrote: "The day of ideas, thoughts, sentiments, words quickened to a spiritual meaning, must of necessity come after, and be prepared by a long and weary drill in rites, institutions, legilities and heavy laden centuries of public discipline. But God will be the same in this day as in that, in that as in this, cherishing the same purpose, moving on the senses, out of the same feeling, in the schoolmastering era of law, as in the grace of the cross itself." [10]

---

[8] *Vicarious Sacrifice,* p. 58; cf. the extract from the sermon "Deliverance in Christ," *The Spirit in Man,* pp. 257–261; also "A Discourse on the Atonement," *God in Christ,* pp. 196 ff.

[9] *Vicarious Sacrifice,* p. 60; cf. *God in Christ,* pp. 70, 72, 74, 302.

[10] *Vicarious Sacrifice,* p. 62, "There he maintains a government more nearly political and earthly; here more spiritual and heavenly. There he calls himself a man of war; here he shows himself a prince of peace. There he is more legal, appealing to interest, in the terms of this life; here he moves on the affections and covers the ground of eternity. There he maintains a drill of observances; here he substitutes the inspirations of liberty and the law written on the heart. There he operates oftener by force and by mighty judgements; here by the suffering patience of a cross."

The principle of love remains the same throughout the Bible. God is love, and He is a being who was burdened with the sufferings of men, just as Christ was. "It is," Bushnell wrote, "as if there was a cross unseen, standing on its undiscovered hill, far back in the ages, out of which were sounding always, just the same deep voice of suffering love and patience, that was heard by mortal ears from the sacred hill of Calvary." [11] When Christ came, he announced that God's love had sent him, and that this love would be magnified in the sacrifice of life He would make. Christ, Bushnell reminded us, was God manifest in the flesh, who reconciled the world unto himself. Christ, in his vicarious sacrifice, was a revelation in time of the love that had been struggling always in God's bosom. God is just what Christ shows Him to be. [12]

But the third person of the Trinity, the Holy Spirit, must also be active in love in the same way as Christ. The Holy Spirit "suffers all the incidents of love—compassion, wounded feeling, sorrow, concern, burdened sympathy, violated patience—taking men upon

---

[11] *Ibid.*, p. 64; cf. p. 65, Bushnell's discussion of the "exclusiveness of the old religion," which is a contrast, but nonetheless a preparation for the universality of the Christian religion. "... there was no other way to get hold of the low sentiment of the world and raise it, but to begin thus with a partisan, chosen people's mercy, and get himself revealed by light and shade, as between his people and others; creating a religion that is next thing to a prejudice."; also, p. 66, "If he had announced himself, at the very first, as the God alike and Saviour of all men, if he had been forthwith incarnate and had shown himself in Moses' day, by the suffering life and death of his Son, the history would have been a barren riddle only. They were not equal to the conceiving of any such disinterested sacrifice; and the fact that it proposed a salvation for all men would have been enough, by itself, to quite turn away their faith. I verily believe that Jesus, coming thus and then, would not even have been remembered in history." Cf. *Sermons for the New Life,* pp. 14 ff.

[12] *Vicarious Sacrifice,* p. 70; p. 73, "The whole deity is in it, in it from eternity and will to eternity be. We are not to conceive that our blessed Saviour is some other and better side of deity, a God composing and satisfying God; but that all there is in him expresses God, even as he is, and has been of old—such a being in his love that he must needs take our evils on his feeling, and bear the burden of our sin. Nay, there is a cross in God before the wood is seen upon Calvary; hid in God's own virtue itself, struggling on heavily in burdened feeling through all the previous ages, and struggling as heavily now even in the throne of the worlds. This, too, exactly, is the cross that our Christ crucified reveals and sets before us. Let us come then not to the wood alone, not to the nails, not to the vinegar and the gall, not to the writhing body of Jesus, but to the very feeling of our God and there take shelter."; cf. also *Sermons for the New Life,* p. 22; also the manuscript sermon "God Reigns for the Largest Love," (Yale Divinity School Library); "A Discourse on the Atonement," *God in Christ,* pp. 198–203.

him, to bear them and their sins . . ." Only in this way can the Holy Spirit properly be called the Paraclete, Advocate, and Comforter. The Holy Spirit is a person who has the same personal properties of feeling, love, sacrifice as the Father and the Son. The ministration of the Holy Spirit includes the whole range of human history and continues through all the untold generations of time. In this way, the Holy Spirit is enduring not only the pain and suffering of the ministry and crucifixion of Christ, but also must endure the contradiction of sinners throughout all time.[13] The Spirit, Bushnell said, was also an extension of the ministry of Christ. Christ recognized at the conclusion of His ministry that a permanent appearance in the flesh would be a hindrance rather than a help to future generations, and, therefore, He declared a change in administration. The Holy Spirit is also an intercessor, as is Christ, "bathing us inwardly in all Christly sympathy, bearing our burdens of weakness, and sin, and groaning, as it were, his own longings for us into our prayers." But Bushnell did not identify the Holy Spirit with Christ, although His role of intercession was the same.[14]

II. *The Atonement and the Moral Power of God*

Bushnell had said that the vicarious sacrifice of Christ was the mode or instinct of His love. He was involved in vicarious sacrifice before he came into the world. His sacrifice, as a fact in time, was not the chief object of his ministry. This would have made it a mere pageant of suffering, without any dignity or character. Christ's act of sacrifice did not compensate for God's justice. Bushnell is adamant on this point. The sacrifice of Christ took place because this was the nature of Christ's being, "to seek and to save that which is lost."

[13] *Vicarious Sacrifice*, p. 76, "The Holy Spirit works thus in a ministry of love precisely as Jesus did, and the love is just the same kind of love, burdened for men, burdened for enemies, heaving in silent agonies of passion to recover and save; fulfilling in every particular the Christly terms of sacrifice."; cf. Bushnell's projected book "Inspiration by the Holy Spirit," *The Spirit in Man*, pp. 3-35.

[14] Bushnell distinguished their mode of operation by saying that "one operates outwardly, the other inwardly; one before the understanding, the other in it; one making impressions by what is acted before the senses and addressed to thought, the other by groanings and throbs of divine feeling back of thought.", pp. 84, 85. Bushnell also referred to the fact that all "good angels" are in the principle and life of love; "and love in angels works according to its own nature, as truly as it does in God or in Christ," p. 93; cf. the whole discussion of good angels, pp. 91-104; cf. *Sermons for the New Life*, pp. 41, 66, 118.

It was Christ's function to bring about a reconciliation of man. The work Christ accomplished by means of His death was the regeneration of souls, a saving, truth-subjecting, all-restoring, inward change of life. The whole purpose of his life, said Bushnell, was "to work a healing general of the subject, a restoration thus to complete health and the crystal unity of heaven's vital order":

And so, taking all Christ's ministry, from his beginning to the hour of his death, it turns out that he is in a grand work of healing for body and soul, charging on his burdened feeling for all our sicknesses and pains, all the disorder of our transgressions and sins, weary, disgustful, deep in sorrow, circumvented, hated, persecuted and smitten, as it were, of God, yet persisting even unto death; and all this for our peace, or, what is nowise different, for our healing, or complete health.[15]

[15] *Vicarious Sacrifice,* p. 143; cf. "A Discourse on the Atonement," *God in Christ,* p. 203. This is the "subjective view of the Atonement." ". . . Christ [is] a manifestation of the Life, thus a power whose end it is to quicken, or regenerate the human character." Cf. pp. 203–204, "Here, as it has been already intimated, the value of Christ's mission is measured by what is expressed. And if so, then it follows, of course, that no dogmatic statement can adequately represent his work; for the matter of it does not lie in formulas of reason, and cannot be comprehended in them. It is more a poem than a treatise. It classes as a work of Art more than as a work of Science. It addresses the understanding, in great part, through the feeling or sensibility. In these it has its receptivities, by these it is perceived, or perceivable. Moving, in and through these, as a revelation of sympathy, love, life, it proposes to connect us with the Life of God." Bushnell called his view *esthetic,* i. e., Christianity is represented as a power moving upon man, "both to regenerate his degraded perception of excellence, and also to communicate, in that way, the fullness and beauty of God."; cf. pp. 204 ff. "The entering of one such perfect life into the world's history changes, in fact, the consciousness of the race;" p. 206. "Regarding the world, then, even as an upright and sinless world, how great an event it is that the Eternal is incarnated in their history, that the King is among them, expressing, by the mysterious identification of his nature with theirs, a mystery yet more august–the possible union of their nature with His! How memorable his words, teachings, works, and condescensions! And when he withdraws into the deep recesses of spirit again, what name will be dear to them as the name of their Christ! His appearing is a new epoch in their history. He will live in their hearts, life within life. A divine light from the person of their Emanuel will stream through their history. Their words will be sanctified by his uses. Their works will be animated by his spirit. A divine vigor from the Life manifested among them will penetrate their feeling, elevating their ideas and purposes, and even their capacity of good itself.", p. 207. "The manifestation of the Life also revives in man, as a sinner, the consciousness of himself. It is one of the paradoxes realized by sin, that, while it makes a man everything to himself, it makes him also nothing. It smothers the spark of conscious immortality. This world is practically all to him. The grave is dark, and he has no faith to throw a light across on spiritual realities beyond it. But when he that he was in the form of God comes into the human state, when we see one here who visibly is not of us, when he opens here a heart of love, and floods the world with rivers of divine feeling, when we trace him from

186

This conception of vicarious sacrifice will soften any heart, Bushnell asserted. The result will be a confiding communion with God. It was with his characteristic feeling that Bushnell wrote:

> The foremost thing we see in Christ is not the infinite holiness, or sovereign purity; he takes us, first, on the side of our natural feeling; showing his compassions there, passing before us visaged in sorrow, groaning in distressful concern for us, dying even the bitterest conceivable death, because the love he bears to us can not let go of us. In a word we see him entered so deeply into our lot, that we are softened and drawn by him, and even begin to want him entered more deeply, that we may feel him more constrainingly.[16]

the manger over which the hymns of heaven's joy are ringing, to the cross where his purpose to save embraces even death for man; and then, when we see that death cannot hold him, that he bursts into life again as a victor over death–following such a history transacted, in our view, we begin also to conceive the tremendous import of our own, the equally tremendous import also of our sin. If God, to renew the soul moves a plan like this, what is it to be a soul, what to desecrate and destroy a soul? The conscious grandeur of his eternity returns upon the transgressor, and he trembles in awe of himself–himself the power of an endless life.", pp. 211, 212. Cf. also "A Discourse on the Atonement," p. 191, "And I affirm, without hesitation, that whenever the question is about *the end* of Christ's work, that end to which he stands related as the wisdom and power of God, the answer of the scripture will be, that he comes to renovate character; to quicken by the infusion of the divine life; in one word, that he comes to be a Saviour, as saving his people from their sins."; also, pp. 191, 192, where Bushnell referred to Hebrews 8, "The eight chapter of the Epistle to the Hebrews opens with a look toward sacrifice, describing Christ as a 'priest' 'having somewhat to offer', but still as 'having obtained a more excellent ministry' than the priests of the law, and brought in for us a 'better covenant'. How better? Because it has a more transforming power in the life, because it fulfills a better and higher design, writing the law in the heart–'*I will put my laws into their mind, and write them in their hearts*'. Here the objective, ritual view passes into the subjective, and reveals the fact that it has and was designed to have a renovating power in character;–thus, becoming a 'new' and 'better covenant'. The aim of Christ's work, said Bushnell, was to change and transform the moral sentiment of man's being; cf. pp. 212, 213, ". . . when God appears in His beauty, loving and lovely, the good, the glory, the sunlight of soul, the affections, previously dead, wake into life and joyful play, and what before was only a self-lifting and slavish effort becomes an exulting spirit of liberty. The body of sin and death that lay upon the soul is heaved off, and the law of the spirit of life in Christ Jesus–the Eternal Life manifested in him, and received by faith into a vital union–quickens it in good, and makes it free."
[16] *Vicarious Sacrifice*, p. 146: "Going along with him in his ministry, and seeing how he works; always competent to the thing he undertakes, unsealing eyes born blind, banishing foul spirits, commanding the white skin of lepers to redden into health, hearing every forlorn sufferer's prayer, unable to be even touched in the hem of his garment without sending out some healing virtue, we have the feeling produced that we, too, can be healed, that the grip of retribution fastened upon us by our sin, all the bad causalities of our inward disorder, can be loosened." See *Sermons for the New Life*, p. 149.

187

Christ became, therefore, the moral power of God—a power to "pierce, and press and draw, and sway, and . . . crystalize the soul." [17] Christ was able therefore to bring about an internal new creation. Bushnell found in the New Testament more than adequate support for his position. The New Testament writers, he said,

conceive him as a wondrously detergent power in souls, "washing and making white," "cleansing from sin," "purging the conscience."

They conceive him going through the sick, disordered mind, even as some healing medicine, or miracle, goes through the hidden maladies of bodies, to search out and expel disease.

They call him a power of leaven, brought into the world to work; heaving in the general mass and willful stupor of it, till all is leavened.

They call him the day-star, because he heralds the mind's day and the expulsion of its dreadful night; and the light, because the instant flash of that element strikes farthest into God's physical empire, and changes most the face of it; and the sun, because the exhaustless heat of that central fire in the sky, has power to keep the planet in habitable order, and even to vivify the otherwise dead matter of it in processes of growth.

They call him Life itself, because the quickening spell of it, among the world's dead atoms, carpets the ground with beauty and fills the air itself with hovering motion.

They conceive him as a fire that is already kindled, in the rubbish of the world's prescriptive falsities and wrongs, whose burning nothing can stop.

His kingdom and the resistless moral power if his gospel, they resemble to lightning, darting from east to west, and flashing across all boundaries.

His word they compare to the swing of an earthquake, "shaking not the earth only but also heaven"—shaking down, that is, all stoutest fabrics of error and prescriptive wrong, and leaving nothing to stand, but that immortal truth and good that can not be shaken.

They describe him in his cross as an immense, world-compelling attraction, moving such control in the once dead feelings and convictions of sin as will "draw all men unto him," even as the whirlpool draws all drifting objects and even passing ships into its vortex.

He is even to be a chariot of thunder in the clouds—"coming in the clouds of heaven in power and great glory"—by that oriental sign of royal majesty showing that the kingdom of God is come with power. [18]

---

[17] *Vicarious Sacrifice,* p. 160; for a discussion of Bushnell's exegesis of Biblical passages which are usually used to assert a satisfaction theory of the Atonement, see pp. 162–166. Bushnell interpreted them to mean an appeal for man to "work a change inwardly in his life." It is, said Bushnell, a great difference between the idea that God is transformed and that man is transformed. Reconciliation refers to man and not to God, cf. p. 165; also pp. 169, 173–182; *Sermons for the New Life,* p. 175; "A Discourse on the Atonement," *God in Christ,* pp. 213 ff.
[18] *Vicarious Sacrifice,* pp. 180–182; cf. "A Discourse on the Atonement," *God in Christ,* pp. 215 ff.

Bushnell referred to the Incarnation as the meaning of the vicarious sacrifice. Because love is the principle of existence, God chose to reveal Himself in the Incarnation. But the Incarnation does not belong to God's "attributive" power, i. e., that kind of attribute or perfection we ascribe to God by our own intellectual refinements.[19] The moral power of God is to be considered as divine power and not as attributive power. It belongs not to an infinite, abstract and unseen being, but to a power who lived among men, a power which became "the grandest, closest to feeling, most impressive, most soul-renovating, and spiritually sublime power that has ever obtained in this or any other world." God Himself had come into human life in the person of Jesus Christ, and had expressed His divine power by means of human acts.

Bushnell discovered that the development of Jesus' life showed a cumulative growth of the moral power of God. Before His public ministry, He was morally good, He confessed no sin, but there was nothing which characterized Him as the moral power of God. The vague presentment He had of His "Father's business" developed into a definite consciousness of a calling. He perceived that He was to go down "into the hell of the world's corporate evil." He would be wounded by the malice of the world. He would bear the burden of the sin of the world as a charge upon his love. By the agony of sacrifice, including a most bitter death, he would reconcile men to God and establish the eternal kingdom of God in their hearts. The meaning of Christ's ministry and mission becomes clearer after the Resurrection, when we are able to conceive of Him as the Incarnate Word. We are now able, Bushnell said, to recognize that the righteousness and love of God are in Him, and that He had come to save the world. From the vantage point of the resurrection, everything in his ministry becomes clear:

The wonderful authority becomes more wonderful, in the right of a superior nature to give it sanction, the severity becomes majesty; knowing who the teacher is, what before was truth brightens into a glorious wisdom; the soft-looking innocence of the life becomes a kind of general transfiguration; the agony, that seemed to be wanting in magnanimity, becomes the love-groan, as it were, of his mysterious nature; the crushing defeat of the death breaks into immortal victory, Whatever, in a word, seemed weak, distracted, contrarious, takes on a look of progressive order,

[19] Cf. *Vicarious Sacrifice*, p. 187. Also, "A Discourse on the Atonement," *God in Christ*, p. 215, 216; cf. Bushnell's *The Character of Jesus forbids his Possible Classification with Men.*

189

and falls into chime, as a necessary factor in his divinely great character. And so the merely human beginning grows into what is more and more visibly superhuman, dying into boundlessness and glory, as the sun when it sets in the sea. The rising and the ascension put us on the revision, and helped us to conceive who was.[20]

This power of love begetting love is a greater power now than it was then, and, furthermore, reported Bushnell, it has a greater hold of the world now than then.[21]

It penetrates more and more visibly our sentiments, opinions, laws, sciences, inventions, modes of commerce, modes of society, advancing, as it were, by the slow measured step of centuries, to a complete dominion over the race . . . If in some particular century the gospel seems to suffer a wave of retrocession, it is only gathering power for another great advance. Bad power dies, right power never. Prophecy, or no prophecy, such a Christ of God could not come into the world, without a certainty coming in his train, that all the kingdoms of the world shall become the kingdoms of our Lord and of his Christ, and he shall reign forever.[22]

Bushnell was anxious to maintain that Christ was neither "a form of thought nor a proposition." and that he could not be defined in terms of a logical system. His reality is what He expressed by means of His moral nature and His vicarious sacrifice. The reality of the power of Christ's life must be seen in terms of the life itself and in no other way. The moral and sacrificial uniqueness of Christ must be maintained, and Bushnell attempted to do this by means of the following assertions:

1. The moral power of Christ was different from all other evidences of moral power.[23] Christ combined moral power with his person, in such a way that men consciously felt that they could learn about

---

[20] *Vicarious Sacrifice,* pp. 207, 208; Bushnell, very interestingly, referred to Lincoln in somewhat the same way, "A certain grotesqueness and over-simplicity, in spite of all our favoring judgments, kept off still the just impression of his dignity, and suffered us to only half believe. But the tragic close of his life added a new element, and brought on a second revision; setting him in a character only the more sublime, because it is original and quite unmatched in history. The great name now of Abraham Lincoln emerges complete, a power of blessing on mankind, and a bond of homage in the feeling of his country forever."; cf. *Sermons for the New Life,* pp. 286 ff.

[21] *Vicarious Sacrifice,* p. 211; cf. the sermon, "The Power of God in Self-Sacrifice," pp. 346–363, *Sermons for the New Life.*

[22] *Vicarious Sacrifice,* pp. 211, 212.

[23] *Ibid.,* pp. 214, 215; cf. the sermon, "Christ as separate from the world," *Sermons for the New Life,* pp. 434–456; also the sermon "The True Problems of Christian Experience," *Sermons for the New Life,* pp. 243–262.

morality only by learning about his person. There was a heroic quality to His life, in the sense that He gave His life because of the love He had for His enemies. This was a further indication to Bushnell that the moral power of Christ was a "supernatural flowering on earth, of a glory that he had before the world was." The greatness of Christ's power lies in the fact that He displayed a sense of the holy and of men's relations to a holy God.[24]

2. Christ humanized God to men. The incarnate life and history of Jesus Christ met man at that one point where he was unable to conceive of God as anything but an attributive power:

God is in Christ, consenting to obtain the power, by which he will regain us to himself, under our own human conditions. He is in our plane, acting with us and for us, interpreted to our sympathies by what he does and is, in social relationship with us. His perfections meet us in our own measures, not in the impossible measures of infinity; and so he becomes a world-king in the world, and not above it and far away from it. We know him, in just the same way as we know one another. He becomes the great Head Character in human history, by living in it Himself—such a kind of power, as being once in it, can never be gotten out of it, any more than if it were a new diffusive element in the world's atmosphere.[25]

God was, therefore, no longer a theosophy or a theophany, but a God-human, a God-man, who had been born into the human race.

---

[24] *Vicarious Sacrifice*, pp. 217, 218, "All true martyrs we conceive to be God's heroes; but what martyr ever bore witness to the truth, whose death had not some reference to the original, transcendent martyrdom of the Son of God? Heroes throw their life upon their cause, by inspiration from it; he had meat and drink and home for his houseless body, in the work he had taken upon him, and knowing that he must die for his cause, he could say 'how am I straitened till it be accomplished'. Heroes are men who go above all the low resentments; he could even pray the prayer of pity and apology for his enemies, when dying under their hands. Great souls are not flurried and disconcerted by the irruption of great dangers; behold the solid majesty or this man's silence, this provincial man, this country mechanic, when so many fierce accusations, by so many fierce conspirators in high life, are hurled against him. Heroes that die, and bear themselves nobly in the terrible hour of their conflict, are commonly caught without much warning, and are fortified by the tremendous excitement of the hour; Christ was facing death for at least three whole years, and waiting for his time to come; yet never weakened, or swerved, by the doom that he knew to be on him, but comforting his great mind constantly in the hope that, when he should be lifted up, he would draw all men to him." Cf. the sermon "The Power of an Endless Life," *Sermons for the New Life*, pp. 304–325, in which Bushnell dealt explicitly with the work of Christ. Bushnell contrasted Jesus Christ with Socrates. In reference to Socrates, Bushnell spoke of "the superficial, almost flashy merit of his power."
[25] *Vicarious Sacrifice*, pp. 220, 221.

Even more, God came directly into our bodies, by the healing of His inward touch. There was no greater advance in the development of human sensibility than the human life which contained the teachings, healings, tender condescensions, and sufferings of the divine man, Jesus.

3. Christ was able to attract the confidence of the guilty. We are able to identify ourselves, therefore, in our guilt, with Jesus Christ:

> But the incarnate Saviour, taking his place with us in our bad level, after the manner just described, stops the natural recoil of our guilt, and marries even our self-condemnation to confidence. Great as our guilt is, Christ, we see, can be our sponsor for all the wrong and damage of it. As the guilt kept him not away from us, so it shall not keep us away from him. Nay as it even drew him after us, shall it not also draw us after him? True we have sinned, our sin is upon us, and not even his forgiveness can ever annihilate the fact of our sin; but if he has come over it all to be the righteousness of God upon us, may we not come away from it, and be the righteousness of God in him? [26]

4. God suffered because of evil. Bushnell recognized that when he asserted this he was challenging the theological thought of his time. It was considered rationally inconceivable that a God who suffered on account of evil could also be infinite and all-sufficient. The theologians contemporary to Bushnell insisted that if God were sovereign and supreme, he could not suffer in any way. These same theologians went on to say that when Christ suffered on the cross, it was only the human nature that suffered. It could never be the divine. [27]

God suffered, Bushnell said, because of His moral perfection. He would not be perfect if He did not feel that which was bad, base, wrong, cruel, destructive, and everything that was opposite to perfection. God was displeased with the wrong. This displeasure was an experience opposite to pleasure for God, and, in a real sense, it was a kind of suffering. Furthermore, Bushnell added, God loathes all baseness and impurity and hates all unrighteousness. What are

[26] *Ibid.*, pp. 222, 223.
[27] *Ibid.*, pp. 223–224, Bushnell wrote, "It was very natural that the coarse, crude mind of the world, blunted to greater coarseness and crudity by the chill of guilt in its feeling, should be over-much occupied in conceiving God's infinity and the merely dynamic energies and magnitudes of his nature; the sovereignty of his will, his omnipotent force, his necessary impassibility to force external to himself, his essential beatitude as excluding all inflictions of pain or loss. Hence it has been very generally held, even to this day, as a matter of necessary inference, that God is superior, in every sense, to suffering."

192

these emotions but kinds of suffering? So it is with "compassion, pity, sympathy, indignations suppressed, wounds of ingratitude, and bonds of faith violated by treachery." All of these are instances of divine suffering, the greatest and most real suffering in the world. Bushnell drew the obvious conclusion: The Infinite God does not need to be impassible! [28]

The suffering of God to which Bushnell referred is the moral suffering of God. God is a being whose moral nature is "pervaded and charactered" by love. Love is, however, a principle so essentially vicarious that it "mortgages the subject to suffering." God as love must experience the burdens of love:

He must bear the lot of his enemies, and even the wrongs of his enemies. In pity, in patience, in sacrifice, in all kinds of holy concern, he must take them on his heart, and be afflicted for them as well as by them. In his greatness there is no bar to this kind of suffering. He will suffer because he is great, and be great because he suffers. Neither is his everlasting beatitude any bar to his suffering; for there is nothing so essentially blessed as to suffer well. Moral greatness culminates in great and good suffering; culminates also in blessedness, for there is a law of compensation in all moral natures, human as well as divine, divine as well as human, by which their suffering for love's sake becomes always a transcendent and more consciously sovereign joy.[29]

Christ's life verifies the moral suffering of Divine Love. Christ's agony is moral suffering, a suffering of a burdened love and of a holy and pure sensibility, "on which the hell of the world's curse and retributive madness is just about to burst." There is no physical suffering other than that which results from moral and mental suffering. In agony, there is no fear, no panic; it is only the moral pain of His love, sharpened by the crisis of His love.

The physical suffering of Christ on the cross is the symbol of God's moral suffering. God's nature is revealed to man through the life and history of Jesus Christ. And so it is in the experience of Christ's pain of the cross—this demonstrates the moral suffering of God. Bushnell wrote:

The moral tragedy of the garden is supplemented by the physical tragedy of the cross; where Jesus, by not shrinking from so great bodily pains,

[28] *Vicarious Sacrifice*, p. 225; cf. the sermon "Loving God is but Letting God Love Us", *Sermons on Living Subjects*, pp. 37–54. Bushnell modified this a bit by stating that God is a being physically impassible, *Vicarious Sacrifice*, p. 228.
[29] *Vicarious Sacrifice*, p. 226; cf. also the sermon "The Immediate Knowledge of God," *Sermons on Living Subjects*, pp. 114–128.

which the coarse and sensuous mind of the world will more easily appreciate, shows the moral suffering of God for sinners more affectingly, because he does it in the lower plane of natural sensibility. And yet even the suffering of the cross appears to be principally moral suffering; for the struggle and tension of his feeling is so great that he dies, it is discovered, long before the two others crucified with him, and sooner than, by mere natural torment, was to be expected.[30]

Jesus Christ was, therefore, the revelation of a suffering God, but also the embodiment of the "Great Moral Power of God."

III. *Law, Right and Government*

The problems of the relationships of law, to justice and righteousness concerned Bushnell next. There was a law before God's will came into existence, Bushnell said, which was in existence even before His act of creation. His law is the necessary, everlasting, and ideal law of *Right*. The perfections of God, being self-existent and eternal, were supported by this self-existent law. The perfections of God, therefore, existed in strict conformity to the moral law of Right. Bushnell wrote:

Otherwise, if God's perfections came forth only after and out of his will, and after the institution of his government, then he began to will and to institute government, without any perfections, and even without any moral standard—becoming all righteousness, and commanding all right, before even the ideal law of right had arrived.[31]

[30] *Vicarious Sacrifice*, pp. 228–229; the passage "My God, my God, why hast thou forsaken me" has no reference whatsoever to Christ bearing the penalty of man's sin. Rather it reflects the divine abhorrence to sin, p. 229; cf. also p. 230; also, the sermon "The Physical Suffering, or Cross of Christ," *Christ and His Salvation*, pp. 248–270, especially pp. 258 ff; even pp. 244 ff.

[31] *Vicarious Sacrifice*, p. 235; cf. "A Discourse on the Atonement," *God in Christ*, p. 218, "For it is even a fundamental condition, as regards moral effect on our character, that, while courage and hope are given us, we should be made, at the same time, to feel the intensest possible sense of the sanctity of the law, and the inflexible righteousness of God. What we need, in this view, is some new expression of God, which, taken as addressed *to us*, will keep alive the impression in us, that God suffers no laxity. In a word, we must be made to feel, in the very article of forgiveness, when it is offered, the essential and eternal sanctity of God's law–His own immovable adherence to it, as the only basis of order and well-being in the universe." Also p. 236, Bushnell indicated in which way this may be conceived. We recognize our own moral nature in reference to His, for we exist in His image: "I think of space, for example, and this eternal, necessary idea of space goes with me, compelling me to see all outward extensions, or distances in it. I think of cause, and this necessary idea

It must be maintained, Bushnell insisted, that God's own nature was in law before He Himself became the lawgiver. He became a lawgiver, therefore, only because He was already within the power of the law. God was, however, not obligated to any governing force above or beyond Himself, because the law was ideal and not governmental. There could be no command upon God, other than that of the idea of *Right*. This was God's righteousness, that is, the sum of all His perfections and the foundation for all that He directed and maintained through instituted government. The moral idea of Right is the "monarch principle of the soul;" as such it put all moral natures under an "immediate, indefeasible, bond of Sovereignty." Moral natures are possible only because they are set before the idea of *Right*.

Bushnell could make the claim that it did not matter whether we knew God or not, because there was a fixed standard of obligation prior to His moral commandments. He clarified his point in this way:

> The simple idea of right, if we accept the authority of it, and set ourselves to it for a total homage and conformity, will be a complete regulation for the life—for every thought, and act, and disposition—and will fashion us in a completely harmonic character and state of righteousness. It only can not do this after we have fallen away from it, and been thrown out of spiritual order, by the shock of our disobedience. Then it will even require a salvation to restore us.[32]

The idea of Right must be the same to every human creature, wherever he may be. It is the same for the Gentile as for the Jew,

compels me, or qualifies me, to see all goings on of change, under terms of causation. These ideas are, in fact, forms of the mind; forms to which it adverts in all thinking, and without which it could not think at all. The same is true of the ideas of time, and number, and quantity. Being in the form of time, I am put on thinking when; of number, on thinking, how many; of quantity of thinking how much. So I think of truth, in general idea, and having that form of thought developed, I begin to think what particular things are true. In the same way is developed the grand, all-regulative, Moral Idea of Right; which to simply think is to be put in everlasting obligation. For it is the distinction of this idea, that it is the Monarch Principle of the soul. It puts all moral natures under an immediate, indefeasible bond of sovereignty. They become moral natures because they are set before this idea of right. Animals think no such thought, and are never set before this idea. They probably have the ideas of space and cause, and number, but right is of a higher range; else if they could think it, they would be moral natures in common with us."; cf. the argument, pp. 218 ff., "A discourse on the Atonement," *God in Christ*.
[32] *Vicarious Sacrifice*, p. 237; cf. also pp. 220 ff, "A Discourse on the Atonement," *God in Christ*.

for the heathen as well as for the Christian. The idea of Right is the same for all created souls, even as it is for God.

Bushnell then expanded the concept of Right to include the law which existed before governments came into being. This law is common to all moral natures and it makes possible all moral distinctions. It is the law of our conscience. It is man's moral natures which is the fact of his kinship with God. It is man's moral nature which is responsive to the eternal and necessary principle of Right.[33] But God's righteousness is also to be united to this same eternal and necessary principle of Right:

> All moral beings, united thus in their homages to right, will be united also in love; love to each other, and love to the law, by which they are set in society and everlasting chime together, as in ways of mutual right-doing. Indeed the necessary and absolute Law of right, thus accepted, is very nearly answered by the relational law of love; so that any realm of being, compacted in right, will as certainly be unified in love, doing and suffering, each for each, just what the most self-immolating, dearest love requires. Even God, in such right-doing, will bend himself to any most expensive, lowest burden of sympathy, for the benefit and well-being of such as are humblest in the order of their dignity.[34]

What happens to the disobedient among the race?, questioned Bushnell. He asserted that the internal state of the disobedient will be immensely changed; "they will be chafing in the bitter consciousness of wrong, doing wrong to each other, feeling wrong, contriving wrong, writhing in the pains of wrong." Self-restoration is not possible. In addition, however, the law itself is made of less consequence, it "desecrated, trampled, and mocked . . ." For this reason, it is necessary for God to act to bring about self-restoration. He is able to accomplish this because of His relationship to the law. He considered Himself elected, by virtue of His own transcendent powers of will, to assume the charge of a Ruler. He thereby instituted governments. In this way He has repaired the broken law. In this way He will also undertake to redeem and restore the fallen race. God's righteous love will unite man to Him. Therefore, God's instituted government and God's redeeming sacrifice will work to-

[33] Cf. *Vicarious Sacrifice,* p. 238, and *Building Eras in Religion,* pp. 290, 316, 331.
[34] Cf. Bushnell's argument, *Vicarious Sacrifice,* pp. 239–241; also the sermon "Christian Ability," *Christ and His Salvation,* pp. 161–179; also "A Discourse on the Atonement," *God in Christ,* pp. 222 ff.

gether for very nearly the same purpose.[35] Bushnell clarified this point:

> Legislation wants redemption for its coadjutor, and only through the divine sacrifice, thus ministered, can it ever hope to consummate the proposed obedience. Redemption also wants legislation, to back its tender appeals of sacrifice, by the stern rigors of law. Both together will compose the state of complete government.[36]

Instituted government, which is founded by God, is the locus of God's administrative activities. It becomes, according to Bushnell, a religious polity for the world.

> It is a large creative outfit and providential management, where contrivance, and counsel, and statute, and judgment, and all that belongs to an administrative polity may get ample range of opportunity. And here we find the instituted government of God... God undertakes, in this, to be its Guardian and Vindicator, making specific applications, adding retributive enforcements, casting soul and body, as far as contrivance may, and arranging the whole economy of causes, to throw the strongest possible motives on the side of right, and against the choice of wrong, or continuance in it.[37]

Included with in the government God initiated are the "machinery of discipline and reconciliation," which are more than the means of legal enforcement in a society. Bushnell added the incarnate mission of Christ to the initiated government of God, all Christian causes,

---

[35] *Vicarious Sacrifice,* p. 243; cf. the sermon "Conviction of the Son by the Cross," *Christ and His Salvation,* pp. 116–138; also *Nature and the Supernatural,* pp. 234 ff. Cf. *Vicarious Sacrifice,* p. 244: "To this end he will organize a complete frame of statutes, and penalties, and motivities general, for the will, such as He, the infinite Lord, and Head Power of the worlds, may count worthy of his wisdom and universal sovereignty–the same combination, we may well enough suppose, that we have to admire in his word and Providential order now. In this manner, or in some other closely related, we shall see that He has taken the government upon his shoulder." See also Bushnell's argument pp. 244 ff.

[36] *Vicarious Sacrifice,* p. 245; cf., "Precisely how, or by what plan, the restoring agency will operate, we, of course, do not know. Doubtless it will involve the grand, principal fact, that God is in vicarious sacrifice; and, if that is best, he will go forward in just the same ways of sacrifice, and the same revelations of love, that he has made in the suffering life and death of Christ. For since he is grounded, as respects all his perfections, in the eternal law of right, now cloven down, he will love the principle itself, and love its adherents, and love, for the law's sake, as well as for their own, all the transgressors and enemies who may haply be recovered to it. And so we shall have on foot a grand work of redemptive sacrifice, that has no reference whatever to claims of justice previously incurred."

[37] *Ibid.,* pp. 252–253.

and all of the missions of the Holy Spirit, the Church, the word, life, death, resurrection, and eternal judgment. All of these are intelligible to God and will bring about the final accomplishment of the Right.[38]

Bushnell elaborated on the relationship of the law to instituted government:[39]

1. The Law and the obligation demanded thereof did not originate with God's will. Neither are they created by His will. The law was right before God enacted it. An example of this relationship is the Decalogue. A first principle, the principle of Right, lies behind it and gives it the possibility of coming into existence.

2. Instituted government initiated the concept of justice and legal sanctions. Instituted government rules by the statutes and penalties enacted by God. These are the means by which He maintains His administration.

3. Instituted government is the "co-factor" of redemption. The soul, living under sin, cannot forget that it is in sin. The structure of reality condemns man for his sin. This occurs because of the idea of duty in the scheme of life. Man's moral sense is, however, heightened by the arrival of justice. Bushnell described the efficacy of justice in the following way: "For it is a great mistake to imagine that the sanctions of justice are valuable only as intimidations. They are God's strange work, and the fearful earnestness they show raises our moral impressions, or convictions, to the highest pitch of tensity." The Scriptures, too, help to enforce and sharpen moral conviction. A knowledge of sin may be brought to consciousness by the Holy Scriptures. In this way, the Scriptures help us to achieve the necessary presupposition for the reception of God's grace.

4. Righteousness and justice must be distinguished. The righteousness of God is the rightness of God before the eternal, self-existent law of Right. The justice of God is the "vindicatory firmness" of God, which maintains his own instituted law. The first is obedience to a law before God's will, the second is the retributive vindication of a law that is under and by God's will itself. God must govern by no capricious rule, and therefore must maintain the character of justice for His government as He maintains a character of righteousness for Himself.[40]

---

[38] *Ibid.*

[39] *Ibid.*, pp. 254–261.

[40] *Ibid.*, pp. 259–260; cf., "One is without option, before immutable, unconditioned, everlasting law; the other is what God wills and does, in the world of

198

5. The law which existed before government was impersonal. God's instituted government is intensely personal and becomes ultimately just like God. The institutional aspect of government will eventually be lost, and we will be able to equate the government with God as King.[41]

IV. *Forgiveness and Justice*

The forgiveness of God, or the free justification of God, introduced a problem for Bushnell in terms of the integrity of law and justice. The theories of judicial satisfaction assumed that Christ's life and death brought about the "ground" of justification. God had two dispensations, one which came before the work of Christ had been accomplished, the other after. These dispensations were related to one another as mercy was to justice, forgiveness to punishment, and justification to condemnation. The theory of judicial satisfiction insisted that God, who began to rule by law, but failed to achieve His desired results, was forced to introduce Christ. It was Christ who rescued the guilty from the penalties of justice. He did this in order to satisfy God's justice. The integrity of the law was thereby maintained.

Bushnell felt is was necessary to revise the entire conception of

conditions, that is of means and measures. God must be righteous; God will be just. That he must be, because it is right; this he will be, because he has undertaken to maintain the right and govern for it. There is the character by which he rules; here is the reason of polity by which he rules. Without that, he could not be himself; without this he can not administer a government that will command his subjects. Righteousness is necessary to the endowment of his person; justice is necessary for a wholly different reason; one for the reason of character, the other for the reason of polity. Nothing can ever dispense with that; this can be tempered only by that which conspires with it, working for the same ends. Righteousness in God accordingly is satisfied only with righteousness in men; justice is satisfied with whatever makes good the dishonors of violated law, working with it, to fulfill its end."

[41] Cf. *Ibid.*, p. 261, "We do not like, in fact, to call it a government, for that is not relational enough to meet our feeling, but we drop the institutional conception, taking up the personal, and calling it King–God is King, that is government enough; and we prefer to let our mind be occupied wholly with his royalties and the homage due to his attributes. More intensely, because externally personal, the government is still to become; for Christ will be visible Messiah, that is visible King, King of Righteousness and so of Peace; whereupon, beholding the government now upon his shoulder, we shall crown him gladly with our invocation–'Give the King thy judgments, O God, and thy righteousness unto the King's son'."

God's mercy and justice. There is a "wrath-principle" in God, he said, which insists upon right overagainst wrong. However, there is no law in God's nature which will require Him to execute what will exhaust His passions. Bushnell clarified his position: "It is only that girding power of justice that puts him on the work of redress, and that armature of strength upon his feeling, that enables him to inflict pain without shrinking. And then, at just this point, comes in another function, equally necessary; viz., wisdom, counsel, administrative reason, which directs the aim, tempers the degree, and regulates the measures and times, of the pain."[42] There cannot be, therefore, any sense of justice in God which does not permit this same justice to be tempered by mercy. God does not punish the disobedient exactly as he deserves. God is free to do what He wants to do with the wrong-doer. He has perfect liberty to do better to the wrong-doer than he deserves. This is not a fault in His justice. God treats the evil-doer as He wants, and does so in order to advance the interests of character and society and government.

Bushnell added that there was no priority in time of God's justice and mercy. Both worked together for one common result, and that was the redemption of man.[43] The antagonism between the two

---

[42] *Ibid.*, pp. 269, 270; "A Discourse on the Atonement," *God in Christ*, p. 225, "... Christ ... fortifies and sanctifies the law through his obedience."; also, pp. 226, 227, "For though God is under no obligations to another, he is yet under obligations to goodness to devise, do, bear, forbear, suffer, all which the conception or idea of infinite goodness and love contains. He is really under the same law of obligation that we were under and cast off, and it is the glory and greatness of his nature that he delights eternally to acknowledge this law. Christ is the manifested Life revealing this everlasting obedience of the divine nature. All that he does and suffers is but an expression of the homage, rendered by God himself, to that which we reject; and the only object of his mission is to bring us back into a like free obedience to the same lovely requirement. His poverty and patience, his weary, persecuted life, his agony, his cross, his death, exclude from these all thought of penal suffering or vindictive chastisement, regard him simply as supporting, thus, the call of duty, and signifying to mankind the self-renouncing and sublime obedience of the divine nature—what an expression of love to the right, and homage to the law! How sacred now is law!—how sacred, yet how lovely! Why, the punishment of all mankind, even for eternity, could not signify as much."
[43] In this context, Bushnell spoke about the fall of man, specifically in terms of the "mythic tree," cf. *Ibid.*, pp. 271, 272., "Then, whether we understand the mythic tree, or test-tree of the garden, to be the law before government, or to be some instituted precept in which it is presented more specifically, the sin of the sin is, in either case, the casting off of the former; that which carries with it a revolution of character down to its deepest principle. And the 'death' that followed was the moral dying that must come with

modes of God's actions—the law of God and the justifying power of Christ—is not a real one. They work together, within the context of government, to reconcile fallen men to God. In order to bring about this objective, law enforces obligation and raises choice to the possibility of love and therefore to salvation:

> And so much is there in this twofold action that without some such grip of law and justice on the soul, no grace-power of God could ever win it back; and without the grace-power felt in its blessed attractions, no mere law-and-justice power could beget any thing closer to God than a compelled obedience, or fear that hath torment. There was in fact an antecedent necessity of their conjoined working, that, in the due qualifying of each other, they may complement what would otherwise be a fault in each.[44]

Bushnell asked whether a superior God was found in the New Testament, that is, a God who solely dispensed grace? The answer must be in the negative, said Bushnell, because the New Testament

such a revolution–no death of God's infliction, but a declarative death, connected with the fall out of principle. Then follows what is called the promise, and what is called the curse–the promise first and the curse afterward–that as the new hope, this as the new state of wrath and penal discipline. And both together, having one and the same general aim, are inaugurated, as the right and left hand, so to speak, of God's instituted government. They are to have a properly joint action; one to work by enforcement, and the other by attraction, or moral inspiration; both having it as their end or office, to restore and establish the everlasting, impersonal law." Cf. also "A Discourse on the Atonement," *God in Christ*, pp. 228–229, "If we look upon it as the very end and aim of Christ's mission, to recover man to God and obedience; or, what is the same, to re-establish the law as a living power in his heart; then, of course, everything he does and suffers, every labor, weariness, self-denial and sorrow becomes an expression of his sense of the value of the law–every pang he endures, declares its sacredness. So that if he offers pardon, free pardon, to every transgressor, we shall never connect a feeling of license, but shall rather feel a sense of the eternal sanctity of the law, and have a more tremulous awe of it in our conscience, than we should if every transgressor were held to punishment by the letter of it."

[44] *Vicarious Sacrifice*, p. 273; cf. Bushnell's exegesis of Biblical passages which deal with justice and mercy, p. 279: "We shall find also, both in the Old Testament and the New, declarations made of God and of his Son, that represent both in the same general combination of attributes; asserting themselves, at once, both in all the rigors of justice, and all the tender concern of a forgiving sacrifice and sympathy. Thus we have from the Old–'The Lord, the Lord God, merciful and gracious, long suffering and abundant in goodness and truth, keeping mercy for thousands, forgiving iniquity, transgression, and sin, and that will by no means clear the guilty, (that is the incorrigible).' And again, answering exactly to this we have from the New–'Tribulation and anguish upon every soul of man that doeth evil, (continue incorrigible in it) of the Jew first, and also of the Gentile. But glory, honor, and peace, to every man that worketh good, to

is nothing but a new edition of the Old Testament, an enlarged and improved report of God. Both the Old Testament and the New Testament describe the same God, but do so in terms of different stages of human thought and development. God is just in both the Old and the New Testaments, although in the Old Testament justice appeared as a bondage. In the New Testament, justice was a deliverance from bondage because, as Bushnell said, "of the incarnate person who could fitly represent to men's feeling the dear charities of God, and show the rites fulfilling their idea in his own complete and all sufficient sacrifice." [45]

However, God's justice had to be maintained, insisted Bushnell, because it was necessary to God's administrative character. Nonetheless, Bushnell questioned:

Is the weight of God's justice heaviest, when it is according to some formally exact standard of measurement conceived for it by theologic opinion—a standard it must meet, in order to be itself justified? Must He be a precisionist in order to be passed as just? On the contrary he seems to me to be most grandly just, when he holds his firmness in a certain way of liberty—most grandly merciful, too, when he dispenses mercy, as one taking counsel of justice. He should seem, in his justice, to to say that he will suffer no jot or tittle of the law to fail; and then to make the saying still more certainly good, he should, for the law's sake, add such argument of love and mercy, as will restore both jot and tittle and, if possible, the whole broken body of the law. [46]

V. Christ and the Law

The life and sacrifice of Christ and the act of forgiveness effected by Christ signified nothing, said Bushnell, unless there was an accompanying inward change which took man out of his bondage and brought him into the liberties of love and adoption. The primary concern of Christ was to heal the souls of men—to reconcile them to God. [47]

the Jew first, and also to the Gentile.' And what have we, in fact, but a complete summing up of all such combinations in these two words, 'the wrath of the Lamb?' "

[45] *Vicarious Sacrifice*, p. 280.

[46] *Ibid.*, p. 281.

[47] *Ibid.*, pp. 297 ff; cf. "A Discourse on the Atonement," *God in Christ*, p. 236, "Looking now, at the death of Christ, in this manner, we are made, first of all, to feel, whether we can explain it or not, that it has a marvelous power over our impressions, concerning ourselves and our sins, the law of God and His

Bushnell dealt next with the term *honor* because, as he said, it is a favorite word in the discussions regarding the doctrine of the Atonement. He recognized that sin dishonored the law and broke it down, and made man disrespect the law. Therefore, there was the necessity for punishment. This was considered as the self-asserting act of God, in behalf of the law, by which he invested it with honor. God deepened and intensified the law, and He did so to such a degree that it was able to become a moral force. But Christ too, by His sacrifice, magnified the precept of the law. Bushnell described the work of Christ in relationship to the law in the following way:[48]

1. He restored men to the precept of the law. The forgiven man is restored to all of the statutes of God's instituted government. The forgiven sinner was brought to a love of the law, in such a way that his obedience became an inspiration. Christ restored man to a free conformity with the law. "Christ beholds it from the first moment onward, doing nothing and wanting nothing, in all the immense travail of his incarnate ministry and death, but to commend the Righteousness and Beauty of it, and regain lost men to that homage which is at once their own blessedness and its everlasting honor."

2. Christ honored the precept by His work of salvation which brought men to righteousness. Salvation meant that the original order of the law was restored within us:

[Christ] proposes, indeed, to be a Savior to men; but the gist of the salvation, both to us and to him, is that heaven's original order is to be restored in us, and made solid and glorious, in the crowning of God's instituted government forever. Every thing that we see therefore, in the incarnate life and suffering death, is God magnifying the honors of his law by the stress of his own stupendous sacrifice. Such an amount of feeling, put into the governmental order, commends it to our feeling; and also turns our feeling into awe before it. The law is raised as precept, in this manner, to a new pitch of honor, and the power of impression given to it, by the vicarious sacrifice and more than mortal heroism of Jesus,

character. It brings an element of divinity into everything, sheds an air of solemnity and grandeur over everything. It is even more awful to the guilty conscience itself, than the thunders of Sinai. And, then, secondly, we shall be able also, I think, to see that the whole effect, contemplated under the laws of art, is produced by the fact that the Life, thrice sacred, so dimly shadowed before in the victims of the altar, is here yielded, as a contribution from God, to the pacification and reconsecration of His realm."; cf. the sermon, "Salvation by Man," *Christ and His Salvation*, pp. 271–292; also "The Bad Conscience taken Away," *Christ and His Salvation*, pp. 293–311.
[48] *Vicarious Sacrifice*, pp. 299–321.

is the principal cause of that immense progress in moral sensibility and opinion, that distinguishes the Christian populations of the world.[49]

3. Christ added authority and honor to the law-precept, by being, in His own person, the Incarnation of it. The law was impersonal in itself. It was abstract and cold and made people "numb with its frozen authority." But when it was incarnate in Christ, it became personal, and addressed human convictions with a human voice. Christ represented God's being perfectly:

> ... Christ is not, as many seem to fancy, a mere half-character of God incarnate, a kind of incarnate weakness in the figure of a love-principle, separated from every thing else in God's greatness, necessary to the tonic vigor of love. Being the incarnation of God, the full round character of God as he is must be included—authority, justice, purity, truth, forgiveness, gentleness, suffering love, all excellence. All these, in fact, belong to God's character, and they are here brought nigh, brought into concrete expression, thus to be entered, by Christ, as a complete moral power, into souls.[50]

In Jesus Christ, the instituted government of God had become a person.

4. Christ conferred his "deific obedience" upon the law; that is, he acknowledged His own obligation to the law. The eternal and absolute law of Right, which formed the basis for God's moral perfection, became obligatory for Christ, too. Bushnell then made the rather startling statement that the same law of Right made God suffer goodness for his enemies, and even brought about the vicarious sacrifice of Christ.[51] Bushnell meant by this that Christ was under obligation

[49] *Ibid.*, p. 301; Bushnell referred to the Civil War in this context: "In our four years of dreadful civil war, what immense sacrifices of blood and treasure have we made; refusing to be weakened by sorrow, or shaken by discouragement, or even to be slackened by unexpected years of delay. Failure was prophesied on every hand; compositions were proposed without number. Yet nothing could meet our feeling but to save the integrity of our institutions, and forever establish the broken order of the law. All the stress of our gigantic effort hinged on this and this alone. No composition could be endured, or even thought of, that did not settle us in obedience, and pacify us in the sovereignty of law; and, to the more rational of us, nothing appeared to lay a sufficiently firm basis of order, but the clearance somehow of that which has been the mockery of our principles, and the ferment even, from the first, of our discord. The victory we sighed for, and the salvation we sought, were summed up in the victory and salvation of law. Failing in this everything would be lost. Succeeding in this all sacrifice was cheap, even that of our first-born." Cf. "A Discourse on the Atonement," *God in Christ*, pp. 242–243; also *Vicarious Sacrifice*, p. 302.
[50] *Vicarious Sacrifice*, pp. 303–304.
[51] *Ibid.*, p. 306; cf. "A Discourse on the Atonement," *God in Christ*, pp. 251 ff.

204

to become the Redeemer. As He fulfilled that obligation, He conferred honor upon the law. Bushnell went on to explain that the eternal law of Right was "only another conception of the law of love." As the righteousness of God fulfilled the Right, so the affirmation "God is Love" was another equally valid conception of His eternal perfection. Bushnell described how right and love were related:

> The two principles, right and love, appear to exactly measure each other. One is the law absolute, or ideal, commanding the soul, even if it were to exist in solitude; the other is the law relational, grounded on the sense of relationship to other beings, who may be socially affected by our acts. Thus every one who will be and do right, in the large and complete sense of the principle, will as certainly love all beings, whether God or men, whether friends or enemies, whether deserving or unworthy, with whom he finds himself in relation. The law of love appears to be, in some sense, a law of revelation, as the law of right is not. And yet the law of love is just as truly grounded in nature, commands the assent of natural conviction just as invincibly, when it is once stated. The only reason why it is not propounded universally as a principle of natural morality, is that the close relationality of it is cross to our humanly selfish habit. We can talk of being right, and are willing to think of that as a duty, because we can put a lower, merely conventional, and market sense on the word, that accommodates our self-approbation; but we shrink from the law of love, and do not propose it in our schemes of ethics, because we do not consciously recognize and practically own the brotherhood of other beings.[52]

Love to God is Right and Right to Him is Love. This was the formula Bushnell used. As He is the law of love, He will suffer the pains of love and will go beyond all terms of mere justice and desert. He will insert Himself into man's miseries, and even into their guilt in order to bring them relief. This is the nature of eternal obligation. The law of love, therefore, is with God "as an eternal, necessary, immutable law, existing in logical order before his will, and commanding, in the right of its own excellence, his will and life." All of God's plans, decrees, and creations, conform necessarily to this law of love. Christ's Incarnation and vicarious sacrifice were not, therefore, optional to Him, but were obligatory. He had to become the incarnate Word and the Savior of sinners. The law of love, or the love-principle, as Bushnell called it, was necessarily vicarious.

> Christ came just because the law he had been in from eternity sent him, and his incarnate appearing was but the necessary outcoming in time of God's eternal Love. He descended to the lot of men just because he had

[52] *Vicarious Sacrifice,* pp. 306, 307.

them in his heart. His object was only to minister. His compassions, even before he came, were tinged all through with sorrowing tenderness. His emotional nature was stung and wounded every day, after he came, by the scenes of wrong and cruelty he was compelled to look upon, the sicknesses, and pains, and deaths, and torments of spiritual disorder to which he ministered. The storms of the world's madness gathered round him in his work, and the inward storms of mental agony rolled heavily over him sometimes in his private hours. But his effort was to simply fulfill such a ministry to lost men as would gain them back to God and eternal life. And doing all this, going even to the cross for love's sake, in a perfectly simple devotion, what will more certainly follow than that even the law thus gloriously fulfilled in his ministry, is itself raised into power by the honor he confers upon it? [53]

Two points need to be observed. First, that the law fulfilled by Christ's vicarious love and ministry was exactly the same that man's sin had cast off and desecrated. The violated law came back upon man to overwhelm him when Christ showed us the goodness which was in it. Second, in the suffering and sacrifice of Christ, there was nothing new expressed, except the revelation of that eternal and perfect law which was at the foundations of the world. Bushnell related the sacrifice of Christ to creation:

This same agony and passion heaved in the breast of God's virtue, even from before the world's foundations. God was suffering in feeling for the ages to be, even before the evil was. In his counsel of creation he could not think of wrong, and disorder, and pain breaking loose, without being exercised for it according to its nature. There was a losing side of pain, in his goodness, just because it was good; only the loss was never a true loss, because it was eternally repaid by the willingness to lose for love's sake. The Gethsemane of his compassions kept company with his joys, and the conscious goodness of one was high enough to exalt the conscious bliss of the other. All this now appears, in the specially human facts of Christ and his passion. The law that was being thus sublimely fulfilled, in God's suffering love from eternity, is only now fulfilled to human view, by the suffering ministry of Jesus. [54]

[53] *Ibid.*, pp. 315–316; cf. also Chapter I, Part I; Bushnell quoted Edwards at this point, *Vicarious Sacrifice*, p. 310; cf. Jonathan Edwards, *Miscellaneous Observations; Vicarious Sacrifice*, p. 310, "We had no claims to lay upon him, any more than our enemy has a claim upon us, that we shall sacrifice our peace, or life, to his benefit. It was simply obligation to the grand, everlasting, essentially vicarious principle of love, an obligation to be gracious, and do by his disobedient subjects, since he could well do it, better than they deserve; which if he could not consent to, he must be quite another and less approvable character before the standards of his own perfect mind." Bushnell also quoted Anselm, p. 311, and Bellamy pp. 311, 312.
[54] *Vicarious Sacrifice*, p. 318.

206

VI. *God's Rectoral Honor*

There was still another aspect of forgiveness which Bushnell wanted considered, and that was what he called, "God's Rectoral Honor Effectively Maintained."[55] God was the administrator of instituted government, and as such, was practically the government Himself. However, if God's magisterial character (His Rectoral Honor and Justice) were in any way reduced by the bestowal of free justification, the consequences would be fatal, said Bushnell. "How shall God be just and have respect in the character of justice, unless he executes justice?," Bushnell asked. The usual answer to this question Bushnell found in terms of a substitutionary theory, with the concept of penal suffering, expiation, judicial satisfaction, ransom, purchase, bearing the curse, payment of the debt, and so on. A unique New England interpretation of the theory was that, if Christ had borne the punishment of the world, no principle of justice in God would allow Him to inflict that same punishment upon the transgressors again. Therefore, Christ, with His sacrifice on the cross maintained the righteousness of God without punishment. Christ, by His death, demonstrated God's abhorrence to sin. The righteousness of God was maintained even though punishment of the sinner was not exacted.[56]

Bushnell dealt with this theory, and questioned whether the idea of God's abhorrence of sin was the same as the idea of God's punishment:

Abhorrence is a word of recoil simply and not a word of majesty. There is no enforcement, no judicial vigor in it. I may abhor what I am only too weak, or too much in the way of false pity, to handle with the due severity. It does not even require a perfect being to abhor sin, especially in the wicked forms of it—that is to draw back from it, as being disgusted and shocked by it. But there is no such drawing back in justice. Justice moves on in the positive vigor of the wrath-principle, girded with inflexible majesty, for the doing upon wrong of what wrong deserves. To put forward an expression therefore of God's abhorrence to sin, as a substitute for justice, is to give it the weakest possible substitute.[57]

Furthermore, Bushnell insisted that Christ's suffering in no way expressed an abhorrence to sin. To what in the transaction of the cross can God's abhorrence fasten itself?, Bushnell asked. He wrote:

[55] *Ibid.,* Chapter VI.
[56] Cf. *Ibid.,* p. 365 for a list of the forms of the substitutionary theory. Cf. "A Discourse on the Atonement," *God in Christ,* pp. 200–202.
[57] *Vicarious Sacrifice,* pp. 367–368.

If he is put in our place to suffer the penalty of our sins, then we can easily see abhorrence to our sins expressed in his suffering. But mere severities and pains laid upon him, even though God violated his own deep sympathies and loving approbations to do it, can only show the fact of something very abhorrent somewhere, and is much more likely to raise abhorrence in us, than to signify God's abhorrence to us.[58]

It is characteristic of every abhorrence theory, said Bushnell, that there is reference to Christ as being a satisfaction for sin. The use of the abhorrence theory was to avoid the repulsive idea of a penal character in Christ's suffering. However, the judicial displeasure of God remained in the suffering of Christ on the cross.

Bushnell dealt also with the most traditional interpretation of the satisfaction theory, which said that God, as a ruler, must execute justice because He is just, if not upon the guilty, then upon Christ as their substitute. This was almost to assert that God's justice was so immovably set on having its due of pains and penalties, that it would be satisfied in having them, apart from every relationship to justice. It was this aspect of the doctrine which was so odious to Bushnell. The doctrine did not improve, said Bushnell, when the pains and penalties which justice obtained for satisfaction were not exacted, but yielded by consent. Then we have a kind of justice, he said, which was willing to get its pains and penalties by contract! Nor does the doctrine become any better when it was asserted that the justice of God was satisfied from within Himself by punishment dispensed upon Himself. What kind of ruler do we have, asked Bushnell, who, to make sure of justice, took all punishment out upon Himself? Furthermore, the justice gotten in this manner was insipid and useless "for the purposes of government."

There was also the problem of the two contrary impulses in God, justice and compassion. The divine being seemed to suffer because of the conflict between these two separate and distinct sensibilities. Bushnell questioned whether a theory based upon this distinction was satisfactory, if in terms of justice the divine being Himself suffered? Bushnell concluded that the real difficulty with such a theory was with the word *justice,* which appeared to have a double meaning:

A sufficient discrimination here would have shown that the absolute justice pertaining to ethical natures is a fiction, without any shadow of reality. It is almost incredible, that a really intelligent writer should throw himself upon the axiom, 'God must be just,' 'God is inexorably obligated

[58] *Ibid.,* p. 369.

to do justly,' without perceiving that we assent to it for no other reason than that the words 'just' and 'justly' mean 'righteous' and 'rigteously'. God can not of course do any thing unrighteous, or, in that sense, unjust; that is God must keep his integrity. Is that the same thing as to say that God has no option left but to stand by retributive justice and do by all men exactly as they do to others? Calling 'the impulse to punish' justice, has he no liberty left, but to follow that impulse, just as far as it must go to be exhausted? [59]

Righteousness and justice must be distinguished at all times. Righteousness, as defined by Bushnell, is "a character grounded in the absolute, unconditioned law of right existing before government." Justice is "a rectoral, politico-judicial character, maintained by the firm vindication of government." Furthermore, a distinction must be maintained between the wrath-principle and justice; "the wrath-principle being only that moral sensibility, or passion, that impels a moral nature to the infliction of evil in redress of wrong, and steels it against the restraints of false pity;" justice is "a due infliction of such evil, according to the ill desert of the wrong." [60]

VII. *The Atonement and Justification by Faith*

Bushnell believed that this interpretation of the Vicarious Sacrifice of Christ was similar to the Biblical doctrine of the "Justification by Faith." When we are justified by faith, Bushnell said, we are "carried back into the recesses, . . . of God's eternity—back of all instituted government, back of the creation, back of the statutes, and penalties, and the coming wrath of guiltiness, and all the contrived machineries and means of grace . . . and rested with God on the base of His antecedent, spontaneous, immutable rigtheousness." [61] In the righteousness of God we are raised into the primal law which God created in all minds. We are united to God in the antecedent glories and liberties of his eternal character. The bondage and fear of our guilt is left behind. In God's righteousness, we share the confidence of His integrity. How artificial and weak in comparison, said Bushnell, is that conception of justification which only means that justice is satisfied in Christ's pains, and that faith, seizing on that fact, con-

[59] *Ibid.*, pp. 379–380; cf. the sermon, "The Gentleness of God," *Christ and His Salvation*, pp. 28–50.
[60] *Vicarious Sacrifice*, p. 381.
[61] *Ibid.*, p. 428 cf. "A Discourse on the Atonement," *God in Christ*, pp. 270 ff.

cludes that punishment is escaped. This is justification without righteousness; that is, the soul has not really obtained righteousness, it only appears to be righteous.[62]

The righteousness of God was, for Bushnell, the ground of mercy. Christ, by means of His sacrifice, became the moral power of God. He became the righteousness of God "declared." In the original and normal state of being, the righteousness of God was a power "all diffusive, a central, radiating orb—Sun itself of Righteousness." Man could not be righteous by his own works, but had to receive righteousness from God. He was to have his "righteoussing" in God, as Bushnell put it. This was why sin was so incapacitating for man. Sin separated the soul from God's life-giving character and inspirations. "Having Him no more, as the fontal source of righteousness, it falls off into an abnormal, self-centered state, where it comes under fears, and legal enforcements, and judicial wrath, and struggles vainly, if at all, to keep its account even, or recover itself to its own ideals. Works of the law, dead works carefully piled, will-works, works of supererogation, penances, alms, austerities of self-mortification—none of these, nor all of them, make out the needed righteousness."[63] In this state, man felt a need for the need for the Infinite Creator, that is, to participate in God's original state of being. Christ makes this possible for man:

He comes to men groping in a state of separation from God, consciously not even with their own standards of good, and, what is more, consciously not able to be—self-condemned when they are trying most to justify themselves, and despairing even the more, the more they endeavor to make themselves righteous by their own works—to such Christ comes forth,

[62] Vicarious Sacrifice, p. 428; cf. also p. 274, "O, how manifest it is, my hearers, as we go over this great subject, that God is full, and His grace free, to us all. What infinite pains does he take, to bring down His love to us. And yet, how does our poor human understanding labor and reel before this great mystery of godliness–height, depth, length, breadth, greater, all, than we can measure! God's loftiest work, in fact, that in which He most transcends our human conceptions, is the work in which he is engaged to save us. Creation is a mystery, the universe is a great deep; but, O! the deepest deep, in all the abysses of God's majesty is here–in the work He does to unite us into Himself. Herein is love. Herein we see that His strongest desire is to have us come unto Himself, and be one with Him forever. O, let us believe this amazing truth, this truth so full of divinity, that God's bosom is indeed open to us all. Let us hear Him say, 'Come and be forgiven.' 'Come, O, ye darkened and humiliated souls, come up out of your guilt, break your bondage, lay off your shame, and return to your Father'."
[63] Ibid., p. 432.

out of the righteousness of God, and also in the righteousness of God, that he may be the righteousness of God upon all them that believe, and are so brought close enough to him in their faith, to receive his inspirations. And this is the state of justification, not because some debt is made even, by the penal suffering of Christ, but because that normal connection with God is restored by his sacrifice, which permits the righteoussing of God to renew its everlasting flow.[64]

Bushnell considered justification not to be an accomplished fact, until there was faith in the subject. Faith was not the belief that Christ had come to even our account with justice, nor was it the belief that He had obtained a surplus merit, which was offered, over and above, as a positive righteousness. Faith was not either belief in the historical facts of Christianity. Faith was only the "trusting of one's self over, sinner to Savior, to be in him, and of him, and new charactered by him." The sinner was justified in the sense that he was justified to life. "The true account of it is that Jesus, coming into the world, with all God's righteousness upon him, declaring it to guilty souls in all the manifold evidences of his life and passion, wins their faith, and by that faith they are connected again with the life of God, and filled and overspread with his righteousness." Justification by faith produces a life of perfect liberty and confidence. Man is no longer trying to attain righteousness by himself, but receives it now derivatively. This, Bushnell said, is the strength of the Christian faith. It demonstrates to man how to be free from the pursuit of goodness. Bushnell expressed the Christian hope in this way:

In it we do not climb, but rest; we goad ourselves into no impossibilities, groan under no bondage that we can not lift; sink into no deep mires because we try to struggle out. We have a possible righteousness, because it is not ours but God's; Christ received by our faith, to be upon us and for us, all that we could wish to be for ourselves. This is the transcendent distinction, the practically sublime glory of our gospel, our great all-truth —Justification by Faith. Here is conquered the grandest of all problems, how to put confidence in the bosom of guilt, and settle a platform of virtue, that shall make duty free and joyful under all conscious disabilities.[65]

Bushnell recognized that this doctrine was Luther's discovery. He described Luther's atempt to justify himself by acts of self-morti-

[64] *Ibid.*, pp. 434–435.
[65] *Ibid.*, pp. 435–436; cf. *Christ and His Salvation*, p. 353, also the sermon "Christ Bearing the Sins of Transgressors," *Christ and His Salvation*, pp. 393–412.

fication, fastings, penances, alms, vigils, and so forth. When Luther came to the awareness that Christ would accept him just because he was guilty, Bushnell believed that he had found the true meaning of the Gospel: "At that point broke in, what light and confidence! His emancipated soul burst off all its chains in a moment, and took, as it were, the range of heaven in its liberty. He was new himself, the world was new, the gospel was new. It had not entered into his heart to conceive the things that were freely given him of God, but now he has them all at once. Justification by faith, justification by faith—his great soul is full of it; he must preach it, he must fight for it, die for it, know nothing else." [66]

VIII. *The Vicarious Sacrifice (Revised)*

The second volume dealing with the doctrine of the Atonement, *Forgiveness and Law,* which was published in 1874, was a tribute to Bushnell's intellectual honesty. He wrote in the introduction, "It seems required of me, by the unexpected arrival of fresh light, that I should make a large revision of my former treatise, . . . and especially of the Parts III and IV of the same." Because of this "arrival of fresh light," Bushnell proposed an amendment or virtual substitution of the latter half of his book on the Atonement. *The Vicarious Sacrifice* intended to exhibit the work of Christ as a reconciling power on men. Bushnell, in *Forgiveness and Law,* proposed a different exposition, "composing thus a whole of doctrine that comprises both the reconciliation of men to God and of God to men."

Bushnell began his revision with a discussion of the nature of forgiveness. In the New Testament, he said, it will be observed that forgiveness by God and forgiveness by men are set forth mutually, one by the help of the other.[67] One kind of forgiveness matches and interprets the other. True forgiveness, that is, forgiveness similar to God's forgiveness in Christ, presupposed first, a sympathy with the wrong-doing party so that one would take virtually his nature, and second, "making cost" in that nature by suffering, or expense,

---

[66] *Vicarious Sacrifice,* p. 436.
[67] Horace Bushnell, *Forgiveness and Law, Grounded in Principles Interpreted By Human Analogies,* p. 35. Bushnell used the texts, "Forgiving one another, even as God for Christ's sake hath forgiven you," "Forgive us our trespasses as we forgive them that trespass against us," in this context; cf. the sermon, "Christian Forgiveness," *Christ and His Salvation,* pp. 372–392.

or painstaking sacrifice and labor. The sympathy must be the kind that brought about an identification with the wrong-doer, "to understand and, as it were, be the man himself." The "making cost for enemies" involved a complete propitiation on behalf of the wrong-doer. Suffering and atonement (that is, propitiation) is the necessary correlate of forgiveness, wrote Bushnell. "Whosoever longs to live in the bright cordiality of brotherhood, and have the true enjoyment of his kind, must atone himself into the gentleness and patience of love all the way." We are required not only to be well-doers, but atoners also.[68]

This fact of our moral natures, that is, that we are to propitiate the wrongs of others, comprehends all moral natures, even the highest moral nature. "Christ, in all that pertains to his propitiation and his forgiveness to enemies, furnishes the ideas and helps we work by in ours, and we are even to allow that we have no complete adequacy without them; but our propitiations and forgivenesses, when these are wrought, suppose analogical properties in our very nature, by which Christ may set us on working correspondently with himself, and forgiving our enemies even as he does his."[69]

Bushnell was insisting in *Forgiveness and Law,* as he had in *Vicarious Sacrifice,* that the redemption of man depended upon the very nature of God, which was characterized by righteousness. God in Christ effected the Atonement for man, because He is righteous and must go beyond the boundaries of strict justice. God was not too holy to forgive sin, rather forgiveness was the primary mode of the expression of His holiness. The depth of His holiness was matched by the depth of His forgiveness.[70] His main intention in *Forgiveness and Law* was to show that there was no antagonism between the demands of the Law and the promises of the Gospel. Bushnell asserted that no forgiveness, whether by man or God, obliterated the fact of a wrong. "The bad act stands forever, plainly

[68] Bushnell gave a number of examples of the way forgiveness is to be given, *Forgiveness and Law,* pp. 42–48; p. 48: "... human forgivenesses are possible to be consummated only by the help of some placation or atonement, or cost-making sacrifice. The forgiving party must be so far entered into the lot and state of the wrong-doing party, as to be thoroughly identified with him, even to the extent of suffering by him and for him. Some alternative must be taken by the man who will truly forgive, that has power to liquefy the indifferences, or assuage the stern, over-loaded displeasures, of his moral and morally injured, morally revolted nature."

[69] *Ibid.,* pp. 52–53.

[70] *Ibid.,* p. 56.

enough, for nothing can efface or any way alter what is done. The law and its sanctions also stand as the eternal morality. And the penal sanctions work on still in the man by natural causation after he is forgiven, till they are worn out or winnowed away by the supernatural causations of grace in his life." [71] There is, however, an essential relationship between law and grace. It is of the essence of this relationship that although grace more than fulfills the demands of the law, the law is not thereby destroyed. Both law and grace exist within separate and distinct spheres, and are autonomous within these spheres. They both serve the objective to build character.

Bushnell said that the forgiveness of sins was a purely personal matter, in which the love and feeling and offended holiness of God were involved. All wrongs, as personal offenses, were therefore violations of the law. Forgiveness, although personal, had no power to right the injuries of broken law. The law itself, because it was impersonal, had no power to forgive. Even God, the administrator of the law, had no power to annul the wrong or the damage done to it. Forgiveness made a man right before God, but not before the law.

We must always recognize, said Bushnell, that Jesus Christ was insistent on keeping the commandments, and that faithful obedience to the commandments was the test of the character of His disciples. He wrote:

The law, by itself, makes nothing in us answer to its own high intentions, and is never expected, simply as law, to become a footing of salva-

[71] *Ibid.*, pp. 57–58. Bushnell met the objection that his concept of forgiveness excluded the Trinity acting in the redemption of man. It may be objected, he said, that, when we are propitiated towards our enemy, by the cost we make for him, the whole process takes place within ourselves, and the forgiving grace is not obtained of us by the intercession or mediation of another; whereas Christ obtained the forgiveness of sin for us by what he does before God, acting in our behalf. Bushnell met this objection by saying that if Christ acted *before* God, in such a way that he was other than God, this would be tritheism and not Trinity. Christ must be the same in substance with God and must not be *other* than God: "The three are still the one, and the three-folding is but a plural in so many finite forms, used representatively as personations of the infinite One." Bushnell said: "All God's forgiving dispositions are dateless, and are cast in this mold. The Lambhood nature is in him, and the cross is set up, before the incarnate Son arrives. His own love bows itself to endurance, by the prescriptive habit of his eternity, and the forgivenesses shown us in their formative era, so to speak, under the great transaction of Calvary, are in fact the everlasting predispositions of his nature. The cross, *ab aeterno*, is in them –'the Lamb that was slain from the foundation of the world'."

tion. But it is to make a beginning of moral impression, or enforced obligation, afterwards to be consummated in the state of allegiance to Christ, and the keeping of his commandments; where the old enforcements are substituted largely by a service in liberty; where, in fact, a new character born, answering both to the law and the commandments by which the law was to be fulfilled.[72]

Bushnell defined *law* as "a rigidly unpersonal, abstract, statutory code of conduct, based in the everlasting, inherent, moral imperative, that underlies it, and gives authority both to the Supreme Legislator and his legislations." On the other hand, a *commandment* was "a less statutory, less tabulated, and more flexibly personal word than the word law." When a commandment was used by Christ, it commanded in the sense of enjoining, and enjoined in the sense of a personal authority, that is, in terms of what a person might become. The commandment was concerned to rectify the character of the individual. The law, on the other hand, was not expected to result in any complete change of character. Rather, it existed to enforce principles, the first obligations necessary to character. The law unfolded or initiated the moral sense and broke the confidence of guilt, by revealing the danger of obedience.

The commandments functioned, on the other hand, in a much broader context; that is, in terms of "God's measures." Furthermore, when man was obedient to the commandments, he left the area of the tabulated, impersonal and statutory way of rule and passed to the way of the personal. "In simply being what it is, it is commandment, and word, and way, and yoke, made easy; for it is the living and dying Christ in whom all the authorities and captivating majesty of good are constrained."

The word is a word of Christly inspiration—take my yoke, take up my cross, walk in my way, as I live, live with me, as I die, be joined to me in death. Our life code is given in the person of Jesus, and in that *living book* gets authority to be our commandment. And it is a way of commandment that leaves us free, nay that makes us free. Legal obedience is gone by forever. Impulse, inspiration, duties that are meat and drink— these are the tide-sweep of the new life quickened in us. The Son makes us free, and therefore we are free indeed. The Spirit goes with the word and commandment, as it does not with the law, wafting us onward, and where the Spirit of the Lord is there is liberty. Nay the law itself, if we use that word, being in us no more by enforcement, is become the perfect law of liberty. And so the result is that when we are engaged to keep the

[72] *Forgiveness and Law,* pp. 99–10.

commandment of Jesus, we have it keeping us, floating us on, tiding us in upon the divine fullness where we rest.[73]

What is more, the commandments were offered to faith whereas the law was not. The commandment had no penal sanction whatsoever, but spoke directly to faith, offering promise and hope, "it enlarges, lifts, kindles with energy such as belongs to the Mighty Great One whose commandment and way of life it has chosen."

How, then, are law and the commandments related to one another? The law did not bring righteousness by itself, rather it led necessarily to failure. The law, however, did bring knowledge of sin. The commandments, on the other hand, brought deliverance from sin. The knowledge of sin was necessary to the deliverance of sin, and, in this way, the law and commandment worked together.

The expectation was, and is, that a beginning made under the latter and the legal intimidations, will stamp in such imprints of authority and obligation, and raise such storms of disorder and wild remorse within, when they are violated, that the subject, driven out of all confidence in himself, will be casting about for almost any deliverance from the dreadful precipitation that is thrusting him down. Whereupon it is the plan to bring him out and up by his faith in the commandment, or second stage of discipline, into a state of new-born life. So that, between the two, and by one as truly as the other, the great final end of liberty and holy character will be consummated.[74]

The law could never be abolished. It had to be fulfilled in the commandment as if it had never been broken. The law, however, belonged to the natural order, whereas the commandment belonged to the supernatural. The law of God can never be taken away:

A thousand crosses, ransoms, atonements, would leave it exactly where it was. The taking away of sin was possible, but no taking away of the law. The sacrifice of Calvary itself, set against the law, would have had as little effect on it as upon the principles of Euclid. Therefore we must never allow to be slid into our secret apprehension, back of thought, any most latent feeling that God is at work in his Son to mend, or mitigate, or get us by, the law. It is whole as it ever was. Broken oft, as in figure, it is yet not flawed; condemning still and always everything in principle it has condemned; certain to outlast the world, even as it lived before the world in the eternal bosom of God.[75]

[73] *Ibid.*, pp. 113, 114.
[74] *Ibid.*, pp. 116, 117.
[75] *Ibid.*, pp. 119, 120.

The law therefore was a schoolmaster which brought man to Christ. As a factor in the discipline of man it was not supported by judicial sanctions, but only by such casual, ungraduated sanctions as will duly enforce the discipline. Finally, coercive discipline, under which we find ourselves, is consecrated by Christ's incarnation and death.[76]

IX. *The Passible God*

The descriptive title Bushnell used for his book on the Atonement is suggestive of his entire point of view: "The Vicarious Sacrifice Grounded in Principles of Universal Obligation." In later editions of the book, when *Forgiveness and Law* became his second volume on the Atonement, the title was changed to include "Interpreted by

[76] *Ibid.*, pp. 134 ff; cf.: "I use the term penally coercive, because there is a law sanction in the discipline, coming back upon actions, in a certain way of retaliation or retributive consequence, without being a substantive measure of their ill-desert; the object being not any making up of award, but the making us aware of what we are doing and becoming. It is the lesson we take in our schooling, to make us understand, stage by stage, ourselves and the law, and to be an efficient element in securing our obedience.", pp. 134, 135; also p. 138, "And no matter at what period in life, whether early or late, the call to repentance may be made, there is never to be a calling away from the law; for the cogencies of the law are always wanted as truly as the grace of the commandment. They work together, and are of right never to be separated; for the killing factor, so conceived, has a really beneficent office, indispensable to the true result." Also, p. 139, "There is accordingly no justice work done here, as we perfectly know. We do not live in a scheme of awards, but in a scheme of probatory discipline. Persons are not treated alike, nor wrongs alike, neither is anything kept in the scale of desert. God reserves the liberty in his own hands, to turn our experience here in what way of stress or modified comfort will best advance his good purpose in us. At the same time, while nothing is being done with us here in the terms of justice, we are duly notified and certified of a time future, when our present mixed way of discipline will be over, and we shall be carried on with our bad ways uncorrected, if so it must be, to be settled on the hardpan basis of justice pure and simple, receiving every man according to his work."; in terms of *justice* Bushnell here said, "And yet the word *justice* does not once occur in the New Testament, neither does the word *just* in any single case where it relates to Christ and his death, save in the little expression 'that he might be just', where it should be translated 'that he might be righteous'. Meantime it is sufficiently clear that God himself does not rate his justice as the fore-front attribute of his nature. He does not say, with sundry teachers who are in the particular type of sensibility that most readily admires this nearly political attribute, justice first, then love and pity afterward. He is willing to have us think of him as slow to anger, but not as slow to righteousness, or love, or patience. And when he is constrained to let some fire-tempest fall on men, he will call it 'his work, his strange work, his act, his strange act'.", pp. 141, 142.

Human Analogies." The phrase was well chosen, because Bushnell attempted, with his theory of the Atonement to bring the sacrifice of Christ "closer to our feeling and perception." Vicarious sacrifice, as applied to the Atonement meant that our Lord "simply engages at the expense of great suffering and even of death itself, to bring us out of our sins themselves and so out of their penalties." Christ took our sins upon Himself, by bearing them in His heart, in the tenderness of his more than human sensibility. But the sacrifice and the cross are Christ's "simple duties." They are not any superlative, optional kind of good, outside the common principles of virtue, but are "grounded in principles of duty and right that are universal." The vicarious sacrifice is "only just as good as it ought to be, or the highest law of right required of it." Love is essentially vicarious, whether it applies to man or God. Nothing more is necessary to comprehend the vicarious sacrifice of Christ but the familiar principle of love. This is, as Bushnell said, everywhere accepted as the fundamental law of duty. At the point of vicarious sacrifice, man is able to "look into heaven's eye itself, and read the meaning of all heavenly grace." Christ was therefore *under obligation* to do and suffer just what He did.

The Incarnation is the great act of identity of God with the human race. For this reason, Bushnell could readily say that Christ was God fulfilling the obligations of God and He suffered throughout His life even as God the Father suffered before Him. The entire Trinity was involved in the Atonement. God is not any better than He ought to be, and the essence of His perfection is that He is just as good as He ought to be. In the burdens of Christ on the cross, God the eternal Father suffered, too. Here one of Bushnell's favorite and dominant themes emerged, the idea of the passibility of God. Bushnell wrote, "Whatever we may say, or hold, or believe, concerning the vicarious sacrifice of Christ, we are to affirm in the same manner of God." In that magnificent passage, Bushnell reminded us that "there is a cross in God before the wood is seen on Calvary." It is this cross, Bushnell insisted, which Christ crucified reveals and sets before us. The whole Trinity is involved absolutely in the Atonement.

Bushnell's conception of the vicarious sacrifice of Christ is, in essence, the "moral view" of the Atonement. The life and sacrifice of Christ consists in what He does to became a renovating and saving power. Christ did not come to earth in order to die, but He died because He was already here. He came just because the law, which had been from eternity, sent Him. His incarnate appearing was the necessary appearance in time of God's eternal love. He descended to man, because this was God's manner of demonstrating His love. Christ suffered death on His own accord, not as an act of obedience, but on account of His obedience in maintaining right. The primary objective of Christ is, therefore, "the healing of souls," that is, to reconcile them with God. Bushnell could, therefore, speak of the "Christed consciousness of the disciples":

It is not the account of their Christian experience, and of the gospel as related thereto, that Christ has done something before God's throne, and wholly apart from all effect in them, to make their acceptance possible; and then that the Holy Spirit, by a divine efficiency in them, changes their hearts. No such theologic gospel of dry wood and hay is the gospel of the apostles. They find everything, in their human nature, penetrated by the sense, and savor, and beauty, and glory of Christ. Their whole consciousness is a Christ-consciousness—every thing good and strong in them is Christ within. Worsted in all their struggles of will-work and self-regeneration, they still chant their liberty in Christ and say—"For the law of the Spirit of life in Christ Jesus hath made me free." Their joy is to be consciously Christed, fully possessed by Christ; to have him dwell in them, and spread himself over and through all the senses and sentiments, and willings, and works of their life.[77]

It is difficult to put the work of Christ in a dogmatic formula, Bushnell asserted. Christ's mission can never become a theorem, or a form of thought, but it is rather the process of reconciliation itself. The work of Christ consisted in exactly the whole life of Jesus—all that He said and did. Christ, by means of His life and teachings, becomes the moral power of God. This identification of Christ with God reaches its highest point when Christ "humanizes God to men." The revelation of a suffering God, Bushnell maintained, permitted Christ to become the "Great Moral Power of God;" "so that whoever believes in his name takes the power of it, and is transformed radically, even at the deepest centre of life, by it,—born of God." [78] Christ's life and death provide the *moral power* for the transformed life. This is in essence Bushnell's "moral theory" of the Atonement, that is, that the objective of the Atonement was the ethical good of mankind.

It was Bushnell's major intention to direct the doctrine of the

[77] *Vicarious Sacrifice*, pp. 158–159.
[78] *Ibid.*, p. 230.

Atonement away from the argument which held that "God creates all law by His will, and can make anything right, or obligatory, by His enactment." Bushnell wanted to get the doctrine away from those theologians who supported the theory of penal substitution in all of its many forms, as related to justice, penalty, righteousness, forgiveness, etc. He wanted to bring the doctrine into the realm of eternal law, where it could relate itself directly to the consciousness of right and wrong, that is, to the ability of man to make an ethical decision.

The possibility of moral discrimination allowed Bushnell to introduce the topic of law as related to instituted government. One cannot resolve Christ's work under "political analogies":

> What is said of law and justice, under the analogies of human government does not appear to hold, without qualifications not given. It can not be that such analogies of law, and justice, and penalty, and pardon, prepared in the civil state, are not to be used in religion. Like all other analogies of the outward life, they were designed to be. And yet there are few close observers, I suspect, who have not sometimes been so far impressed, by the fatalities discovered in attempts to resolve Christ's work under this kind of analogy, as to seriously doubt whether any thing reliable can be thus accomplished. There certainly can not be, unless the analogy is carefully qualified by others, such for example as those of the family, the field, the shop, the market. There is also another kind of qualifier, that is obtained by getting a partially distinct footing for the subject, in a province of thought which is not under such analogies.[79]

What Bushnell asserted is that *before* God's will, there is "that necessary, everlasting, ideal law of *Right*." To think is to be obliged by it. Obedience to this law makes a complete society until disobedience brings in confusion and disorder. God, then, institutes "government and redemption together." Instituted government inaugurates justice and penal sanctions, thereby appealing to man's moral nature all over again.

Christ's sacrifice pushes everything off the basis of justice:

> The justice satisfied is satisfied with injustice! the forgiveness prepared is forgiveness on the score of pay! the judgment-day award disclaims the fact of forgiveness after payment made, and even refuses to be satisfied, taking payment again! What meantime has become of the penalties threatened, and where is the truth of the law? The penalties threatened, as against wrong doers, are not to be executed on them, because they have been executed on a right doer! viz., Christ.[80]

[79] *Ibid.*, p. 233.
[80] *Ibid.*, p. 293.

But, nonetheless, Christ has demonstrated His respect for the law. Christ is able to combine His own moral influence with natural retributive forces. What has occurred, therefore, is that the moral influence of Christ and the natural laws of morality work together. Bushnell related Christ to the law in the following way:

... Christ has set the law precept in a position of great honor and power, enduing it with such life and majesty, in men's convictions, as it otherwise never could have had. (1) He proposes, we have seen, no remission of sins which does not include a full recovery to the law. (2) All that he does and suffers in his sacrifice, he as truly does for the resanctification of the law as for our recovery. (3) In his incarnation, he incarnates the same, and brings it nigh to men's feelings and convictions, by the personal footing he gains for it in humanity. (4) He honors it again by his obedience, before the eyes of mankind; the grandest fact of human knowledge.[81]

Bushnell referred to his distinction between the natural and the supernatural to clarify this point. There is first a natural order of justice, and then a supernatural order of mercy interacting with it. The cooperation of these two realms is very difficult to trace. But, said Bushnell, there was no judicial sanction which could be verbally stated which was more exact or closer to the truth of justice than that which is in fact asserted in the penalties denounced. There was a constant "going on of justice and mercy—the natural order and the supernatural—moving with locked hands, sometimes issuing a deliverance, and sometimes a finality of retribution." But neither of them violate the *everlasting and fixed ordinance*. The executive laws of justice are natural, he said, but the person of Christ, His character, His moral power, His death, and sacrifice belong to the supernatural realm. The mercy of God in Christ's sacrifice works together with the retributive causes of justice, to bring forth a result which one could not effect alone, that is, the conversion of man. Bushnell was quite insistent that the order of justice was not violated, rather it functioned according to the natural structure of things. "Even as Christ came to nature in miracle, as a higher first term, doing all his mighty works without stopping, or suspending any law, so much more easily may it be true, that his new creating and delivering work of mercy, operating only by moral power, falls in conjunctively among the retributive causes of nature, and without any discontinuance turns them to a serviceable office, in accomplishing its own great

[81] *Ibid.*, p. 321.

designs."[82] The mercy of God and the retributive causes of justice always work together, to bring about the conversion of man.

Christ had entered practically into the condition of evil and was made subject to it. This condition of evil was called the "curse" because it referred to the expulsion from paradise of the primal pair. The effects of sin were therefore its "curse" upon us. The laws of retribution, "set in deep and firm in the economy of nature itself," were God's appointed ministers of justice. Everything, therefore, including the whole realm of causes, function as an organ of God's moral retributions. When sin broke out, all of the causes in nature worked against it. As sin is itself against the will of God, and as everything centers in that will, a shock of discord ran through the general framework of life and experience:

> The crystalline whole of things is shattered, as it were by some hard blow, and the fragments begin to grind heavily upon each other. The soul itself, lacerated by its own wrong, winces for pain, like an eye that has extinguished sight by gazing at the sun. The passions, appetites, fears, aspirations are pitched into a general quarrel with each other, and especially with the reason and the conscience; and the will, trying to usurp control of all, when it can not sufficiently master any thing, falls off its throne, as a tyrant plucked down by revolt. The body suffers a like shock of disorder, and true health vanishes before the secret crowd of infections, twinges, and immediate combustions, that steal into the flesh, and traverse the bones, and go burning along the nerves. Evil becomes a kind of organic power in society, in the same way; a kingdom of darkness, a conspiracy of bad opinions and powers usurped for oppression, under which truth and goodness and right and religion itself are, either badly perverted, or cruelly persecuted. The very world, made subject to vanity, groans and travails every where, waiting for some redemption that can redeem it from itself.[83]

Corporate evil is what the Scriptures called the "curse." Directly into the "curse" has Christ come in the Incarnation. Christ became a true member of the race, and was subject to all the liabilities of the corporate world into which He had come. He entered into man's humanity in a real way, not as a "dainty, and merely ideal embodiment." The world was to him just as it is to us. He is joined to all the corporate woes and judicial disorders of the curse:

> He is 'grieved,' he 'groans in spirit,' he 'has a baptism to be baptized with' and he is 'straitened' by the dreadful pressure of it, till it be ac-

[82] *Ibid.*, pp. 284–285; also pp. 294–295.
[83] *Ibid.*, pp. 385–386.

complished. He is 'troubled in spirit,' he cries 'now my soul is troubled,' and finally, when all his work is ended, and there is no longer any active ministry to divert or occupy his attention, he sinks, at once, into a dreadful superhuman agony and horror of darkness, moaning heavily—'My soul is exceeding sorrowful even unto death!' Now in all these incipient agonies, and finally in the last great agony of all, his trouble is mainly mental, as we can see for ourselves.[84]

On the cross, when He dies, he had already been repulsed in a dreadful but moral way by the curse and judicial horrors of evil. Christ had never undertaken to bear God's punishments for us, but He came down simply in love, to "the great river of retributive causes where we were drowning to pluck us out."

Christ was careful to respect God's instituted government and law in his vicarious work. We must observe, said Bushnell, that although He had all powers to stop the retributive causes and strip away the whole instituted order of justice, He did not do it. Neither would He discontinue any of the laws of nature by His miracles. Bushnell concluded:

He is a being strictly supernatural, and his work in the deliverance of transgressors is also supernatural; but in coming to them, in their thraldom, to lift them out by his divine love and sympathy, he only masters the bad causes, but does not stop them. It could as well be imagined that a strong magnet, lifting its iron weight into the air, discontinues, or annihilates the law of gravity. Nothing in short is so conspicuous, in the vicarious suffering and death of Christ, as the solemn deference he pays to God's instituted justice in the world, and even to the causes from which he comes to redeem.[85]

Forgiveness and Law maintained the characteristic emphases of Bushnell. He asserted the "moral view" of the Atonement, but added that he was now to interpret "all that is prepared and suffered in the propitiation of God and the justification of men" in relationship to the moral pronouncements of human nature and society. He stated that nothing could be true of God or Christ, which could not be made intelligible by human analogies. One cannot interpret God, he said, except in terms of what one finds in his own personal instincts and ideas. There is a "grand analogy" or an identity between our moral nature and that of God. Such a position led Bushnell to make the statement that, "He is brought so close to us that almost every thing that occurs in the workings of exigencies of our moral

[84] *Ibid.*, pp. 387-388.
[85] *Ibid.*, p. 390.

223

instincts may even be expected in his." [86] The statement is, however, quite in accord with Bushnell's conception of the relationship of the natural to the supernatural realms. The individual is located within that structure of reality which God is employing to redeem man. The individual, furthermore, is placed directly into the very process which is effecting the reconciliation of man to nature. However, Christ does nothing in His love and vicarious sacrifice which one man is not expected to do for another. It is exactly at this point that the world (including man and nature) is redeemed. The principles of salvation are principles of "universal obligation." Man becomes one with God when he permits himself to be drawn into the suffering of Christ. The "moral view" of the Atonement thereby makes suffering the supreme expression of what it means to be human—and at the same time, nature is reconciled to the supernatural.

[86] *Forgiveness and Law,* p. 35.

CHAPTER VII

Conclusion:
The Accomplishment of Horace Bushnell

I. *American Liberal Theology in the 19 Century*

Horace Bushnell has been designated as the father of American liberal theology.[1] This assertion may be verified in terms of the task that confronted him, to deliver the religious life of his day from the bondage of inflexibility and obscurantism, and to restore it to naturalness and reality! Bushnell's biographer, Theodore T. Munger, enumerated the four major contributions of the Hartford theologian to American religious thought. He brought relief, Munger wrote, from 1) a revivalism that ignored Christian growth, 2) a conception of the Trinity bordering on tritheism, 3) a view of miracles that implied a suspension of natural law, and 4) a theory of the atonement that failed to recognize the law of human life.[2] Charles H.

---

[1] Cf. John W. Buckham, *Progressive Religious Thought in America,* pp. 6 ff; Theodore T. Munger, Horace Bushnell, *Preacher and Theologian,* p. 413; Williston Walker, "Bushnell," *Encyclopedia Britannica,* 11 ed.; William Warren Sweet, *Makers of Christianity,* pp. 295 ff.; Walter Marshall Horton, *Realistic Theology,* (New York: Harper and Brothers, 1934), pp. 26 ff; Ernest Trice Thompson, *Changing Emphases in American Preaching,* Chap. 1, "Horace Bushnell and the beginning of American Liberalism," pp. 9–49; A. C. McGiffert, *The Rise of Modern Religious Ideas,* (New York: The Macmillan Company, 1915), p. 277; S. Smith, *Changing Conceptions of Original Sin,* pp. 162–163; cf. Bushnell's conception of his role from "God's Way with a Soul," the few notes he left for an autobiography, quoted from Munger, *op. cit.,* pp. 379–380: "My figure in this world has not been great, but I have had a great experience. I have never been a great agitator, never pulled a wire to get the will of men, never did a politic thing. It was not for this reason, but because I was looked upon as a singularity,–not exactly sane, perhaps, in many things,–that I was almost never a president or vice-president of any society, and almost never on a committee. Take the report of my doings on the platform of the world's business, and it is naught. I have filled no place at all. But still it has been a great thing even for me to live. In my separate and merely personal kind of life, I have had a greater epic transacted than was ever written, or could be. The little turns of my way have turned great changes,–what I am now as distinguished from the merely mollusk and pulpy state of infancy; the drawing-out of my powers, the correcting of my errors, the winnowing of my faults, the washing of my sins; that which has given me principles, opinions, and, more than all, a faith, and, as the fruit of this, an abiding in the sense and free partaking of the life of God."

[2] Munger, *op. cit.,* p. 387.

Hopkins, the historian of the Social Gospel in America, pointed to Bushnell as the great liberalizer of mid-nineteenth century American theology. He did more than any other, said Hopkins, to break down the extreme individualism of the Old Puritanism and to direct the "New Theology" to its unique emphasis upon the Social Gospel.[3] Ernest T. Thompson, in his massive study of the changing emphases in American preaching, found that Bushnell oriented his theology about moral intuition, religious feeling, the facts of religious experience, overagainst the prevailing dogmatic interpretations of Scripture taken as literal scientific fact, logical deductions arrived at from unexamined assumptions, and metaphysical speculations remote from life; "In a word he brought theology from the realm of mere logic to the realm of life." [4] John W. Buckham, the historian of 19 and 20 Century Congregationalism, called Bushnell the father of the constructive theology which developed in the Congregational Church at the turn of the 20 Century. The reason for this, Buckham designated, was Bushnell's 1) restoration of the organic nature of the Christian community, 2) replacement of the narrow rationalism of New England theology with a theology of experience, 3) destruction of the dividing wall between nature and the supernatural, and revealing them both as "parts of one system," 4) recovery of Christ as the central light of Christianity.[5] Bushnell did indeed enable Christian theology to emerge from its inflexibility and obscurantism!

However, if Bushnell is the father of American liberal thought, it must be recognized that America had been particularly provincial in theology, especially in terms of any direct influence from the European continent. Bushnell broke through American theological isolationism, but did so *not* directly because of any knowledge of German theological thought. It was through Coleridge's *Aids to Reflection* (the book to which American and British religious liberalism owes more than to any other writing), that Bushnell was able to develop a theology adequate for the "modern" 19 Century world in which he lived and worked. It is to Bushnell we must go for the classic formulation of the "New Theology," that particular formulation of the Christian faith in America which displayed a distrust of abstract reason and a confidence in moral faith and

[3] Charles Howard Hopkins, *The Rise of the Social Gospel in American Protestantism 1865–1915*, (New Haven: Yale University Press, 1940), p. 5.
[4] Thompson, *op. cit.,* p. 44.
[5] Buckham, *op. cit.,* pp. 3–32.

religious intuition, a theological approach which a half-century earlier had effected a revolution in Germany. Bushnell has been called the "Schleiermacher of America," [6] and received this designation because he, more than anyone else in America in the 19 Century, created a new theology, a theology of the modern world, in which the timeless truths of Christian experience could be expressed. He challenged men to a new way of thinking, and accomplished this task in the midst of a confused and rigid theological scene: in the midst of the "stern, ironlimbed speculative logic of our New England theology."

As Bushnell emancipated New England theology from a confining rationalism, and replaced it with a theology of experience, he did so by demonstrating the superiority of intuition to reason and spirit to form and dogma. He bridged the chasm between these two poles of theology by his "Essay on Language," which may be regarded as the indispensable preface to all of his work. Both orthodox and Unitarian New England theologians take themselves too seriously, he intimated. The true basis of theology is not built upon words and logical concepts, because they have merely a symbolic, analogical truth, mixed with inevitable error. Seeking for an explanation of the ineptitude and stagnation in theology, Bushnell found it at length in the very nature of language, supplemented by its inadequate aids, grammar and logic. A great many of the theological dilemmas which are ours, Bushnell said, resulted from the misuse of this instrument of communication. The true basis of theology is not to be found in any "tortured reading" of the Scriptures, but in a *Perceptive Power in spiritual life . . . an immediate experimental knowledge of God."* "Words of thought or spirit" are related to the truth only as form to spirit, he added. Doctrines and creedal formulations can only be "proximate representations" of the truth. The language of poetry and paradox express more adequately the truth about God than does the logical structuring of ideas. The Holy Scriptures would be affected initially. They could no longer be studied as "magazines of propositions" but as "poetic forms of life." No more will it be imagined, Bushnell stated, that poetry and rhythm are accidents or figments of the imagination of the human race. Rather than this, we shall know, he said, that poetry is the real and true state of man, "the proper and last ideal of souls." The theology which would

[6] Horton, *op. cit.,* p. 27.

emerge from such a method could not be based upon any creedal formulation, but the believer would be permitted to embrace many creeds simultaneously, as moments in a complex truth, essentially inexpressible. It would be less clear than the older theology, because it would initiate from a "humbler state of mind." Theological knowledge would not be made up of a scheme of wise sentences, rather it would be "a Living State." The discovery of Truth will rely upon inspiration and not upon reflection. This, then, is Bushnell's starting point, and to evaluate Bushnell properly, one must be cognizant of the fundamental position the theory of language had in his entire theological system. Bushnell's entrance into the company of New England theology had been compared with Copernicus appearing among the Ptolemists. Whatever creative energy Bushnell gave to the theology of his time is based upon the new language he gave to theological statements. He exchanged definition in theology for expression. It is this theme which is his initial contribution to American theological thought. Religion was to be freed from the tyranny of words. New avenues of expression were to be made available to the Christian believer. "Spiritual realities" could be addressed to faith, feeling and the imaginative reason. The essential mood of American liberalism was expressed here too. The attempt to be always irenic, the disparagement of clarity in the use of religious language, the disavowal of theological systems, the ability to embrace mutually contradictory proposals, are all set forth with energy and enthusiasm.[7] The temper of Bushnell's audience was romantic, and he responded to their sensitivities.

Once Bushnell had a language for theology, he could then proceed to construct a system. It is correct to assert that Bushnell disallowed theological systems in favor of intuition or, as he said, "inbreathings of the divine love and power." But Bushnell had a method by which the insights of Divinity, which replaced Theology, could be interpreted and unified. He did not condemn theological systems outright; he did condemn, however, the theological systems operative in New England during his time. He perceived that to crucify the "instinct of system," was to crucify the intelligence. "I have a certain conviction, whether I can show the reasons or not, that we must have something, somehow held and exercised, that may be called theology."[8] He refrained ultimately

[7] Ibid., p. 28.
[8] Christ in Theology, p. 80.

from the condemnation of theology, and at length, contributed to its advance. He found a theological system which was suited to his own spiritual aspirations in terms of the principle which lay at the basis of language, that is, that the world of the spirit pervades all of what we call the natural world, that *man* who has the capacity for the spirit, belongs to the supernatural realm as surely as God belongs to it.

Bushnell assaulted the conception of two separate realms, which held apart the spiritual and the natural, and revelation and reason. The result of this separation for New England theology was that the natural world became more and more estranged from the spiritual or the supernatural, and became drearily dualistic. Bushnell enabled New England theology to break down the dividing wall between nature and the supernatural, and to include both as the "one system" of God, all governed by the divine purpose, all revealing the divine presence in various degrees. The proposition of *Nature and the Supernatural* was that the restriction of the supernatural from the natural order was alien to the Christian faith. Bushnell felt that the segregation of one from the other resulted in the supernatural receiving an arbitrary and unreal character. New England theology which upheld itself as the guardian of supernatural religion, had, in effect, created a frigid dualism between the supernatural and nature. Bushnell recognized this error and sought to show that "man himself belongs primarily and chiefly to the supernatural realm." Personality, he said, was a spiritual reality, and was the factor in man which elevated him above nature. Man possessed personality, and therefore did not come under the law of cause and effect, but instead under the moral law. If this one point is clearly apprehended, all the difficulties of our subject are at once relieved, if not absolutely and completely removed, Bushnell said. Man is rooted in nature, but is sovereign over nature. Man, as a sovereign volitional agent, is able to act upon the chain of cause and effect in nature from outside of nature. Nature is a secondary realm of being; it is only the "stage, field, medium, vehicle, for the universe; that is for God and his powers." Man does not suspend any of nature's laws; he only applies them in new combinations. God was able to effect change by new combinations of nature's elements and forces, never by the suspension or disruption of nature's laws. A naturalistic tendency in Christian theology could not do justice to the redemptive power of the Christian faith, said Bushnell. Furthermore, it threatened to leave God out of the universe altogether, or at least to restrict his actions to the operations of the natural law. A miracle becomes, therefore, "a supernatural act, an act, that is, which operates on the chain of cause and effect from without the chain." The disorders and deformities of creation provide "anticipative consequences" of man's lapse into spiritual deformity. The "dark things" of nature—pain, disease, danger, plague, insanity, mutabilities—are disciplinary dispensations adapted for moral uses. By trial and testing, they aid the development of character.

Christianity, of course, is affected. The world, said Bushnell, is governed supernaturally in the interest of Christianity.

Finding now, that we ourselves are supernatural creatures ... what shall we think of God's relation to nature? If it be nothing incredible that we should act on the chain of cause and effect in nature, is it more incredible that God should thus act? ... Strange as it may seem this is the grand offense of supernaturalism, the supposing that God can act on nature from without, on the chain of cause and effect in nature from without the chain of connection, by which natural consequences are propagated—exactly that which we ourselves are doing as the most familiar things of our lives.[9]

The world has been brought to a state of disorder by man's misuse of his freedom. Redemption for man is only possible through the supernatural interposition of God. This meant, therefore, for Bushnell, that our world "taken in the whole comprehension of its import ... is nothing but a vast, supernatural, reciprocal Providence in which our God is reigning as an ever present, ever mindful counselor and guide and friend, a Redeemer of our sin, a hearer of our prayers."[10]

Bushnell's constant appeal to nature and its laws was purposive. He rejected the view of nature that included God but was not transcended by Him. His method, however, was not to bring the supernatural down to the realm of the natural, but instead to elevate the natural to the supernatural. Man is freed from the false dichotomy between the material and the spiritual. By virtue of the consciousness of his freedom, man could be identified with God. Nature, therefore, as a co-factor with the supernatural, became "a vast anal-

[9] *Nature and the Supernatural*, pp. 58–59.
[10] *Ibid.*, p. 408; cf. p. 19, "The world was made to include Christianity; under that becomes a proper and complete frame of order; to that crystallizes, in all its appointments, events, and experiences; in that has the design or final cause revealed, by which all its distributions, laws, and historic changes are determined and systematized."

230

ogon of the world of spirit". All things were divine thereby. Bushnell's major contribution, therefore, was the new definition he gave to man—and he united him with God.

Bushnell was the first theologian in New England to bring the modern sense of nature into his thought. The theological task which he set for himself and which informed his system, that is "the wide hypothesis of the world, and the great problems of life and sin and supernatural redemption and Christ and a Christly Providence and a divinely certified history and of superhuman gifts entered into the world and finally of God as related to all . . .," [11] was no more than the attempt to interpret nature spiritually. What Bushnell saw was that not only was this God's world, but God was in His world. Every one of his treatises was an effort to bring nature and the supernatural into some kind of relevant unity. Bushnell did not deny a certain antithesis between nature and the supernatural, but he defined the supernatural in such a way that the two could be embraced in the one category of nature when viewed as the order of God in creation. The supernatural is the realm of freedom, and it is as natural as the physical realm.

The problem remained for Bushnell to translate his conception of the relationship of the realms of nature and the supernatural into the traditional theological ideas of his time. This possibility was always alive, for New England theology did not conceive that its formulations were absolute, although it was exceedingly reluctant to make changes in its theological definitions. The Congregational Order, based upon democratic principles of equality, permitted every responsible Christian to articulate his faith, and encouraged redefinition and re-formulation. The Unitarian movement, in spite of its brilliant leaders and social alertness, was constantly threatened with the dissolution of its corporate unity. [12] In the midst of these movements, Bushnell came on the scene, and undertook to reinterpret the basic truths of the Christian faith and to restate them in terms of life itself, that is, in terms of his conception of nature and the supernatural. Bushnell had already applied this conception to the category of the family in *Christian Nurture*. The immediate occasion for the volume was the problem of revivalism within the New England Churches, and the theological confusion the revivals evoked. Bushnell, primarily the pastor and only later the theologian, saw

[11] *Ibid.*, pp. iii–iv.
[12] Cf. Munger, *op. cit.*, pp. 385–386.

that the Church was in grave jeopardy if the extreme individualism of the revivals was not altered. Salvation became relevant solely to adults. Children were poor substitutes for adults, and if salvation was relevant to them, it was only in terms of the adult conditions for salvation. The sacraments, particularly Baptism, as Bishop Brownell reminded the Congregationalists, had lost its meaning. The Holy Spirit was hidden behind sentimentalism and emotionalism, and its presence was determined beforehand by the effectiveness of the revivalist. Superstition was widespread, and the prevailing spirit of the time bordered on the peripheral and heretical. The major problem for Bushnell as the pastor of a growing Hartford church, was the place of children in the church.

Bushnell asserted that there existed an "organic relation" between the parent and the child, and that children were to be included in the faith of their parents, "partakers with them in their covenant." By virtue of the parents' faith, children were brought into a "peculiar" relationship to God. The child growing up in a Christian home was "ingrafted" into the life of God by becoming an organic participant in the life of the family. The process of becoming a Christian was therefore a simple developmental one, *without* any need of an extraordinary and unnatural crisis of conversion. Christian nurture replaced revivalism in New England, and Bushnell, in effect, was simply reminding Christians in New England of one of the fundamental principles of the Puritans, that is, that children in the Christian household participated in the Christian community from the beginning, and were to "grow up in the Lord."[13] Bushnell provided the churches with a doctrine of Christian growth, and turned the direction of thought in the churches to the young. He rejected at the same time that theory of religion which constructed the world in halves: "The kingdom of God is to stretch itself side by side with the kingdom of darkness." The individual had to be dragged into the church by conquest as a result. Furthermore there could be no normal expectation of the possible advancement of human society and the universal prevalence of Christian virtue. The dualism which underlay the theology of revivalism was extravagant and unreasonable, said Bushnell. The growth of Christian virtue nonetheless required a struggle with evil. In spite of the struggle of the soul with an innate "pravity," Bushnell insisted that the life of God was the life of the

[13] Cf. *ibid.*, pp. 70 ff; cf. Smith, *op. cit.*, pp. 142–143.

race. The Christian faith flows normally into the life of successive generations and forms an organic spiritual continuum. Christian Nurture—"growth, not conquest is . . . the true method of Christian progress."

The doctrine of the Trinity too, demonstrated Bushnell's conception of the relationship of nature to the supernatural. The real point of controversy between the Orthodox and the Unitarians did not relate so much to the being of God and to the nature of man. The real dispute with the Unitarians was over the fall and the depravity and regeneration of man. The Unitarians protested against these doctrines as they did the concept of hell proposed earlier by Jonathan Edwards. However, the point of attack seemed to be the denial of the Trinity. The success of the Unitarian movement was in terms of the denial of the Trinity, which was made to appear as a tritheism, or at least as a logical contradiction, that three are one and one is three. The Orthodox New England theologians had not properly understood the Nicene formula of the Trinity, and their teaching on the subject was extremely confusing.[14]

God in Christ did not defend the traditional orthodox definition of the Trinity, but it did clarify the theological issues involved which would have led the church to embrace a tritheism. Instead of affirming three metaphysical persons in the substances of the Godhead, Bushnell allowed for an "instrumental Trinity" which was sufficient for faith and adequate for practical religious usages. The Trinity was taken out of the realm of speculation by Bushnell and placed instead in the realm where it could become an aspect of Christian experience. Bushnell did not attempt to fathom the internal nature of God. Rather he assumed the strictest unity and simplicity of God's nature, and discovered that God could not be "sufficiently revealed to us" without *evolving a Trinity of* persons. By so doing, Bushnell brought God and the fullness of His being into humanity. The Trinity was a necessary truth because the personalities of the Godhead (the *dramatis personae* of revelation) were directly related to human capacities and wants. The doctrine of the Trinity must be maintained because it produced mutuality between God and man, and was the most effective means by which God could communicate His love to us. The idea too of an immanent God, whose presence might be intuitively apprehended through all of nature, provided

[14] Cf. Munger, *op. cit.*, pp. 390–391.

all that the human heart required for its personal needs. God is a personal unity, however, who reveals Himself as Father, Son, and Holy Ghost. The three persons of the Trinity are realized in experience, if not comprehended by human reason. This was, therefore, Bushnell's Trinity of manifestation.

In his work, *The Vicarious Sacrifice*, Bushnell argued that the Atonement had to be understood in the light of the Incarnation. The prevalent theories of the Atonement in New England were scholastic doctrines, which had little to do with the human situation. It was not the theory of the maintenance of general justice or the idea of the propitiation by Christ of the sins of a perverted humanity, which was needed. More than this, the New England Christian needed a doctrine that would help him to become personally just before God. The Atonement as an act of God for and on behalf of man had long been under-emphasized. The Incarnation provided Bushnell with the doctrine he needed to reassert the life of Christ as a manifestation in humanity of the eternal God, who entered into the world to re-engage the world's love to Him. The Incarnation emphasized the divine Fatherhood and the obedient Sonship. It was this theme which meant that the life and death of Christ were related to the possibility of man developing his divineness; man possessed the ability to become "Christed." The Atonement was interpreted, therefore, in terms of the vicarious suffering that is inherent in all true love, and became a part of every Christian's duty. The perfect realization of humanity could be found in Christ, who did not die on the Cross to satisfy some demand of government or even the commands of an angry but lawful God. Christ suffered to "bring us out of our sins," that is, to enable man to realize his oneness with God. The Atonement is, therefore, a moral achievement. The character of man is renovated, and man is able to love sacrifically, both God and his fellow man.

When Bushnell spoke of "the Character of Jesus, forbidding his possible classification with men", he distinguished Christ's *character* as being essentially different from that of man. The Atonement was oriented to the Incarnation, but it was the demand that every man should become "Christed," which highlighted the nature of the Incarnation. One becomes a "Christed man" when one reflects in his own character the character of the Master. By the power of Christ, Bushnell meant much the same as what he meant by *personality,* a human power released by His resurrection. Christ is therefore, "The

234

Gospel of the Face," revealing the essential human meaning of the Gospel. Christ "humanizes" God to men.[15] God must, of course, be a passible God, because only a suffering God can radically transform the character of man:

Here then it is, in the revelation of a suffering God, that the great name of Jesus becomes the embodied glory and the Great Moral Power of God. In it, as in a sun, the divine feeling henceforth shines; so that whoever believes in his name, takes the power of it, and is transformed radically, even at the deepest centre of life, by it,—born of God.[16]

Bushnell united the natural and the supernatural realm into the "one system of God." Nature, when differentiated from the super-natural, meant nothing and revealed nothing. But when nature and the supernatural were inter-dependent forces, or powers, then nature became the realm in which God revealed Himself. Gone now is the antithesis between the material and the spiritual, the visible and the invisible, and the natural and the supernatural—for all of nature shares in the supernatural. It is this thought which Bushnell gave to New England theology, which marked the major develop-ment in American theology in the 19 Century.

[15] *Vicarious Sacrifice,* p. 159, "It is not the account of their Christian experience, and of the gospel as related thereto, that Christ has done somthing before God's throne, and wholly apart from all effect in them, to make their acceptance pos-sible; and then that the Holy Spirit, by a divine efficiency in them, changes their hearts. No such theologic gospel of dry wood and hay is the gospel of the apostles. They find everything, in their human nature, penetrated by the sense and savor and beauty and glory of Christ. Their whole consciousness is a Christ-consciouness,–everything good and strong in them is Christ within. Wor-sted in all their struggles of will-work and self-regeneration, they still chant their liberty in Christ and say, 'For the law of the Spirit of life in Christ Jesus hath made me free.' Their joy is to be consciously Christed, fully possessed by Christ; to have him dwell in them, and spread himself over and through all the senses and sentiments, and willings, and works of their life."

[16] *Ibid.,* p. 230; Munger regarded Bushnell's emphasis upon the Incarnation as the most important contribution made to New England theology, *op. cit.,* pp. 402–403, "The Incarnation has enfolded and drawn up into itself the atonement, where man becomes one with God in Christ Jesus. Sin does not draw God down to endure its penalty, or to maintain his government; rather does He enter into humanity,–having it eternally in himself,–in order to save and regene-rate it by participation in its life. This was Bushnell's teaching, and since his day the eye of theology in New England has been fixed on the Incarnation as the central doctrine; and there it stands awaiting full development, and in natural alliance with all thought. Theism is shaping itself for its easy admission, and Humanity is opening its eyes to its own divineness. The realized ideal of the union and oneness of the two will probably not be henceforth a subject for debate and definition, but will be regarded as a fact in the development of human history."

Bushnell changed the entire face of Orthodoxy. A great many of the aged theories were discarded in favor of new truths. A theology imprisoned about such ideas as total depravity, reprobation, a penal atonement, a mathematical Trinity, vanished along with the hell that had been prepared for all those who rejected God, or had never heard of Him. In its place came a theology of experience, adequately responsive to moral needs, which is both natural and supernatural, and which insists upon a unity and humanity in the Godhead, which is the motivation for a revelation which offers salvation to all men.[17]

II. *The Transition to the New "Theology" (The Social Gospel)*

The biographer of Horace Bushnell gave this final estimation of his work:

There is little occasion to compare Bushnell with the great doctors of theology before him, but he had what they had not,—a unifying law of thought that delivered him out of the antinomies into which they led the church while seeking to deliver it from existing ones. He was a theologian as Copernicus was an astronomer; he changed the point of view, but pointed the way toward substantial unity in theological thought. He was not exact, but he put God and man and the world into a relation that thought can accept while it goes on to state it more fully and with ever-growing knowledge. Other thinkers were moving in the same direction; he led the movement in New England, and wrought out a great deliverance. It was a work of superb courage. Hardly a theologian in his denomination stood by him, and nearly all pronounced against him.[18]

Subsequent developments in American theological thought have given evidence of Bushnell's impact upon the direction Christian thinking has taken. Walter Marshall Horton, writing in 1934, described what he called "realistic theology," which he felt would replace the Liberal theology of the earlier part of the 20 Century. In this context, he said of the theology of Bushnell that it was essentially identical with that liberal theology which was "passing away before our eyes." Horton was aware, however, of the new influences which had come to mold liberal thinking since Bushnell's day: evolutionary natural science, Biblical criticism, and the new social conscience. The remarkable thing about all three of these

[17] Munger, *op. cit.*, pp. 409–410.
[18] *Ibid.*, p. 413.

236

influences, continued Horton, was that they "proved amenable to interpretation in terms of Bushnell's ideology." He wrote:

Nature and the Supernatural had nothing in it which was in the least in-
consistent with the acceptance of Darwinian evolution, or any other scientific theory, unless one were to interpret these theories as implying— what certainly could not be proved—that the world of naturalistic cause- and-effect, as scientifically analyzed and described, was the whole real world. *The Essay on Language* made it possible, in principle, to accept quite calmly all the most radical results of Biblical criticism, since it made plain the distinction between the eternal ideas of the Bible, which must always be grasped by intuition and experience, and its temporary thought- forms and modes of expression, of whose secondary and transient character Bushnell was convinced long before it was proved by the critics. Finally, in his *Christian Nurture* and other practical writings, Bushnell had already transcended the individualistic psychology and ethics of the rationalistic school, and arrived at a view of the social dependence and social respon- sibility of the individual, quote consonant with the views arrived at much later by social psychologists and social reformers. None of his basic con- cepts had to be unlearned or discarded; they had only to be expanded to cover new accessions of knowledge and to express new social aspirations. In 1914 as truly as in 1849, when Bushnell's first important writing, *God in Christ,* was published, the one great idea of an immanent God, whose presence may be intuitively apprehended throughout the length and breadth of nature and in all the institutions of civilized society, proved adequate to express the whole Gospel and solve all theological problems.[19]

The impact of Bushnell's theology upon later American theologians may be summarized in terms of the following theological emphases which were present in the beginning of the 20 Century: 1) the im- manence of God; 2) the idea of evolutionary growth; 3) the inherent goodness of man; and 4) the historical Jesus.[20] These four theological ideas might characterize what has generally been called the "Social Gospel" movement in America, which was America's most unique contribution to the great ongoing stream of Christian thinking. One of the leaders of this movement defined the Social Gospel as "the application of the teaching of Jesus and the total message of the Christian salvation to society, the economic life, and social institu- tions ... as well as to individuals."[21] The Social Gospel, or social

[19] Horton, *op. cit.,* pp. 30–31.
[20] Cf. H. Shelton Smith, *Faith and Nurture,* (New York: Charles Scribner's Sons, 1941), pp. 4–26; also Hopkins, *op. cit.,* p. 5; also Cross, *op. cit.,* Chapter X, "The Uses of Theology."
[21] Shailer Mathews, "Social Gospel," *A Dictionary of Religion and Ethics,* ed.

Christianity, as it was also designated, involved a criticism of conventional Protestantism, a progressive theology and social philosophy, and an active program of social reform and renewal. From the foregoing study of the theology of Horace Bushnell, one is able to trace those theological motifs which led in a direct line to the Social Gospel in America. To see the relationship between the theology of Horace Bushnell and the Social Gospel in its clearest light, it is of value to look first at that development in American theology which consciously attempted to build upon Bushnell's thought, a movement known as the "New Theology."

Charles H. Hopkins maintained that the "New Theology" was the bridge between Horace Bushnell and the Social Gospel.[22] Indeed, the "New Theology" could have been written by Bushnell himself. The term, the "New Theology," appeared to have been used first by Theodore T. Munger in the extended introduction to his book *The Freedom of Faith*. Munger attempted to present a picture of the developments within American theology in the period following Bushnell. The "New Theology," or progressivism, as Munger also called it, asserted its belief in a personal God, accepted the "theory of physical evolution as the probable method of creation," insisted upon free will, accepted the new Biblical criticism, and preached a living Incarnation active "in all the processes of human life." It sought to replace the excessive individualism of orthodoxy with a truer view of the solidarity of the human race, and asserted the significance of the social philosophy of human nature which is proposed in the Bible.[23] The New Theology maintained that the spiritual world was real, but also related to the material world. It denied, however, that the material provided the only field of knowledge and the only force which was operative in the world. Munger wrote about the New Theology:

It asserts the reality of the spiritual as above the material, of force that is other than that lodged in matter, of truth realized in another way than by induction from material facts, however fine their gradation, of an eter-

Shailer Mathews and G. B. Smith (New York: Macmillan Co., 1921), pp. 416–417.
[22] Hopkins, *op cit.,* p. 5; "However, the great liberalizer of mid-nineteenth century American theology was Horace Bushnell, from whom the social gospel of Washington Gladden and others was to stem directly.", p. 61. Washington Gladden himself agreed with this designation, cf. *Recollections*, (Boston: Houghton, Mifflin and Co., 1909).
[23] Theodore T. Munger, *The Freedom of Faith* (Boston: Houghton, Mifflin and Co., 1851), pp. 6–38.

nal existence and a human self-consciousness correlated in mutual know-ledge and freedom and power. It makes these assertions on scientific grounds and as inductions from phenomena, and therefore claims for itself the possession of knowledge that is such in reality.[24]

The New Theology accepted the designation "the religion of hu-manity" for itself, and maintained that the main relationships of the human race are to God, and that these relations constitute a theology, that is, a science of God. This conception of theology was unlike the Old Theology which "stands on a structure of logic out-side of humanity." The New Theology, on the other hand, recog-nized the fact that God was "revealing himself in the whole life of the world, in the processes of history, ... in the ordained relations of life, in the play of every man's mind." It thus magnified the man-ner in which God revealed himself to man. It brought God and man face to face; but it was the whole of God and the whole of man who came into contact with one another. Munger wrote:

It thus allies itself not only with the Scriptures, and with philosophy and science and human consciousness, but it awakens a sense of *reality*, the securing of which lies at the basis of the Incarnation,—the divine life made a human life, the Son of man eating and drinking, a *living* way, that is, a way lived out in very fact in all the processes of human life, and so leading to eternal life.[25]

The New Theology also insisted upon an ethical interpretation of religious dogma, a moral God, a moral divine government, a moral atonement and a faith that involved moral action. It was more con-cerned with the "logic of life" than of system, and refuted the charges of inconsistency with the statement that it had no interest in a logical scheme that stood outside of the "ordinary thought" of men. It is rather evident that this kind of a theological approach was much dependent upon the thought of Horace Bushnell, as indeed, Munger himself revealed in his biography of Bushnell.

To summarize then, the theology of Horace Bushnell altered the direction of American theological thought in the following ways:

1. The immanence of God:

The development of liberal theology in America was closely re-lated to the decline of New England Calvinism, particularly of the

[24] *Ibid.*, pp. 26, 27.
[25] *Ibid.*, pp. 31–32.

type represented by Jonathan Edwards. The transcendent God of New England orthodoxy was replaced by an immanent God whose presence was apparent throughout nature and in all of the institutions of civilized society. God, who had once been distant and wholly removed from the world and man, now became identified with the processes and operations of the world. Subsequent liberal theology developed the idea that the world process was a unified and dynamic order of events, and that God was its indwelling reality. The principle of continuity (between God and the world and society) was maintained rather than the orthodox principle of discontinuity. The natural and the supernatural were interdependent realms or systems of powers. Together they constituted "one order". God was the indwelling reality of one organic and developing world-process. Nature is the manifestation of this one reality; "the rigid unity of the system of God."

The doctrine of the immanence of God broke down the traditional distinction between the sacred and the secular, the spiritual and the material, with the result that Christianity became a natural religion. God had revealed himself in creation, in history, in man, and in Christ. God worked through all human institutions as well as through men. All life was sanctified as God unfolded himself in human institutions. The basic laws of the Christian faith could be verified inductively and religion itself was a produce of evolution. In the universe, humanity was considered "the crown of creation." Christ became, therefore, the head of humanity. Christ completed and explained the revelation which began at creation. The union of the heavenly with the earthly could best be seen in the person of Jesus Christ.

George A. Gordon's *The Christ of Today* is an illustration of the attempt to reconstruct theology in terms of the conception of Christ as the head of humanity. Gordon said that it appeared the modern world was ready for a new conception of Christ. There was the indication everywhere, Gordon found, of the coming acceptance of Christ's absoluteness for mankind.

Christ is the creator of our human world. The worth of the individual, the reality of social union, the sanctity of home, the infinite meaning of love, the eternal validity of our ideas of righteousness, freedom, and God, all the ultimate realities of our human world, are the creation of Christ.[26]

[26] George A. Gordon, *The Christ of Today*, (Boston: Houghton, Mifflin and Co., 1895), p. 30; cf. also *Ultimate Conceptions of Faith*, (Boston: Houghton, Mifflin

240

To appreciate fully the consciousness of Christ, he said, it is imperative that we know the method of physical science, the fruitful ideas of philosophy, Christian history, and historic theology, and the new biblical learning, the classical literatures and religions of the world. In addition to all of this, one must have an original power, a venturesome spirit, not to ascend into heaven to bring Christ down or descend into the depths to bring Christ up, "but [to] . . . fathom the significance of the word that is nigh our humanity." [27] The great new beginning of theology is, therefore, "the consciousness of Christ as the authentic revelation of the character of the Infinite." If the consciousness of Christ is accepted as "the measure of truth" or as "the ruling philosophy of human life," then the Augustinian, Calvinistic, and Edwardean theology must be abandoned. This type of theology made God a "partial" God, a God who "sincerely contemplates only the selection of a number." The kind of theology Gordon proposed, was a theology that asserted that God had a purpose of love and mercy for the *entire* race of man. Christianity became, therefore, the absolute religion because the revelation of God in Christ was the authoritative and final revelation of God. For this reason, the whole of western civilization was under the spell of the consciousness of Christ.

Not indeed so intensely, nor so nobly, but yet as truly, as in the apostolic age, is our entire Western civilization under the dominating consciousness of Christ. I venture the statement that it is almost as impossible to think of God and man and human society, through any other medium than Christ, as it is to look up at the stars, or abroad upon the earth, in any other way than through the world's enfolding atmosphere. Our whole thought of God and man; our entire working philosophy of life; our modes of intellectual vision, types of feeling, habits of will; our instinctive, customary, rational, emotional, institutional, and social existence,—is everywhere encompassed and interpenetrated by Christ. [28]

and Co., 1903); cf. also the following articles, "The Contrast and Agreement between the New Orthodoxy and the Old," *The Andover Review,* Vol. XIX, no. 109, January, 1893; "The Collapse of the New England Theology," *Harvard Theological Review,* Vol. I, no. 2, April, 1908; "Some Things Worth While in Theology," *Harvard Theological Review,* Vol. III, no. 4, October, 1910.

[27] Gordon, *The Christ of Today,* p. 32.

[28] *Ibid.,* p. 50; cf. *Ultimate Conceptions of Faith,* pp. 238–248, "Between the physical organism of man and his environment there is an increasing harmony. Natural selection means nothing less. . . . The time may come when there shall be no more pain. . . . A better economic condition has come; a better still is bound to come. . . . God's world-plan is the education of mankind; that is the great assumption of religious faith. . . . And along with this vision of the educative purpose of God for the individual life there is the sense of the world-process for

Christology is therefore *not* born of imagination, it is the serious attempt to express the indubitable fact of Christ's Lordship over mankind.

Christ, however, was primarily an ethical Christ. Metaphysical speculation about the nature of Christ was irrelevant to theology, said Gordon. The original Biblical message was that of a "transcendent ethical Personality" founding a kingdom through the influence of *life* rather than the power of ideas. There was therefore, said Gordon, no place in the evangelical faith for a metaphysical construction of the person of Christ. He indicated that there was a profound difference between the Sermon on the Mount and the Nicene Creed—the one belonged to the world of Syrian peasants, the other to a world of Greek philosophers. The picture of an ethical Christ is a "popular" way of looking at Christ. First of all, it emphasizes eternal life as the final objective of the gospel. Second, it is a view which poses no problems for the Christian intellect. Third, it presupposes courage, because critical scholarship is beginning to question how much of the evangelical narrative is truly supernatural. Last, it reduces the problem of the miraculous to a dead issue—the miraculous is quietly ruled out, "and the ethical remains as the real and imperishable." The apprehension of Christ through moral feeling is the way to reach his true character, Gordon said. The ethical character of Christ, however, presupposes, said Gordon, the "personal reality" of Christ. Christ is more than an exalted ethical figure, for "it is impossible to account for character in any human being without the assumption of a personal spirit whose character it is. Character must be the character of some one; and Christ is not merely an exalted ethical habit, but a being to whom that exalted ethical habit belongs." [29]

The imitation of Christ then is the task of humanity. His followers and disciples are those who are trying to become as He was, and learn the art of right living from him. This truth—the imitation of Christ as the locus of the Christian faith—had been lost again and again in Christian history. Augustine's and Calvin's excessive em-

the recovery of sight to the blind. History is seen to be inexorably just, and for this reason infinitely kind. . . . The ancient blunder of self-seeking will not always be repeated; the joy of existence will not forever be sought for, against the whole protest of the past, in impossible fields. Light will, in the overwhelming majority of cases, be welcome, and darkness will be disowned. . . . Optimism is a faith that has good foundations."

[29] Gordon, *The Christ of Today*, p. 58.

phasis upon the evil in human nature, asserted Gordon, has reduced man to such a position that he could never feel himself a candidate for "the purity and elevation of the New Testament morality."

Finally, Gordon defined God in terms of Divine Fatherhood. God, therefore, became responsible to man to act always as a parent, with a sense of "sacred obligation" to care for human life. In this way, human society could be moulded to the moral standard of Jesus Christ. This ideal was *not* an impossible one. Gordon concluded,

This great revival of the moral faith inspired by the Incarnation is the first distinct and enormous gain in the appreciation of the Person of Christ. There has been lodged in the conscience of this century a sense of the obligation resting upon the disciple to imitate and reproduce the character of his Master. Nothing could be more hopeful for our poor race than the hearty acceptance of this high faith, than the sincere acknowledgment of this obligation.[30]

2. The idea of evolutionary growth:

The idea of growth or evolutionary development served the Christian faith in a positive way. Evolutionary science introduced the principle of unity into the universe, and as it did, it laid the basis for a developmental conception of religion and drew God down and into the processes of creation as its constant and all-pervasive factor. Regeneration itself became a natural process which could be traced in the developmental processes of every human being. Furthermore, as the individual developed in time, so too did religion. Religion evolved as an integral part of the history of civilization. Human history, therefore, ultimately had to issue forth into a moral age. Revelation in the Bible, furthermore, was considered to have evolved from the Old Testament to the New, "from the patriarchs to Christ." The evolutionary principle operative throughout the universe was the same principle operative within the Christian faith.

An "organic" theory of society was developed on the basis of the conception of evolutionary growth. The unity of mankind was based on the idea of the indwelling of the divine Father in all men and institutions. Mankind was bound together in an organic brotherhood. No man lived apart from his fellow man. Humanity possessed a unity and a continuity similar to that of nature. The Christian God made "all men of one blood." There was a God in history just as

[30] *Ibid.,* p. 55.

there was a God operative in the physical universe. The Christian ideal was to bring about "moral order which includes all men in one brotherhood subject to the Divine Fatherhood." But Christianity is a revelation of God which is part of the growing spiritual life in man. The doctrines of the Fatherhood of God and the Brotherhood of Man formed the basis for a social Christianity. Redemption had to include the entire human race. The Kingdom of God was the regenerated society, just as the child of God was the regenerated individual. Regeneration was not, however, the restoration of man to a state of innocence; it was rather the process of spiritual evolution by which God created a new humanity in Christ. The goal of this spiritual evolution was the gradual humanizing of the kingdom. Evolution had prepared mankind for the idea of a Reign of God toward which all creation was moving. The Christian conception of life includes the belief that the Kingdom of God *is* a present reality. The salvation of the "organic life of society" was therefore assured.

Lyman Abbott was the great popularizer of the new theology of Evolution. He wrote that "the object of Christianity is human welfare; its method is character-building; *its process is evolution;* and the secret of its power is God." Abbott's position was clearly demonstrated in two of his most popular works, *The Evolution of Christianity* (1892) and *The Theology of an Evolutionist* (1897). Christianity was defined as a spiritual force in the history of mankind. There was, Abbott said, a growth of revelation from the Old Testament to Christ. This development was the actual working out of the same evolutionary principle which was operative in the physical realm. Christianity is, therefore, said Abbott, the life of God in the soul of man. Christianity, as the highest form of religion, is a personal consciousness of God, and as such, it is a human experience, but an experience of a relationship with One who transcends humanity. Christianity is distinct from the creeds and worship of the church. Christianity may be a social experience, and when it is, it is the contemporary consciousness of God in a great number of individuals which produces a social or communal life. The Christian faith "is a life, not an opinion about life. It is not a definition of God, it is fellowship with Him; not a definition of sin, but sorrow because of sin; not a definition of forgiveness, but relief from remorse; not a definition of redemption, but a new and divine life." [31]

[31] Lyman Abbott, *The Theology of an Evolutionist,* (Boston: Houghton, Mifflin

Evolution is described as "God's way of doing things." Theology is, therefore, the attempt to explain God's way of doing things. The science of theology and the science of evolution have the same ultimate end, affirmed Abbott. Both attempted to furnish an orderly, rational, and self-consistent account of phenomena. The supposed inconsistency between science and religion was really an inconsistency between two sciences. The theologian and the scientist have given different, and to some extent, inconsistent accounts of God's way of doing things. Abbot was conscious of the tension between science and religion. He directed his writings, however, not to disbelievers in evolution, but to believers in evolution, in order to show them that their belief was not inconsistent with the Christian faith.

However, a position which accepts the new science of evolution must also reject much of what is found in what Abbott called "the old faith." The old faith referred to a conception of God, whose nature was such that He resided outside of nature and outside of men, and who operated upon men and nature from this vantage point. Abbott called for modern man to alter his conception of God in terms of a position he referred to as "theistic evolution." "Theistic evolution" may be summarized in Abbott's own words:

I reverently and heartily accept the axiom of theology that a personal God is the foundation of all life; but I also believe that God has but one way of doing things; that His way may be described in one word as the way of growth, or development, or evolution, terms which are substantially synonymous; that He resides in the world of nature and in the world of men; that there are no laws of nature which are not the laws of God's own being; that there are no forces of nature, that there is only one divine, infinite force, always proceeding from, always subject to the will of God; that there are not occasional or exceptional theophanies, but that all nature and all life is one great theophany; that there are not occasional interventions in the order of life which bear witness to the presence of God, but that life is itself a perpetual witness to His presence; that He transcends all phenomena, and yet is the creative, controlling, directing force in all phenomena.[32]

Abbott agreed with the evolutionist rather than with the theologian when it is asserted that God's way of doing things is in terms of a continuous and unbroken progression. All life for Abbot was

and Co., 1897), p. 2; cf. also *The Evolution of Christianity* (Boston: Houghton, Mifflin and C., 1894), *Christianity and Social Problems,* (Boston: Houghton, Mifflin and Co., 1896).

[32] Abbott, *The Theology of an Evolutionist,* pp. 9–10.

divine, and he affirmed that God acts in life as a continuous and progressive development which follows basic laws. He favored this position overagainst one which asserted that some things were done by divine forces and according to natural laws, while others were done by special interventions of a Divine will, acting from outside natural laws.

Theology and the science of evolution are growing together, Abbott asserted. Both the religious and the scientific world have come to believe in a greatly lessened number of divine interventions. Science has reached these three conclusions, Abbott said: first, there is but one force, manifesting itself in different forms; second, that this force is never increased or diminished in amount, only varied in form; and third, that this force, if we believe it to be directed to intelligent ends, is sufficient to account for all the phenomena of nature and life, so that there is no reason to believe in any interventions from without. He believed that the theology of the future will gladly accept these conclusions, instead of resisting them and endeavoring to discover some evidences of interventions, which constantly lessen in number if not in magnitude. It, too, will affirm that there is only one force, the "Infinite and Eternal Energy from which all things proceed." It will affirm that this Infinite and Eternal Energy is never increased or diminished; that, in other words, God, who varies infinitely in His manifestations, varies in no way in His real life. It will affirm that there are and can be no interventions in this resident force, this Infinite and Eternal Energy, for if there were there would be a second God, superior to the God who resides in the universe and controlling Him. And finally, it will affirm that this Infinite and Eternal Energy is itself intelligent and beneficent,—an infinitely wise and holy Spirit, dwelling within the universe and shaping it from within, much as the human spirit dwells within the human body and forms and controls it from within. Scientifically this is the affirmation that the forces of nature are one vital force; theologically it is the affirmation that God is an Immanent God. "Resident forces" and "Divine Immanence" are different forms of the same statement. According to this view, it is not correct to say that "God, the one Force, did somehow bring into being the earliest forms of matter with resident forces." [33]

It is, therefore, correct to say, said Abbott, that all "later forms of existence," including life and consciousness, reason and con-

[33] *Ibid.*, pp. 12-13.

science, are the manifestations of God's power in the sense that they are revelations of His presence. The Divine Spirit which resides in Nature transcends Nature, as the human spirit which resides in the body transcends the body. The Divine Spirit which is manifested in all phenomena is more than the sum of all phenomena, as the human spirit which is manifested in all the activities of a life is more than the sum of those activities.

The theistic evolutionist believes, therefore, that "God is the one Resident Force, that He is in His world; that His method of work in His world is the method of growth; and that the history of the world, whether it be the history of creation, of providence, or of redemption, whether the history of redemption in the race or of redemption in the individual soul, is the history of a growth in accordance with the great law interpreted and uttered in that one word evolution." [34]

3. The inherent goodness of man:

No idea in the traditional New England theology was more repugnant to the liberal theologians of the late 19 Century than the depravity of man. Overagainst this pessimistic conception of man, there was proposed the doctrine of the inherent divinity of man. Man had within him the seeds of divinity which permitted him to grow "godlike by the gradual unfolding of his own inner nature." Conflict and violent change were foreign to human nature. Man's proper response to God was to approach God by the free and natural unfolding of his highest powers. Religion, and the Christian faith, did not attempt to change human nature, but only to develop the full capacities of human nature from within. Christ was the divinely human Ideal. He came not to reveal divinity to us, but to evoke from us our latent divinity. Christ was, therefore, "the secret of spiritual evolution," the pattern of the ideal in whom spiritual evolution was completed.

The doctrine of the inherent goodness of man provided cosmic sanction for the belief in the ultimate triumph of good. There was a growing spiritual life in man, beginning in the early dawn of human history, when man first came to moral consciousness. This spiritual force freed the world of superstition and prejudice, and purified it for the realization of the highest ideals of justice.

An obvious illustration of a theologian who supported the doctrine

[34] *Ibid.*, p. 15.

of the inherent goodness of man, and who related it to a social Christianity, was Washington Gladden. He was first attracted to the ministry by a religion "that laid hold upon life with both hands, and proposed, first and foremost, to realize the kingdom of God in this world." No problems of human life could be considered outside the realm of the Christian faith, he said. The Christian law of love must be a check upon the inhuman tendencies of material forces. The Christian faith must be related to every aspect of life, and particularly it must be applied to the common affairs of men.

Gladden recognized that there was a growing interest in the question of the individual as he was related to the social organism. The Christian man, in the face of the pathological condition of much of society, must ask himself the question whether the reconstruction of society rather than simply its repair was not needed. The social ailments, Gladden said, were constitutional, and the remedies must reach the "seat of the disorder." But society possessed the characteristics of an organism, and if any remedies were to be applied, it had to reach the soul of the organism. Only a radical solution to the problems of society was relevant. Society had to be transformed, but the transformation had to recognize that society was a living thing which had all of the characteristics of a physical organism. For this reason, Gladden said, "its life may be replenished; possibly its vital forces may be directed into new channels, but the structural principles must remain essentially the same. The one lesson that the social reformer as well as the theological reformer needs to learn is the lesson of evolution." [35]

Gladden criticized Orthodox Protestantism for its failure to recognize the "organic filaments" by which a man is vitally bound to the community. Orthodox Protestantism had made religion too much of an individual matter, and for that reason, it had been oblivious to the social matrix in which every individual was found. Gladden spoke of this situation in the following way, a passage which lucidly displays his confidence in the perfectibility of man:

Their [representatives of Orthodox Protestantism] defective conduct arose from their failure to comprehend their vital relations to their fellow men. That the essence of religion is righteousness they would not deny,

---

[35] Washington Gladden, *Social Salvation*, (Boston: Houghton, Mifflin and Co., 1902), pp. 5-6; cf. also *Applied Christianity*, (Boston: Houghton, Mifflin and Co., 1886); *The Church and Modern Life*, (Boston: Houghton, Mifflin and Co., 1908); *Recollections*, (Boston: Houghton, Mifflin and Co., 1909).

but the social nature of righteousness they do not understand. The breadth and comprehensiveness of the law of love has not been brought home to them. They think of God as a Moral Governor, and conceive of his kingdom in this world as the maintenance of a certain rectoral justice between man and man; these, therefore, who keep well within the requirements of common honesty are not transgressors, and have nothing to repent of. Within those requirements there is room for a great deal of indifference and hard-hearted disregard for the welfare of our neighbors. And I think that those who scrupulously keep to the letter of their contracts, who always pay their debts, who can never be accused of misrepresentation or fraud, but who, standing on these principles of common honesty, push their advantages relentlessly, and are willing to profit by the misfortune or the ignorance of those with whom they deal, are rather worse hated, in their generation, than the recognized sharpers and swindlers. This may seem a hard judgment, but there is a profound reason for it. For the conception of the divine fatherhood, which has been gaining possession of the mind of Christendom, has greatly modified our ideas of obligation and sin, and our ideals of character. The discord between the selfish soul and the Father whose name is love is seen to be a far more serious thing than disobedience to a Moral Governor whose reign consists in the maintenance of rectoral righteousness. The same insight shows us what is the root of all the trouble between ourselves and our fellow men.[36]

The essence of sin, said Gladden, is "the defect of love." The Christian experience is radically defective if love is lacking, for it is love which fulfills the law. But the Christian life had to include the social dimension, because it is only here that the commandment to love could be made concrete. The law of love was to govern all of life—it defined man's relations to his fellowman in the church and at home, but also in industry and commerce and politics. Religious conversion, therefore, was to be more than a change in the religious sentiments. It involved a change in one's social relationships as well. Gladden said, "Salvation is just that getting into right relations; and no man is in the way of salvation until he has in some dim way grasped that idea, and tried to realise it."[37] Gladden concluded by saying that the view of the Christian life which puts the whole emphasis upon individual experience is seen to result in defective conduct and in morbid social conditions.

There was, therefore, Gladden said, no possibility of separating the individual from society. Man's spiritual world is the social world. The fundamental fact of theology is the assertion of the Fatherhood

[36] Gladden, *Social Salvation,* pp. 8–9.
[37] *Ibid.,* p. 10.

of God, which made the Brotherhood of Man the necessary response on the part of the Christian. An individual could no longer exist isolated from the society in which he was found. "No individual," Gladden said, "is soundly converted until he comprehends his social relations and strives to fulfill them; and the work of growth and sanctification largely consists in a clearer apprehension of these relations and a more earnest effort to fill them with the life of the divine Spirit. The kingdom of heaven is *within* us and *among* us." [38]

God is in his world and we are co-workers with Him. In all of the struggles of life He is present, working according to the counsel of His perfect will. Gladden wrote:

In the gleams of light which sometimes break forth from the darkness of the conflict we discern his inspiration; in the stirrings of good will which temper the wasting strife we behold the evidence of his presence; in the sufferings and losses and degradations which wait upon every violation of his law of love we witness the retributions with which that law goes armed. In the weltering masses of poverty; in the giddy throngs that tread the paths of vice; in the multitudes distressed and scattered as sheep having no shepherd; in the brutalized ranks marching in lock-step through the prison yard; in the groups of politicians scheming for place and plunder,—in all the most forlorn and untoward and degrading human associations, the One who is never absent is that divine Spirit which brooded over the chaos at the beginning, nursing it to life and beauty, and which is 'nearer to every creature he hath made, than anything unto life itself can be'. [39]

God has a perfect social order in mind for the common life of man. He is seeking to lead his children to this goal, so that "He may give them plenty and blessedness and abundance of peace as long as the moon endureth."

4. The historical Jesus:

An emphasis upon the historical Jesus was a unique feature of American liberalism at the beginning of the twentieth century. The ethical apprehension of Christ became more and more the fashion in Protestant theological circles. The greatest theological discovery, even in liberal Christianity, was the emphasis upon Jesus as a human being, a human being who was concerned with ethics and social reform. Jesus did not need any Christiological formulation. The whole purpose of His coming was to promulgate a new law of con-

[38] *Ibid.,* p. 12.
[39] *Ibid.,* p. 21.

duct for man. Harry Emerson Fosdick expressed the liberal sentiment about Jesus when he said: "They [his theological predecessors]
started with the certainty that Jesus came from the divine realm and
then wondered how he could be truly man; we start from the
certainty that he was genuinely man and then wonder in what
sense he can be God." [40] When asked to compare the Sermon on the
Mount with the Nicene Creed, the response was usually that the
theological beliefs which went into the former belong to ethical
concerns; the latter is speculative and metaphysical. This was conceived to be the difference between moral and metaphysical Christianity. The ethical teachings of Jesus were social in intention. The
discovery of the Jesus of history furnished the Social Gospel movement with ethical and religious formulae by which it constructed
for itself a rationalistic and autonomous foundation for a conception of the Kingdom of God. The ethics of Jesus provided a frame
of reference within which either a theistic or a humanistic social
creed could be constructed. The social teachings of Jesus, however,
depended upon his religious presuppositions. The doctrine of the
Fatherhood of God was the central point of Christ's teachings. The
idea of the Brotherhood of Man was derived directly from it. Jesus
taught that the goal of humanity was "the realization of brotherhood
interpreted in the light of the common fatherhood." Man could contribute to the building of the Kingdom of God, and the evidence
of this was the love of God as it was made manifest in all of human
affairs and institutions. The Kingdom would be built by men on
earth: it would be "an ideal social order in which the relation of men
to God is that of sons, and to each other that of brothers." [41] Jesus
meant that the Kingdom would come gradually, by means of an
evolutionary process, but it would come to society as a whole. The
three laws of the Kingdom were service, sacrifice, and love. The
social convictions of Jesus included the value of life, the solidarity
of the human family, and the necessity of "social sacrifice," that is,
the necessity of the strong to "stand up for the weak." Jesus believed
in the absolute worth of every human individual, and this innate
value of man was to be the ultimate norm by which all of social
institutions were to be judged.

[40] Harry Emerson Fosdick, *The Modern Use of the Bible,* (New York: Harper,
1924), p. 256.
[41] Shailer Mathews, *The Social Teachings of Jesus* (An Essay in Christian Sociology), (New York: Hodder and Stoughton, George H. Doran Co., 1897), p. 54.

The theological emphasis of the historical Jesus immediately brings to mind the figure of Walter Rauschenbusch, who was the chief architect of the Social Gospel in America. In 1907, he published *Christianity and the Social Crisis,* which became the text book for Social Christianity. In this work, Rauschenbusch analyzed the social and ethical implications of the Old Testament. He asserted that the Hebrew prophets were interested in the moral, social, and political life of the nation. Jesus was the "divine founder of a new society." Rauschenbusch demonstrated the great chasm which existed between the socially impotent Christianity of his time and the social relevancy of the Early Church. He suggested that the contemporary church had the task to christianize the social order in the confused world in which it lived.

His second book, *For God and the People: Prayers of the Social Awakening,* was written in 1910. It gave expression to Rauschenbusch's conviction that the social dimension of the Christian faith must be based upon a valid religious experience. The religious emotions issuing from such an experience, however, must have conscious social expression. This book was written in order to recognize the role that prayer was to play as the basis for the new social consciousness. The Lord's Prayer, said Rauschenbusch, was the great prayer of social Christianity, because it possessed a unique "social consciousness."

Christianizing the Social Order appeared in 1912, and spoke of the social and ethical teachings of the historical Jesus:

> Christianizing the social order meant bringing it into harmony with the ethical convictions which we identify with Christ. A fairly definite body of moral convictions has taken shape in modern humanity. They express our collective conscience, our working religion. The present social order denies and flouts many of these principles of our ethical life and compels us in practice to outrage our better self. We demand therefore that the moral sense of humanity shall be put in control and shall be allowed to reshape the institutions of social life.[42]

In this book, Rauschenbusch subjects the social and economic order of his world to a moral analysis, and, as a result, he indicted capitalism as spiritually antagonistic to Christianity. He spoke of "our semi-Christian social order," and insisted upon social justice and economic democracy as minimum requirements upon which a Chris-

[42] Walter Rauschenbusch, *Christianizing the Social Order,* (New York: The Macmillan Co., 1912), p. 125.

252

tian social order could be built. Using the term "social evolution" he indicated some of the fundamental lines along which society must move in order to approximate the ideal of the Kingdom of God in all of life.

In 1916, a little manual appeared, entitled *The Social Principles of Jesus,* which was published by the YMCA. This was probably the most popular of Rauschenbusch's works. Jesus was the heart of the new social teachings. Although Jesus did not lay down any rules of conduct which were forever binding, and although he did not have any formalized social or political doctrine, He did stress the value of the human personality. The fundamental principle of Jesus is "the absolute worth of every human being"—this is the ultimate norm by which all social institutions and the social activity of the individual are to be measured. Social regeneration is to come through the dissemination of the spirit of "reverence for personality" throughout society. Beginning with individuals, it expanded to groups in society, as well as institutions, instilling in all of them Christ's spirit of brotherliness. In this way, the Kingdom of God could become a reality in our time, Rauschenbusch said. It is this Kingdom which is the great social objective laid on the conscience of every Christian man and woman.

The last and the most significantly theological of Rauschenbusch's works was *A Theology for the Social Gospel,* which formed the Nathaniel W. Taylor lectures at Yale University in 1917. In this work, Rauschenbusch realized the need for a "systematic theology large enough to match the social gospel." His greatest attention was given to the doctrines of sin and salvation, but he also discussed revelation, inspiration, prophecy, Baptism, the Lord's Supper, eschatology, the atonement, and the conceptions of God and the Holy Spirit. The heart of the work, however, remained the concept of the Kingdom of God. Sin, he said, is the treasonable force which wrecks the ideal of the Kingdom. Sin can be transmitted socially, through the group, by the group's justification and idealization of the wrong, and by means of the influence of economic profit in the propagation of evil. There are collective superpersonal forces of evil in society which converge into the Kingdom of Evil. These forces can be redeemed only by coming under the law of Christ. The Kingdom of God has been initiated by Christ, and all ethical and social religion must relate itself to this ideal. "We love and serve God when we love and serve our fellows, whom he loves and in whom he lives. We rebel against God and repudiate his will when we set our profit and ambition above the welfare of our fellows and above the Kingdom of God which binds them together." [43]

The Kingdom of God had a divine origin. Its progress and consummation are also within God's control. The Kingdom is always a present and a future reality—"always pressing in on the present, always big with possibility, and always inviting immediate action." The function of the Kingdom of God is the Christianizing of the social order. Jesus Christ initiated the Kingdom in this world. The ethical principles expressed by the life, teachings and spirit of Jesus Christ are the highest expressions of the aspirations of man found throughout the history of mankind. Christianizing the social order means to bring it into harmony with the ethical convictions of Jesus Christ. [44] Nonetheless, Rauschenbusch recognized that men are human and for that reason a Christian social order could not be perfect and could never be realized. What was necessary, said Rauschenbusch, was to insist upon perfection—in this way present-day conditions would be improved appreciably. Certain aspects of the social order have already been "Christianized." Rauschenbusch found that they were the family, the Church, education, and politics. The structure of the family had passed through an ethical transformation, a process which could truly be called Christian, insisted Rauschenbusch. The institution of the family had been a restraining influence upon the lives of civilized men throughout history. The Church, in like manner, as it has passed from a tyrannical institution to a liberating life-force, had passed through a Christianizing process. The educational system had also passed from an aristocratic institution to an institution serving all peoples. This, too, Rauschenbusch said, was a Christianizing process. The state, too, had undergone a transformation from the position of a specially privileged class to that of an order which permitted liberty and equal rights. The Christianizing process was very apparent if a comparison were made with past evidences of inequality and oppression, Rauschenbusch said.

The Kingdom of God is present in the world. However, it is also a future possibility; that is, it can come into being when every aspect of the social order comes under the spirit of Christ. The final con-

[43] Walter Rauschenbusch, *A Theology for the Social Gospel,* (New York: The Macmillan Co., 1917), p. 48.
[44] Rauschenbusch, *Christianizing the Social Order,* p. 125.

summation of the Kingdom must be a cooperative venture between God and man, Rauschenbusch insisted. The regeneration of society can only come about through the activity of God and the spirit of Christ; nonetheless, Rauschenbusch called for man's participation in the regeneration of society. The call of Jesus to men is to seek the Kingdom of God here and now. Social regeneration is not to be postponed to a future era.

The process of the Kingdom was also to be seen in evolutionary categories. Social institutions are the results, said Rauschenbusch, of a long series of social configurations in the history of a civilization. Social institutions, therefore, are to remain as they are—until the spirit of Christ can be imposed upon them. Religion and ethics must cooperate with the evolutionary processes which are constantly changing the social order.

The Kingdom of God, in accordance with the teachings of Jesus, projects towards that social order which will guarantee to every individual person his free and full development. Every form of personal oppression, even when it is found in economic, social and religious forms, must be destroyed. The Kingdom of God implies a "progressive reign of love in human affairs." Love tends toward "the progressive unity of mankind, but with the maintenance of individual liberty."

Rauschenbusch's idea of salvation must be considered from this viewpoint. The Kingdom of God insists upon the Christian transformation of the entire social order, as well as of the individual. Rauschenbusch spoke about the "progressive social incarnation of God," which meant that the divine life of Christ had to get control of humanity. Christ had set in motion "the historical forces of redemption which are to overthrow the Kingdom of Evil." The entire life, ministry, and death of Jesus Christ was interpreted by Rauschenbusch in terms of the establishment of the Kingdom of God. He was not interested in the metaphysical problems of the traditional doctrines of the Trinity and Christology. Rather, he insisted upon the new "religious personality" which was evidenced by Jesus' life. Jesus' divine quality came from the perfect realization of the will of God in His life. Jesus' personality, which is His divinity, was a new type of humanity, and was, therefore, the true revelation of God. Jesus, Rauschenbusch claimed, was "a perfect religious personality, a spiritual life completely filled by the realization of a God who is love." The uniqueness of Jesus' personality could be seen by the unique way he experienced God, a God who was "the Father in heaven who forgives sins freely, welcomes the prodigal, makes his sun to shine on the just and the unjust, and asks for nothing but love, trust and cooperative obedience." Every individual was able to derive this consciousness of God from Jesus and by doing so could be recipients of God's spiritual power. In this way, said Rauschenbusch, man was able to free himself from the forces of evil in social life.[45]

The goals of the social gospel (freedom, equality, cooperation, etc.) had to be clearly expressed in every theological formulation about God. The conception of God had to be democratized and was to become the theological foundation for the concern for social unity. Rauschenbusch found that such a conception of God, that is, a God who had a social feeling, went back to the conception of God held by the Old Testament prophets. Rauschenbusch maintained that an "imperialistic" conception of God, that is, a God who had been given autocrative and monarchical power, went back to the time when the church was existing in a feudalistic society. Economic and political despotism influenced the church's conception of God. Jesus democratized the conception of God. God became a God of Love. This permitted God in turn to be loved by man. Jesus, said Rauschenbusch, removed the conception of God from the realm of coercion and despotism to the realm of family solidarity and love. Jesus' idea of the Fatherhood of God permitted man to be free. That, he said, was the source of St. Paul's assertion that when man became a Christian he no longer was a slave, but a son who could say, "Our Father."

Jesus' death must be seen in the context of Jesus' relationship to God during all of His life. Jesus' death, Rauschenbusch said, was the "culmination of His life, its most luminous point, the most dramatic expression of His personality, the consistent assertion of the purpose and law which had ruled Him and formed Him." God was in the personality of Jesus. The experiences of the cross were, therefore, directly related to the mind of God. Rauschenbusch said: "If the principle of forgiving love had not been in the heart of God before, this experience would fix it there." Jesus also altered the relation between God and humanity. Humanity was out of harmony with God and God was therefore forced to oppose it. Christ was the first

[45] Rauschenbusch, *A Theology for the Social Gospel*, pp. 151–154.

256

man to live fully within the consciousness of God. By drawing others into his own realization of God's will, Jesus enabled man to love God freely. By so doing, Jesus altered the relationship between God and humanity; that is, a relationship which was no longer antagonistic but one which expressed the cooperative unity of wills.[46] Rauschenbusch concluded by writing this about the death of Jesus:

In this way the death of Jesus has taken personal hold on countless religious souls. It has set them free from the fear of pain and the fear of men, and given them a certain finishing quality of strength. It has inspired courage and defiance of evil, and sent men on lost hopes. The cross of Christ put God's approval on the sacrificial impulse in the hearts of the brave, and dignified it by connecting it with one of the central dogmas of our faith. The cross has become the motive and the method of noble personalities.[47]

Bushnell's fate as a theologian was that of a mediating thinker. He did his work and served the Church of his time. But he also helped a generation of younger Christian leaders to make intellectual decisions which permitted them to direct the Church of their time. Bushnell's ministry, therefore, had its sacrificial aspect. He was superseded by later theologians and their systems, but they were enriched by the contribution of his articulation of the Christian faith. Indeed, all of Christendom remains in his debt.

[46] *Ibid.*, pp. 248–258.
[47] *Ibid.*, pp. 278–279.

BIBLIOGRAPHY

I. The Published Writings of Horace Bushnell:

A. BOOKS

Building Eras in Religion. Literary Varieties, III. New York: Charles Scribner's Sons, 1881. 459 pp.

✓*The Character of Jesus: Forbidding his Possible Classification with Men.* New York: Charles Scribner, 1861 (1860 c.) 173 pp.

Christ and His Salvation: In Sermons Variously Related Thereto. New York: Charles Scribner. 1864. 456 pp.

Christ in Theology: Being the Answer of the Author before the Hartford Central Association of Ministers, October, 1849, for the Doctrines of the Book entitled "God in Christ." Hartford: 1851. 348 pp.

Christian Nurture. (Isaiah liv. 13.) New York: Charles Scribners, 1861 (1860 c.). 407 pp.

Discourses on Christian Nurture. (Approved by the Committee of Publication.) Boston: Massachussetts Sabbath School Society. 72 pp. Introductory note and two discourses.

Forgiveness and Law, Grounded in Principles Interpreted by Human Analogies. New York: Scribner, Armstrong, & Co., 1874. 256 pp.

God in Christ. Three Discourses delivered at New Haven, Cambridge and Andover (with a preliminary Dissertation on Language). Hartford: 1849. 356 pp.

Moral Uses of Dark Things. New York: Charles Scribner & Co., 1868. 360 pp. Revised in 1881 and in 1903.

Nature and the Supernatural, as together constituting the One System of God. New York: Charles Scribner, 1858. 528 pp.

Sermons for the New Life. New York: Charles Scribner. 1858. 456 pp. Revised in 1903.

Sermons on Living Subjects. New York: Scribner, Armstrong & Co., 1872. 468 pp.

✓*The Spirit in Man. Sermons and Selections.* New York: Charles Scribner's Sons, 1903. 473 pp.

The Vicarious Sacrifice, Grounded in Principles Interpreted by Human Analogies. New York: Charles Scribner, 1877. In two volumes. I., 552 pp; II., 269 pp.

The Vicarious Sacrifice, Grounded in Principles of Universal Obligation. New York: Charles Scribner & Co., 1866 (1865 c.). 552 pp.

Views of Christian Nurture and of Subjects Adjacent Thereto. Second
edition. Hartford, New York, and Boston: 1848 (1847 c.). 251 pp.
Women's Suffrage: The Reform Against Nature. New York: Charles Scribner, 1869. 184 pp.
Work and Play; or Literary Varieties. New York: Charles Scribner, 1864.
464 pp. Revised in 1881 and in 1903.

B. ARTICLES, PAPERS

"Abjuration of America." *Hours at Home,* I. (July, 1865), 244–245.
"Addressed to Rev. Dr. Hawes." Letter dated Hartford, April 3, 1854. *The
New England Religious Herald* (Hartford), June 1, 1854. Published in
Cheney, *Life and Letters of Horace Bushnell* (1880), p. 337.
"Addressed to the North Consociation of Hartford County." Letter in
The New England Religious Herald (Hartford), January 9, 1847. 1 ½
columns.
"An Argument for 'Discourses on Christian Nurture.'" Pamphlet addres-
sed to the Publishing Committee of the Massachusetts Sabbath School
Society. Hartford, 48 pp. Republished in *Views of Christian Nurture*
(1848).
"III. Bad Government or Bad Men in Power." *Hours At Home,* IV. (April,
1867), 481–488. Republished in *Moral Uses of Dark Things* (1868).
"California, its Characteristics and Prospects." *The New Englander,* XVI.
(February, 1858), 142–182. Reprinted in pamphlet. San Francisco: 1858.
"Christian Comprehensiveness." *The New Englander,* VI. (January, 1848),
81–111. Republished in *Building Eras in Religion* (1881).
"The Christian Trinity A Practical Truth." *The New Englander,* XII. (No-
vember, 1854), 485–509. Republished in *Building Eras in Religion*
(1881).
"A Church without a Bishop." Letter addressed to *The Religious Herald,*
Hartford, of March 20, 1844.
"The Conflagration." Letter from Dr. Bushnell, dated Hartford, November
1, 1871. In *The Advance* (Chicago). Thursday, November 16, 1871.
V., No. 219.
"Correspondence." Letter dated New York, January 15, 1855. *The New
England Religious Herald,* January 18, 1855.
"Correspondence." Letter in reply to one from the North Church and
Society, signed by all the members of the Church and Society (May 17,
1858). Dated Hartford, June 15, 1858. Addressed to Normand Smith,
A. M. Collins, and others. *The New England Religious Herald,* July 8,
1858.
"Dinstinctions of Color." *Hours At Home,* VII. (May, 1868), 81–89. Re-
published in *Moral Uses of Dark Things* (1868).

"The Doctrine of Loyalty." *The New Englander,* XXII. (July, 1863), 560–581. Republished in *Work and Play* (1864).

"The Evangelical Alliance." *The New Englander,* V. (January, 1847), 102–125. Republished same year in pamphlet form. New York: Baker & Scribner. 32 pp.

"Hartford Park." *Hearth and Home,* I. (Saturday, February 6, 1869), 101–102. Reprinted in Cheney, *Life and Letters of Horace Bushnell* (1880).

"How to Make A Ripe and Right Old Age." *Hours At Home,* IV. (December, 1866), 106–112.

"Inspiration by the Holy Spirit." Paper published in *The Spirit in Man* (1903).

"The Kingdom of Heaven as a Grain of Mustard Seed." *The New Englander,* II. (October, 1844), 600–619. Republished under the title, "Growth, not Conquest, The True Method of Christian Progress," in *Views of Christian Nurture* (1848).

"The Law of Feeding as Pertaining to Souls." *The Advance* (Chicago), Vol. I, Thursday, February 13, 1868. No. 24.

"The Learning How to Feed." *The Advance* (Chicago), Vol. I, Thursday, February 20, 1868. No. 25.

"A Letter from Dr. Bushnell." Dated Geneva, October 7, 1845, 2 columns. *The Religious Herald* (Hartford), November 8, 1845.

"Letter from Dr. Bushnell." Dated San Francisco, May 19, 1856. *The Independent* (New York), July 3, 1856. 1 column.

"Letter to Henry W. Longfellow." Dated Hartford, December 28, 1871. First printed in Samuel Longfellow's *Final Memorials of Henry Wadsworth Longfellow* (1887), pp. 178–179. See also the edition of *Longfellow's Life* (1891), III. 192–193. Again reprinted in Colonel T. W. Higginson's *Henry Wadsworth Longfellow* (American Men of Letters Series), 1902, pp. 245–246.

"A Letter to His Holiness, Pope Gregory XVI." Dated London, April 2, 1846. Ward & Co., 27 Paternoster Row. 1846. 24 pp.

"Letter to the *Courant,* Hartford." Dated St. Anthony, Minn., August, 1859. Published in Hartford, Friday, August 12, 1859. ½ column.

"Meaning and Use of the Lord's Supper." *The Advance* (Chicago), Vol. I., Thursday, March 5, 1868. No. 27.

"Moral Uses of Dark Things." I. Of Night and Sleep. *Hours At Home,* IV. (February, 1867), 289–297. Republished in *Moral Uses of Dark Things* (1868).

"Movement for A University in California." A Statement to the Public by the Trustees of the College of California, and an Appeal by Dr. Bushnell. San Francisco: 1857. 23 pp.

"The Natural History of the Yaguey Family." *Hours At Home,* II. (March, 1866). 413–418.

"X. Of Insanity." *Hours At Home,* VI. (December, 1867). 97–106. Republished in *Moral Uses of Dark Things* (1868).

"VI. Of Oblivion, or Read History." *Hours At Home,* V. (May, 1867), 97–105. Republished in *Moral Uses of Dark Things* (1868).

"II. Of Non-Intercourse between Worlds." *Hours At Home,* IV. (March, 1867), 385–393. Republished in *Moral Uses of Dark Things* (1868).

"XI. Of Physical Danger." *Hours At Home,* VI. (January, 1868), 193–201. Republished in *Moral Uses of Dark Things* (1868).

"VIII. Of Physical Pain." *Hours At Home,* V. (September, 1867), 385–394. Republished in *Moral Uses of Dark Things* (1868).

"VII. Of the Animal Infestations." *Hours At Home,* V. (August, 1867), 307–315. Republished in *Moral Uses of Dark Things* (1868).

"V. Of the Condition of Solidarity." *Hours At Home,* V. (May, 1867), 97–105. Republished in *Moral Uses of Dark Things* (1868).

"XII. Of the Mutabilities of Life." *Hours At Home,* VI. (February, 1868), 296–305. Republished in *Moral Uses of Dark Things* (1868).

"IX. Of Things Unsightly and Disgustful." *Hours At Home,* VI. (November, 1867), 1–9. Republished in *Moral Uses of Dark Things* (1868).

"IV. Of Want and Waste." *Hours At Home,* V. (May 1867), 1–9. Republished in *Moral Uses of Dark Things* (1868).

"XIII. Of Winter." *Hours At Home,* VI. (March, 1868), 406–414. Republished in *Moral Uses of Dark Things* (1868).

"(The Oregon Question.) Addressed to the Editor of the *London Universe,*" March 3, 1846. Signed, "An American." 3 columns. Reprinted in *The Religious Herald* (Hartford) of April 4, 1846. 3 ⅓ columns, under the heading, "Dr. Bushnell in London."

"Our Gospel A Gift to the Imagination." *Hours At Home,* X. (December, 1869), 159–172. Republished in *Building Eras in Religion* (1881).

"Position and Power." Occasional, No. 2. Boston: The American Tract Society. 8 pp.

"Progress." *Hours At Home,* VIII. (January, 1869), 199–210.

"Remonstrance from Dr. Bushnell." Letter addressed to the General Association of Connecticut. *The New England Religious Herald,* June 19, 1852. 1 ⅛ columns.

"Reply to Dr. Taylor." Signed "Constans." *The Christian Freeman* (Hartford), December 12, 1844. 4 columns.

"Report of the Committee Concerning the Proposed Public Park." (Addressed) to the Honorable, the Court of Common Council of the City of Hartford, November 14, 1853. 8 pp.

"Review of the Errors of the Times." *The New Englander,* II. (January, 1844), 143–175. Reprinted in pamphlet form—*Review of the Errors of the Times: a charge, by the Rt. Rev. T. C. Brownell, D. D., LL. D., Bishop of the Diocese of Connecticut.* Hartford: 1844, 51 pp. (including prefatory note by the author).

"Science and Religion." *Putnam's Magazine,* I. (March, 1868), 265–275.

A Series on the subject of Prayer, appearing in *The Advance* (Chicago):

1. "Prayer Accorded as a Right of Petition." Thursday, April 13, 1871. *The Advance,* Vol. IV., No. 189.
2. "Ends for Which Prayer is Instituted." Thursday, April 27. IV., No. 191.
3. "By What In a Prayer Does It Prevail?" Thursday, May 18. IV., No. 194.
4. "Prayer as Related to Second Causes." Thursday, June 8. IV., No. 197.
5. "Prayer as Related to God's Will." Thursday, June 29. IV., No. 200.
6. "Prayer in the Name of Christ." Thursday, July 13. IV., No. 202.
7. "The Prayer of Faith." Thursday, August 3. IV., No. 205.
8. "Induement with Character through Prayer." Thursday, August 31. Vol. V., No. 209.
9. "The Testing of Prayer." Thursday, October 3, 1872. Vol. VI., No. 265.

"Spiritual Economy of Revivals of Religion." *The Quarterly Christian Spectator,* X. (February, 1838), 131–148. Republished in *Views of Christian Nurture* (1848), and *Building Eras in Religion* (1881).

"Taste and Fashion." *The New Englander,* I. (April, 1843), 153–168.

"To the Editor of the *New England Religious Herald.*" Letter, *The New England Religious Herald* of October 16, 1847. 3 $^{1}/_{10}$ columns.

"To the Editor of the *Religious Herald.*" Letter dated December 14, 1843. $^{7}/_{8}$ column. *The Religious Herald,* Hartford, December 20, 1843.

"To the *Religious Herald,*" Hartford. Letter of January 24, 1844. $^{1}/_{8}$ column.

C. ADDRESSES, LECTURES

"An Address before the Hartford County Agricultural Society." Address delivered October 2, 1846. Hartford: 1846. 24 pp. Republished as "Agriculture in the East," in *Work and Play* (1864).

"The Age of Homespun." Discourse delivered at Litchfield, Conn., on the occasion of the Centennial Celebration, 1851. *Litchfield County Centennial Celebration.* Hartford: 1851, pp. 107–130. Republished in *Work and Play* (1864).

"American Politics." (John xix. 12.) Sermon, *The American National Preacher* (New York, December, 1840), XIV. 189–204.

"Barbarism the First Danger." (Judges xvii. 13.) A Discourse for Home

Missions. New York: The American Home Missionary Society, 1847. 32 pp. Republished in *Work and Play,* second edition.

"Building Eras in Religion." Sermon delivered at the Dedication of the Park Church, Hartford, Conn., on Friday evening, March 29, 1867.

"The Capitol Site." Speech in *The Courant* (Hartford), Monday, January 8, 1872. Extracts. 1 ½ columns.

"The Census and Slavery." (Isaiah xxvi. 15.) Sermon. A Thanksgiving Discourse delivered in the Chapel at Clifton Springs, N. Y., November 20, 1860. Hartford: 1860. 24 pp.

"City Plans." Address written for the Public Improvement Society of Hartford. Published in *Work and Play* (1864).

"Common Schools." Sermon. A Discourse on the Modifications demanded by the Roman Catholics (Leviticus xxiv. 22), delivered in the North Church, Hartford, on the day of the late Fast, March 25, 1853. Hartford: 1853. 24 pp. Republished in *Building Eras in Religion* (1881).

"Concio Ad Clerum: A Discourse on the Divinity of Christ." Address delivered at the Annual Commencement of Yale College, August 15, 1848. Published as second article in *God In Christ* (1849).

"Crisis of the Church." Sermon delivered at the North Church, Hartford, Conn. (Published by request.) Hartford, 1835. 36 pp.

"The Day of Roads." (Judges v. 6.) Sermon. A Discourse delivered on the Annual Thanksgiving, 1846. Hartford: 1846. 35 pp. Republished in *Work and Play* (1864).

"A Discourse in Atonement." Address delivered before the Divinity School in Harvard University, July 9, 1848. Published as third article in *God In Christ* (1849).

"Discourse in Memory of Rev. Dr. Noah Porter." Psalms lxxi. 9. (In Memorial of Noah Porter, D. D., late of Farmington, Conn., comprising the Discourses of President T. D. Woolsey, Rev. Levi L. Paine, and Horace Bushnell, D. D., occasioned by his Death.) Farmington: 1867. 75 pp.

"A Discourse on Dogma and Spirit, or the True Reviving of Religion." Address delivered before the Porter Rhetorical Society, at Andover, September, 1848. Published in *God in Christ* (1849).

"A Discourse on the Moral Tendencies and Results of Human History." Oration delivered before the Society of Alumni in Yale College, on Wednesday, August 16, 1843. Published by request of the Society. New Haven: 1843. 39 pp. Another edition, New York, New Haven, Hartford: 1843. 32 pp. Republished as "The Growth of Law," in *Work and Play* (1864).

"A Discourse on the Slavery Question." (Acts xxvii. 41.) Sermon delivered in the North Church, Hartford, Thursday evening, January 10, 1839. (Published by request.) Hartford: 1839. 32 pp.

"The Fathers of New England." Oration delivered before the New England Society of New York, December 21, 1849, and published at their request. New York: George P. Putnam. 1850. 44 pp. Republished as "The Founders Great in their Unconsciousness," *Work and Play* (1864).

"God's Thoughts Fit Bread for Children." (Psalms cxxxix. 17.) A Sermon preached before the Connecticut Sunday-School Teacher's Convention at the Pearl Street Congregational Church, Hartford, Conn., Tuesday evening, March 2, 1869. 39 pp. Republished in *The Spirit in Man* (1903).

"The Great Time-Keeper." (Genesis i. 14). Sermon, *The American National Preacher*, XVIII. (January, 1844), 1–9. Republished in *The Spirit in Man* (1903).

"The Moral Uses of Great Pestilences." (Deuteronomy xxix. 24.) A Discourse delivered in the North Church, Hartford, on the Occasion of the National Fast, August 3, 1849. *The American Literary Magazine*, V. (August, 1849), 81–94. Reprinted in pamphlet. Hartford: 1849. 16 pp. Revised and published as "Of Plague and Pestilence," *Moral Uses of Dark Things* (1868).

"The Moral Uses of the Sea." (Genesis i. 10.) Sermon delivered on board the packet-ship *Victoria*, Captain Morgan at sea, July, 1845. Published by request of the Captain and Passengers. New York: 1845. 20 pp. Revised and republished under the title, "Of the Sea," in *Moral Uses of Dark Things* (1868).

"The New Education." Address delivered at the Annual Commencement of the Sheffield Scientific School, New Haven, July 18, 1870, *Hours At Home*, XI. (September, 1870), 421–434. Republished in *Building Eras in Religion* (1881).

"The Northern Iron." (Jeremiah xv. 12.) Sermon. A Discourse delivered in the North Church, Hartford, on the Annual State Fast, April 14, 1854. Published by request. Hartford: 1854. 29 pp.

"An Oration Pronounced before the Society of Phi Beta Kappa, at New Haven, on the Principles of National Greatness." Oration, August 15, 1837. New Haven: 1837. 27 pp. Republished under the title, "The True Wealth or Weal of Nations," in *Work and Play* (1864).

"Our Obligations to the Dead." Oration delivered at the Commemorative Celebration, held July 26, 1865, in honor of the Alumni of Yale College who were in the Military or Naval Service of the United States during the Civil War. *Addresses and Proceedings at the Commemorative Celebration*, New Haven: 1866, pp. 9–38. Republished in *Building Eras in Religion* (1881).

"Parting Words." (Jeremiah xxii. 10.) Sermon. A Discourse delivered in the North Church, Hartford, July 3, 1859. Published by request. Hartford: 1859. 25 pp.

"Politics Under the Law of God." (Isaiah xxx. 11.) A Discourse delivered in the North Congregational Church, Hartford, on the Annual Fast of 1844. Hartford: 1844. 23 pp.

264

"Popular Government by Divine Right." (Jeremiah xxx. 21.) Sermon delivered on the late National Thanksgiving (November 24, 1864), in the South Church, Hartford, before the Congregations of that and the South Baptist Church. Hartford: 1864. 16 pp. Republished in *Building Eras in Religion* (1881).

"Prosperity Our Duty." (2 Chronicles xxxii. 30.) Sermon. A Discourse delivered at the North Church, Hartford, Sabbath evening, January 31, 1847. (Published by request.) Hartford: 1847. 24 pp. Republished in *The Spirit in Man* (1903).

"Pulpit Talent." Address delivered before the Porter Rhetorical Society of Andover Theological Seminary at their Anniversary, September, 1866. *Hours At Home*, III. (October, 1866), 485–499. Republished in *Building Eras in Religion* (1881).

"Religious Music." (I Corinthians xiv. 7.) Discourse. Hartford: 1852. pp. 5–31.

"Religious Nature and Religious Character." (Acts xvii. 27.) Sermon, *The Monthly Religious Magazine*, XXXV. (March, 1866), 156–169. Republished in *Sermons on Living Subjects* (1872).

"Revelation." Address delivered before the Porter Rhetorical Society at Andover, Mass., on Tuesday afternoon, September 3, 1839.

"Reverses Needed." (Proverbs xxiv. 10.) Sermon. A Discourse delivered on the Sunday (July 28, 1861) after the Disaster of Bull Run, in the North Church, Hartford. Hartford: 1861. 27 pp. Republished in *The Spirit in Man* (1903).

"Society and Religion." (Jeremiah i. 10.). A Sermon for California, delivered on Sabbath evening, July 6, 1856, at the Installation of Rev. E. S. Lacy as Pastor of the First Congregational Church, San Francisco. Hartford: 1856. 32 pp.

"Speech for Connecticut." Address. Being an Historical Estimate of the State, delivered before the Legislature and other invited guests at the Festival of the Normal School in New Britain, June 4, 1851. Hartford: 1851. 43 pp. Republished as "Historical Estimate of Connecticut," *Work and Play* (1864).

"Speech Made by Dr. Bushnell at the General Association of Connecticut" (New Haven), in June, 1854. Quoted (2 columns) in *The New England Religious Herald,* July 6, 1854.

"Spiritual Dislodgements." (Jeremiah xlviii. 11.) A Sermon of Reunion, preached in the North Church, Hartford, February 22, 1857. Hartford: 1857. 21 pp. Republished in *Sermons for the New Life* (1858).

"The Stability of Change." Address delivered at the Commencement of Western Reserve College, Hudson, Ohio, August 9, 1842.

"Thanksgiving for Kansas." Sermon delivered November 26, 1857, in Hartford. (Numbers xi. 10.)

"Training for the Pulpit Manward." Address delivered at the decennial anniversary of the Chicago Theological Seminary, before the Rhetorical Society, Wednesday, April 29, 1868. *Hours At Home,* VII. (July, 1868), 193–203. Republished in *Building Eras in Religion* (1881).

"Twentieth Anniversary." (Philippians i. 5.) Sermon. A Commemorative Discourse delivered in the North Church, Hartford, May 22, 1853. Hartford: 1853. 32 pp. Published in Cheney, *Life and Letters of Horace Bushnell* (1880), p. 279.

"Unconscious Influence." (John xx. 8.) Sermon. Published by request. London: 1846. Republished in *The American National Preacher,* XX. (August, 1846), 169–179, under title, "Influence of Example," And again in *Sermons for the New Life* (1858).

"Uses and Duties of Stormy Sundays." (Psalms cxviii. 8.) Sermon, *The American Pulpit,* II. (October, 1846), 123–133.

"The Value One Man Has to Another." (II Corinthians xii. 14.) Sermon, *The Advance* (Chicago), Vol. I., No. 1. Thursday, September 5, 1867. Republished as "The Property Right We Are to Get in Souls," in *Sermons on Living Subjects* (1872).

"The Vital Principle." Lecture delivered at Western Reserve College, Hudson, Ohio, August 9, 1842. Published as "Life, or the Lives," in *Work and Play* (1864).

"A Week-day Sermon to the Business Men of Hartford." (Acts xxvii. 15.) In the Supplement to *The Courant,* Hartford, October 31, 1857. 5 ½ columns. Republished in *The Spirit in Man* (1903).

"What it is to Preach Christ." (II Corinthians iv. 6.) Sermon, *The Advance* (Chicago), Vol. I., No. 18. Thursday, January 2, 1868. Republished as "The Gospel of the Face," in *Sermons on Living Subjects* (1872).

"Work and Play." An Oration delivered before the Society of Phi Beta Kappa, at Cambridge, August 24, 1848. Cambridge: 1848. 39 pp. Republished in *Work and Play* (1864).

D. APPENDAGE: UNPUBLISHED MANUSCRIPTS

"The Church Catalogue of Rome" (Sermon manuscript in the Yale Divinity School Library).

"Duty Not Measured by Our Own Ability" (Sermon manuscript in the Yale Divinity School Library).

"God Reigns for the Largest Love" (Sermon manuscript in the Yale Divinity School Library).

Journals (Manuscript in the Yale Divinity School Library).

"On Moral Agency" (Sermon manuscript in the Yale University Library).

"Power from on High" (Sermon manuscript in the Yale Divinity School Library).

"Remarks to His Students on leaving Yale College" (Manuscript address, Yale Memorabilia Collection, Yale University Library).

"Revelation" (Sermon manuscript in Harvard University Library).

"Sermon on Hosea 6: 3" (Sermon manuscript in Yale Divinity School Library).

"The Word 'Grace' Revived" (Sermon manuscript in Yale Divinity School Library).

II. Sources Used:

ABBOTT, LYMAN. *Christianity and Social Problems*. Boston: Houghton and Mifflin Co., 1896.

Christ's Secret of Happiness. New York: T. Y. Crowell and Co., 1907.

The Evolution of Christianity. Boston: Houghton and Mifflin Co., 1894.

The Great Companion. New York: Grosset and Dunlap, 1904.

In Aid of Faith. E. P. Dutton and Co., 1891.

The Industrial Problem. Philadelphia: G. W. Jacobs and Co., 1905.

Jesus of Nazareth: (his life and teachings; founded on the four gospels, and illustrated by reference to the manners, customs, religious beliefs, and political institutions of his times). New York: Harper's, 1869.

Kingdom of God on Earth (sermon), delivered at the diamond jubilee of the Congregational Home Missions Soc., May 14, 1901.

The Personality of God. New York: T. Y. Crowell and Co., 1905.

Reminiscences. Boston: Houghton and Mifflin Co., 1915.

The Rights of Man; a study in 20 Century problems. Boston: Houghton and Mifflin Co., 1901.

A Study in Human Nature. Chautauqua Press, 1885.

The Theology of an Evolutionist. Boston: Houghton and Mifflin Co., 1897.

ALEXANDER, JAMES. "Large Cities," *Christian Spectator,* I., No. 2 (1828), 20–28.

ANDREWS, W. W. *Remarks on Dr. Bushnell's "Vicarious Sacrifice"*. Hartford: Case, Lockwood and Co., 1866.

Appeal of the Association of Fairfield West to the Associated Ministers connected with the General Association of Connecticut. New York: Baker, Goodwin and Co., 1852.

ARCHIBALD, WARREN SEYMOUR. *Horace Bushnell*. Hartford: Edwin Valentine Mitchell, 1930.

BACON, BENJAMIN. *Theodore Thornton Munger*. New Haven: Yale Univ. Press, 1913.

BAINTON, ROLAND. *Yale and the Ministry*. New York: Harper and Bros., 1957.

BAKER, RAY STANNARD. *The Social Unrest.* New York, 1910.

BENNETT, JOHN. "After Liberalism—What?", *Christian Century* (1933), 1403–1406.

Biblical Repertory and Princeton Review, 1848, 1853.

Biblical Repository, IV, 3 (1849).

BODEIN, VERNON PARKER. *The Social Gospel of Walter Rauschenbusch and its relation to Religious Education.* New Haven: Yale Univ. Press, 1944.

BRASTOW, LEWIS, O. *The Modern Pulpit—A Study of Homiletic Sources and Characteristics.* New York: Macmillan Co., 1906.

BRIGGS, G. W.,"Bushnell on Christian Nurture," *The Christian Examiner and Religious Miscellany,* XLIII (1847), 435–451.

BROWNELL, THOMAS. *Errors of the Times.* (A charge delivered to the clergy of the diocese of Connecticut, at the annual convention held in Christ Church, in the city of Hartford). Hartford: Case, Tiffany and Co., 1843.

BUCKHAM, JOHN WRIGHT. *Progressive Religious Thought in America.* Boston: Houghton and Mifflin Co., 1919.

Bushnell Centenary (Minutes of the 193 Annual Meeting, General Association of Connecticut, Hartford, June 17, 18, 1902). Oxford Press, 1902.

"Bushnell's Christian Nurture," *The Church Review and Ecclesiastical Register,* I (1848–1849), 228–245.

CARTER, PAUL A. *The Decline and Revival of the Social Gospel.* Ithaca, N. Y.: Cornell Univ. Press, 1954.

CHENEY, MARY BUSHNELL. *Life and Letters of Horace Bushnell.* New York: Harper Bros., 1880.

CHESEBROUGH, AMOS S. *Contributions of C. C., Now declared in full as Criticus Criticorum.* (by request). Hartford: Brown and Parsons, 1849.

Christian Observatory, III (June, 1849).

COLE, ARTHUR. *Social Idea of the Northern Evangelists.* New York, 1854.

COLERIDGE, SAMUEL T. *Aids to Reflection.* London: Bohn Library, 1913.

CROSS, BARBARA M. *Horace Bushnell: Minister to a Changing America.* Chicago: Univ. of Chicago Press, 1958.

Das Theologische Seminar der Deutschen Baptisten. Fünfundsiebzigstes Jubiläum. Rochester, 1927.

A Dictionary of Religion and Ethics. (Ed. Shailer Mathews and G. B. Smith). New York: Macmillan Co., 1921.

DREW, S. S. "An Estimate of Horace Bushnell," *Contemporary Review* (August, 1879), 823.

EATON, L. "Eli Todd," *The New England Quarterly,* XXVI (1853), 435–453.

Encyclopedia Britannica (11 ed.).

FISKE, JOHN. *The Idea of God.* Boston: Houghton and Mifflin Co., 1898.
Outlines of Cosmic Philosophy. Boston: Houghton and Mifflin Co., 1874, II Vols.
Through Nature to God. Boston: Houghton and Mifflin Co., 1899.
The Unseen World, and Other Essays. Boston: Houghton and Mifflin Co., 1876.

FOSDICK, HARRY EMERSON. *The Modern Use of the Bible.* New York, 1924.

FOSTER, FRANK H. *A Genetic History of New England Theology.* Chicago: Univ. of Chicago Press, 1907.

GIBBS, JOSIAH WILLARD. "Historical and Critical View of Cases in the Indo-European Languages", *Christian Spectator*, IX (1837).

GLADDEN, WASHINGTON. *Applied Christianity.* Boston: Houghton, Mifflin and Co., 1886.
Being a Christian (what it means and how to begin). Boston and New York: The Pilgrim Press, 1910.
The Christian Pastor and the Working Church. New York: Charles Scribner's Sons, 1898.
Christianity and Socialism. New York: Eaton and Mains; Cincinnati: Jennings and Graham, 1905.
The Church and Modern Life. Boston: Houghton, Mifflin and Co., 1908.
How Much is left of the Old Doctrines? Boston: Houghton and Mifflin Co., 1899.
The Labor Question. Boston, New York: The Pilgrim Press, 1911.
The New Idolatry, and Other Discussions. New York: McClure, Phillips and Co., 1905.
Recollections. Boston: Houghton, Mifflin and Co., 1909.
Ruling Ideas of the Present Age. Boston: Houghton, Mifflin and Co., 1895.
Social Salvation. Boston: Houghton, Mifflin and Co., 1902.
Working People and Their Employers. New York: 1885.

GOODRICH, SAMUEL. *Recollections of a Lifetime.* New York, 1857.

GOODWIN, HENRY M. *Christ and Humanity.* New York: Harper and Bros., 1875.

GORDON, GEORGE A. *Aspects of the Infinite Mystery.* Boston: Houghton, Mifflin and Co., 1916.
The Christ of Today. Boston: Houghton, Mifflin and Co., 1895.
"The Collapse of the New England Theology," *Harvard Theological Review*, I, No. 2 (April, 1908).
"The Contrast and Agreement between the New Orthodoxy and the Old," *The Andover Review*, XIX, No. 109 (1893).
The Genius of the Pilgrim. Boston; New York: The Pilgrim Press, 1913.
Humanism in New England Theology. Boston, New York: The Pilgrim Press, 1920.

Immortality and the New Theodicy. Boston: Houghton, Mifflin and Co., 1897.

My Education and Religion. Boston: Houghton, Mifflin and Co., 1925.

The New Epoch for Faith. Boston: Houghton, Mifflin and Co., 1901.

Religion and Miracle. Boston: Houghton, Mifflin and Co., 1909.

"Some Things Worth While in Theology," *Harvard Theological Review,* III, No. 4 (October, 1910).

Through Man to God. Boston: Houghton, Mifflin and Co., 1906.

Ultimate Conceptions of Faith. Boston: Houghton, Mifflin and Co., 1903.

HAWES, JOEL. *A Sermon Delivered at the Dedication of the North Congregational Church of Hartford.* Hartford, 1825.

HEATH, WILLIAM. "The Baptist and Pedobaptist Theories of Church Membership," *The Christian Review,* XII (December, 1847), 529–551.

HEININGER, HAROLD R. *The Theological Technique of a Mediating Theologian.* Chicago: Distributed by the Univ. of Chicago Libraries, 1935.

HODGE, CHARLES. "Bushnell on Christian Nurture," *The Biblical Repertory and Princeton Review,* XIX (October, 1847), 502–539.

Essays and Reviews. Bangor, 1849.

HOPKINS, CHARLES H. *The Rise of the Social Gospel in American Protestantism (1865–1915).* New Haven: Yale Univ. Press, 1940.

HORTON, WALTER MARSHALL. *Realistic Theology.* New York and London: Harper and Bros., 1934.

MATHEWS, SHAILER. *Christianity and Social Process.* New York and London: Harper and Bros., 1934.

The Social Gospel. Philadelphia: The Griffith and Rowland Press, 1910.

"Social Gospel," *A Dictionary of Religion and Ethics,* ed. Shailer Mathews and G. B. Smith. New York: Macmillan Co., 1921.

The Social Teachings of Jesus (An Essay in Christian Sociology). New York: Hodder and Stoughton, George H. Doran Co., 1897.

McGIFFERT, ARTHUR C. *Christianity and History.* New York, 1909.

The Rise of Modern Religious Ideas. New York: The Macmillan Co., 1915.

The Methodist Quarterly Review (January, 1849).

MILLER, PERRY. *Errand into the Wilderness.* Cambridge, Mass.: Belknap Press of Harvard Univ. Press, 1956.

MUNGER, THEODORE T. *The Appeal to Life.* Boston: Houghton, Mifflin and Co., 1887.

The Freedom of Faith. Boston: Houghton, Mifflin and Co., 1891.

Horace Bushnell, Preacher and Theologian. Boston: Houghton, Mifflin, and Co., 1899.

Lamps and Paths. Boston: Houghton, Mifflin, and Co., 1885.

On the Threshold. Boston: Houghton, Mifflin, and Co., 1881.

MYERS, A. J. WM. *Horace Bushnell and Religious Education.* Boston: Manthorne and Burack, 1937.

NEVIN, JOHN W. "Educational Religion," *The Weekly Messenger of the German Reformed Church,* XII (New Series: June 23—July 14, 1847).

New England Religious Herald, August 7, 1847, V., pp. 383–393; June, 1848, pp. 273–283.

The New Englander Magazine, II (October, 1844); VI (May, 1848).

"The New Theological Controversy," *The New Englander Magazine,* V (1847), 613–614.

North Church Records. Hartford, State Historical Library.

Three articles signed "Omicron," "What Does Dr. Bushnell Mean?" *New York Evangelist* (1848).

PARKER, EDWIN POND. *The Hartford Central Association and the Bushnell Controversy* (An Historical Address given before the Hartford Central Assoc., Feb. 3, 1896). Hartford: Published by the Association, the Case, Lockwood and Brainard Co., 1896.

PARKER, THEODORE. *Discourses on Religion.* Boston: American Unitarian Association, 1842.

PAUL, ROBERT S. *The Atonement and the Sacraments.* New York: Abingdon Press, 1960.

Pioneers of Religious Liberty in America (Being the Great and Thursday Lectures delivered in Boston in 1903). Boston: American Unitarian Association, 1903.

POND, ENOCH. *Review of Dr. Bushnell's "God in Christ."* Bangor, 1849.

PORTER, NOAH. "Bushnell on Christian Nurture," *The New Englander Magazine,* VI (1848), 126–134.

RAUSCHENBUSCH, WALTER. "Christian Socialism and the Brotherhood of the Kingdom," *New York Press* (June 3, 1894).
Christianity and the Social Crisis. New York: The Macmillan Co., 1907.
Christianizing the Social Order. New York: The Macmillan Co., 1912.
"A Conquering Idea," *The Examiner* (July 21, 1892).
Dare We be Christians. New York; Boston: The Pilgrim Press, 1914.
For God and the People: Prayers of the Social Awakening. New York, Boston: The Pilgrim Press, 1910.
"How Rich Have I a Right to Be?", *Inquirer* (May 10, 1894).
The Kingdom of God. New York: Samuel Z. Batten, 1894.
"Relation of the Church and State," *Proceedings of the Baptist Congress,* VII (1889), 139–140.
The Social Principles of Jesus. New York: Association Press, 1916.
A Theology for the Social Gospel. New York: The Macmillan Co., 1917.
"Review of Horace Bushnell's Discourses on Christian Nurture," *The Christian Observatory,* I (July, 1847), 323–330.

ROGERS, A. KATHRYN. *The Social Gospel and the Idea of Progress*. Chicago: Distributed by the Univ. of Chicago Libraries, 1937.

SHARPE, DORES ROBINSON. *Walter Rauschenbusch*. New York: The Macmillan Co., 1942.

SINGER, ANNA M. *Walter Rauschenbusch, and his Contribution to Social Christianity*. Boston: R. G. Badger, 1926.

SMITH, H. SHELTON. *Changing Conceptions of Original Sin*. New York: Charles Scribner's Sons, 1955.
Faith and Nurture. New York: Charles Scribner's Sons, 1941.

SMYTH, NEWMAN. *Christian Ethics*. New York: Charles Scribner's, 1892.
Old Faiths in New Light. New York: Charles Scribner's Sons, 1879. (Second Edition).
The Orthodox Theology of Today. New York: Charles Scribner's Sons, 1881.
The Place of Death in Evolution. New York: Charles Scribner's, 1897.
Through Science to Faith. New York: Charles Scribner's Sons, 1902.

SPERRY, WILLARD L. *Religion in America*. Cambridge: University Press, 1945.

SPRAGUE, WILLIAM (ed.). *The Man of Business considered in his Various Relations*. Philadelphia, no date.

STRONG, JOSIAH. *My Religion in Everyday Life*. New York, 1910.

STUART, MOSES. "The Sonship of Christ," *The Biblical Repertory and Princeton Review*, VI (1835).

SWEET WILLIAM W. *American Culture and Religion*. Dallas: Southern Methodist Univ. Press, 1951.
Makers of Christianity (from John Cotton to Lyman Abbott). New York: Henry Holt and Co., 1937.

TAYLOR, NATHANIEL. *Lectures on the Moral Government of God*. New York: Austin and Smith, 1859.
Practical Sermons. New York: Clark, 1859.

THOMPSON, ERNEST T. *Changing Emphases in American Preaching*. (The Stone Lectures for 1943). Philadelphia: The Westminster Press, 1943.

TRUMBULL, H. CLAY. *My Four Religious Teachers*. Philadelphia: The Sunday School Times Co., 1903.

TUCKER, WILLIAM JEWETT. *My Generation* (An Autobiographical Interpretation). Boston: Houghton, Mifflin and Co., 1919.

TYLER, BENNET. *Letters to Dr. Bushnell on Christian Nurture*. Hartford, 1848.

WALKER, WILLISTON. "Bushnell," *Encyclopedia Britannica* (11 ed.).
Great Men of the Christian Church. Chicago: The Univ. of Chicago Press, 1908.

Abbott, Lyman 9, 14
Abhorrence theory 208
Absolute Being 164
"Aids to Reflection" 18
American Romantic movement 19
"An organic whole" 134
Analogical 54
Analogy, department of 54
Andover 139
Anselm 72, 206
Arius 171
Athanasius 170, 171
Atonement 14, 29, 30, 179, 180, 182,
   185, 203, 213, 218, 234
-, moral government theory of the 179
-, moral view of the 180, 218, 223
-, penal theory of the 180
-, satisfaction theory of the 188
-, subjective view of the 186

Bacon, Leonard 32
Baptism 143
   See also "Household baptism"
Baptists 121
Bartol, C. A. 160
Bellamy 206
Biblical criticism 39
Briggs, G. W. 131
Brootherhood of Man 244, 250, 251
Brownell, Thomas C. 108, 232
Buckham, John W. 226

Calvin 172
Chesebrough, Amos S. 160
Childhood, plastic nature of 113
Christ 92
- and the law 202
-, deity of 146
-, divine-human union in 155

Christ, doctrine of 140
-, ethical 242
-, ethical apprehension of 250
-, imitation of 242
-, moral influence of 221
-, moral power of 190, 191
-, morality of 95
-, pre-existence of 141
-, two distinct natures in 155
-, vicarious sacrifice of 42
Christian
- education 124
- experience, formulated 139
- family 26
- knowledge 139
- nurture 14, 111, 112, 113, 117, 123,
   129
- nurture, covenental conception of
   110
Christly Providence 66
Civil War 181, 204
Coleridge, Samuel T. 18, 226
Commandment 215, 216
Commemorative sermon 34
"Comprehensive" 107
- approach 33
- approach to Christian theology 101
"Comprehensiveness" 137
-, theological 34
"Condition privative" 75, 77, 103, 133
"Confession agreed on at the Savoy"
   60
Congregational
- Associations 37
- Church 9, 226
- Order 231

Dark things of nature 103, 230
Davenport 78

Deformity, a realm of 83
Depravity
–, human 137
–, natural 131
–, theory of 129, 135
Divinity 62, 65, 146, 228
"Doctrinal Articles of the Church of England" 60
Dogmatic 60
Dynamic 163

Edwards, Jonathan 10, 17, 206, 233, 240
Episcopal Church 24
Eternal
– generation 171
– virtue 182
Ethical, see Christ, Personality
Evolution, theistic 245, 247
Evolutionary growth 237, 243

Fatherhood of God, see God
Fenelon 138
Finney, Charles 33
Forgiveness 80, 199, 212, 214
Fosdick, Harry Emerson 251
Free intelligences 70
Freedom of the will 85

Gladden, Washington 14, 248
God
–, Absolute 176
–, fatherhood of 243, 244, 249–250, 251
–, government of 197, 199, 203, 204, 223
–, immanence of 237, 239, 243
–, impassible 153, 193
–, Infinite 193
–, justice of 202
–, kingdom of 41, 105, 251, 253, 254, 255
–, knowledge of 151
–, law of 201
–, moral power of 185, 189, 210, 219
–, passible 179, 217, 218, 235
–, personality of 163
–, rectoral honor of 180, 207
–, righteousness of 198, 210

God, sovereignity of 122
–, suffering of 193
–, system of 67, 73, 99, 134, 229
–, transcendent 12, 165, 240
–, unity of 165
Godhead 141
Goodness of man, inherent 237, 247
Gordon, George A. 14, 240
Grand analogy 223
Guyon, Madame 138

Harvard Divinity School 139
Hawes, Joel 22, 37
Hodge, Charles 27, 130, 132
Holy Spirit 44, 106, 158, 184, 185
Honor 203
Horton, Walter Marshall 236
"Household baptism" 119, 120
Howe, John 172
Hume, David 47, 48

Imaginative reason 31
Impersonation
–, double 157
–, finite and relative 158
–, three-fold 176
Incarnate Redeemer 100
Incarnation 56, 64, 88, 105, 141, 150, 152, 158, 162, 168, 176, 189, 204, 205, 218, 222, 234, 238
Instituted government 197, 198, 207
Instrumental 168
Intellectual department 52
Intuition 57
Irenaeus 121, 122

Jesus
–, character of 98
–, historical 237, 250
–, personality of 90
– the central figure of Christianity 89
– the Divine Word 89

Justice 199, 217
– and righteousness 194
See also God
Justification
– by faith 105, 209, 211, 212
–, ground of 199
Justin Martyr 121

274

Knowledge, experimental 139
    See also Christian, God, Sin

Language 29, 46, 49, 50, 53, 59, 162
- for theology 228
-, noun- 51
- of intelligence 51
-, physical 51, 52
-, speculative 34
Law 75, 76, 86, 87, 194, 195, 198, 215, 216
- and gospel 76
-, eternal 220
-, moral 87
-, natural 86, 87
- of liberty 77
- of love 205
- of nature 81, 97, 137
- of organic connection 115
-, works of the 210
    See also Christ, God, Organic
Law of Right 196, 198, 205
-, eternal and absolute 204
-, ideal 194
Liberalism 10
Literal 54
Locke 53
Logos 53
-, Divine 85, 156
- world, a 65
Luther 165, 211, 212

Magisterial character 207
Miracle 85, 96, 97, 230
Modern science 39
Moral, see Atonement, Christ, God
    Law, Right, Suffering
Munger, Theodore T. 20, 62, 160, 225, 235, 238
Mystic being 61
Mystic's insight 62

Natural 178, 221, 224, 240
- order 216
- privaty of man 114
- realm 13, 85, 97
Naturalism 47
Nature 13, 14, 39, 66, 69, 80, 83, 85, 98, 107, 134, 229, 231

Nature, brutality of 103
    See also Law
Neander 61
Neo-Orthodoxy 9
Nevin, John W. 131, 132
New Divinity 17
New England Theology 10, 17, 18, 35, 61, 102, 179, 226, 227, 228, 229, 231, 238, 239
New Light 10, 35
New-School 35
Nicene Creed 170, 171
North Church in Hartford 20, 34, 108
Nurture
- of the Lord 112, 124
    See also Christian

Obedience, deific 204
Old Puritanism 226
Old-School 35
Organic
- forms 126
- law of character 120, 122
- relation 116
- theory of society 243
- unity 126
- unity of the church 26
- unity of the family 125, 128

Pantheists 47
Parker, Theodore 80
Penal substitution 220
Perfectibility of man 248
Person 144, 145
-, threeness of 169
Personality 229, 234
-, transcendent ethical 242
    See also God
Persons, plurality of 159
Plato 85
Poets 59
Porter, Jr., Noah 130
Powers 71

Rauschenbusch, Walter 9, 19, 252
Reconciliation 197
Redemption 84, 230
Revelation 38, 40, 56, 147, 173

Revelation, dramatis personae of 31
–, instrumental three of 162
– of God in Christ 105
   See also Supernatural, Trinity
Revival movement 26
Revivals 22, 35, 108, 109, 131
Right 198, 220
–, concept of 196
–, idea of 195, 196
–, moral idea of 195
–, principle of 198
   See also Law of Right
Romantic 228

Sabellian 177
Salvation 203
Satan 77, 78
Satisfaction, judicial 199
   See also Atonement, Christ
Saybrook Platform 60
Self-expression, capacity of 149
Sin 80, 83, 84, 114
–, knowledge of 198
–, original 132
Slavery 41, 42
Social Gospel 14, 226, 237, 251, 252
Social Gospel movement 9
Spirit 127
Spiritual Regeneration 106
Stuart, Moses 174
Substitutionary theory 207
Suffering, moral 193
   See also God
Supernatural 13, 14, 39, 66, 69, 80,
   84, 107, 134, 178, 216, 221, 223,
   231, 240
– action 85
– agency 86
– agents 74
– creature, man as a 68
– divine ministration 89
– force 83
– gospel 107
– interposition of God 230
– realm 13, 97, 224, 229
– revelation 46, 96

Supernatural world 86
Supernaturalism 38, 46, 67
Supernaturally 99, 137
Swedenborg 83

Taylor, Nathaniel 17, 136
"The Ostrich Nurture" 124
Theological realism 9
– systems 64
Theology, constructive 226
–, liberal 9
– of evolution 244
– of experience 46
–, realistic 236
Things and persons 70
Things and powers 70
Thompson, Ernest 26
Transcendent Being 178
Transcendentalism 38–39, 39, 40, 101
Trinity 10, 29, 30, 31, 37, 56, 106, 143,
   144, 150, 160, 161, 162, 164, 167,
   169, 170, 171, 174, 175, 176, 177,
   184, 214, 218
–, economic 178
–, instrumental 160, 233
– of generation 170, 172
– of manifestation 14, 31, 177
– of persons 146
– of revelation 162
Twesten 173
Tyler, Bennett 27, 108, 129, 132, 136

Unitarian 10, 33, 48, 136, 145, 152,
   155, 156, 168, 227, 231, 233
Unitarianism 39
Unnature 84
–, state of 82

Vicarious sacrifice 43, 180, 182, 183,
   184, 189, 204, 205, 218
   See also Christ

Westminster Assembly 37
Westminster Confession 60, 172

Yale 15, 29, 139, 179

276 *(1)*